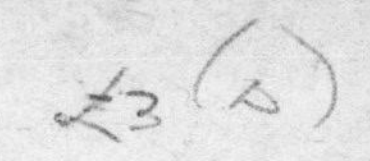

D1420986

ALL OVER THE PLACE

By Compton Mackenzie

Novels and Romances

SINISTER STREET
SYLVIA SCARLETT
GUY AND PAULINE

CARNIVAL
FIGURE OF EIGHT
CORAL
THE VANITY GIRL
ROGUES AND VAGABONDS

THE ALTAR STEPS
THE PARSON'S PROGRESS
THE HEAVENLY LADDER

HUNTING THE FAIRIES
WHISKY GALORE
KEEP THE HOME GUARD TURNING
THE MONARCH OF THE GLEN

THE RED TAPEWORM
POOR RELATIONS
APRIL FOOLS
RICH RELATIVES
BUTTERCUPS AND DAISIES
WATER ON THE BRAIN

VESTAL FIRE
EXTRAORDINARY WOMEN

EXTREMES MEET
THE THREE COURIERS

OUR STREET
THE DARKENING GREEN

THE PASSIONATE ELOPEMENT
FAIRY GOLD
THE SEVEN AGES OF WOMAN
THE OLD MEN OF THE SEA

THE FOUR WINDS OF LOVE:
THE EAST WIND Book One
THE EAST WIND Book Two
THE SOUTH WIND Book One
THE SOUTH WIND Book Two
THE WEST WIND Book One
THE WEST WIND Book Two
THE NORTH WIND Book One
THE NORTH WIND Book Two

History and Biography

GALLIPOLI MEMORIES
ATHENIAN MEMORIES
GREEK MEMORIES
AEGEAN MEMORIES
WIND OF FREEDOM
MR ROOSEVELT
DR BENES

PRINCE CHARLIE
PRINCE CHARLIE AND HIS LADIES
CATHOLICISM AND SCOTLAND
MARATHON AND SALAMIS
PERICLES
THE WINDSOR TAPESTRY
THE VITAL FLAME

Essays and Criticism

A MUSICAL CHAIR
UNCONSIDERED TRIFLES
REAPED AND BOUND
LITERATURE IN MY TIME

Children's Stories

SANTA CLAUS IN SUMMER
TOLD
MABEL IN QUEER STREET
THE UNPLEASANT VISITORS
THE CONCEITED DOLL
THE ENCHANTED BLANKET
THE DINING-ROOM BATTLE
THE ADVENTURES OF TWO CHAIRS
THE ENCHANTED ISLAND
THE NAUGHTYMOBILE
THE FAIRY IN THE WINDOW BOX
THE STAIRS THAT KEPT ON GOING DOWN

Play

THE LOST CAUSE

Verse

POEMS 1907
KENSINGTON RHYMES

ALL OVER THE PLACE

Fifty Thousand Miles by Sea, Air, Road and Rail

by

COMPTON MACKENZIE

1949

CHATTO AND WINDUS

LONDON

PUBLISHED BY
CHATTO AND WINDUS
LONDON
*
CLARKE, IRWIN AND COMPANY LTD
TORONTO

SECOND IMPRESSION

PRINTED IN GREAT BRITAIN BY THE
SHENVAL PRESS LONDON AND HERTFORD

TO
CHRISTINA MACSWEEN
after twenty years with my
handwriting

FOREWORD

In the autumn of 1945 I was asked, in a letter signed by Major J. L. Shaw for the Historical Section of the Defence Department of the Government of India, to write for the general reader a history of the contribution India had made to victory in the Second World War. I was ill at the time, and I declined the invitation on the plea of bad health and ignorance. To my surprise I received another letter which, in asking me to reconsider my refusal, said that the Indian Government would make it possible for me to obtain first-hand knowledge of battlefields from Tunis to Hong Kong and, moreover, was willing to wait until my health allowed me to undertake the necessary tour. Major Shaw added that he was coming to England and would be glad to talk matters over with me.

By the time this letter reached me I was in St. Mary's Hospital and in no mood at all for adventure. I had just written a second refusal when General Sir Ian Hamilton came in one afternoon to see how I was getting on. I told him about the offer and said how much I regretted having had to turn it down.

"What?" he exclaimed. "You've jolly well got to go. You've jolly well got to round off your career by learning something about India."

I was then planning the design for my autobiography *The Keyboard*, which I had decided to write in octaves of eight years. In due course, granted the time, I should reach the eighth octave, and it seemed imprudent to reject this opportunity to acquire for that volume so much valuable material. With that veteran beside my bed, I, all but a day 30 years younger than he, felt ashamed to suggest that I was too old to undertake the fatigue even of such an Odyssey. After all, the veteran himself had commanded at Gallipoli when he was 62.

So when John Shaw arrived at the hospital I told him that if I could postpone my departure from England until the autumn of 1946—the date accepted by my doctors—I was ready to tackle the job.

Some weeks later Lieut.-General T. W. Corbett, the Director of the Historical Section, came to England and after a long evening with him and John Shaw at the Cavalry Club I realized that, however formidable it might be, I had taken on what looked like proving the most enthralling job of my life. At this date it still seemed probable that 10 years would elapse before the Indian Army passed entirely from the control of British officers, and the division of that

Army between India and Pakistan was not yet even a conjecture for the immediate future. It was hoped that a book like mine would serve a useful purpose in bringing before the Indian public and the British public the magnitude of the Indian achievement and the vital part it played in the final victory over Germany and Japan. To get it written and published as soon as possible seemed of major importance then.

Since that memorable evening with Tom Corbett and John Shaw in the Cavalry Club the rapid march of political events has made early publication less important, and it has also led to a change in the scope and character of the book itself. *Indian Epic* will still be a history for the general reader of the Indian achievement in the war under the direction of British officers ; but it will also be the swan-song of the old Indian Army, and, I dare to hope, a bugle-call to the new Armies of India and Pakistan. So, it has been decided to make the history a larger book than was originally contemplated and not attempt to rush it out.

Brigadier W. E. H. Condon, who has succeeded Lieut.-General T. W. Corbett as Director of the Historical Section, and Field-Marshal Sir Claude Auchinleck agree with my proposed extension of the date of publication in order to write the larger book ; and they have also agreed to the publication of the present diary in advance of *Indian Epic*.

There was a certain amount of natural opposition in India to a British author's being invited to write this history of the Indian achievement, particularly a British author who had not even visited India. This opposition died down as soon as it was fully realized that the book was not an official publication and that it would have to hold its own in the open market without subsidy. I hope that the pages of the diary will convince those who supposed a previous experience of India to be indispensable that on the contrary such a lack of experience was an advantage, because prejudice could not exist. Let me add that the more I see of India the more thankful I am that I was able to start my task with an absolutely open mind.

I did not keep my diary with any notion at first of publishing it. It included a lot of notes about the details of battles and campaigns most of which I have excised, though here and there I have left them in because the entry for the day would have been meaningless otherwise. I have also suppressed the details of most of the conversations I have had with officers of the Indian Army of every rank. The value of these frank talks was to me inestimable and the history will benefit accordingly, but it was obviously out of the question to include them in a diary. This is not to suggest that I expect to pull my punches in *Indian Epic*. Truth is being suppressed nowadays by Bureaucracy as the Dormouse was suppressed by the Mad Hatter and the March Hare. A halt must be cried to this lunatic secrecy. Truth may live at the bottom of a well, but there is no reason why she should be drowned in a teapot. Meanwhile, officials armed with the Official Secrets Act will find nothing in this diary to alarm them. It is extremely, perhaps excessively, discreet.

Nevertheless, after cutting out military details and confidential discussions, a lot remains which I hope may amuse readers who have not had the good fortune to travel as widely as I have at a time when circumstances at home make travel seem more than ever enviable. I am not pretending to offer a piece of literature. The contents of this volume have been dictated or hastily written when too often the last thing I wanted was either to dictate or to write a word.

Few men on the edge of 65 can have visited so many places and met so many people within less than 10 months as I have had the luck to visit and meet in that time, and I beg that the inevitable occasional inaccuracy in spelling the names of these places and people may be forgiven. I am working hard now at the book to which the journeys recorded in this diary were the prelude, and I must send that prelude to press with only the most superficial revision. The irony of fate has ruled that this revision should coincide with the culmination of the lamentable strife between Hindu and Muslim that succeeded Independence Day. For nearly a year my mind has been enriched and stimulated by the mighty deeds performed by Hindus, Sikhs and Muslims in a fraternity of valour which is unique in human history. Within a few yards of where I write these words the unarmed Muslims of the East Punjab are being cut down by the swords of Sikhs who themselves have hardly escaped with their lives from the armed Muslims of the West Punjab.

Below is a Muslim letter which gives a painfully vivid impression of Simla in September 1947. Hindus and Sikhs are writing similar letters in the West Punjab.

" *Since five days we have taken refuge in our room. The room is surrounded with Hindus and Sikhs and with whose horrible attitude and noise of breaking the shops and slogans.*

We are bitterly terrified and are in disgusting position.

Yesterday we tried to be very bold on account of being hungry to get the rations, but the moment the ration shop opened countless Mohamadans sprang from their shelters and the bomb was dropped which caused numerous casualties, hence we returned to our refuge hopelessly.

Under these circumstances we request your honour that we got no hope of having a narrow escape from Simla. The Sikhs have turned very furious and their behaviour show that they have girded up their loins to take bitter revenge of Mohamadans. Which they do. Here we are about 35 members excluding two children of seven years and four years old along with their two old mothers.

Our wisdom is gone. We have got no courage to stand. Neither we hope of our future lives. Could you very kindly arrange to save 39 lives by means of convoy or any other source to reach Pakistan area. Please for God's sake do something and save us."

I try to believe that this is a fever which will soon pass, but my experience of Greece has taught me that the evil spirit of revenge is the least easily exorcized of all evil spirits, and that, although the demand of an eye for an eye and a tooth for a tooth *must* ultimately turn the body politic into a mutilated corpse, revenge remains sweet, sweeter indeed than life itself.

Yet not always. An elderly Hindu in Simla whose house in Lahore has been looted and whose fortune in Pakistan is in jeopardy has provided food for Muslim refugees, sheltered Muslim refugees in his own home, and even provided penicillin out of his own pocket for the wounded.

Simla
September 1947

CONTENTS

MAPS

ILLUSTRATIONS

The illustrations of Nepal, Tunis and Italy are reproduced by courtesy of Major Peter Goodwin

EN ROUTE

October 1st, 1946. LONDON TO BOMBAY

We reached platform 15 at Euston just as the train was coming in and were lucky to get comfortable seats.

It was raining at Liverpool, and the *Lancashire* waiting for the tide was not alongside the quay with the result that the luggage got into a sad confusion and the passengers spent an anxious afternoon and evening wondering whether they had all their stuff. I found I had been given a pleasant cabin to myself on the boat deck and C.* had a cabin to herself on the upper deck. The *Lancashire* was a regular troopship before the war, and we shall be spared the horrors of the amateur troopship. We sailed from Liverpool at midnight on the top of the tide.

October 2nd. AT SEA

Cool, but nothing much in the way of a sea. We were off Land's End about dusk. I am next door to Major-General A. C. Curtis who commanded 13th Brigade of 1st Burma Division in the 1942 retreat and later did great work in command of 14th Indian Division, training people for jungle fighting.

C. and I are at the Purser's table. With us are Ernest Pearson of Burma Oil and G. K. Robertson, a jolly Scot from Angus who is in some shipping house in Calcutta and had been a Gunner right through the Burma campaign. He was born on the same day as Francis Brett Young and his wife was born on the same day as Jessie Brett Young. I have a Tennyson birthday book which was given to me in 1886 in which the first entry was Tom Hughes, the author of *Tom Brown's Schooldays*. Sarasate, Charles Hallé, Henry James and other celebrities of the nineteenth century wrote in it. Then in 1890 I lost it and it did not turn up again till C. was clearing out an old hamper in Barra in 1943 when Bob Boothby† was staying at Suidheachan. So I started it again with Bob's name. I wonder how many names I shall collect on this tour.

October 5th. AT SEA

C. and I had drinks with the Captain before dinner. Lady Messervy, wife of Lt.-General Sir Frank Messervy, and Mrs. Douglas

*Christina MacSween, my secretary.
†Robert Boothby, M.P.

Gracey, wife of Lt.-General D. D. Gracey, were there. Captain Kirbyson said he didn't like the look of the sky as we were going down to dinner and prophesied fog. We got it all right. No sleep till 4 o'clock, and at one time the ship was hove to.

October 6th. GIBRALTAR

We reached Gibraltar early in the morning, and here the troops left us, about 100 of them in all. The weather was as perfect as the Mediterranean can be in October. There was a following wind from the west when we sailed about lunch time.

October 8th. AT SEA

Weather more exquisite than ever. The clouds are reflected in the water like milk. We were off Bizerta at sunset. Later on we passed Pantellaria in the moonlight with one light winking. In the afternoon I had a long talk with Vidyavati Devi of Vizianagram, who is returning from a Congress of Women at Interlaken where she was representing India. The Maharani is President of the Women's Rights League or whatever it is called in India. She spoke of Pethick-Lawrence as "God's good man". A delightful personality and extremely young-looking to be a grandmother.

October 9th. AT SEA

We sighted Gozo with Malta behind about midday. I won the sweep on the day's run. Cocktails with the Captain. Liar dice after dinner in the Captain's cabin with himself, Colonel Kirkland, Robertson, and Commander John Dalison, R.N. The last named is on his way to Delhi to be Intelligence Officer at Naval H.Q. He's a really good painter. The sea all day was the authentic thick oily blue of 'Mare Nostrum'. I never remember the weather's being so warm at this time of the year in the Mediterranean.

October 12th. PORT SAID

I woke up to find the ship approaching Port Said. There was a line of feluccas on the starboard side, and I heard a small boy say "look, mother, those boats are queueing up". We passed the aircraft carrier *Patroller*, homeward bound from the Pacific. Her decks were thronged with men in shorts, all the colour of Red Indians. There was a loud Cockney shout from one of them as we passed, "Oi! you're going the wrong way!" I decided not to go ashore, but practically everybody else in the ship went except the mothers on B deck. They all spent far more money than they meant to.

An orange moon was rising as we glided into the canal and I

never saw the man in the moon so clearly. The beauty of the night nearly led to my undoing because I sat on the deck too long and my leg started to get busy. However, two strong doses of salicylic managed to stave off the pain and I told everybody to shoo me into the saloon at sunset. Salicylic acid is the synthetic coal-tar equivalent of the salicylic acid secreted by the willow. Query. Does the willow generate this anti-rheumatic acid to protect itself against the effect of its own damp mode of life?

October 13th. AT SEA

I woke more or less without pain to find the *Lancashire* clearing Port Suez and being overtaken by the Dutch liner *Tagelberg* crowded with troops for Java. It was pretty hot, and at sunset the Red Sea was like a mirror of green and gold and orange. I have been reading Nehru's book *The Discovery of India*. It is a remarkable example of the best English prose apart from being a most lucid exposition oı a point of view with which I find myself in complete sympathy.

October 14th. AT SEA

The weather is pretty sticky, but there is a southerly breeze and we have been spared the horrors of a following wind which the Captain had expected. So far the voyage has been a miracle of weather. Somebody overheard a knowledgeable woman on B deck telling the children that four porpoises were flying fishes.

October 17th. ADEN

We are due in Aden at noon. A rain squall coming up from the south-west has cooled everything considerably. There is a tender silvery sky northward. Apparently it is an unusual—indeed almost a unique experience—to see Aden under cloud, and I found it much more beautiful than I'd expected and the diversity of line fascinating. The aircraft *Indefatigable* was lying there. Captain Michael Stephenson, R.N., who commanded an aircraft-carrier in the war and is now on his way to be N.O.I.C. Karachi, and John Dalison in gold lace and ribbons, set out to visit *Indefatigable* and delighted us all by sitting down simultaneously with a bump when the pinnace sent for them started unexpectedly.

There was a shower of rain. The sunset was sublime. For an hour before it the sky was pale green above a milky sea, and the effect of the flat land northward was to produce a Dutch seascape in the classic style which gradually turned into a blazing sunset by Turner behind an island as jagged as the Coolins. The whole show was magnificent. Earlier on I noticed as we came into Aden that the clouds were reflected in green bice on leaden blue giving the effect of two kinds of liquid which hadn't mixed.

A few more Indian troops came on board. We sailed about dinner time. The air was very damp. To bed about 1 a.m. A decrescent moon was riding like a boat on a broken sea of cumulus.

October 18th. AT SEA

A most exquisite day—the very perfection of weather. The sunset was remarkable not for the conventional blaze of golden scarlet in the west but for the reflection of it in the east where a large cloud the colour of loganberry-fool hung in an arch over a spectrum of blues ranging from an ultramarine bar just above the horizon up to the palest cerulean. The night was brilliant with stars, Sirius flashing white and green as I never saw it flash before.

October 21st. AT SEA

The children's party was amusing. A delightful little Abyssinian boy who got on at Port Said and a lovely little Indian girl were the stars. The Captain told me a terrible story about one of his previous voyages when two small children pushed another child of four into a bath, turned on the hot tap, and killed it. The two mothers of the culprits and the mother whose child was killed were completely distracted. The mother of the dead child would not allow it to be buried at sea in the ordinary way, and they had to make a coffin out of an apple-box. Bunny Watkins told a story of a mother who said to her small child, "if you're not good I'll throw you out of the porthole". She then left the child in charge of a small older brother, and he *did* throw the kid out of the port, presuming that to be the right way to deal with bad behaviour.

Dalison was talking about the names missionaries gave to people in West Africa. He asked one native what his name was and he replied "Pods". "What's your first name?" "Senna."

INDIA

October 23rd. BOMBAY

Up very early to find the ship coming into Bombay harbour. We were met by Brigadier W. E. H. Condon, Director of the Historical Section and Major J. L. Shaw. Lt.-Colonel J. S. Wolfe Barry, G.1 to Major-General Eric Goddard, brought me a letter from the General to say the Q.M.G. had suddenly descended on Bombay and carried him off and that we were to stay at Government House instead of Gun House. I left C. with Lt.-Colonel Wolfe Barry to deal with the luggage and drove on with Condon and Shaw to the Taj Hotel where we went up to Mr. and Mrs. Hardingham's room. Hardingham is head of Collins until Jackson Marshall comes out in mid-winter. Iced coffee and a gimlet revived me, but it was piping hot with much humidity. C. and the Colonel got back from the harbour about 11.30 and we all lunched in the hotel surrounded by various of our late shipmates. I enjoyed my first pawpaw and a really good banana.

About 16 o'clock we were driven to Government House and found ourselves housed in a delicious bungalow at the edge of the cliff. We were met by a charming young A.D.C., Paul Methuen. My bearer Gulaba Ram picked by Condon looks like being a treasure. He is a Dogra hill man from the Simla district, speaks English well and has a useful knowledge of dialects. At dinner-time the entrance to music of His Excellency and Lady Clow attended by the bodyguard across a red carpet from their part of Government House up marble steps to the dining-room was suitably impressive.

October 24th. BOMBAY

I was up and about at 7, watching the green bee-eaters at work. Wagtails were running about the lawn, and I watched a nest of young kites in the conifer growing out of a cliff, father kite being very attentive to mother kite. Miniature Brimstones were fluttering about everywhere and a sort of chipmunk with a tail like the wire brush of a baby's bottle was playing in the trees.

At noon the car arrived to take us to lunch at Gun House, where we found Lieut.-General Douglas Gracey and his wife Cecil with whom we had made friends in the *Lancashire*. I had a long talk with Gracey who commanded 20th Indian Division in Burma and has just left Pindi to command 1st Corps in Karachi. He had strong views about Imphal which he thought could have been held with less casualties. On the other hand, he admitted that the violence of the fighting and the complete smashing of the Japs in the long run had probably been all to the good from the point of view of the 14th Army's advance. He spoke highly of General Sir George Giffard and said his work had not been sufficiently appreciated. He was strongly in favour of plain speaking in the book, whoever might be offended. He did not have a high opinion of Stilwell as a general and was severe on the Ledo Road as a white elephant. Roosevelt insisted on it with his eye on the future of America in China. Only two convoys passed along it before the Atom Bomb, and already the road is reverting to jungle. He said we had lost India because we never learnt to say "please" and "thank you" at the right moment. I found his mind keen and I look forward to another long talk with him in Karachi.

We got back to Government House at 16 o'clock and after C. and Gulaba had repacked we saw the heavy luggage off to the station whence Condon and Shaw will take it with them up to Simla.

October 25th. BOMBAY TO POONA

I left Government House at 9.45 to visit the dockyard and naval barracks. It was Divali, the Hindu New Year and Feast of Lights, so the men were on holiday. The barracks occupy the original Portuguese fort on the island, dating back to 1600. They are entered through a rococo gateway, and there is a large vertical rococo sundial which Captain Cooper was only just in time to save from being knocked down for a proposed extension of the sick bay. He saved also the two big banyans in the courtyard. Afterwards Jasper Teale took me along to the Yacht Club where we met Rear-Admiral Rattray. Over coffee he and I discussed the possibility of a sloop's meeting us at Rangoon and taking us by way of the Andaman and Nicobar Islands to Penang. He was interesting on the subject of North Sentinel, an outlying island where two or three hundred negrito pygmies still live and whence they used to swim across to Port Blair and shoot convicts with poisoned arrows in order to get their identification discs as a treasured decoration. Apparently the Japs left North Sentinel severely alone.

During lunch at Government House, Sir Andrew expressed disapproval of Cunninghame Graham as a romantic and I said it wasn't reasonable to disallow a man's realistic approach to life merely because he had a good profile. I've had this battle before over Don Roberto who in point of fact was no more a romantic than I am.

We had a hurried departure by the Deccan Queen to Poona at 17.10 because the luggage car was late at Government House. However, Gulaba got our stuff safely on the train with a minute to spare. The Deccan Queen is India's star train, rather like the Brighton Belle or whatever it's called from Victoria. We had an interesting journey with two friendly Indians who insisted on giving us tea. One was a rice merchant who had lost everything when Rangoon fell and the other was a dealer in oilseed and spices who gave us cloves and cardamom seeds after tea. Later on we enjoyed whiskies and soda together. The railway journey through the Ghats in the gathering dusk was most impressive, and it was tantalizing when darkness obliterated the mountainous scene. We reached Poona at 20.10 feeling pretty tired and found comfortable quarters at the Turf Club.

October 26th. POONA

I woke early with sharp rheumatism in my knee which seemed rather ridiculous in allegedly dry Poona after damp Bombay. Horses were being exercised on the racecourse. At 10 we drove off to Headquarters of 4th Indian Division and met Major-General Maurice Chambers, Major-General T. W. Rees and Lt.-Colonel W. Stewart of the 2nd Gurkhas. Chambers, who is to be our guide to-morrow, went off and I had a long talk with Rees and Stewart. 'Pete' Rees is a short dark stocky Welsh-speaking Welshman, the youngest of a parson's very large family. It was he who in command of 19th Indian Division captured Mandalay. He now commands 4th Indian Division. After tea Stewart took us along to the 1/9th Gurkhas where various V.C.O.s* and N.C.O.s came in to tell me stories of the deeds for which they had been decorated. One Subedar-major was so eloquent that I could follow his story from his gestures. I think it was in Tunis that he had killed six Germans before they got his kukri away from him and hit him on the head with it, but with the wrong side of the kukri, he added with a broad grin. He pretended to be dead and thus had managed to get away, but, he told us regretfully, he had had to leave his kukri behind him.

After a pleasant lunch with Lt.-Colonel Dick Whittington and the officers of the 1/15th Punjab Regiment, we got back to the bungalow about 15 o'clock and I went off with Colonel M. H. Board, R.E., to see the site of the Indian War Memorial at Kharakvasla. The site for the proposed Memorial is really magnificent. I climbed a steep hill for a view of a countryside which offers a classic composition of hill, dale, woodland and water in every direction. The lake in the

* Viceroy Commissioned Officers.

foreground is to be raised another sixty feet and it is to be a combined training ground for Indian Air Force, Navy and Army at a cost of £11,000,000.

October 27th. POONA TO KOLHAPUR

Major-General Chambers and Colonel Clark arrived to escort us to Kolhapur. Maurice Chambers commanded 25th Indian Division at the capture of Rangoon. 'Clickety' Clark, a C.L.O. or Civil Liaison Officer between the Military and Civil Authorities in the matter of demobilized soldiers, is a single-hearted enthusiast passionately devoted to the Mahrattas and their history. He is depressed by his job's coming to an end next March. He tried his best to give me the names of trees and flowers as we passed, but preferred questions on old Mahratta customs. The road climbed about 2,000 feet at one point with a magnificent view below of a strath checkered with the various greens of tobacco, millet, groundnuts, sugar-cane and more rarely rice. The road was now shaded most of the way by banyan trees, with here and there a *nim* the light-green leaves of which are used like lavender and here and there small teak trees of no use as timber. We reached the travellers' rest-bungalow on the outskirts of Satara just before 13 o'clock and ate our picnic lunch to the accompaniment of tinkling cow-bells. Plague has reached Satara which accounts for the encampment of hovels on either side of the road into the town. The Commissioner, who is a high caste Brahman called Bhidi, arrived at the bungalow, having been telephoned for to investigate rioting at Mahad where the bazaar had been burnt. Bhidi is an attractive personality. His headquarters are at Belgaum. Colonel Clark left us when we drove on to Kolhapur after lunch to reach the Residency about tea-time.

Colonel Hervey gave a dinner-party for us. Among the guests was Princess Indurnati, who has been a widow since she was eleven but cannot marry again. She was a sister-in-law of the late Maharaja, whose death has set a problem to the Resident because there are at least half a dozen claimants to the throne. The Princess is a handsome woman in the grand style and wears her sari looped up between the legs. This Mahratta fashion is preserved as a relic of Amazonian exploits in the past on horseback.

The night was warm and the insects were more numerous than any we'd seen yet, including blister flies and a queer kind of hump-backed earwig. I slept like a log till nine o'clock.

October 28th. KOLHAPUR TO BELGAUM

Immediately after breakfast we drove up with Maurice Chambers and Angus Blyth through lovely country to the fort of Panhala which the Mahratta hero Shivaji defended against the forces of the Mogul in 1660 and which is now used as a summer resort by the Resident of Kolhapur. The story of the Mahrattas is fascinating, similar in many ways to the story of the Highlands. We sat on an arcaded balcony and looked down almost a sheer 1,000 feet to an immensely wide view, a cool breeze blowing and an exquisite peace diffusing itself. A framed inscription on one of the walls spoke of the building as 'this pure palace.' I revelled in that smell of immemorial stone where the sun rules and dankness is banished. In Capri there is a little church, Santa Maria di Citrella, built on what was the site of a temple of Venus on the edge of Monte Solaro. Sitting in this loggia of Panhala I could have fancied I was there again. On the other side there is a brilliant garden full of cannas and hibiscus, cosmos and zinnias. We saw a 200-feet cliff at the edge of which it was customary to stand the condemned prisoners in sacks from which only their hands emerged. In due course they became giddy and fell over of their own accord. This process was known as *tamtak* or mesmerization. We saw the three astonishing granaries each as large as a cathedral. We then drove back the 14 miles to Kolhapur through the bazaar, which in reading over this diary after an experience of many bazaars remains in my memory fuller than any of Eastern romance.

Before lunch we called in to see the cheetahs : Kolhapur is famous for its cheetah hunting. There are only six left and no more are being imported from Africa. It was a surprising sight. Each of these lovely cats was lying on a charpoy big enough to allow the syce to sleep with his charge. One of the cheetahs growled when I went to stroke it, but another rolled over and purred and I scratched it under the chin. The syce put over its eyes the leather hood which the cheetah wears like a falcon when it is taken out to hunt. The hood is slipped off when the prey is in sight and for a quarter of a mile the cheetah is the fastest creature on legs; but if he does not catch his prey in the first rush he stops. He will not hunt doggedly.

At lunch in the Residency we met the Prime Minister, Sir Thomas Austin, and Dr. and Mrs. Garipathy. He is a Coorg from South India and a graduate of Edinburgh ; she is a Rajput, a beautiful, exquisitely dressed and most intelligent woman, greatly interested in Greece.

At 14.30 we drove on to Belgaum after an all too short stay in good company and lovely surroundings. The drive was interesting all the way and particularly toward the end when we were travelling through low jungle-covered hills in which there is some of the best big-game shooting in India. We stopped for a moment beside the road near a place called Sutkavri where Maurice Chambers who is himself an old Mahratta talked regretfully of bygone week-ends in the rest-bungalow, of sport with tiger and bison, and of the fishing he had had in the river near by. As I was wondering when we were going to see our first monkeys, C. walked up the road to present three little children sitting on the roadside with three annas. The youngest child yelled at the sight of her to such good effect that it startled a group of monkeys hidden in a tree above and they went scrambling along the branches in a panic, great grey fellows called langurs.

It was late tea-time when we reached the house of Colonel Ralph Isaacs, Commandant of the Mahratta Regimental Centre. One or two Indian officers came in for drinks before dinner and then the four of us dined quietly together—Maurice Chambers, 'Ike', C. and myself. This is an old-fashioned bungalow without sanitation, but cool and pleasant and thanks to D.D.T. more or less insectless. Our host, a man of boundless geniality, had given up his own room to me. About eleven o'clock it began to rain heavily. I again slept like a log.

October 29th. BELGAUM

After breakfast we set out to go all over the regimental centre. The experience was continuously fascinating. We saw recruits drilling, learning to use the bayonet, shooting and swimming. Then we visited the King George Royal Indian Military College which was formerly the headquarters of a course for senior officers. The classrooms are cool and comfortable and we listened to a debate between some of the older boys who will be going up to the Academy at Dehra Dun next year as cadets. The latter is the equivalent of Sandhurst and Woolwich in one. We did not neglect the junior classes and I made the usual fatuous jokes that one does make on these occasions. From there we went on to the V.C.O. Mess where I talked to officers back from every theatre of the war.

Our next visit was to the Regimental School where the young recruits being given intelligence tests competed against one another in quiz teams. The N.C.O. would say, "I am going to start a garden. What do I want first?" Then one of the young recruits from each team would run to a table beside the instructor and the first who found a card with the picture of a spade had scored for his side. We passed on to the physical training ground to watch a gymnastic exercise and a squad being drilled by a boy Havildar-major with a tremendous voice for his size. Then we stopped at various classes being held in the open air for basic English, carpentry, geography, art, etc. In the last we found that the best book of paintings had been done by the boy Havildar-major. We looked in at the boys' club which is run by themselves, and from there we went to see the women's school. Here the wives of sepoys were being taught to read and write in Mahratta. There was much opposition to this at first among the men themselves, and indeed there is a good deal of opposition still. While the mothers were at their lessons the small children were being looked after in a crèche. The head-mistress is the wife of one of the senior V.C.O.s.

From the women's school we went to the hostel which is run on the interest from the sum subscribed for a War Memorial after the First World War. The children were at tiffin when we passed through the dining-room and their manners would have set an example to children of the same age at home. The whole experience was moving because this place was the fruit of the genuine devotion that the British officers feel for their Mahrattas, and the reflection that it might so soon come to an end weighed heavily on our host who has had 33 years' service. He runs a farm for the men to learn something of agriculture while they are still soldiers. They made three-quarters of a ton of sugar last year. They have first-class strains of Rhode Island Red and Leghorn fowls, turkeys and geese. At the swimming pool I noticed that the British officer acting as instructor was playing water polo with the boys. No man is accepted for the regiment who cannot swim. Much of the schooling at the hostel is done at the Catholic school of St Paul's where the Indian priest gave his word that no religious instruction would be attempted. This promise has been kept strictly. There are only eight attendants at the nice old Anglican church. Colonel Isaacs is anxious to hand it over to the Catholics who have no church here, but this is being opposed.

After tea we drove to the Parade Ground to sit in the pavilion and watch the Retreat which had been arranged. The Parade Ground is laterite almost as deep in colour as red Devonian sand-stone. On the far side from the pavilion is a screen of trellis work from behind which emerged the drums, bugles and band of the Fifth Mahratta Light Infantry, dressed in khaki with black and blue striped *pagris*. The big drum was played by an Anglo-Indian, the son of a drummer in a Highland regiment. A ceremonial fanfare was blown, and the rain which had been threatening cleared away at the sound of the bugles. The band retired, and after a display of physical training, sixty-four dancers, wearing a skilful arrangement of coloured turbans and coats but all in white trousers, performed the Lezim dance. Each dancer held a curved piece of wood from which was suspended a series of heavy metal discs like miniature cymbals but shaken like bells. The performers danced in four sets of sixteen. Two men stood in the middle, one of them sounding at intervals a weird note on a large, slim, circular brass horn round his shoulder and the other beating a drum. From time to time the war cry of the Mahratta was chanted in honour of their great leader Shivaji whose fort we had visited the day before. The rhythm and colour of that wonderful Lezim dance will be for ever memorable. I was sad when it finished and the dancers retired to sit under the trees on the right side of the parade ground and watch the Malkhamb which is the recognized recreation of every Mahratta village. Three great poles with a gilded knob at the top of each and greased with castor oil were set up by orderlies. Then about three dozen magnificent figures of men wearing nothing but orange-buff loin-cloths performed a series of bewildering acrobatics which included revolving, outstretched on the gilded knob, merely by movement of the stomach muscles. I wish these Mahratta dancers and acrobats could be brought over to London for the Military Tournament. Their performance would electrify Olympia. The Malkhamb was followed by a display of massed P.T. by the Boys' Company (ages 15 to 17) perfectly carried out. The Boys' Company attached to every Regimental Centre in India is a comparatively recent development of military training which Field-Marshal Sir Claude Auchinleck has fostered with enthusiasm. He has presented Colours to most of the Companies. They take part in ceremonial occasions, and all wear the same grey-blue uniform. In due course they pass on into the Regiment as recruits and have been an outstanding success everywhere.

When the boys had retired behind the screen three sentinels emerged dressed in the scarlet and white uniform of the Regiment more than a century ago and remained absolutely motionless for about twenty minutes while the drums, bugles and band marched and countermarched, playing among other tunes *John Peel*. This was followed by a beautifully executed slow march, with dusk turning the men's *pagris* to violet. The sound and the scene were almost unbearably poignant. I had a lump in my throat, and I knew that Maurice Chambers and Ralph Isaacs had the same, for to both of them this show was seeming the end of an old song.

The bugles sounded the Retreat. The drums, bugles and band vanished behind the screen. The three motionless sentinels came to life and vanished too. It was now the edge of night. One of the most moving ceremonies I have ever witnessed was over.

We drove back to " Ike's " bungalow to change for dinner. I

was to be a guest of the Mess and C. was dining with the ladies. Before dinner we went to the house of Mr. Bhidi, the Commissioner, for drinks, and there we met his daughter with a delicious baby and a nice husband who is a surgeon in the R.I.N. The graceful hospitality of Indians is so warming to the heart.

The Mess dinner was impressive, about forty officers sitting at the long silver-gleaming board. I sat between the Colonel and the handsome young Raja of Savantvadi who is a Captain in the Regiment. Opposite the Colonel's chair was an alcove beyond the table in which were the drums and colours guarded by a sentry with fixed bayonet, dressed in the scarlet of pre-war days, who never batted an eyelid or twitched a muscle all through dinner. Round the walls were photographs of successive Commandants of the Regimental Centre, a hirsute frieze from the Dundrearies of the 'fifties, through the smaller whiskers of the 'sixties, the beards of the 'seventies, the mutton-chops of the 'eighties, the heavy moustaches of the 'nineties, down to the toothbrushes of to-day. Field-Marshal Montgomery's grandfather was among them. The band played a selection of Scottish tunes, and after dinner we were joined by the ladies who listened to the band in scarlet playing melodious old musical-comedy selections in an open pavilion in the garden of the Mess. I felt I was in a scene of some Drury Lane drama of 1895. Colonel Isaacs was good enough to give a holiday on the morrow, at my request and his suggestion, to everybody who had taken part in that wonderful afternoon. It was a wonderful evening too, and a wonderful experience in every way, all too feebly recorded in this diary.

October 30*th*. *BELGAUM TO BANGALORE*

We most regretfully said good-bye to Maurice Chambers and Ralph Isaacs and left Belgaum about 10 by the narrow-gauge train for Bangalore.

For the first part of the journey the line ran through the Kanara jungle, but I saw only one big grey monkey. We lunched at Hubli and dined just before dusk at Harihar before coming to which we crossed the Kistna over a high bridge, so narrow that one looked down on the water on either side of the train. A quadrilateral of dark rain was over the hills away to the left. In the foreground stood a sort of burnt-umber town and the river was the colour of pale aquamarine in the sunset. I was glad to see the new moon through the open window in Harihar station. We bedded down for the night about 9 o'clock.

October 31*st. BANGALORE TO MYSORE*

We were up at dawn to find ourselves at a station called Goolhari on the platform of which were a dozen or so red-faced monkeys looking exactly like waiting passengers. I gave one of them the remains of an orange which it carried up to the top of a station building over which another one chased it. Then I saw just below the carriage window a large monkey looking at me, but I had nothing left except a banana skin which I threw to him. He picked it up, pulled it apart, and finding nothing inside threw it away with a comical expression of disgust. Then he gazed at me reproachfully and seemed to sigh. I tried to atone by throwing a piece of chocolate to him. He picked it up, sniffed it in disgust, and threw it away.

We reached Bangalore at 7.10 and it was decided we should start for Mysore about 11 o'clock.

Major Philip Poonoose of the Rajputana Rifles was to be our guide, philosopher and friend for the next part of the tour. A Syriac Christian from Travancore, he enlisted in 1914 and must be one of the first Indians to be given the King's Commission. We left Bangalore soon after 11, Poonoose expressing the gloomiest forebodings about the ability of our car to reach our destination. He had wanted to drive us in his own car, a big new Ford, but the authorities had refused to give him the petrol. The first part of the drive took us through an attractive country of fertile lowland from which weird outcrops of rock would shoot up abruptly from time to time. We reached Seringapatam about lunch-time, and walked round the fort to see the breach made upon that fourth of May in 1799 and the memorial to the fallen. We also visited the dungeons where Tippu Sultan kept the British officers he had captured earlier chained to the walls. The niches for the elbows are still to be seen. It was here that Colonel Baillie died, but others survived, including General Baird who some six years later had the pleasure of leading the unexpected assault across the river Cauveri in the blaze of noontide and later of discovering the body of Tippu Sultan himself. Highlanders and Madrassis were most prominent in the storming of Seringapatam under the command of General Harris. I think the only English regiment was the 12th Foot (Suffolks). It is when one reads through the names on a memorial like this that one realizes the extent to which England drew upon the Highlands during the first century of aggressive imperialism. In the Napoleonic Wars 10,000 officers and men went to fight from Skye alone. Two hundred men from Glen Strathfarrar fought in those wars. Fifty fought in the Crimea. Two fought in the First World War. They were almost the only men left in the Glen.

It was blazingly hot even at this time of year and we were glad to get back into the shade of the car. The mosque and adjacent Hindu temple stand now just as they did in the days of the siege. A cannon ball damaged one of the minarets of the mosque, and that's about all.

The road on to Mysore showed increasing signs of prosperity. Rice and sugar cane were everywhere, and many plantations of coconuts. We reached the Government Guest House about 16 o'clock and were welcomed by Mr. R. J. Rego who is head of the State Guest Department. The Guest House is 100 years old and luxuriously equipped. The Maharaja expressed a desire to see me, and at 17.30 I drove off to the Palace which looks like the largest wedding cake in the world. In the entrance hall stand half a dozen tigers and three enormous bison shot by His Highness, and on the wall hangs the head of a rogue elephant whose tusks repose on the floor underneath while false ones are set in the head because the weight of the originals was too much for the wall to stand. I also had a look at the armoury and saw some of Tippu Sultan's tiger-fanged knuckledusters, and what looked like a large pair of scissors eighteen inches long which when opened became three separate daggers. I also had a glimpse of the Durbar Hall and noticed the blue-glass-lined gallery in which the purdah ladies can watch the ceremonies without being seen. H.H. received me in the music room the end of which was taken up by a large electric organ. He was dressed in white with a turban of bluish-grey, silver and gold. He was wearing some rich jewelled rings. He has a pleasant, quiet, precise way of talking, and he much surprised me by saying that he had been taking in *The Gramophone* ever since 1932 when he was thirteen years old. He had secured all the earlier numbers since, and told me that the intimacy of the paper had been one of his great pleasures and that my own writing about music had meant much to him. He then went on to say he wished to start a Medtner Society and to subsidize other recordings at from £5,000 to £7,000 a year. He had just written to Captain S. T. Binstead, his Trade Commissioner in London, instructing him to get into contact with myself, Christopher Stone and Alec Robertson for advice about the founding of the Society, so he was pleased when I turned up in Mysore.

When I got back to the guest house, Mr. Rego drove us to Brindavan where the State has a beautiful hotel overlooking the gardens and the great dam which was entirely the work of Mysore engineers. The gardens are usually illuminated only at the week-ends, but the lights were turned on for our benefit, and the spectacle of fountain after fountain playing over great parterres of superb cannas and turning gold, green, purple, mauve and crimson was astonishing. At 21 o'clock we returned to the guest house and were given a sumptuous dinner with the chirruping of a myriad frogs for an orchestra.

November 1st. MYSORE TO OOTACAMUND

The private Secretary of His Highness, Sir T. Thumboo Chetty, a Catholic, arrived at 8.30 to show me St. Philomena's Cathedral which was built and endowed by the late Maharaja. Before we left he took me aside to say that His Highness wanted to present me with £1,000 immediately for any purpose connected with the gramophone I chose to spend it on. I told Sir Thumboo that I did not feel I could give the attention that would justify me in accepting H.H.'s munificent offer at the moment but that when I had finished my job out here I should like to return to Mysore for a visit and see more of this State which is an example to the whole of India of good administration. Nobody who has seen Mysore could feel the slightest doubt of India's future.

I forgot to note yesterday that when we arrived at Mysore there was a message for me to ring through to Bangalore. I talked on the 'phone with General Snelling who told me he had had a message from Condon that some M.P. would be asking presently what my emoluments were for this job and letting me know the official reply given by the India Office. They were afraid I might see some alarmist report in the Indian Press and be worried. This was thoughtful of Bill Condon.

To come back to the Cathedral. It is modelled on St. Patrick's, New York, which was modelled, I think, on one of the French cathedrals. Underneath is a reproduction of a catacomb on a small scale with a relic of St. Philomena which was taken out for me to kiss by Father Mary Joseph, a most agreeable young Indian priest. The Cathedral was full of birds and Father M. J. told me it was difficult to get rid of them. I said I was sure St. Francis would have wanted to keep them. Their presence added much to the light and airy space of this graceful building. There were pews in the south transept for a few people, but the rest of the cathedral was an expanse of marble. When it was built it overshadowed a nearby mosque, and young Muslims, to show their resentment, made a habit of breaking into the offertory-box in the catacomb. One of them was caught by a priest and given a thrashing which resulted in a riot and the burning of the West door. However, all has been peaceful for a long time now.

We started for Ooty at 9.45 and soon after leaving Mysore Poonoose bought from wayside vendors some green coconuts of which we and our drivers drank the milk in the jungle later on before we made the long ascent of the Nilgiris. I have to admit that my first experience of fresh coconut milk and flesh was a little disappointing. It was also my first experience of the jungle, but that was certainly not disappointing. Red-faced rhesus monkeys and grey langurs were plentiful. Great gothic ant-hills, one after another, rose beside the road. The brilliant flowers of trees and shrubs made me curse my ignorance of the tropical flora. This is famous elephant and tiger country. We saw where the former had been feeding on the bamboos, but it was the wrong time of day to get a glimpse of the great beasts themselves. We emerged from jungle and began the spectacular ascent to Ooty. I cannot begin to attempt a description of the views of clouds and mountains on the winding way up. It was a scene for Shelley.

A porcupine ran across the road in front of the car. They are disliked because they do so much damage to the potatoes which are grown in these hills for the whole of Southern India. We passed a big quinine plantation and factory, a certain amount of coffee, and many tea gardens. Then we reached a rolling downland to which gorse and broom had been introduced and finally arrived at Winchcombe, the home of our host, Lt.-Colonel E. G. Phythian-Adams. He is a delightful bachelor of 63 and a famous hunter. Unfortunately the mist descended just as we arrived and obliterated the view which on clear days displays a panorama for 108 miles. Our host's sitting-room is hung with tiger-skins and many heads of deer and bison. The chairs are covered with leopard-skins; there are stools of elephants' feet, and innumerable other trophies of his prowess as a shikari. Had we been a month earlier we should have seen the whole place covered with strobolanthes, which is a kind of blue Canterbury bell, and this happens only every six years. Major Poonoose had told us that the Nilgiris (Blue Hills) were called after the eucalyptus which has been widely planted. I did not believe this, because the blue gums could not have arrived here until well into the nineteenth century. Colonel P. A. set my doubts at rest by telling me that it was the strobolanthes which had given the hills their name. A large black langur frequents this country, one of which we saw on the way. I sat up till eleven listening to tales of hunting and of the old Madrassi Army for whose history he is an enthusiast, and of which he has been the C.L.O. for the last five years. It came on to rain hard during the night.

November 3rd. OOTACAMUND

The rain is still coming down in buckets, and Phythian-Adams cannot show me his view, which is maddening for him. His disappointment recalls my own when Martin Secker arrived for the first time in Capri in a dense fog and brought with him a large telescope which I could not test for three days.

The weather cleared slightly and we said goodbye to our perfect host and drove the seven miles from Winchcombe to Ooty where we were to lunch at Arranmore, the officers' hostel generously lent by the Maharaja of Jodhpur. I noticed everywhere plantations of *acacia dealbata* and, of course, masses of red and blue gums. We passed a picturesque band of Todas on the road. They are handsome aborigines, few in number, with large beards and aquiline features. We had heard them chanting at some tribal ceremony from Winchcombe. Arranmore is most efficiently run by Lady Stow, the widow of a well-known I.C.S. official. I walked round the garden which reminded me of a good West Cornwall garden. Our lunch was a beauty. I never ate a better chicken vol au vent or tasted more delicious green peas. I was gratified to hear that my article about the origin of Snooker was framed in the Ooty Club. When I was asked to hand the Cup to Joe Davis at Thurston's in 1938 I seized the opportunity to tell how on a rainy afternoon in 1886 a Gunner subaltern took out the pool balls at the Ooty Club and invented Snooker. Freshmen at Woolwich used to be called snookers. This subaltern was afterwards General Sir Neville Chamberlain. I wrote an article for the *Billiard Player* and had a letter from the General to say that my account was exactly accurate and how glad he was that the many false claims for the origin of snooker were now finally contradicted.

After lunch we set off to drive down the other side of the Nilgiris to Metapalayam. Until beyond Koonoor a heavy mist obscured most of the view, but gradually it lightened to reveal a superb wooded gorge down which the road wound between great waterfalls. I saw my first mongoose. At the bottom of the descent the sun was blazing furiously, and the road ran through an immense colonnade of areca palms. Metapalayam was garish and hot. We had tea at the railway buffet, where for the first time I saw and felt an old-fashioned punkah. Our train to Madras left at 17.50. We said good-bye to dear Poonoose with much regret; he had been splendid company. We had dinner at Eroda at 21 o'clock, but neither of us could eat much after that lunch at Arranmore. Gulaba had the beds ready when we got back into the train and in spite of the swinging I slept pretty well as far as Madras, which we reached about seven in the morning.

November 4th. MADRAS

Government House is now seven miles out of Madras, agreeably situated in a large level park full of deer.

Brigadier Mackay called for us after breakfast, and we drove with him to the docks where I met Commander J. L. Leitch for whom in 1916 I got a commission as Sub-Lieutenant R.N.V.R., to help in the control of the port of Piraeus. We were glad to meet again and by an odd coincidence I was wearing the very same white coat and trousers I used to wear in Athens 30 years ago. We went up on the roof to get a bird's-eye view of the harbour which is entirely artificial. After that we went on to visit Fort St. George and the oldest Anglican church east of Suez. It was built in 1678. I could easily have spent the rest of the day studying the tombstones and cenotaphs, almost every one of which is a piece of history. Archdeacon White showed us round, and I signed the Visitors' Book which is kept in the Treasury with much beautiful old silver. The Visitors' Book had many interesting names, and in turning over the pages I noticed as far back as 1906 the name of Douglas MacArthur. The Archdeacon had been unaware this signature was in the book.

After leaving Fort St. George we drove round Madras for a while before going to lunch at the Club. The noise and colour of Madras are fascinating. The Club is a remarkable building part of which goes back to 1780 and the rest to 1844. It was amusing to find the crows flying into the dining-room and trying to pinch the food from the sideboards. C. was feeling rather seedy and I sent her home after lunch while I went off to see various members of the Provincial Government at the Secretariat. Brigadier Mackay was with me.

The first interview was with Raghava Menon, Minister for Motor Transport and Food, a bright-eyed, direct member of Congress who had been jailed in 1942. He said at once that he was not interested in the book because he and his party had not considered it their war. I didn't bother to argue this point, but asked him if I was to understand that he and his party would prefer to forget all about the Indian Army and consign it to oblivion. He hesitated to reply in the affirmative and I went on to ask what India proposed to do in ten years' time if she were suddenly invaded by another power, let that power come from any point of the compass. He would be a rash man who would venture to prophesy that such an invasion were an impossibility. Menon agreed with this. And then I asked him point blank if he was ashamed of the Indian Army. I said we might have missed most of Homer, Herodotus and Thucydides if political partisanship had been allowed to determine the writing of epic or history. I saw he was wavering and I pressed him harder, going so far as to ask if he had the remotest idea of what the Indian Army *had* done. Finally, when I made my farewells after a lively twenty minutes, he wished the book all possible success. Mackay told me he had been much interested in watching Menon's gradual change of attitude.

The visit to the next Minister was less successful because he wasn't sure whether I was Mackenzie King or myself and I didn't waste much time with him. Avinashilingam Chettiar, the Minister for Education, was agreeable but vague. So was Kurmayya, the Minister for Public Information, who is a member of the depressed classes. My next interview, with Kotie Rerry, the Minister for Hindu Religious Endowment, was most entertaining. He is a good-looking man with a black Ramsay MacDonald moustache, and I could have fancied myself talking to an enthusiastic Gaelic Leaguer when we discussed the cultural value of home industries. I could assure him sincerely that I was in complete agreement with every one of his aims and we parted on very good terms. In his bureau I shook hands with Jiri, the Minister for Labour, who I am told is the most competent of all the Ministers. I liked the look of him much, and wished he could have spared the time for a talk. The Minister for Local Administration was Daniel Thomas, a Christian. He was well up in my books and had brought down one of them for me to sign. The Christian element is strong in Madras where St. Thomas the Apostle is believed to have landed on the so-called Mount, the only small earthly protuberance in miles of flat watery land. The mark of his footstep is supposed to be visible on marble, about the authenticity of which I fear St. Thomas himself would be a bit sceptical.

The interviews came to an end with Prakasam, the Prime Minister, an old man of 75 with a twinkling eye and benevolent countenance. The Secretariat is like a great beehive, with petitioners buzzing outside the door of every Minister's bureau.

Sir Archibald Nye, the Governor and late Vice-C.I.G.S., has a firm grasp of the situation here already. It is always refreshing to meet a man with a rapid and clear-cut mind. Lady Nye told me a good war story of Winston's successfully dodging a tête-à-tête with

Henry Robinson Luce, the Editor of *Time*, all through the day at Chequers and of Luce's getting more and more annoyed. When she went to say good night to the "Old Man", she noticed that Luce was sitting with him in a corner at last and supposed that Winston had been defeated. Not at all. He was moving ash-trays and matches about the table and talking to Luce about the Battle of Omdurman!

November 5th. MADRAS TO BANGALORE

A cobra had been caught in the park and its poison fangs taken out; so we saw it displaying its coils at the prodding of its captor who was given the conventional reward of a rupee which seems low pay. Brigadier Perouet, a Jerseyman, arrived at 9 to take me to Avadi, some twenty miles from Madras. Here I was handed over to Brigadier S. Greeves, known as Sam the Sudden, who has just been promoted Major-General and is moving to Delhi as D.A.G. Greeves is a rich personality, an M.C. with bar in the old war and a D.S.O. with bar in World War II when he was one of Gracey's Brigadiers in 20th Indian Division.

Avadi is 27 square miles of Slough Dump with palms instead of elms. It was to have been the main supply base for the invasion of Malaya and is a superb demonstration of the heartbreaking waste of war. We lunched at the *General Wade*, Ye Olde English Inne in miniature. There is another called *The Cob House* with a swinging signboard and a thatched roof. Both are run as canteens for officers. I had a talk with some Third Gurkha officers and V.C.O.s, and we had tea at a hostel run by some kind women in green dresses, where a tame mongoose sat on my knee. He had lost one eye from a dog. The car broke down, and we took to a jeep to complete our tour of this vast place. Greeves was considerate and would not allow anyone to show me his particular shed in detail. I noticed one hangar for bulldozers which looked half as big as Olympia and was the same shape. They were presenting the wireless sets to the railway stations in South India, and Madras hopes to get for nothing what is left of this immense dump. I saw enough tinned food to feed a country for a month. If I had not been in the company of such an exhilarating personality the spectacle of so much waste material would have been a gloomy one.

We had dinner early with the A.D.C.s at Government House and left for Bangalore at 21.10. The broad gauge train rocked more than the narrow gauge, but I was so tired that I fell asleep again immediately every time I was woken up.

November 6th. BANGALORE

My visit came at a difficult time for Bangalore because Southern Command was moving up to Poona. Nevertheless Brigadier Marsland, the Sub-area Commander, contrived to make admirable arrangements. I had a talk with Lt.-General Sir Rob Lockhart, and we were half an hour late for Marsland, who was waiting to take me to meet representatives of 2nd Indian Group, R.A.F. I was much struck by the intelligence of these young Indian airforce officers under the stimulus of which it suddenly occurred to me that the proper way to finish off my tour was to go on from Hong Kong to Japan and visit 4th Indian Group which had just relieved the 2nd.

After this we went on to the Regimental Centre of Queen Victoria's Own Madras Sappers and Miners, which was to some extent a repetition of the Belgaum morning.

After lunch we saw more of the Sappers and Miners Training Centre including a dear little hospital presided over by an Indian lady doctor. We were beguiled by two newly born babies asleep in cots and some enchanting convalescent children.

November 7th. BANGALORE

I drove with Brigadier Marsland to Hebbal, where we were shown the Motor Transport Training Centre. From here we went on to Jallahalli which had been designed as a hospital town to accommodate the wounded from the final attack on Japan but is used now for non-medical purposes.

We lunched at the 72nd Brigade Mess. I then went on to see the presentation of a saluting gun to the Maharaja of Mysore on the polo ground. The Mysore Lancers in full dress of dark blue with white facings and blue and white pennons were a welcome sight after so much mechanization of cavalry. Everything was refreshingly pre-war, the pavilion full of people dressed up to the nines among whom Colonel Hill in a grey tailcoat and grey top hat was the very spirit of once upon a time. Presently the state landau of the Maharaja drove on to the ground, His Highness was dressed in a white frock coat with a green and gold turban. Footmen behind held a large green and gold parasol over him, and the bodyguard in a blue and yellow uniform followed. The gun covered with the Union Jack was unveiled by Sir Rob Lockhart whose speech was broadcast through loudspeakers. His Highness made a speech of thanks in reply. When he had finished he stood to take the salute at the march past of the Mysore troops, during which all of us in the pavilion stood too. It was a good show. The two Colours of the First Battalion were crimson and dark-blue and the two Colours of the Second Battalion were crimson and yellow. The Fourth Battalion, being a kind of Home Guard, had no Colours. The band was playing in the middle of the ground, and I was told that owing to the difficulty of replacing instruments during the war any of them was likely to crack at any moment.

November 8th. BANGALORE TO BOLARUM

At 5 o'clock to the moment Brigadier Marsland's orderly roused me. Sir Philip Gaisford had been amused about this because the orderly had informed him of his intention the evening before and when Gaisford had said his own servants would do it, the orderly saluting had declared firmly that he had his orders. And that was that.

We got away from the Residency about a quarter to six to drive through a wet morning twilight to the aerodrome, escorted by Marsland's Indian A.D.C. At 6.45 exactly the plane took off for the 300-mile flight northward. The small biplane had a familiar air and I asked tentatively if it was a Dominie. It was, but it is called a Rapide out here. I made my first flight in a Dominie from Renfrew to Barra.

I was very tired and dozed a good deal of the way. In any case there was little to see, because the N.E. monsoon made the sky a monotone of grey. The big water reservoirs all over the countryside were full, and there seemed so many of them that it was like flying over South Uist. We crossed the mighty Kristna, the water of which was a lovely grey-green like a cowslip's spathe. At Secunderabad aerodrome we were met by Colonel Bruce Steer, who drove with us to Flagstaff House, Bolarum, where we were welcomed by our hosts, Brigadier J. C. Martin and his wife who are both from Edinburgh. Two Siamese cats greeted their President with extreme courtliness.

November 9th. BOLARUM

Round noon various representative officers came along to Flagstaff House. Major-General El-Edroos who commands the forces of His Exalted Highness the Nizam of Hyderabad was one visitor. He is an Arab, a superb figure of a man, a soldier of the finest quality, and exactly my notion of what Othello should be.

Dinner with Major-General Claud Pert and Mrs. Pert was jolly.

November 10th. BOLARUM

We left Flagstaff House at 9.30 and drove to the office of Brigadier L. Gilbert in Hyderabad where we were met by Colonel Ali Ahmed, a Turk from Central Asia who was to act as our guide for the morning drive round Hyderabad. I shall always remember General El-Edroos at the telephone trying to be patient with some bureaucrat at the other end. "No, I am not in the least angry", and as he said this his left hand was strangling bureaucracy with a magnificent gesture of repressed rage.

The drive round the great city of Hyderabad was absorbing and I wished we could have had a much longer time here. We went up to see the late Nizam's Palace, Heaven's View, which is only used now when the Viceroy visits Hyderabad. Colonel A.A. told us a story of one of the Arab officers in H.E.H.'s Bodyguard who went berserk during the war after a party and attacked the Palace single-handed under the impression that he was helping the Turks by attacking Moscow. The top of the morning's interest was our visit to the Golconda Fort which we entered by the Fath Dowaza (Gate of Victory) heavily spiked to protect it against the battering of elephants. Beside it was an old cauldron which once upon a time held the boiling oil used in defence. The Kohinoor Hill lies outside the Golconda Fort, which formerly was the diamond market of the East. The small rocky hill where I understood Colonel Ali Ahmed to say the great diamond was found looks like an abandoned Cornish tin mine. We had a cup of tea in the Colonel's Mess after we had marvelled at the great domed tombs of Moslem saints and sultans. We saw the Elephant tree, so called because the trunk of it looks like an elephant. We were told that it is the only tree of its kind in existence but I should like a botanist to confirm that. I thought it was a kind of baobab. It is hollow inside, but we shirked climbing down the latter to explore further.

The Hall of Privacy is a dream of oriental architecture. The four houses of a bygone Sultan's four wives stand in each corner and his own house stands in the centre. A sort of shrubby white verbena and an orange-buff bougainvillea were in prodigal bloom among the fretted woodwork and sculpted marble of one lonely silent courtyard after another. When we were nearing an end of this all too brief exploration of Golconda, Colonel Ali Ahmed moved five old gun barrels on a swivel which spurted rust-brown water over him. So before lunch he had to go and change at his house and we were introduced to his wife, his young son and a lovely little girl of seven, Dilkruz. The boy had enchanting manners and spoke perfect English beautifully.

We reached Brigadier Gilbert's picturesque house, which was the old Residency, about 13.30. Dr. M. G. Naidu and Mrs. Sarojini Naidu were there, two Indian officers and their beautiful wives, and

Colonel R. Lawrence, the Military Secretary. Mrs. Naidu was in glorious form, and I had the pleasure of sitting next to her at a superlative lunch which included a masterpiece of a curry. She said of an A.D.C. who had been given an administrative job that it was like making a duster out of a piece of chiffon. Mrs. Gilbert, who came over with us in the *Lancashire*, was the perfect hostess, and between the good talk and the good food I've seldom enjoyed myself as much.

At 16 o'clock we drove out to the Maijram where General El-Edroos had kindly arranged for us to see the Arab Bodyguard do their musical rifle drill in full uniform—red breeches, blue coats, green breast-plates and orange-yellow headdress. The instruments of the band included *mizmars* which are made of two eagle's legs with reeds, *sournayas* like chanters, and five kinds of drums. The drill was an exhilarating performance and the general effect like clockwork figures on a musical box. We had tea at the Mess afterwards and drove back to Bolarum reaching Flagstaff House about 18.30.

I had been working on the diary for about half an hour when our host rang up to tell us to come back to Hyderabad where a farewell buffet party was being given to Sir Arthur Lothian the Resident. It was like one of those invitations or commands people received in the Arabian Nights when they were taken through dark byways to alight before a dark doorway passing through which they found themselves in the middle of a banquet. At the end of our drive we suddenly found ourselves in the midst of marble and music, fairy lights, jewels, dancing and champagne. It was the house of Raja Dhanrajgir, and it was certainly some party. Unluckily rain fell and so his guests could not wander about the illuminated lawns. I was photographed with the Raja and the two Ranis, the junior of whom was an Indian film star.

After we got back to Flagstaff House I sat up with my host and heard something about his work as liaison officer between Stilwell and Alexander. He had had a tough time, being wounded, catching scrub typhus and getting his neck broken in a car accident. Mrs. Martin was out there, too, doing canteen work. A bomb had taken all her hair off, though there was no sign of such a disaster now. His daughter, 16 years old at the time, had also been wounded, and his son was fighting there as a subaltern in the Royal Garwhal Rifles. Such a family record must be unique.

November 11th. HAKIMPET TO NEW DELHI

We left Hakimpet at 10.20 in a converted Dakota of Tata Airways, coming down for lunch at Nagpur and also at Bhopal and

Gwalior. Before we passed over Agra the pilot invited me to sit beside him and I had my first view of the Taj Mahal, the Jumna, and the Red Fort, from 4,500 feet up. Some idea of the difference air has made to travel in India may be gathered from the fact that Gulaba had to leave Bangalore on November 7th in order to meet us in Delhi with the luggage four days later. We reached the Willingdon Airport at 17.20 and were met by Bill Condon with news that the Commander-in-Chief wanted me to spend the night in Delhi and that I was to dine with the Viceroy the next evening before going on to Simla. We had a pleasant evening at the Chief's.

November 12th. NEW DELHI TO KALKA

The Chief left early for Secunderabad in the morning. I had a long talk with General Sir Geoffrey Scoones, who commanded 4th Corps. He was extremely frank off the record about Imphal. Condon asked his advice about a conducting officer when we go to Burma, and he suggested Brigadier K. Bayley who was B.G.S. of 4th Corps for over a year, and is now commanding the Independent British Brigade at Meerut.

After tea Bill Condon took C. and myself for a drive round Delhi which ended in our climbing up the steepest and tallest steps I have yet encountered to the top of the tower on the famous Delhi Ridge. In the evening we dined with the Viceroy, whom I had not met since he was a Major in the Black Watch in October 1916. I told him that most of Whitehall had notified Chatto's that they expected to see *Indian Epic* before publication, and he said, "Don't let anybody tinker with your book. It has nothing to do with Whitehall." He told me that if I wanted to consult any books his were at my service. At dinner he told a good story about a private and a sergeant at the first battle of Ypres who were walking up towards the line together through the mud and rain. At last the private asked if they couldn't sit down for a minute and rest. "Rest?" exclaimed the sergeant. "What do you want a rest for now? You'll be dead in half an hour."

As we were going off to catch the train for Kalka one of the A.D.C.s told me that H.E. would like me to stay with him on my return to Delhi from Simla. We had a quick drive to the station because the curfew was on and the streets were deserted. The journey up to Kalka was comfortable.

November 13th. KALKA TO SIMLA

We left Kalka by car at ten o'clock, and after a seemingly interminable series of green loops reached Simla at lunch-time which looks as if a giant jigsaw puzzle with a view of Grindelwald on one side and Golders Green on the other had been upset over a jumble of mountains. I am staying with Brigadier and Mrs. Condon at Bemloe. The sunset was a roseate wonder in a cloudless sky after which the temperature went down to 45 degrees.

November 14th. SIMLA

I spent the morning in the Historical Section offices working out the details of the Middle East tour with Brigadier Condon, Lt.-Colonel A. E. Cocksedge and Major John Shaw.

November 16th. SIMLA

C. had a terrific day of re-packing, and I was taken aback to be told that we had to have yellow fever injections for Eritrea and the Sudan. C. who had spent the morning doing accounts at the Historical Section was nearly whisked off to some bacillary G.H.Q., 20 miles away, to be done on the spot. It was finally decided to have it done in Karachi. India has the mosquito that carries yellow fever, but so far yellow fever has not reached India, and they are wise to insist on not allowing anybody who has been in Africa to land in India without a certificate of inoculation.

November 17th. SIMLA

In the morning we went to see our future abode at Snowdon, the house of the Commander-in-Chief. The original house was enlarged by Sir George White from a smaller one lived in by Lord Roberts. Then Lord Kitchener obtained a grant to make the Commander-in-Chief's house really worthy of him, and he must have spent a lot of money on the synthetic Tudor and Jacobean interiors with their red corrugated iron roof. The ornate ceiling in the drawing-room is papier mâché made from the military files accumulated in years. There is a large ballroom with a stage, and a squash court right in the middle of the house. The view is magnificent—a fifty mile range of the Himalaya beyond a series of lower peaks. The garden is well planted and full of birds. This is an appropriate place in which to write *Indian Epic*, among the ghosts and portraits and heraldic shields of bygone Commanders-in-Chief. A swan song could not have a better setting.

I had a long talk with Wavell's son, Archie John. He was a Major in the Black Watch and lost a hand in Burma. He is doing Army Education work up here. He told me of his father's hairbreadth escapes in planes during the war. A most attractive young man—sensitive, humorous, completely natural, and an obvious artist.

November 18th. SIMLA TO NEW DELHI

Gulaba went on with the luggage at 12.30. Condon, C. and I followed by rail motor at 17.35. I sat in front between an interesting Parsee called Warden and the driver, a Punjabi Mussulman in a Balaclava helmet. It was too dark to see anything of the scenery, but once or twice a jackal sneaked away in the light of the engine. We dined at Barog just before 20 o'clock. It was very cold and so was the food.

We left Kalka at 22.45 hours arriving in Delhi at 6.50. Major Peter Goodwin who is head of the photographic section at Simla had secured us comfortable quarters in the train. He hopes to visit Tibet this winter. A signpost on the road past Snowdon says 'To Tibet', but that road loses itself in the hills not many miles on.

November 19th. NEW DELHI

We were met by Captain J. Scott, one of the Viceroy's A.D.C.s, and I was installed in the Dufferin suite. Upstairs, C. is in the Minto suite. I spent the morning catching up with diary and writing one or two letters. In the afternoon I went out with Bill Condon to the Chief's House. Here I had a long and a most interesting talk with General Bruce Scott who commanded 1st Burma Division in the 1942 retreat. He spoke highly of Curtis. He said the Chinese fought only one real battle, and that was at Toungoo, where they burnt a large area around the centre they were holding. The fire was a hundred yards away from the only supply dump left to them and to our own retreating forces. Bruce Scott said it was saved by a miraculous effort made by one supply company commanded by a son of Bill Condon. He had a low opinion of Chinese discipline, and thought Stilwell thickheaded. Stilwell never could grasp why we were not advancing instead of retreating.

Commissions in the Burma Rifles were given to the employees of MacGregor's timber company, and the stars for their shoulder straps were cut out of evening socks. Bruce Scott insisted that the Burma Rifles had been unfairly criticized and that in the circumstances they had fought admirably. It was a hard business to have to retreat and leave their families and homes in the hands of such a foul enemy. He spoke with enthusiasm of the Cameronians. One night he found his tent pitched near a stinking dead cow. "Who pitched my quarters by this bloody dead cow?" he shouted. Presently a Cameronian sergeant sent a chit to say, "General's bloody dead cow safely out of the way!" A fatigue party had buried it.

After that long talk with Bruce Scott I had a talk with Auchinleck. It was agreed that, after I come back from the Middle East at the end of December, I should go and stay with the Jam Saheb at Jamnagar. H.H. had already invited me when I met him earlier in the afternoon, but I said then that I didn't think it could be managed. So it is a bit of luck that the Chief is going there himself for a brief holiday. The Jam Saheb is a magnificent Rabelaisian figure whom I first met in Ireland as long ago as 1924. He was then a quiet solemn young man much in awe of his uncle the great Ranji.

I dined with Pandit Nehru. Mrs. Naidu was there with an attractive and witty daughter who lives in Hyderabad. There were no Europeans except myself, and before dinner people kept coming in and going out of the house in an agreeable Bohemian atmosphere. Nehru is a man of altogether unusual charm. I had a longish talk with him alone after dinner and I offered to hand over all my material to an Indian if one could be found to write *Indian Epic*. Questions were always being asked in the Assembly about my qualifications and why an Indian author had not been chosen. Nehru said that the country had had to be "infected" with Nationalism, and that I would understand why that had been necessary in order to make it nation-conscious. He thought I should pay no attention to the sharpshooting in the Assembly. I'm afraid that the rest of the talk must remain unrecorded.

November 20th. NEW DELHI TO LAHORE

Condon and I went off at 10 to R.A.F. Headquarters and saw Air Commodore McCloughry. He promised every help possible in the way of planes, but the problem of maintenance is becoming insuperable. From McCloughry we went to see Commodore J. Lawrence, R.N., the Chief of Staff to the Vice-Admiral, Sir Geoffrey Miles, who is away. The Commodore was helpful and promised to do all he could to secure a sloop in mid-February to take me round the Arakan creeks and on by way of the Andaman and Nicobar Islands to Penang. The trouble is refitting. The Commodore sent for John Dalison, who thought that a trip in the sloop would be a grand opportunity for him to fill in some gaps in Naval Intelligence. I hope he will be able to manage this. He and his wife and Susan are living uncomfortably and expensively in a Delhi hotel at present.

November 21st. NEW DELHI TO LAHORE

There were twenty-six people at lunch, including three members of the Government. The most picturesque was Chazanfar Ali Khan in a blue European suit with a magnificently arranged turban that seemed to float across the room, Liaqat Ali Khan was also there.

I sat next Mr. Bhabha, who is the Minister for Works, Mines and Power. He has an agreeable sardonic wit. Sir George Abell was on the other side.

We had dinner early in the Tiger Room with Colin Mackenzie, the Assistant Military Secretary, Freddy Burnaby-Atkins, and Mr. and Mrs. Philip Mason. Mason as Philip Woodruff wrote that excellent novel *Call the Next Witness*. We were due to leave Delhi for Lahore in the Frontier Mail at 21.15, but it was considerably late, so we did not have to rush through dinner and could enjoy some capital conversation. We reached the station five minutes before the train started round about 23 o'clock. A very dirty dusty coupé, much knocked about by British troops.

November 22nd. *LAHORE*

We were nearly two and a half hours late at Lahore and were met by our kind and charming hostess Mrs. Bruce, the wife of Major-General J. G. Bruce, with Captain Narindar Singh, 60 years old and looking exactly like Phelps, the late Provost of Oriel, and Kashi Ram. The two latter are working with the C.L.O. on demobilized soldiers' welfare. Captain Narindar Singh and I were joined by Miss Tehmina Masters, a Parsee girl of extreme competence, subtle charm, and much humour. Her parents died recently, and she was getting her young brother on his feet in Amritsar to carry on the family business of making mineral waters. She and I and Narindar Singh visited the Employment Bureau where the official in charge showed us his filing system in a bureaucratic rapture. When we escaped at last from dockets and files I was given a glimpse of the Emperor Jehanghir's famous tomb and some of the surroundings of Lahore.

After lunch at Flagstaff House we went to the village of Narli about twenty miles away, driving along a road two feet thick in dust. We met there Mrs. Setti, a merry matron who manages to look after her husband and a young family and spend most of every month driving round outlying villages to deal with cases of hardship, on a salary of 100 rupees a month. At Narli the chairs were set out on the equivalent of the village piazza and I talked with a number of old pensioners. From Narli we went on to Gawind where the chairs were on a platform outside the school. We talked to more ex-soldiers, and then we had tea in the courtyard of the schoolmaster's house. Hardboiled eggs and some capital aubergine fritters. The schoolmaster's wife, who prepared the splendid tea, was too shy to preside herself because she did not speak English, but C. and I were introduced to her before we left. We drove back in the dusk and the dust.

November 23rd. LAHORE

I left Flagstaff House at 9.30 to visit No. 1 Group R.I.E.; it was rather too much machinery and dust, but I enjoyed seeing the men about to be demobilized learning trades. Soap-making is one of the most popular. At 11 o'clock I went on to visit the Regimental Centre of the 8th Punjab Regiment. Colonel J. F. Scotland the Commandant, a large genial man, showed me round with an infectious enthusiasm. He rivals Colonel Isaacs at Belgaum with the farm he is running, and showed me a patch of sugar cane from which he expected to make Rs.3000 clear profit. I was shown a real beauty of a model house for ex-soldiers costing Rs.2500. I feel it is impertinent to praise the devoted work done by the Commandants of these Regimental Centres, but I must set on record my deep admiration of what they have done and are doing. Where the idea originated that Indian Army officers are particularly prone to blimpery I do not know, but it's bad biology.

After lunch C. had to deal with packing and I went with Mrs. Setti, Miss Masters and Captain Narindar Singh to the village of Khamman. This is a largish community, and there I got a closer view of village life than in either of the previous two I had seen. It was a long business walking down alley after alley and occasionally looking in at farmyards and houses. I was shown a small austere Sikh temple close by which was a little mosque. The adobe fretwork done by the women was attractive. In the courtyard of one house was a pole with a sort of straw parasol over it for the pigeons to sit upon. I was given a bag of popcorn to eat with a lump of brown molasses sugar. Popcorn dipped in sugar used to be a speciality of the Spa at Scarborough fifty years ago. We drove back along the side of the canal and were held up quite a long time by one of the gates being locked.

Major Peter Petit who is going to be my conducting officer in Eritrea, Damascus and Libya, arrived with his wife in a station-wagon from Campbellpore. They were going up to Simla and joining us in Karachi.

November 24th. LAHORE TO DHARMSALA

We left just after 9 for Dharmsala, 160 miles away, Gulaba staying behind to take the other half of the luggage on to Karachi. Colonel Hutchins drove the station wagon with the rest of our luggage, and Bruce kindly lent me his orderly. We stopped to visit the Shalimar Gardens, an exquisite piece of Mogul architecture, but unfortunately the fountains were not playing. The old havildar at the gate had been in the Viceroy's Bodyguard when Minto was

Viceroy. The first part of the drive was across the dusty Punjab plains. We met many camels. In Balata, one of the towns through which we passed, all the inhabitants were busy with various kinds of ironwork on either side of the main street. Twenty miles further on the inhabitants of Dina Nagar were working in the same way with wood. Beyond Pathancot, the road grew more and more beautiful all the time, and the last sixty miles ran through as lovely country as ever I saw. It was like the Highlands on a much larger scale. The Himalayan peaks run right along the northern horizon, rising to about 17,000 feet. There was not much in the way of wild life except an occasional monkey and lots of green parakeets. I saw a blue jay, which is supposed to be lucky. We did not reach Dharmsala, 5,000 feet up, until 15.30 where we had tea with the Deputy Commissioner, who is an Indian, and met various locals including Major Bhakshi of the Dogra Regiment, a fine old military figure of the past.

After tea we set out to visit the village of Chetru, five or six miles back on the way we had come. We left the car at a bridge and walked across a paddy field for a while until we reached a roughly paved path up the hillside to this typical Dogra village. We went over the house of a water carrier, which was extremely clean and tidy; there had been no warning of our visit. A man who had been badly wounded in the back by a shell in Libya was brought to me, and we heard that his pension was only 12 rupees a month, because as an army cook he was not a combatant. This seems hardly reasonable. He was unable to work as his lung had been affected. Later on Captain Kirpa Ram of the 11th Territorial Battalion of the 17th Dogras, the local squireen, took us to his attractive house higher up and gave us drinks.

It was dark before we left Kirpa Ram's house, when we were shown round the cow stalls and buffalo stalls by lantern light. His small grandson, aged five, walks two miles to school and back each day. Before leaving I was presented with a brace of Himalayan pheasants. The cock is black and white with a bright red eye and the hen is brown. Then we were lighted down the hillside and across the paddy field back to the car.

The whole experience had an Arcadian fascination about it.

November 25th. DHARMSALA TO JULLUNDUR

We left Dharmsala soon after 9 for Jullundur, 182 miles away and reached the Commissioner's House there just before 5 and found him and his wife rather worried because he was expecting me at 15 o'clock to go to a birthday party of the Maharaja of Kapurthala. The Commissioner is C. N. Chandra. Baradari is an old house where

Henry Lawrence lived for three years from 1846. I pleaded dust and fatigue, and my hosts let me off. So I rested until a pleasant dinner party that evening.

November 26th. JULLUNDUR TO LAHORE

We set out soon after 9 to visit the Dogra Regimental Centre where Colonel Bristowe had arranged a grand display of jungle warfare. There were lots of good bangs, swinging upside down over water obstacles by rope, and crawling through a dense thicket of tree dahlias. A demonstration of holding a defensive position in a village for 24 hours was in progress.

From the Dogra Centre we went on to King George's Royal Indian Military School for the sons of Indian soldiers. I visited every class room. I was much struck by the small Sikh temple in a corner of the grounds, where the Sikh members of the school worship. We went on to lunch with Brigadier and Mrs. Farwell at Flagstaff House—one of the most attractive Flagstaff Houses we had seen. A particularly delightful young Sikh major, Jogindar Singh, was present and two other agreeable Indian officers. Our host is the Sub-area Commander, and as usual one was aware of the respect and affection that the Indian officers have for the senior British officers.

At 2.30 we set out to see the village of Liddar, picking up Mr. and Mrs. Chandra in their car on the way. Here we watched people working at looms, sitting in shallow pits in the shade of the trees. We walked all over the village and saw the smithy under a spreading acacia tree. I talked with various old pensioners. We enjoyed beer in one hospitable house and disappointed another hospitable house by not having time to wait for tea. We were sorry to part from our kind hosts who had taken so much trouble to make us comfortable. From Liddar we drove on as fast as we could with beaming genial Khashi Ram to Beas. Here we picked up Miss Masters and Narindar Singh. There was no time to visit the village we had intended to visit here, and we drove on to Amritsar, where various prominent municipal personalities interrupted a council meeting to give us a marvellous tea at the Club. Chilli sandwiches and various new and delicious kinds of cakes and sweets. It had been planned that we should visit the famous Golden Temple of the Sikhs, but much to my disappointment time did not allow this to be done. As it was we did not reach Government House in Lahore until 19.30, relieved to find there was no formal dinner-party.

November 27th. LAHORE TO KARACHI

We reached the airport at 8.30 and left for Karachi at 9.30, coming down at Quetta for half an hour on the way. The approach by air is formidable indeed. Barren mountains up to 10,000 feet high almost encircle the level plateau on which Quetta lies and one flies among them thankful that all is calm and clear. It was brilliantly sunny and icy cold when we landed at the airport. The thermometer goes down to 22 degrees at night.

We reached Karachi at 15.45 and were met by Captain Langmead, Douglas Gracey's G.3, and Nawabzada Major Amir Khan who is a son of the Nawab of Hoti.

November 28th. KARACHI

Major-General C. H. Boucher, of the 2nd Indian Airborne Division, arrived at 10 o'clock to drive me out to H.Q. of 14th Indian Paratroop Brigade, I walked round for two hours, talking in turn to V.C.O.s and N.C.O.s of the 1/12th Frontier Force Regiment, the 4/6th Rajputana Rifles (Outram's), and the 2nd Gurkha Company of the Indian Paratroop Regiment. Boucher was one of the stars of the Eighth Army and did a good escape in Italy.

November 30th. KARACHI

Dear ebullient Amir Khan came dashing in at 8.30 to say we were due to attend a practice parade at the Baluch Regimental Centre for the ceremonial attestation of recruits to-morrow, I gulped down two bananas while dressing, and we were not more than ten minutes late, Amir gallantly taking all the blame. I was invited to take the salute for the march past of the Battalion. Then Colonel Fellows the Commandant took me to see Black Bull farm which is a harder agricultural proposition in that dry sandy Karachi soil than Isaacs had at Belgaum or Scotland at Lahore. I went round the training centre, and here as everywhere else soap-making was the most popular choice. I also watched the various stages of the demobilization process. I saw too the various amenities. In charge of the recreation and reading rooms I met Naik Bhandari Ram of the 16/10th Baluch Regiment who won a V.C. in Burma. He's a Dogra from the Simla hills with a gentle voice and manner. I think it was in this room that there was hanging the sword of Naik Fazal Din, a Punjabi Mussulman, of the 7/10th Baluch Regiment, who was awarded a posthumous V.C. in March, 1945. A Japanese officer ran him through the chest with his sword and as he withdrew it Fazal Din snatched it from him and killed the officer with his own sword. Then he killed two more Japs with the sword and waved on his platoon to capture the enemy position. He died at the Regimental Aid Post.

Lunch was at the Baluch Mess in Karachi and when it was over we saw some Khotak dances on the lawn. It is not fair to see them by daylight in such a setting. They are meant to be danced round a bonfire at night. Tabors and a pair of instruments between a flute and a chanter provided the music. The most effective dance was a wedding dance with handkerchiefs called the bulbula.

When we got back to the hotel we found that Peter and Rachel Petit had arrived.

December 1st. KARACHI

We left the hotel at 8.45 and drove over a sandy waste to the airport. The flying boat *Castor* was airborne by 10.15, but after flying over the sea for an hour and a half one of the engines went wrong and we had to return to Karachi. We ate the lunch we should have eaten on board at the airport and then came back to the Palace Hotel. It was a tiresome anticlimax and we all felt very tired. My diary for these last crowded days is evidence of that. As I stop dictating I hear we are to be called at 4 to-morrow morning. The four of us recuperated after this shock by eating lots of oysters, which were served without the shell. They are the pot-bellied Blue Point type, which is not my favourite.

IRAQ, EGYPT, ERITREA, LIBYA, SYRIA

December 2nd. KARACHI TO BAHREIN

It was a long dark bumpy drive in the bus to the airport where the customs formalities gone through yesterday had to be repeated. The medical formalities were confined to having our pulses felt for about a couple of seconds. We had breakfast and were airborne about 8. I was too tired to pay any attention to the savage coast of Baluchistan and dozed in my comfortable seat most of the way to Dubah where we came down to fuel. We went ashore, drank some excellent lemonade and took on with us four dignified Arabs half an hour later.

Our next port of call was Bahrein where we were told that another engine had gone wrong and that we were likely to be there for at least four hours. So we were driven in a hard-seated transport bus along a bad road to see a pool among the date groves, full of large stately fish and small turtles, into which small boys dived for coins. Among the passengers were two Chinese officers, one of whom had his wife with him and a delightfully well-behaved small son. There was also an American lady who was in a state of gloom because she would miss the train at Basra for Baghdad and Istambul and would have to wait nearly a week for another one. This had happened to her twice in three weeks, and she was fierce in her criticism of B.O.A.C. The *Castor* is over ten years old and is to be scrapped at the end of the year. She had been at the Narvik evacuation and also at Crete and had taken part in the recapture of Rangoon. Morgan the purser has been with these flying boats since they were started and has met every contemporary V.I.P. except Stalin and Roosevelt as passengers. The only V.I.P. he disliked was . . . well, readers will have to guess.

On the way back from the pool to the Rest House we passed a gathering of wild dancers bare to the waist, with a band and three banners. They were practising with noisy groans for Mohamar, the Muslim day of mourning on December 5th. When we got back to the Rest House we found we should have to stay there for the night because the engine wasn't ready. It was a poor dinner and the place was black with flies. I was given a bedroom to myself and I was so tired that I fell asleep before I had finished undressing. C. shared a room with the nice wife of some oil man in Basra who had flown to Bombay and back to fetch an Aberdeen bitch called Sally, an agreeable animal laudably obsessed with a mission to snap up as many flies as possible.

December 3rd. BAHREIN TO HABBANIYA

We were called at 4.30 a.m. I was the first down in the dark to find the eating-room black with flies. I turned on the fan and opened the windows which got rid of a good many. At 6, when we were due to start, Captain Blackaller came in to say there was bad news of heavy fog at Basra. We breakfasted at the Rest House. Then we went down to the landing stage where we sat about until half an hour after sunrise, when it was decided that by the time we reached Basra the fog would have lifted. So on we went, flying over the Garden of Eden and looking down at the Euphrates and the Tigris. It was as well we hadn't started earlier ; a Skymaster had had to circle for 40 minutes before coming down at Basra. Here we had coffee by a cheerful fire and were off again half an hour later.

We came down on the lake at Habbaniya at about 12.30 fully expecting to hear that a plane would take us on to Damascus. However (I am afraid I must say as usual) the R.A.F. were completely vague about everything when Peter Petit rang up to enquire about the prospects for getting on. We decided it would be best to continue our journey in the *Castor* as far as Cairo, but meanwhile some other passengers had gone on board and with the conked-out engine he was carrying the Captain wouldn't take the risk of a bigger load. So Rachel Petit went on to Cairo alone, while P.P., C. and myself hung about the embarkation office and filled up forms to say we had nothing dutiable in Iraq until Wing-Commander Fraser, the Intelligence officer, came along in a car, drove us to the Cantonment, and gave us a capital lunch in the Officers' Club. After a lot of telephoning it was finally decided that the only possible way of getting anywhere was to take the Service Dakota to Lydda in Palestine. C. was tired and a bit upset after the fly-blown food at Bahrein. So she retired to bed and had a much needed rest preparatory to flying in the discomfort of a Service Dakota next morning.

At 18 hours I went along to have drinks with Colonel Luce who commands the Levies and had kindly invited four of his Assyrian officers to meet me—Rab Kheila (Leader of the Force) Zaia Gewergis M.B.E., Rab Tremma (Leader of 200) Odisho Nathan M.B.E., Rab Tremma Soski Paulos, Rab Emma (Leader of 100) Baijan Peco M.C.

These Assyrians were instigated by us in the First World War to rebel against the Turks and have been a responsibility we have been trying to get rid of ever since. They are nearly all Nestorian Christians except a few who are Catholics. I fancy that the Syriac Christians in the south-west of India are a kindred stock. They spoke English well, and reminded me of Indian V.C.O.s. They gave me a vivid account of the Iraqi revolt in April-May '41. There were about 750 of them and they seem to have put up a good show, but they said the A.O.C. in his despatch never mentioned them and took all the credit for the R.A.F. ground staff. They claimed casualties off the Iraqis up to 2,000. Their own casulties were 22. One platoon of the Assyrian Levies was occupied in guarding the company of Arab Levies who wanted to join the Iraqis. This whole Habbaniya business is mystifying.

I got to bed by midnight and in spite of the minute ants running all over the bed and a stray cockroach or two went to sleep at once, having arranged to drive round the battlefield before catching the Service Dakota at 10.30.

December 4th. HABBANIYA TO LYDDA

I was up and dressed by 8.30, but the heavy downpour of rain since 6 now turned into a mist and there was no visibility for visiting a battlefield. At 9 o'clock Wing-Commander Fraser came along to say that the Dakota had broken down at Shaiba and would not be leaving until the afternoon. At 11 Squadron-Leader Stapleton came along to say it would not leave before 19 o'clock, which means landing in the dark at Lydda and doesn't sound too good a prospect. P.P. is now trying to get us driven to Bagdad this afternoon to catch a Misr plane to-morrow morning at 6.45 from Baghdad to Cairo, abandoning the idea of reaching Damascus first. The whole business is a muddle and this place is like an enormous lunatic asylum. It was built before the war at a cost of £7,000,000 and the lease with the Iraqi Government has to be renewed in 1948. There is no training school here now and only four planes. So the ground staff of 2,000 really have nothing to do. Besides the ground staff there are 5,000 civilians occupied in maintaining the station. Ten years ago the whole place was desert; now it is beautifully planted with avenues of gum trees already 30 feet high. There are yachts on the lake, squash courts, cricket and football fields, a race course, cinema theatres, everything to keep people amused except the female form for the absence of which pin-up girls are not perfect compensation.

Women are not allowed on the station because the thermometer goes up too high in summer. So the atmosphere is unhappy. I doubt if the training of the R.A.F. is capable of turning out men to run a station like this properly. It is a sad contrast to the Regimental Centres in India.

P.P. has just come in to say that the Dakota is on its way and that we shall leave here at 19 o'clock for Lydda. Incidentally, I always thought that loofahs were some form of marine life. I asked if the gourds growing along the verandah outside my bedroom were edible and was told that they were loofahs. They are the pods of *Luffa Aegyptica.*

After hurrying down to the aerodrome to be there by 19 o'clock, we finally got off at 21.30. The Dakota was draughty, ramshackle, foully uncomfortable, and frightfully cold because we had to fly at 10,000 feet to get out of bad weather, and the heating didn't work. The machine was full of Erks and a couple of Waafs. At 1 a.m. after three and a half hours of misery we landed at Lydda on one wheel and put up at the Transit Rest House after a welcome snack.

December 5*th. LYDDA TO CAIRO*

The beds were hard and bumpy and the toilet arrangements were squalid. We were up by 7, but had to hang about till noon before Group-Captain Morrison, who was extremely kind and patient, managed to secure an Anson in which we flew to Heliopolis. Lydda is close to Tel Aviv and while we were waiting for the plane Jewish terrorists a few miles away drove a lorry laden with explosives into the camp at Sarafand where it exploded.

At Heliopolis we were met by Colonel Ross Majentie, the liaison officer with India, and Major Bishop who is Number Two to Brigadier MacCormack, the Public Relations Officer. We reached Shepheard's Hotel in time for lunch. We paid 120 piastres for bedrooms without baths. The noise of motor horns outside was incessant. From the Club we went to G.H.Q. to discuss the future programme with Brigadier MacCormack, who told me he had just invented a slogan for air travel: *Travel by Air If You've Time to Spare.* He was pessimistic about our ability to carry through the programme mapped out for us.

December 6*th. CAIRO*

Severe pain all day.

December 7th. CAIRO TO KHARTUM

After a baddish night alleviated by the kindness of Rachel Petit who sat up with me to give C. a chance to sleep I managed to get dressed and also to leave Shepheard's Hotel, where the bill was almost £20 for two nights. We were airborne in a B.O.A.C. Durban flying-boat at 11 and, stopping half an hour at Luxor and Wadi Halfa, reached Khartum at 18.30. I slept nearly all the way.

I was quite fit by the time we were due to go to dinner with the Kaid—Major-General W. D. Stamer. An extremely pleasant evening. We had a delicious melon ice.

December 8th. KHARTUM

I had a perfect night and at 9 went round with Peter Petit to see Major Scott (K.R.R.), the G.2. Later on Scott took us round to Arber of Public Relations. Arber said he should never forget what a relief it was, after the Italians had declared war, to see the 3/5th Mahrattas marching into Khartum, so trim and jaunty with their green hose tops and scarlet hackles, looking as if the world was theirs. This battalion arrived a couple of months ahead of any other. If the Italians had had the transport they could easily have taken Khartum at the beginning.

At 11.30 escorted by Behari Effendi of the Sudan Defence Force we drove to Omdurman, which is all café au lait and neat compared with Indian towns of the same kind. They were shooting a couple of mad dogs as we passed. The florid cemetery of those who fell in the battle is on the outskirts of the town. We drove on across the desert to the site of the battle. It's an arid and desolate spot. We saw a couple of sand devils—the equivalent of a water spout in sand. Behari told me his name meant "sailor", and then added apologetically, that is of course to say "slave dealer".

The Grand Hotel is good, and the prospect from the terrace beside the Blue Nile is delightful. Even in December Khartum is 94° in the shade and blazing in the sun. It must be terrific in May. We had a capital lunch with plenty of olives.

At 8 o'clock I went off to supper with the Governor—Major-General Sir Hubert Huddleston. He was still at church when I arrived at the Palace, and I found Lady Huddleston watching a total eclipse of the moon with a pair of opera glasses. The whole disc turned to an unnatural greenish-red colour. We had been told that the natives would start beating drums to frighten away the rat that was supposed to be eating the moon, but sophistication has evidently set in here, for no one seemed to pay much attention to it. Sir Hubert came back from a long sermon by a Church of Scotland minister and we went out in the Palace launch to eat a supper in the middle of the Nile under the emerging moon. Huddleston, who is much esteemed as Governor, is about the only man senior to myself I have met out here. He is Colonel-in-Chief of the Dorset Regiment, and he said how proud he was to find himself next to Thomas Hardy in the roll of the freemen of Dorchester.

I was interested to hear that in one part of the Sudan they produce a blood grapefruit, the rind of which is much deeper in colour. This would be a good line for a fashionable fruiterer if it could be marketed in England. There is an obstinate belief that the blood orange is the result of fertilization by pomegranate pollen. Complete nonsense, of course. In the Palace I saw the stone marking the spot where Gordon was killed, but a new storey has been added since then, and the externals of the tragedy are quite different. A panoply of captured drums, lances, guns and other weapons covers the walls, not to mention the breastplates and helmets of cuirassiers, because the Sultan, whose name I forget, dressed his bodyguard in the same uniform as that of Napoleon III.

December 9th. KHARTUM TO KEREN

We were up early, and at 8 Major Scott arrived to escort us to the aerodrome. It was about half-past nine when we took off in a Wellington to Asmara. At first, the ground below was amber and ochre with occasional splashes of raw sienna. Then the whole desert became a kind of greenish-yellow tabbied silk over which we flew at about 10,000 feet. When we drew near to Kassala we came down to less than 500 feet for P.P. to take some photographs and caused a good deal of alarm to the goats and camels, and to the human beings living in clusters of beehive huts, or rather haycock huts, for that is what they resemble more. Extravagant rocky shapes rose up from the desert, which as we flew on increased in size to become isolated mountains and reminded me of the scattered bens of Sutherland. For a while the pilot was uncertain of his way and was looking for a telephone wire to guide him out of the fantastic gorges and ravines through which we were roaring into as much space as would give him a chance of gaining the height to fly over the 8,000-ft barrier of mountains. It made us a little anxiously pensive until we reached the air over the high plateau round Asmara, from which after circling round two or three times we landed safely on the small Asmara aerodrome. There was the usual fuss about passports and as we got out of the plane we were solemnly flitted. This is a zone of British Military Administration, and a customs examination for a party like ours seemed otiose. It was 13.45 when we reached the Headquarters of Brigadier Nigel Tapp which had once been the residence of the Italian Governor. Lifeless portraits of Fascist personalities turned out like oleographs lined the corridors. I still think that instead of hanging some of the war criminals we should have paraded them round the world like a menagerie or freak show as a diversion and a warning to the rest of mankind.

About 15.30 Major Jelf and Major Savory arrived to take us down to Keren, a drive of about 60 miles on a continuously well engineered and occasionally spectacular road between great candelabra cactus trees and giant spurges. Every few hundred yards there is a sign-post painted with a skull and crossbones to record a fatal accident at that spot and urge other drivers to be careful. These were the result of our passion for making drivers keep to the left. It was the first thing we did after entering Asmara, and the Italian lorry-drivers were baffled by it. Moreover, the road had been constructed for keeping to the right. At the end of the descent the road ran for a few miles down a fertile valley, where a lot of sisal was being grown, and shortly before reaching Keren we drove between hedges of bougainvillea which seemed to burn like a furnace of magenta. I never saw such a solid mass of hot colour. Beyond the hedges on either side the vegetation was luxuriating in abundance of water. Orange and lemon groves, papaya plantations, and many other kinds of fruit trees wore the lustrous green of happy growth. On a knoll above, the house of the Italian proprietor—Cavaliere Somebody—stood as bare as a bleached bone. They never planted trees near houses on account of the insects.

We stopped for a while half way down to see where P.P. and his First Punjabis came under heavy fire when pursuing the retreating Italians. We reached Keren itself about 18 o'clock and went to the Grand Hotel kept by a Palermitano and Jennie, his Viennese wife, who was the popular manageress of our Officers' Club in Asmara. A high wall, over which tumble musk-roses and bougainvillea, protects the Grand Hotel from the gaze of passers by, and this wall is doubled in front of the entrance so that one goes in through an archway at the side and passes by the janitor's room up some steps into a flowery courtyard surrounded on three sides by the wide verandah of the single-storied hotel.

It is like a stage setting in a provincial Italian opera-house. The hotel bedrooms all have thick walls, small windows, bidets and shower baths; and I discovered later that the Grand Hotel was formerly the *bordello di lusso* of the Italian officers.

December 10th. KEREN

We set out at 10 to survey the incredible battlefield of Keren. My leg was still inclined to protest and I shirked going up to Fort Dologorodoc on the mules which had been provided. From where we stood the view of the battlefield was clear enough. The more one looked at it the more amazing did the achievement of 4th and 5th Indian Divisions seem.

I am doubtful of ever being able to evoke the nightmare scene. Certainly no description I had read of the surroundings of Keren had prepared me for what I was to behold. The barren mountains heaped with greyish-green boulders and the serrated peaks are what you would expect to find if you landed upon the moon. Granite predominates, but there are a good many smooth rounded boulders which I fancy may be basalt. I wish I were a better geologist. We paused for a few minutes to look at the site of the road block made by the Italians in the ravine through which the road curves down to the wide strath called ironically Happy Valley, where so many of our soldiers died. A troop of great baboons with preposterous carmine bottoms and what looked like heavy fur capes gathered on the slope above and barked angrily at us. If we had got out of the car they would have pelted us with stones. The wide level Happy Valley was dotted with thorny *zizyphus cristospina* and acacias whose thin spreading foliage cast a pale shade. Here and there among them were ancient baobab trees whose massive trunks with a tuft of twiggy growth on top seemed like browsing pachyderms. Small pied goats with wagging greedy tails and wanton eyes were all over the place, and from time to time hornbills in plumage of rusty black and off-white, some with red, some with yellow beaks, would alight to peck about in the stony soil.

We came back from the battlefield to lunch with the Spicers just as the siren was sounding to recall the workers to the button factory. Toward the end of lunch a large but slim chocolate-coloured ram came into the dining-room to beg for cigarettes to eat. I gave him a cigar, which he chewed up with particular relish. Edgar was the name of this engaging animal.

I went round to see Colonel Tregaskis, the Civil Affairs Officer, who told me that a branch of the Arab League has just been started here. Huddleston seemed to think we ought to give Eritrea to the Abyssinians. I am sure this would be a mistake. There will inevitably be trouble between the Sudanese and the Abyssinians, whom the Eritreans dislike as much as they dislike the Sudanese. The Italians should be left with what was a model colony. There are only about 800 of them in Keren now, and obviously the place will decay rapidly when they leave. The climate is perfect in winter and I am told that in the hottest season it is reasonably cool in the evening. I went with Major Jelf to see General Antonelli, a fine old Italian cavalry officer of seventy, who is the head man of the 800 Italians left. We had a long talk in Italian. He will soon leave Keren after eleven years in Eritrea to go home to Rome. Later on P.P. and I went round to the Mess of the Sudan Defence Force and did not get back to the hotel till 21 o'clock.

December 11th. KEREN TO ASMARA

We left Keren (which by the way should be spelt Cheren) at 10 hours to drive to Asmara. The chauffeur was a good-looking Italian who had been in Italian Somaliland. Like most Italians he was an absolutely first-rate driver and one was hardly aware of the hairpin bends all the way. At one point we were held back by a lorry for about four kilometres and when we were finally able to pass our driver stopped, jumped out and demanded indignantly "Avete comprato la strada?" (Have you bought the road?) The driver of the lorry pointed to his ears. He was stone deaf. No wonder the road is marked by skulls and crossbones.

Asmara is a typical little Italian town and it is depressing to think of its being handed over to the Abyssinians. There are a Catholic cathedral, a Coptic cathedral and a Mosque. After dinner most of the party went on to the Odeon Cabaret to celebrate the public holiday in honour of the King's Accession. I sat up talking with Tapp until 1.30. He is a friend of John North's and certainly one of the best-informed and clear-thinking officers I have met, with a great admiration for Montgomery and Dempsey, particularly the latter. I gathered things had not been too good in the way of administration here and that Tapp had been sent along to put the house in order. He said that the trouble with British people in a place like Asmara was that many of them were inclined to suffer from megalomania after a time.

It is high time a decision was reached about the future of Eritrea. Otherwise there will be trouble between the Muslims and the Copts, and we shall be left holding the baby. If the Italians want it they should have it. The people all like them, Neither the Sudanese nor the Abyssinians can possibly administer Eritrea, and God forbid that the Egyptians should try.

December 12th. ASMARA TO CAIRO

We had to be up by 6 to catch the B.O.A.C. Lockheed-Hudson plane to Cairo. We stopped at Khartum for an hour and a quarter, and the long flight of nearly 1,500 miles at 10,000 feet was absolutely smooth. The desert north of Khartum is a monotone of beige. The rich variety of browns and yellows one saw east of Khartum is absent. The notion that the Egyptians should administer the Sudan is risible: it would be better if the Sudanese administered Egypt.

We reached Cairo soon after 16 o'clock and had a wearisome time with the ineffable Customs, who wanted to charge duty on the Hermes typewriter. It is really monstrous that the Egyptians should control the nodal point of three continents. The sooner the Suez Canal is destroyed the better. That would give the Egyptians as much importance as they deserve and stop their dreaming about the Sudan. Australia would benefit from the round the Cape route for trade. If the Canal had been destroyed in the autumn of 1939, Mussolini might never have come into the war. Perhaps an opportunity of shortening the war was lost for lack of strategic imagination on a global scale.

We got away from the Customs at last and drove to the Ghezira Club where we met Rachel Petit and her father. After that we all went to the Mena House Hotel which lies just under the Pyramids.

December 14th. CAIRO TO TOBRUK

We were up before dawn to catch the plane for Tobruk, which by the way should be spelt Tobruch. It was blowy and cold when we reached Heliopolis. Police with tin helmets were everywhere, the University having opened again and riots being expected in consequence. Egan, our pilot, was afraid we should have a bumpy passage in the Anson; actually it was smooth. We flew over El Alamein which seen from above is a vast monotone of sand on which the military operations are still intagliated—gun pits, shell craters, slit trenches, wire entanglements, tank traps, and even the tracks of lorries. I say 'even', but considering that the tracks of the Roman chariot wheels are still to be seen in the crusted Libyan soil it is not so remarkable.

We had a good view also of Sollum and the Halfaya Pass, but I have to admit that I get no more from flying over ground in a plane than I should get from a good contour map. The colour of the earth seen from the air is the most rewarding part of flight. Recent rain had dyed stretches of the desert to a richer tawny here and there, and these seemed spread out like immense lion-skins over a paler floor.

The ultramarine of the sea against the sun-bleached sand along the shore was intense. I search for a comparison and can only think of the blue of copper sulphate, but that is an ugly simile and it is better to leave such a hue unparagoned.

We came down over the shimmering pale blue lagoons of Mersa Matruh to refuel and we did not reach the big aerodrome of El-Adem until 14.20 o'clock by which time we were so hungry that we ate with voracity the disgusting lunch provided by the R.A.F. For the first time in my life I had a second helping of boiled potatoes. The meat was something between the tongues and laces of boots: even the badly cooked spuds were more edible.

After lunch we drove the 18 kilometres to Tobruk where we put up at the Officers' Club which rises from the foundations of a Byzantine fort built by Wavell's so much admired general Belisarius. We walked round Tobruk after tea. The harbour is full of sunken ships; there are 132 of every nationality. Four thousand German prisoners are still here. Their morale is wonderfully high, but they are all longing to be home, whatever conditions may be in Germany.

The Officers' Club is a pleasant place, and it being Saturday there was a dance with an admirable orchestra of eight German prisoners. The servants are all German and keep the place spotless. What a parodox that a nation of natural servants should believe themselves natural masters.

When the dance was over I got into a jeep and went to the Pioneer Mess where I sat talking till 2 with some grand fellows and slept well on a bed as hard as a moneylender's heart.

December 15th. TOBRUK

Colonel Guy came round at 10.30 and we drove off to look at the western end of the perimeter. It was covered here and there with a dwarf sage-like scrub, and after the rain grass and small herbs were sprouting in a thin film of green. The whole area is a scene of utter desolation covered with smashed aeroplanes, tanks, lorries, petrol tins, guns and endless heaps of barbed wire. At Acroma we walked round the cemetery of over 3,000 dead which is now being laid out and is to be enclosed with a wall of the same stone as was used for Sollum cemetery. Nearby is one of Musso's pompous quasi-Roman monuments on which various nationalities have scribbled their slogans, the very top one being 'Scotland for Ever'.

After lunch we drove out to the eastern end of the perimeter and saw where the Mahrattas were overrun. One cannot walk far from the road on account of the mines, which it will take years to clear. The anti-tank ditch here looked a feeble obstacle. So far as possible the side of the main road has been cleared to enable the Senussi to drive their flocks of sheep and goats to market on the Egyptian frontier 200 miles away. The flocks appeared to be in wonderfully good order, many of the sheep being piebald or skewbald. There were lots of lambs and kids. One sheep dog was having a rough time being chased by an indignant ewe and was finally butted in the ribs.

We visited an old Italian ammunition store in a series of large underground caves, two of which were used later as an Indian field hospital and are now used as a prisoner of war camp. I didn't see many birds, but there were some wheatears and crested larks and the ubiquitous wagtail which I noticed all over India and would see all over Burma. Guy told me that there were many owls which prey on the desert rats. Asphodels were sprouting, and in September *pancratium maritimum* is plentiful by the sea.

We visited the Tobruk cemetery, which is very large and I should imagine contains more various dead than any of the war cemeteries. The Czechoslovaks and the Poles have both put up well designed memorials, and we have put a less well designed memorial in the centre on which is inscribed "Honour these graves of men who died for their country". A small Union Jack flutters at the entrance. Australians, New Zealanders, South Africans, Greeks, Poles, Czechoslovaks, Yugoslavs, Pioneers from the Seychelles and Mauritius, Palestine Jews, Hindus, Muslims and West Africans lie here. Beyond the British and Allied cemetery is the German cemetery and on the slope of the escarpment two or three hundred yards away is the Italian cemetery. It is a profoundly moving experience to wander among these white wooden crosses or Jewish stars or Muslim slabs facing Mecca. Many of the graves hold unknown warriors, sometimes three or four buried in one grave.

Back in Tobruk I talked with a Subedar-Major and two Jemedars of the 17th Baluchs whose headquarters are at Benghazi. The Dogra company was in Tobruk when we were there. The previous company had been Punjabi Mussulmans who had rebuilt and decorated the smashed up mosque in 25 days. The Subedar-Major took us along to look at the interior. He had married a Turkish girl in Rhodes where the Battalion had been stationed last. The reopening of the mosque had been a great ceremony attended by the Senussis all round. The regimental crest of the Baluchs is painted on the white wall of the mosque in vivid blue. Elsewhere an Anglican church, All Saints, had been built out of a ruined building and consecrated by the Bishop of Cairo a week or two back. The husk of the Catholic cathedral stands abandoned.

We wound up the afternoon by having tea at the recently built Officers' Lido—a tea-room and terrace from which members go down to bathe from the deck of a sunken Greek caique. The sky was covered with golden mackerel clouds—a lovely sight, but not promising well for the weather to-morrow. Driving round Tobruk is more like riding than driving and when we got back to the Club at 17.30 I lay down and slept for an hour and a half.

We dined in Colonel Guy's Mess, which was formerly an Italian N.C.O. Mess. A huge log fire was burning brightly and I had vodka before dinner. I have been immensely struck by the happy atmosphere in Tobruk. Everybody seems to be pulling well with everybody else in agreeable contrast to Habbaniya. Prisoners of war have decorated the whole place. On the white wall of the petrol depot all the Divisional and Corps signs have been painted. The walls of the Mess of the Royal Pioneer Corps have been painted with various ships sunk and wooden frames nailed round them, three feet by two. Colonel Guy's Mess had reproductions of the Victory stamps three feet by two painted on the walls, and the threepenny stamp designed by my nephew Reynolds Stone looked most decorative.

Here's a good desert story. An officer called X was caught with his own and the other armoured cars in one of our minefields during the retreat from Bir Hakeim. They tried to clear a way through, but night fell and in the morning they were overtaken by the German tanks and shot to pieces. X lay down, pretending to be dead, and managed to escape being made prisoner. The retreat had long swept past, when he wandered on across the desert for many weary days and finally reached Buq Buq. Here he undressed on the beach and enjoyed a good swim, after which he lay sun-bathing on the warm sand and fell fast asleep.

When he woke he found himself in the middle of a Boche bathing party. Nobody had paid any attention to his sleeping form and perhaps if he had not grabbed his clothes and tried to make off he might have bluffed it out. However, he was caught and taken along with other prisoners to the cage. He was the last man in the line and, noticing an empty cookhouse by the gate, slipped aside into it. Here he pulled a blanket over himself and lay down in a corner. Unluckily when night fell a guard party came into the cookhouse for a game of cards. One of the players, feeling chilly in the course of the game, spotted the blanket in the corner and X was revealed. He was hauled up before the commandant and told that if he tried to escape again he would be shot. Back he was put in the cage and in a thoroughly depressed mood started fiddling with the padlock of the gate when the sentry had passed by. It was not that he expected any result: it was nervous fidgets. To his amazement the padlock opened. The hook had not caught when the key was turned. He slipped out quickly, and this time he managed to reach our lines.

X was given an M.C. for the two escapes and sent to recuperate at a rest camp near Suez. Here there was a number of Wrens who slept in tents in a wired-in enclosure, which of course was known as the Aviary. One night, coming back from a party and being well ginned up, the companions of X challenged him to demonstrate his skill at escaping by getting in and out of the Aviary. He took on the bet and when he got over the wire he saw a Wren sitting outside her tent in the moonlight. She had been to a party and she was thinking about love, a Jessica without a Lorenzo. And suddenly Lorenzo appeared. They talked for some time and then she invited him into the tent she shared with fourteen other Wrens, all of them respectably fast asleep. When the time came for X to leave his Wren and make his way carefully out of the tent, one of the sleepers woke up and seeing a male shape profaning the sanctity of the tent screamed a shrill alarm. X dashed out and hid in a slit trench, but here he was discovered and barely escaped a court martial. However, in view of his M.C. and a tale in which Boccaccio himself would have rejoiced, X was let off with a reprimand.

December 16th. TOBRUK TO CAIRO

It was blowing from the S.S.E. when we were called at 6.30, but during the 18-kilometre drive to El-Adem the wind moderated and we got away in the Anson by 9.15. The innumerable blues of the sea were damascened with silver between Sidi Barrani and Mersa Matruh, where we came down to refuel. We reached Heliopolis at 14 o'clock. All the way into Cairo lorry-loads of Gyppy soldiers were going past, and a few tanks. The part of Cairo through which we had to pass to reach Mena House was out of bounds to military vehicles, and after lunch at the Ghezira Club we had to take a taxi. I have been sitting on the balcony of my bedroom dictating the diary of the Tobruk days under the gaze of the Great Pyramid hardly more than 300 yards away. Early to bed, very tired.

December 17th. CAIRO TO BEIRUT

We had breakfast at 5.30 and left the Almaza aerodrome by Misr Airways for Beyrouth or Beirut at 7.50. The plane was a Beechcraft, and though small gave one a feeling of confidence in its airworthiness. We flew over the sea through masses of cumulus, all white as snow. The coast of Palestine was not clearly visible and one could not distinguish Haifa. We reached Beirut about 11. The small aerodrome lies among orange-red sand on the outskirts of the town and with a cross wind is rather dangerous. We were met by Howes the Press Attaché and after the usual finicking formalities, which included a fee of three Lebanese pounds for looking at our health certificates, we drove off to the Hotel Normandy, all chromium plate and imitation leather, put up in 1940. Roger Mochadie, the son of the proprietor, aged 21 and looking 42, was very attentive. When we reached our rooms on the third floor a furious battle of words in French was going on between the chambermaid and the sweepers; so we left the scene of action to drive round the town.

After lunch we drove out to the River of the Dog which runs down a narrow gorge to the sea about seven miles north of the town. A series of seventeen inscribed stone plaques beginning with Nebuchadnezzar and going on through Assyrians, Greeks, Romans, French and finally Australians in this war commemorate among the rocks the various armies that have passed this way. Caracalla with the Third Gallic Legion, Napoleon III, Gouraud in the First World War, Allenby, and the Australian advance against the Vichy French in the Second World War are among them. We walked up the gorge and found a few cyclamens in blossom, also *iris sisyrhinchium*. The cyclamen was the arrow-leaved type, pink with a red nose. We were just going to walk up a path to look at the Assyrian steles when a tremendous thunderstorm began, which lasted for the rest of the afternoon and a good deal of the night. The road back to Beirut reminded me of the road through Piano di Sorrento with sugar cane and bananas added to the oranges. The Lebanese Republic has a slight Christian majority and there was an air of Christmas about the shops. The prices here and in Syria are as high as anywhere in the world at present. The hotel bill for C. and myself during our three days' stay was close on £30. In the evening we went to the hotel cabaret where Roger Mochadie stood us crême de menthe and cigars. The dancers were Polish, Czechoslovak and Hungarian. To bed about midnight.

December 18th. BEIRUT TO DAMASCUS

We left at 9.20 to drive the 60 miles to Damascus. We were able to admire the mighty stone-pines and terraced vineyards above Beirut before the weather cheated us of beauty; but most of the ascent of the Lebanon was shrouded in thick mist, and at 5,500 feet the car had to crawl at a snail's pace through sleet and slush past dimly seen slopes of snow. However, when we descended to the wide valley of the Anti-Lebanon the sun came out. We passed grove after exquisite grove of poplars with slim silver trunks and the golden leaves of autumn not even yet fallen from their filigree of boughs. Concrete dragon's teeth had been sown by the Vichy French in the pass before Damascus. I have not been able to find out how successfully they thwart the passage of tanks. When Mahomet drew near to Damascus from the desert east of it, he turned aside from the city because he did not wish to anticipate Paradise by entering it. I can understand his impulse. As we drove into Damascus by the wide road from the west beside that clear bottle-green river which flows through the heart of the city, I thought that I had never come to a place which so completely satisfied every dream of what it should be. Those three lovely words "damson", "damask", and "damascene" have stirred the imagination with such colour from earliest youth that one might well expect to be disappointed. So far from being disappointed I was enraptured.

We put up at the Hotel Ommayed. It was grubby, but the food was good. The crushed wheat in the pilaff was particularly good, and the kidneys were the best I have eaten for a long time.

After lunch, defying the rain which by now had reached Damascus, we drove out to study the advance of 5th Indian Brigade against the Vichy French, and ended up by going to see the house in Mezze where the 3/1st Punjabis had to surrender after 30 hours without food or ammunition. That pinkish house in a high-walled garden will always be haunted. Peter Petit who was taken prisoner from here was able to give me a vivid picture of those hours.

December 19th. DAMASCUS TO BEIRUT

We drove out to see the cemetery of the 3/1st Punjabis and 4/6th Rajputana Rifles which is hardly a quarter of a mile from Mezze House. The inscription over one large square grave says, "35 Indian soldiers are honoured here". They were all too badly mutilated for identification. Presumably this outrage was committed by Senegalese troops, but it reflects gravely on the French officers and N.C.O.s.

We went up the hillside toward the old French barracks and had a superb view of Damascus under a luminous blue and white sky, fruitful Damascus with its golden poplars and fountains and cypresses, its domes and minarets and orchards. Mount Hermon crowned with snow rose from the southern horizon. It was a scene of great beauty. We then drove across a sandy track to the British cemetery which lies surrounded by cypresses in the middle of large plantations of prickly pears. The graves of the First World War have stone headstones and the cypresses are already tall, but the additional space taken in for the graves of the Second World War has only white wooden crosses at present and the young cypresses swing in the lightest breeze. The paths in the first graveyard are edged with rosemary, cut square and as thick as box. Both graveyards are covered with pinkish-mauve chrysanthemums. It was a melancholy thought that the most beautiful war cemetery I have seen should have watched men advancing along the edge of it who would presently rest within it. Some, indeed, must have walked over their own graves.

We got back to the hotel at eleven o'clock and were met by Kirkpatrick and his cultured assistant Dr. S. Sadda who took us on a tour round part of Damascus. The street scenes are fascinating. I recall the elaborately decorated brass shoe-shine stands and the women in fashionable modern dresses with heavy black veils over their heads. We drove down the Street called Straight and had the good fortune to be almost the first to see a 3,000-year-old gate which they have just excavated in the middle of it, showing that the level was originally at least twenty feet below where it is now. Five thousand years of continuous city life! Can any other city in the world compete with this? We went on to the Jerusalem Gate on the south side of the city and saw the window through which St. Paul was let down in a basket. The Greek Uniate Catholics have made an austere little chapel in the Gate, which is entered by a stone wicket nine inches thick. There is an altar in the middle with a cross and two candlesticks, an ikon on the wall and framed accounts of St. Paul's adventures in English, French and Arabic, but oddly enough neither in Greek nor Latin.

Our next visit was to the Tomb of Saladin and his Grand Vizier, Aladin. We crossed a courtyard with a fountain and some orange trees and were admitted by a heavily veiled old woman. The tombs are surmounted by triangular cubes covered with ancient green silk at one end of which are the green turbans of Saladin and Aladin. The walls are covered with blue and green tiles with a design of grapes, and all round are chairs and divans of crimson velvet on which the faithful may sit in contemplation. The Kaiser paid for the renovation of the tomb when he visited the place.

The souks of Damascus are completely Arabian Nights. One crawls down a narrow alley in a car, being bumped by a loaded camel on one side and an Arab on a donkey on the other. Marvellous brocades at £5 a yard made us covetous.

At 12 I was interviewed by eight representatives of the Damascus Press. I told them that it had long been my ambition to write a history of the Crusades and that in a couple of years' time I should like to have a house in the middle of Damascus near the Arab University with a courtyard, a fountain and four orange trees from which I would explore the great castles of the Crusaders—Krak des Chevaliers, Chastel Rouge, Chastel Blanche, and the rest of them. They all applauded this idea and were sure I should be given every facility.

After lunch we set off back to Beirut. The atmospheric effects were indescribably lovely nearly all the way, but we ran into mist again at the top of the Lebanon. Some of the hillsides after the rain were the colour of the Skye bracken in autumn. And always everywhere those slim silver-stemmed poplars with their golden leaves. There was even one poplar growing out of the wall of a house in the densest part of the souk.

We reached Beirut about 16.30 hours, and G. P. Young, the Chargé d'Affaires, who is off to Rio soon, came round to see me. Over a couple of arracks we talked about a lot of mutual friends. Mochadie was anxious that we should see the Cabaret again and particularly a Polish girl contortionist performing on a glass table electrically lighted. The Victor Rabbath band consisted of six brothers, the youngest of whom played alternately the double-bass and the two globular rattles used for the rumba. An odd combination.

December 20th. BEIRUT TO CAIRO

We left Beirut in a Beechcraft plane called Cleopatra at 10.50. Some of our luggage was put in her mouth. It was rather a bumpy flight across a squally sea. We reached Cairo at 13 o'clock and then had to spend three-quarters of an hour dealing with the complications of a transit visa. I hope that one day before I depart from this earth the Sudanese will sack Cairo, and then occupy it permanently. We lunched at the Ghezira Club at 14.30, before driving out to Mena House. We walked over the hill to see the Sphinx which to my surprise was completely unsanded. It looks like a large cat sitting in a bath. I was very tired when I got to Mena House and lay down till dinner time. After dinner I went at once to bed.

December 21st. CAIRO

We left the Hotel at ten o'clock to go down to the B.O.A.C. offices and get our tickets for Karachi. We found that we required an Iraqi transit visa for the night we have to spend at Basra on the way. This involved another three-quarters of an hour going to the Iraqi Legation. At 13.15 we got back to Mena House after a morning wasted on what should be unnecessary formalities. This damned business of passports and visas and customs has been the only wearisome part of our tour. I little thought what a Frankenstein I was creating when I originated the present passport system at Athens in 1916. I shall shake the sand of Cairo from my feet with zest to-morrow morning after another 5.30 a.m. breakfast and the boring rigmarole of customs, passports, and health certificates at the Nile seaplane base. It was a detestable place in the last war and it is twice as detestable now. Obviously Lawrence's passion for Arabian adventure was sustained by a horror of being caught in Cairo. My adventures in Greece were originally inspired by a dread of finding myself in a Cairo office when Gallipoli was evacuated.

December 22nd. CAIRO

We had breakfast at 4.45, which is not a reasonable hour. Cairo was enveloped in mist, and the car was a quarter of an hour late. When we reached the Petits' flat the driver could make no impression on a household wrapped in sleep and finally we drove on to the Nile port without Peter. When we arrived we were told that there was too much fog to be able to start punctually and we followed a pleasant and competent young woman to the houseboat to eat a second breakfast. Peter and Rachel Petit arrived soon after 8 to bid us farewell and in the end the mist cleared sufficiently for us to get away by 9.40. Just as I was stepping aboard the launch a burly middle-aged man came up and told me he was Archie Douglas (Norman's son) on his way to Kenya. He was as thin as a cigarette the last time I saw him. There was no time for more than a quick greeting and we hurried on to our respective flying-boats. We were travelling in *Champion*, which was the first flying-boat to cross the Atlantic and is to be broken up at Durban when she gets back there at the end of the month. Every seat was taken.

Our first stop was Kallia at one end of the Dead Sea. We were soon on our way again. I asked what a patch of green was on the hillside, to be told it was Jericho. Beyond we had a glimpse of the snowy peaks of the Lebanon and below of the pipe-line to Haifa. We kept having to put our watches forward, and though we reached Habbaniya six hours after leaving Cairo it seemed later. When we got back to the plane we found the two seats opposite us occupied by two young Arabs returning to Bahrein from Beirut University. One of them, who gave me his card, was called Hamad M. Al Khahipuh. They were a delightful pair. Habbaniya was cold and the frosty sunset a vast orange-red. We reached Basra about 7 o'clock. The hotel is equipped with aquamarine baths and basins and with comfortable beds but lacks food.

December 23rd. BASRA TO KARACHI

We were called at 3.45 and went on to Bahrein at 5 o'clock. There was a superb scarlet, gold and green dawn over a deep steel-blue sea. The two young Arabs appeared in native costume and were met on the quay by a large family gathering. A great deal of kissing went on between the males. At Bahrein we took on a very old Arab, two middle-aged ones, and two women heavily veiled in black. The two women and one of the men sat on the seat near us and chattered incessantly for an hour. Then they all covered themselves with blankets and slept until the steward brought a large basket of cakes, biscuits and sandwiches which they devoured *in toto*, a complicated business under a veil. There was another large family gathering to meet these Arabs at Dubah. Dubah is rather a fascinating place—just date palms, sand and sea. It is interesting to notice how naturally the Arabs have taken to flying. The same thing happened in the Hebrides. Old people who shuddered at the notion of a sea-voyage hopped into a plane like grigs. Dubah was much warmer then Basra, and when we landed at Karachi six hours later at 18 o'clock the climate was perfection. The medical and customs examinations were expeditiously and pleasantly carried through and not a bit of luggage was opened; but one of our Indian friends was detained for ten days in quarantine because his yellow fever certificate was out of order.

INDIA AND ASSAM

December 24th. KARACHI TO JAMNAGAR

Major Qarishi of the Rajputs arrived in the morning with news from Simla and some welcome mail. At 11 we drove down to the airport and after lunching there left for Jamnagar. It was a pleasant flight in an Indian Airways refitted Dakota with one stop before Jamnagar, which we reached about 15.30. Two and half hours by air for a journey which takes two and a half days by train! We were met by the Jam Saheb's secretary, and after being garlanded with a chain of white chrysanthemums and marigolds we drove to the guest palace.

Twenty-two people sat down to dinner at about 22 o'clock, with as much champagne as they could drink after so many champagne cocktails beforehand, and some marvellous '35 brandy. One was back in 1911, and could imagine that Nijinsky and Karsavina would be dancing *The Spectre of the Rose* at Covent Garden after dinner. I sat between the Maharani of Jaipur and Mrs. Symon. The Maharani of Nawanagar is a small woman in her mid-thirties with three girls and a boy. She is a woman of intellect with a clear-cut personality and much administrative talent. It was 2.45 when I went to bed, and some of the others, including the Jam Saheb himself, were half an hour later.

Christmas Day. JAMNAGAR

H.H. arrived about 10.30 to drive C. and myself round Jamnagar. It is a fascinating walled city, full of temples and mosques, the temples all flying red and white flags. Goats and pigeons were everywhere and green parakeets wheeled screaming round the heavily carved fort. A great flight of demoiselle cranes had arrived the previous evening and we saw them standing about in the estuary. They come here from Siberia.

I was much impressed by the evidence on all sides of the affectionate regard in which H.H.'s people hold him. Nawanagar is a happy state and Jamnagar a happy city. This is an oriental Dingley Dell and Mr. Wardle wears a black silk coat with jewelled buttons. When we got back to the Palace the Jam Saheb sat in the drawing-room to receive Christmas greetings. Among those who came was a Polish woman who has been here since she escaped from Russian imprisonment seven years ago. Her face was tragic, and there were ashes among her fair hair. She had just received a photograph of her grown up daughter whom she had not seen since she was a little girl.

When the guests were gathered for lunch, H.H. went round with his presents. He gave me a pair of enamel and gold links which was just what I wanted and to C. and the other women he gave a dozen handkerchiefs and two scarves of gold tissue made in Jamnagar. We had some wonderful '27 hock at lunch which to a palate denied good hock for five years tasted rather better than nectar.

I was roused at 17.30 from what was more like a stupor than a siesta with news that H.H. was waiting to drive us out to the game preserve on the island in the estuary. Hares, guinea fowl, partridges and quail were on all sides of us, but to H.H.'s disappointment we did not get a glimpse of the cheetal deer. It was flat country with many thickets of low trees and here and there dense bushes of cactus. Indian warblers, bulbuls and rosy doves were the most frequent birds. Sometimes we would pass a tree from which the body of hawk or jackal or jungle-cat or iguana would be suspended as a warning to the rest, but I doubt if the iguana's cold eye would be sufficiently impressed by his brother's bad end to abstain from poaching. When we got back to the Palace in a grey and crimson sunset, I saw the new moon over my right shoulder, an auspicious end to a delightful drive.

Sixty-six of us sat down to Christmas dinner in the banqueting-hall at 22.30 with gold plate and cutlery and great boxes of crackers that Titans might have pulled with one another. After a dinner of Dickensian prodigality, with turkey and one of the best plum puddings I ever ate, there was a dance. I went to bed at 5 a.m. H.H. calls me the Emperor in reference to my always carrying round my air cushion.

December 27th. JAMNAGAR

After an early lunch we drove to a range of low hills where marble is quarried, some thirty miles south of Jamnagar. Here two panthers had been ringed by beaters. We stood on a stone platform facing a glade out through scrub, forbidden to talk above a whisper. H.H. made me take off my white cap and gave me his own topee to wear. The Maharani of Jaipur, who had a new Holland and Holland rifle brought back from England by her husband, was given first shot. After a quarter of an hour of unearthly noises by 200 beaters the female panther broke from the scrub and seemed to be ambling across the glade. Actually she was moving at a very fast pace and after the Maharani had missed with both barrels there was no time for the Jam Saheb to get in his shot. About five minutes later the male panther came across and was also missed. So we drove on about a quarter of a mile and took up a fresh position above a nullah. This time it was the male panther who broke first, but in such a way that it was impossible for anybody to get a shot at him. We waited a long time until the ring of beaters closed in at last without a sign of the female. We now moved on to a tower up which we climbed by wooden steps, and the beating began again. The three motor-cars had been parked in the sunlight up the slope to discourage the panther from turning away from the tower as he crossed the open ground in front. Finally he broke cover and this time the Maharani hit him and Colonel Himatsinhji, the Jam Saheb's brother, followed up with a shot through the head. The panther measured seven feet five inches over all.

H.H. told me afterwards that he never expected to see the female panther again and that the beaters had no doubt deliberately let her through because they liked having panthers about, which at the cost of an occasional goat kept the woodland free from poaching woodcutters.

We drove on to a diminutive shooting-box beside a stream running through a rocky gorge overhung with trees, and there under the shade of a huge banyan covered with red fruit we sat down on a red carpet to a picnic tea, all of us unaware that exactly seventy yards away two panthers were watching us. The head shikari dressed in green is a most distinguished-looking Rajput Major, seventy years old, without a tooth in his head and still able to run uphill as fast as a young man. At dinner H.H. related how in 1918 175 Punjabi Mussulmans had expelled two complete Egyptian Divisions from their Cairo barracks at the point of the bayonet. Later on, I told the Maharani of Jaipur how much I had sympathized with her over that first miss and she said how thankful she had been that her husband wasn't there. She thinks that the desire to kill is leaving her. Indeed, she had made up her mind to give up shooting, but the new rifle had been irresistible. She is a really enchanting young woman and the nearest thing to a fairy princess the material world has shown me. I told her that I had come to the conclusion—regretfully—that I must have been up at Oxford with her grandfather, the Maharaja of Cooch Behar.

December 29th. *JAMNAGAR*

Claude Auchinleck had now joined the party with the Maharaja of Bundi.

We drove to Balachadi, the seaside summer resort of the Jam

Saheb. The road was bordered on both sides for a good deal of the way with sealing-wax-red aloes, which I am told were a source of supply to Beecham's Pills. After lunch we sat looking at the tide coming in, and many birds. The Auk is keen on bird-watching. Some energetic people played golf; Bill Condon, who arrived the day before, was of course among them. I had my first sight of mangroves, which are quite small here and do not increase much because the crabs eat the shoots of the young trees. Just after sunset we started home under a rose-plumed sky across which the demoiselle cranes were winging slowly to roost. In order to preserve the air of a quiet day in the country there was no champagne for dinner, but we enjoyed a peach-fed ham brought by the Merrills which was cooked in champagne.

December 31st. JAMNAGAR TO AHMEDABAD AND NEW DELHI

Bill Condon, C. and I left Jamnagar by air at 8.

We were loaded with garlands of chrysanthemums and marigolds, heavy with morning dew or extra watering.

We reached Ahmedabad at about 10.30 and were met by Lt.-Colonel H. R. S. Houghton of the 2/7th Gurkhas. He drove Condon and myself round the Cantonments and I had an interesting picture of a Kipling set up of once upon a time, for nothing has been changed here except to put in electric light and turn the stables into stores. The huge banyan trees offer shade to the pipe-clayed ghost of that great man Thomas Atkins who laid down his life at Mons and Ypres and on the beaches of Gallipoli. We could still see where the punkahs used to hang in the dormitory of the British N.C.O.s, the old magazines, the gun park, and all the rest of it. The bungalows of the officers are now being sold for anything up to £12,000 to rich business men in Ahmedabad who want to escape from the communal rioting.

After lunch Mrs. Houghton, a charming Australian woman (I don't know why I add the epithet because Australian women, thanks to their naturalness, always are charming), drove Condon, C. and myself and her 16-month son into Ahmedabad, after we had visited her clinic and school for wives. I was entranced by the spectacle of a dozen wives being instructed with unbroken high-pitched eloquence by a young pundit of eleven armed with chalk and a blackboard. When the women turned away from their slates to look at the visitors they were sharply rebuked by their young schoolmaster and bidden to pay attention to the blackboard on which he was demonstrating how to write 'yours' in Gurkhali.

Ahmedabad is the Manchester of India with a seething population of 800,000. Factory chimneys rise from the debris of ancient tombs. We were taken by our hostess to see the Rocking Tower of a mosque, the name of which I have failed to record. There used to be two towers to climb, but they monkeyed about with one of them in order to find out why it rocked, and then they couldn't put it together again for people to ascend. C. and Bill Condon took off their shoes, followed our guide Dr. Baght to the top, and successfully rocked their tower while the other one ten yards away rocked in unison. I doubted the prudence of climbing shoeless up the steep stone steps and therefore missed this insoluble architectural mystery.

From the Mosque we drove to a lake full of crocodiles, but as it was blowing we were not lucky enough to see a single snout. It is an artificial lake made in 1452 by the builder of the Taj Mahal. After the lake we drove to see from the road three windows in a wall, the light behind them, with arboreal patterns in dark brown and white at once exquisitely complicated and exquisitely simple.

We got back to the Cantonment about 17.30 and at 18 o'clock went along to the aerodrome, taking off an hour later and reaching Delhi at 21.30, after a seemingly motionless flight high up in the starry sky. Bill Condon, C. and I wished one another a Happy New Year and went to bed just after midnight.

New Year's Day, 1947. *NEW DELHI*

Condon and I went to pre-lunch drinks in the garden of Dennys Thomas, the Burma Shell representative in Delhi. Several people had figured in the Birthday Honours. One of the new Ladies asked what had impressed me most in the tour so far, and I said "Keren". "Oh, yes?" she went on in a puzzled voice, "And where and what is Keren?"

January 2nd. NEW DELHI

Brigadier Kenneth Bayley of the 52nd Foot (2nd Oxford and Bucks Light Infantry) arrived from Meerut where he is commanding a British Brigade. He is to accompany us as far as the Chindwin. John Shaw and C. went round to the finance people, and it looks as if I shall be heavily down on travelling expenses. Barristers are the only people who know how to wrest their expenses from Governments, which I suppose is what one would expect.

January 3rd. NEW DELHI TO CALCUTTA

We went to the Willingdon airport at 10.30 where we found we were to travel to Calcutta on the maiden flight of the *Indus*, a new Vickers-Viking plane. The airport officials as always were most helpful and pleasant. There was a lot of experimental adjustment of the seating in the aircraft to get the best balance for taking off and coming down. A cold wind with rain started about noon, just before we were airborne, but by the time we made our first call at Cawnpore it was already hot again. We stopped at Allahabad for a poor lunch and reached Calcutta just before dusk, where we stayed with Major-General Roy Bucher in Fort William.

January 4th. CALCUTTA TO JAMSHEDPUR AND BACK

I flew off to Jamshedpur with Bailey at 8 a.m. in a jolly little Waco holding four in all. I enjoy flying in small planes. One has a much better view and one seems somehow in closer accord with the air. The shadow of the plane led the plane westward across the well-cultivated alluvial country outspread below. I noticed ricks of some crop, which from above looked like large champignons. On we went over stream after stream, the shadows of the palms black and sharp in the morning sun. An hour's flight brought us to Jamshedpur where we were met by Mr. K. Khosla, the Secretary of the Tata Iron and Steel Company (Tisco), and driven to the Directors' bungalow for a jolly good breakfast.

Jamshedpur is a fantastic romance of industry. In 1907 it was a haunt of tigers; now it is a city of 150,000, and a garden city at that. The steel works occupy five square miles and the whole place twenty-five square miles. There are some other industrial concerns besides Tisco such as Indian Steel and Wire Products which was started in 1921 and acquired in 1927 by Indra Singh, now a remarkable old Sikh gentleman of over seventy, who gets up every morning at three, takes a five-mile walk, works all day and goes to bed at 21 o'clock. His elder son is Baldev Singh, the Minister of Defence in the Interim Government, and his younger son Ajain Singh manages the business. It was the latter who took us round. I watch the machines which turn out nails, wire, and barbed wire as I should watch an accomplished conjuror.

We passed on from wire products to the Indian Cable Company. This concern is managed by Mr. Edwin Thompson who is the first really good gardener I have met during this tour. I saw with pleasure the purple and white bauhinias he had planted all round the works. After watching the process of cable making, which is a complicated business outside my powers of description, I went round Thompson's own garden with him, and was grateful to find at last somebody who could name a few shrubs.

After the three comparatively minor industrial concerns we went over the largest steel works in the Commonwealth. I felt I was back doing my tour of the Gas Industry among blast furnaces and coke ovens. It is the largest steel works in the Empire. I recall most vividly the high white wall right round the five square miles of steel works, an escarpment of slag, a great crowd of cheerful women getting their pay at the end of the week, the general air of happiness and cleanliness, and the strange effect of always emerging from the surge and clamour of the shops into sunlight instead of a Black Country drizzle. The smoke from the blast furnaces was as colourful as the plume of Vesuvius.

At 14 o'clock we drove out seven miles to an artificial lake they have made, which looks a cross between Loch Lomond and Loch Awe. Nobody would suppose it was made by man. It is an astonishing achievement. I noticed on the road dark men and women carrying various burdens to market. These were aborigines who still use bows and arrows, which gives an idea of the kind of country in which this immense industry has been planted. Above the lake stands the comfortable bungalow of the Directors with a beautiful view of the hills on the other side, but the main veranda looks in the other direction. I asked Mr. Khosla the reason for this, and he told me that it was because from this side one could just see the smoke of the blast furnaces and one of the great chimneys of Jamshedpur.

We flew back to Calcutta at 16 o'clock, doing the 156 miles in under an hour. At the airport I was introduced to Sir Jehangir Jivaji Chandy, the General Manager, on his way out to Jamshedpur. He is what *Time* would call a tycoon of the metallurgical world.

January 5th. CALCUTTA TO DIGBOI

We were picked up after an early lunch by Brigadier Bayley, and left Calcutta at 14 o'clock for Digboi. Lt.-Colonel J. G. Thomson, I.A.M.C., who is doing a survey of the medical side of the war east of India for the Historical Section, had joined us at Delhi and was soon to become an intimate and much valued friend. The compartment we were in had been repainted and was unusually clean. The dining-car had been redecorated with chromium plate and fluorescent lighting. About dusk at Gopalpur the coupling of the coach in front of us broke, fortunately just as the driver was starting. After a great deal of talk the coach was uncoupled and put at the back of the train. We were nearly two hours late in arriving at Parbatipur where we changed into a narrow-gauge train. This was dirty and the lavatory didn't work as the cistern was leaking all the time. However, we were too tired to stay awake and by being late we did not arrive at the Brahmaputra ferry until after 8 o'clock, which was better than crossing in the dank twilight of dawn.

January 6th. IN THE TRAIN. CALCUTTA TO DIGBOI

We had to walk about five minutes down a crowded bank of thick dust and sand to board the ferry boat, which reminded me of pictures I have seen of the Mississippi steamers in the old days. Breakfast was ready laid under an awning on the upper deck, and a very good breakfast it was. A pearly morning mist was hanging over the mighty river. There was a notice entreating upper class pasengers to leave their dogs on the lower deck. The crossing of the river to Pandu did not take long and we walked up the other bank to the waiting train where Major Luscombe, the R.T.O., gave us a warm welcome and put us into a coach to ourselves—once upon a time the headquarters of the Commander of the L.O.C.—two saloons, dining-room, two lavatories, a bathroom, a room for the bearers and a kitchen. What luxury after the train we had left on the other side! We left Pandu at 10 o'clock railway time. The railway uses Calcutta time which is an hour ahead of local time.

The first part of the journey was fascinating for window-gazing. What looked like a eupatorium, with flowers the colour of an ageratum, lined the embankment on either side and seemed to cover the ground wherever the jungle was cleared. I did not notice any of that pretty but pestilent lantana which apparently has not crossed the Brahmaputra. Drongos or king-crows were perched all along the telegraph-wires. They are like large swallows with forked tails four times as long and will tackle the biggest crow. Egrets and cranes were everywhere in the paddy fields from which the rice had already been harvested. People were fishing with nets in the ponds and ditches where quite big fish are found after the flooding of the river. We saw the first elephant we had seen in India. It was doing farm work. Vultures were frequent. We passed many neat little villages, the houses of which had thatched roofs and walls of plaited reeds. We were all fairly tired and retired to bed after dinner at 21 o'clock.

January 7th. DIGBOI

We apparently reached Digboi about 3 and woke to find our coach had been put into a siding. I was up first. I am amazed at my anxiety to get up in the morning nowadays. Thomson left us to go on to Dibrugarh. Captain David Tyler came along to point out the bungalow of Mr. and Mrs. Valentine where we were to spend the night. Valentine is the General Manager of Assam Oil. When we went up to breakfast at 8 o'clock he had already gone off to his work. He is an Aberdonian, and Mrs. Valentine comes from Glasgow. A combination after my own heart.

I drove off with Bayley and Tyler at 10.45 to visit Brigadier Crampton at Panitola about 30 miles away. The road was atrocious and we could seldom move at as much as 15 miles an hour. We noticed two big American dumps where such vehicles as had not been stolen were being sold gradually. We passed a small mountain in the middle of the road and soon afterwards the elephant responsible. He was doing farm work. Elephants fetch 18,000 rupees (£1,350) and eat 600 lbs. of green stuff a day, so two days of the week are spent in sending them out to get the bamboo shoots they eat. They strongly object to working a moment over their allotted time. Bayley saw an elephant who had been laying a bridge (they do everything except clamp the wood together) object to picking up a log after he had done his day's work. Finally he was persuaded just to lay one more. Then they tried to persuade him to lay still another. He protested and dropped the log in the middle of the bridge. When they still pestered him he picked it up and threw it into the river. No overtime for him!

We drove on along a straight, rough, dusty road, most of it beside the railway. There was a line of tin telephone poles, many of which had been bent almost double by lorries. On the other side of the road were the poles of the American telegraph, all the wires of which had been removed, and along the railway were the telegraph wires still in use. We reached a squalid straggling little town with a lot of metal junk and much corrugated iron, appropriately enough called Tinsukia, and a short way out of it came to the bungalow which Brigadier Crampton had inherited from an American colonel. He had also inherited a lot of whisky, a mountain of toilet paper which the Americans call tissue, two fluorescent lamps in the ceiling, and a huge wireless set on which without a moment's delay we tuned in to hear the test match being reported from Australia with perfect reception. Why cannot we make wireless sets like this? The furniture was painted bright blue and the chair covers were bright scarlet.

From the Brigadier's hospitable bungalow we called on Vernon Brown, the Manager of a 1,300-acre tea-garden. After Tinsukia the country is one immense tea-garden. The fine old bungalow dates back to the 'eighties when people built on piles to escape the miasma which was supposed then to be the cause of malaria. By the way, we were all of us on mepacrine by now including Gulaba. Tea, which is a distant relation of the rhododendron and a close relation of the camellia, will not grow on lime. Various leguminous trees are planted thinly above the serried tea-plants to cast a light shade and supply nitrogen to the soil at the same time. V.B. told me that Ceylon and Darjeeling teas were noted for their flavour and Assam tea for its quality. I should have said that quantity was a more obvious attribute.

Vernon Brown showed me some of the leaflets which the Japs dropped over Panitola. They had ridiculous pictures of scarlet-clad Tommies with big teeth such as one used to see in French comic rags during the Boer War. He also showed me a leaflet which we dropped on the Japanese. This was a picture of a naked woman bound to a post and a Jap soldier leering at her. And here is the legend underneath: "The Japanese are rapping (sic) your women and robbing your homes." Could anything be more fatuous than printing this in English in the hope of impressing the local inhabitants?

The story of the superb patriotic effort made by the Assam tea-planters in the war must wait for the book. I shall enjoy rubbing it into those critics at home who maligned the men on the spot out here.

On the way back the sun lit up the peeling bamboo stems so that they looked as if they were hung with metal. This glitter became a commonplace, but I never read any allusion to it in a traveller's tale. As we got into Digboi half a dozen sturdy Nagas went hurrying past bent under great bundles of greenery. This was my first glimpse of those jolly people.

January 8*th. THE LEDO ROAD. DIGBOI TO DIMAPUR (Manipur Road)*

We left Digboi at 9.30 hours for the Ledo Road. Captain Tyler drove me in the first jeep. Sergeant Rose drove C. in the second jeep. Brigadier Bayley followed in the third, and there was a fourth in reserve. After a few miles of shocking road we came to Margherita, so named by an Italian who discovered coal here. This coal now fetches 30 rupees a ton at the pit head. The oil here was discovered by one of the elephants who were turned loose at night. On arriving back to work one morning its legs were covered with black oil ooze. Margherita lies on the other side of the Tirap river which is crossed by a picturesque bridge, and Ledo itself is beyond Margherita. There is a large brick kiln at Ledo and a squalid bazaar. The train runs on beyond Digboi as far as here.

A little way outside Ledo stands a big white signpost about eight feet square right across the top of which is painted in large letters

STILWELL ROAD. Underneath are the names of more than a dozen places and their distances. I noted "Myitkyina 275 miles" and at the bottom of the table "Kuomting 1078 miles."

Presently we came to an airstrip beside the road, and a little way farther on to the left a space completely devoid of vegetation where various explosives had been blown up. A mile or two after this we reached the frontier post between India and Burma, though the frontier has not yet been finally delimited, and beyond it is really No Man's Land for a while. A Sub-Inspector of the Assam Police was in charge.

I am told that the road is to be maintained for 30 miles, but the present system of maintenance is extremely ineffective. However, the splendour of the natural scene made the worst bumps a jeep can give one hardly noticeable. We drove on and on, penetrating the wildest jungle, but every mile or so passing the remains of camps either of workmen or of refugees. There was a Chinese cemetery where the soldiers of the Far East lie under heavy tombstones and headstones covered with Chinese ideographs. In the middle of the cemetery is a tall monolith on which a rising sun is painted. I was puzzled to see this political emblem of Japan, but I presume that for the Chinese it has some religious significance. By the remains of one camp there was a notice board on which was painted TO THE MEMORY OF TOM, THE LOYAL WATCHDOG OF THE ORISSA PIONEER COMPANY. Elephant droppings in the roadway made us hope for a glimpse of a herd, but none appeared.

When we alighted from the jeep to stretch our legs by a particularly grand sweep of the road, the jungle just beyond was loud with the eldrich ululations of black gibbon apes, but these monkeys are shy and we did not catch a glimpse of them. I am told that the females are in labour for three days with their young, and that when the Naga women are near childbirth it is the custom to drive away all the gibbons in the neighbourhood so that the evil influence of their slow parturition may be avoided.

It is not a good time of year for butterflies, but I saw one beautiful creature of dark blue and steel blue and by a puddle in the road about twenty whites with yellow undersides, which I imagine are relations of our Clouded Yellow. I also saw a couple of Cleopatras. That is a Brimstone with a splash of orange on the tips of the wings. The ubiquitous wagtail was often in evidence and many pigeons, but on the whole birds were scarce.

At one point the road ran beside the loop of a sinister rifle-green river called Namchik over which the oil pipe line was carried like a suspension bridge. On the far side rose a steep conical jungle-clad hill. It was down a bridle track on this hill that the stream of refugees slithered in exhaustion after the deathly trail from Myitkyina up the pestilential Hukawng Valley in that tragic Burma spring of 1942, to cross the river and make for Lagopani. That, of course, was long before the road or pipe line was made. By this path, too, came footsore Gloucesters and K.O.Y.L.I.s—stragglers from Alexander's retreat. An official I met told me that the only bit of humour he remembered in connection with the refugees, which was one of the most heartrending episodes in history, was when he went to get a railway ticket for one of the Gloucesters who had been in hospital at Ledo for two months: "You won't get a return ticket, will you, sir?"

It was interesting to see the way the jungle is advancing on the road. First, like 'recce' parties, convolvulus, purple, and white and mauve, throws out its long tendrils, then young tufts of elephant grass establish themselves, and behind them the bamboos consolidate the jungle's gain. Creepers are climbing up all the telephone poles and festoon the wires where they remain. I doubt if the road will even be jeepable after another monsoon.

We stopped for lunch at the cleared site of an old camp, a few hundred yards before Hell Gate, which marks the frontier accepted at present between India and Burma. Here there is a small group of tumbledown huts and sheds where a few debased Nagas are pottering round a wretched huddle of decrepit cars and lorries. We had a capital lunch provided by our kind hosts at Digboi and the only flies were small hover flies, tactfully unobtrusive. At the back of the clearing I found a plantain with a bunch of bright carmine bananas smelling of cucumber. The inside was full of seeds and they were very astringent. I am told the Nagas eat them. The other plantains, which were a feature of the vegetation, had small yellow bananas. We ate some of these on the train. The flavour is good, but they have black seeds and are slightly astringent.

Beyond Hell Gate the road rises 3,500 feet in three miles, and God knows how it was ever made in the time. Bayley had come into my jeep and Tyler had gone into the one C. was in, and Bayley and I kept looking round after we had negotiated a curve through thick yellow mud, with a wall of rock on one side and a thousand foot sheer drop on the other, to see that the jeep behind had not gone hurtling down. Once or twice there was a hole in the road at the bottom of which the jungle was visible, and that was a bit alarming. Nevertheless, it was impossible to feel nervous in a scene of such staggering beauty and grandeur. By great good fortune the day was clear, which is very rare at this time of year, and when we came to the top of the Paunsao Pass we could see across three or four green ranges stained with blue air the Himalayan snows for mile upon mile, ten days' march away and, I suppose, a hundred miles as the eagle flies. It is silly trying to describe views like this. This was the famous Hump over which the American airmen flew, day in day out, with supplies for China. It was a hazardous task. In one day 32 planes were lost in an electrical storm. At this moment two Americans are jeeping right down through Burma to obtain information about lost aircraft and if possible rescue the bones for burial across the Atlantic.

We went on for about a quarter of a mile round the head of the Pass to look down at the Forbidden Lakes which lie in a vast marsh where there are neither birds nor beasts and where the aircraft that crashed will never be found. Until the Ledo Road was made nobody had seen these lakes since 1885 when an American Baptist missionary called Elliot reached them by paddling up the Namchik in a Rob Roy canoe. A truly astonishing feat.

We got back to Margarita just before dusk, and Bayley and I stopped to have tea with Felix Walker the D.C. who had just come in from a ten days' tour of Naga villages. My talk with him was all too brief. He was able to tell me the local name of the tall trees which run straight up for over 100 feet without a branch. They are called in Naga *hellong*, and the wood which is softish is used for making those tea-chests in which my books have travelled so often and so far. Another tree also used for making tea-chests, with flowers like a small clematis, is called *hollock*. *Gonseroi* and *champa* are used for cabinet work, the wood being rather lighter than walnut. Walker told me that head-hunting was still going on among Nagas three days' march away. This head-hunting is connected with fertility rites. The villages have four guard houses and if the head-hunters can get through the guards and capture the heads of women and children these are considered more valuable trophies than the heads of the warriors. The heads are kept in the bachelors' guard houses, together with the hands and the feet. He also told me that the women were great supporters of the attempt to put down head-hunting and that among the Nagas the women, who are most intelligent and do all the work, have a position of much influence. Quite a few of the Nagas are Christians, having been converted by American Baptist missionaries of whom no doubt Elliot was a precursor.

At 21 o'clock we went down to our railway coach to travel through the night to Dimapur or, as it was known during the campaign, Manipur Road. A truly memorable day.

January 9th. DIMAPUR (Manipur Road) TO KOHIMA

The early mist we had been told to expect at Manipur Road did not gather. No morning could have been lovelier, and everybody had slept well. Presently along came Brigadier Michael R. Roberts, the Sub-Area Commander at Shillong, who commanded 114 Brigade of 7th Indian Division in Arakan. It was thanks to him that we had that comfortable railway-coach. He was driving his own staff car and took Bayley, C. and myself on board. Major F. K. Cassels of the Assam Regiment took charge of the transport, which included a wagon with our luggage and several jeeps. We were glad to join up with Thomson again, who brought a supply of atabrine, a variant of mepacrine, from Dibrugarh. The Kabaw Valley, down a part of which we should be driving in due course, produces the worst malaria in the world, but at this time of year one is not so likely to catch it.

We drove round what is left by the relentless jungle of the huge Manipur Dump, eleven miles long and never less than a mile wide. We saw the curious remains of an ancient fort near which are a group of stones like enormous button mushrooms. There are at least two dozen of them and they are obviously of phallic significance. Thomas Atkins used to call this place P— Park. They are carved with various animals and hieroglyphics and are about eight feet high.

Brigadier Roberts solved for me the mystery of what I thought from the train was a mauve eupatorium. No wonder I said it was the same colour as an ageratum. It is an ageratum, and according to popular belief was introduced into Assam by railway sleepers. That story may be due to its profusion along the line. However, I saw it right up the Ledo Road growing to at least twelve feet. I wonder what Queen Victoria would have thought of the behaviour of her favourite border flower. They say it is the only plant with which the lantana cannot compete, and Roberts told me that nothing brings back Arakan to him like the smell of crushed ageratum. It is foul stuff to march through. I must track out the history of this flower when I can get at some books.*

After Nichuguard the scenery became magnificent. It was rather like the Wye Valley carried to the *n*th degree. We drove slowly up through a superb gorge with prodigal vegetation on either side and a river below. Higher up, an immense view of dense jungle was unfolded to lose itself in a blue haze miles away. In this level tract of

*This was not so easy. All the ageratums and nearly all the eupatoriums are American. After wrestling with the *Index Kewensis* and other floral reference-books I am left in doubt whether this pest of Assam, Arakan and North Burma may not be Eupatorium ageratoides.

country there are said to be more elephants than in the rest of India put together. Tigers abound and there are both buffalo and bison. The pick of the fauna is the great Indian rhinoceros, the remnants of which are protected in a reservation. This is the only part where they are still found.

Just beyond the 32nd of the 46 milestones to Kohima the road runs across the low Zubza ridge which marked for a few days the farthest advance any Japanese troops made into India. They were soon turned out by the advance of 7th Indian Division and on the right hand side of the road Frank Messervy had his H.Q. We walked up the bank to have a look at the bamboo beside which his caravan stood. A leopard had left his card close by after a good meal of dog.

We reached Kohima about 17 o'clock and were met by C. R. Pawsey, the Deputy Commissioner. It is a piece of luck that I have been able to meet this remarkable man to whose devoted service among the Nagas we owe the marvellous loyalty they displayed during the Japanese invasion. The Commissioner's bungalow was destroyed, and he is now living in a tiny improvised cottage. C. and I are housed in what amounts to a shack of two rooms made of sheets of corrugated iron full of bullet holes. However, there is a brick fireplace in one of them, and these words are being dictated beside a good fire of logs.

At 16 o'clock Charles Pawsey, driving me in his own jeep, led the way up to the top of the Naga village on the crown of the hill some 500 feet above what is called the Treasury, which is the office of the D.C. The road winds round and round and is swarming with small pigs and minute piglets, mostly black and white. A full-sized pig is no bigger than a large Cocker spaniel. To one part of Assam a pigmy wild hog eighteen inches long is indigenous. The Naga village was entirely destroyed by the various British and Jap bombardments and has now been rebuilt with corrugated iron. This is painted a dull maroon, and the houses have managed to preserve a much better shape than the average tin shack in England. I noticed that two or three of them had what looked like large wings of corrugated iron with two big round holes through them at the gable end of the roof. These I was told were the horns that a Naga who has given a feast of a cow to his neighbours is allowed to put up as a decoration. The Nagas in Government service wear bright red blankets. One of them who took us round the village spoke good English and Hindustani. He told C. he had himself killed six or seven Japs, but added with a smile that he had not taken their heads. The language is difficult. A lot of words as in Chinese depend entirely on intonation. Thus the word *dzu* with one intonation means water, with another egg, and with a third intonation something which makes the women laugh inordinately when asked if they have any eggs. Not only is the language difficult, but there are twenty different languages. One village not far from Kohima has a language entirely its own. The vocabularies, too, are fairly large.

C.'s stockings caused a good deal of mirth among the women. They could not make out whether her face and her legs were a different colour. They felt them, but they were so thin that they couldn't believe they were stockings until she pulled up her skirt and showed them where her leg began. This has a great comic success. They really are delightful people. The young girls' heads are cropped until marriage, and the men grow a sort of small top knot into which they put ornaments and flowers. I saw two boys with marigolds in their hair. Some of the women wear brass ear-rings four inches across. The girls wear thick brass bracelets. We watched them doing some wonderful weaving with cotton. We also watched the hulling of rice by a woman and her daughter, the daughter working with a pestle and the mother shaking the rice rhythmically in a large flat basket sieve with a most graceful action.

INTERLUDE

One of Pawsey's servants has just come in with a stone bottle of *zyu* or rice beer and a glass bottle of the much more potent spirituous type. The rice-beer tastes rather like fermented coconut milk. The potent stuff is good. I wish I could offer a glass to the Coddy* in Barra. It has a kick which he would appreciate. The Nagas won't drink milk. They think the idea disgusting.

KOHIMA

At the very top of the highest peak of the village called Hunter's Hill we came upon a memorial to the men of the First Camerons killed here. Just a plaque with their names, and above it LOCHABER NO MORE. Yet I can say to any Highland wife or mother who laments a loved one lying eight thousand miles and more away from the braes of home that this Naga village is far nearer in spirit to Lochaber than almost any place in between. We came down from Hunter's Hill just before dusk. It had been a wonderful experience. I wish I could spend a long time with these lovable people. It is evident that Pawsey is heartbroken to be leaving them in two or three months. His three servants have been with him twenty years. A pleasant dinner and to bed about 23.30. I needed three blankets.

* John Macpherson, a famous Hebridean figure.

January 10*th. KOHIMA*

After breakfast we jeeped and walked round various parts of the battlefields. The cemetery with 1,100 British dead has been constructed in terraces on the site of what was once the Deputy Commissioner's garden and bungalow. His tennis court was No Man's Land, and the remains of it, even the white markings, are still to be seen. The crown of the hill constituted the Kohima Box which was held through that desperate fortnight in April 1944. At the top of the cemetery is the Memorial to 2nd British Division, which is not entirely satisfactory either from a practical or an aesthetic point of view. On the edge of the perimeter is the Royal Berkshires' Memorial where the Chinese dragon of the regimental badge looks northward away across the Himalayas to China. Just above and close by is the Memorial to the Durham Light Infantry with, as I think a misplaced facetiousness or sentimentality in the circumstances, a signpost inscribed "New Gateshead." On the knoll beyond, called Kuki Picket, is the Memorial to the Royal West Kents—the old Dirty Half Hundred—who were flown in from Arakan with 161st Brigade of 5th Indian Division and fought superbly. The Memorial to the Royal Welch Fusiliers is inscribed *Ond Nid Ym Ofer*, and the famous black flash, a yard high, is painted on the tablet. This, too, is on Kuki Picket. Beyond is where the 4/15 Punjabis and the 1st Queen's of 33rd Brigade in 7th Indian Division held the position while the Bengal Sappers and Miners cleared the crucial road that cut between the ridges of the minefield into which 149 Regt. R.A.C. had run with their tanks. The Memorial to the Punjabis, the 4/1 Gurkhas and the 77th Indian Field Company overlooks that fatal cut in the road where so many lives were lost. Farther along the road are other Memorials to the Royal Norfolks, Dorsets and Royal Scots.

I walked round nearly all the various ridges and hills which saw fighting as desperate as any recorded in history and I have obtained a clear idea of the battle, but I have little hope of ever giving a clear picture of it to the reader. There is no more vivid descriptive journalist than Frank Owen. Yet his account of Kohima in his book *Burma* did not give me the faintest idea of what the place was like and I do not suppose for a moment that I shall be any more successful.

On the east side of the cemetery where the ground was held by the Japanese a stone slab is inscribed "At Kohima in April 1944 the Japanese invasion of India was halted." Beyond this stands the most impressive of the War Memorials. A great rough block of stone bears a copper plate with the names of those who died in 161st

Brigade of 5th Indian Division. At either end of the small semi-circular terrace in which the block is set is the Divisional badge—a ball of fire in red stone and black marble.

Farther along, I was surprised to find a Memorial going back to 1879 to two British Officers and a Subedar-Major of the 44th Native Infantry (afterwards 8th Gurkhas) who were killed on November 22nd of that year and to an officer of the Madras Army Ordnance Service who was killed on October 4th. They were killed not at Kohima but at Konoma, a village some six miles away, between which and Kohima exists an old blood-feud likely to break out at any time if D.C.'s like Pawsey are no longer available. Then I came across a Memorial to a Manipur Raja who burnt Kohima about 1820. This consists of an inscribed headstone with a cow and a dragon and on the horizontal stone slab in front the imprint of the Raja's two bare feet.

After lunch I read Pawsey's collection of papers about Kohima and then devoted three hours to dictation. Bayley and I considered the *zyu* spirit a good aperitif. I went to bed fairly soon after dinner and finished off Pawsey's papers. So far as Intelligence work was concerned it was the old story I have told *ad nauseam*.

January 11th. KOHIMA TO IMPHAL

We left Kohima just after 9.30, driving on a good road through magnificent mountain scenery. Pawsey had said we might meet a Naga wedding party, but we had no luck. However, we passed many parties of Nagas all of whom gave us friendly greetings. The women are top dogs in this part of the world. They do all the work and carry the heaviest burdens, but the men have to carry the babies. At Milestone 77 stands the Memorial to 32 men of the Reconnaisance Corps who came round the corner here in lorries and were all wiped out by a Jap ambush. Across the road is a small notice beside three or four large flat stones placed on a small terrace just above the road with a much larger flat stone standing on end farther up. "This is a 'gino' according to the Mao Naga custom," says the notice. "Nobody should break or remove it. I have spent more than 2000 Rs.—Sibo Monthibo Naga of Makhan."

It is the custom from time to time for some rich Naga to give a feast on these stones which are brought up from the river, about a thousand feet below, and I suppose it is after such a feast that he is allowed to put the horns on his house.

Close to 79 Milestone is a simple wooden cross inscribed "The Manchester Regiment, 2nd Batt." A fleur de lis is painted on the top of the cross. Soon after this we reached the rest house at Maram.

This was built in 1897 and stands about 4600 feet up. In the garden is a huge monolith twelve feet high and fairly wide where the Nagas used to sacrifice cows and celebrate. On the very top of it an orchid is growing. I wonder if there are many instances of orchids growing from stone. On the wall of the principal room in the rest house there is a large wooden plaque with the names of the Officers, N.C.O.s and Men of the 7th Worcesters who were killed round here. This rest house was used by the Japanese as a Headquarters. Later on it became an M.D.S. for the 75th Indian Field Ambulance.

The road ran on above a rich green river, impassable in the monsoon. Round one corner a rusty car was standing on end festooned with convolvulus and decorated with a notice: "This might happen to you!" The trees on either side of the road were full of what looked like mistletoe. After crossing a bridge, which for some inexplicable reason was never blown up by the Japs, we reached the rest house at Karong, built in 1899 and standing 3,600 feet up. Here we ate lunch. At 109 Milestone near Kangpoki we saw the spot where on June 22nd, 1944, 4th Corps and 33rd Corps joined hands. Three miles farther on Bayley gave us a lucid account of the fight for the hills called Liver and Bacon on the left of the road and at Milestone 115 of the fight for the three small hills known as Pip, Squeak and Wilfrid, where on June 10th the river was crossed by the 3/14 Punjabis, waist deep, to get round behind the Japs. Farther on Bayley explained the fight for Hill 3813, when a 5.5 gun which had been damaged and from which three feet of muzzle had been taken off was used with deadly effect at point blank range. This gun was known as the Circumcised Five Point Five.

After an enthralling drive we reached the Residency at Imphal where we were greeted by the Political Agent and his wife, Mr. and Mrs. Gerald Stewart. Stewart was captured by a German raider in the Indian Ocean and finally after spending a fortnight in a supply ship was taken to Japan and interned. The two Brigadiers are being put up at other houses. The Residency is a fantastic house, and it has been made more fantastic by the twenty-five bombs which were dropped all round it. The house is full of stucco Corinthian columns inside and out. The plaster is half down in most of the rooms and the tiled roof which was knocked to pieces has been temporarily replaced by corrugated iron. The Stewarts have been waiting nearly a year for their linen, crockery, and plates which left New Zealand eleven months ago and are apparently still in Australia, together with most of their clothes. I fear our visit is a strain on their hospitality, though nobody would think so.

Christopher Gimson, the late Political Agent, who was here for many years had a passion for lawns. He was a champion tennis player and there are five grass courts of the finest quality. He was a great gramophone fan, and on top of the wardrobe in my room stands an E.M. Ginn horn which he did not take back to England with his collection of records. He also left behind all his copies of *The Gramophone*. It was his custom to give a concert of good music every Sunday evening. I need hardly add that he was a bachelor. After the Residency had been knocked about and nearly every pane in the windows had been broken he continued to live in it quite happily and, though it is cold here at night during the winter, he was unperturbed. The garden here, much of it planted by Gimson, with advice from Kingdon Ward, is really beautiful, and as I sit on the west veranda looking across a wide green lawn to majestic trees I might be in Devonshire, except for the sound of the drums being beaten by the Nagas at their ten days' harvest festival.

After tea we walked along with the Stewarts and Thomson to the market where at least 500 women were sitting on the ground displaying their wares. Half the market is in the open, but in the other half the women sit under long shallow booths, covered with corrugated iron which could give one a nasty cut if one recoiled too quickly from the merchandise. Imphal is the capital of Manipur State, the massive Maharaja of which drives about in a jeep. He is away at the moment. In the garden of the Residency there is a memorial to the five military and civil officers who were beheaded by an usurping Maharaja as lately as 1891. The Manipuri women rule the roost. This market cannot start until they have done their day's work because they insist on selling their stuff themselves. They can be pretty tough, too. A probably apocryphal tale relates that a former President of the Durbar, that is the British Political Adviser to the Maharaja and professional Prime Minister, once annoyed the women about something, for which he was debagged and thrown in a pond. A predecessor of Stewart's (not Gimson) who telegraphed to the Government about some matter connected with the price of rice was shut up in the Post Office and told he must stay there until the answer came back. The President of the Durbar went to his rescue, and he too was shut up in the Post Office by a crowd of 4,000 women. Finally the Commandant of the Assam Rifles went along and he in turn was shut up, and there they all three had to remain until the telegram came from Calcutta, but the women allowed them to have refreshments brought. On a third occasion they surrounded the Residency and kept the Political Agent a prisoner for several days.

On our way back to the Residency we passed the Naga village where the Harvest Festival was going on. We were invited inside and sat for a long while watching little girls and older girls dancing a series of rhythmical movements that symbolised various agricultural work. Two drums were beaten all the time and the men stood round with spears the points of which were hung with greenery. We were offered and drank glasses of rice beer, and it was fascinating to watch the scene in the dusk. Indeed, we did not come away until after 19 o'clock.

I read an extremely dull book written about the Nagas and other hill tribes of Assam by one Alexander Mackenzie. The Khasis, who are the hill tribes round Shillong, chose names for the pleasant sound of their syllables. Thus you will find a Khasi girl called Meltonian Cream and even Mediterranean Sea. This was told me by Mrs. Stewart. My ethnographical fellow clansman never allowed such frivolous details to lighten his pedantic narrative.

January 12th. IMPHAL

We set out at 9.30 to see the battlefields round Bishenpur. At Bishenpur it was resolved to attempt to get up some 2,000 feet above the plain along the Silchar track to see the scene of so much bloody fighting. Brigadier Bayley drove the first jeep with myself, C. and Mrs. Stewart. Brigadier Roberts drove the other with Thomson and Stewart. When we reached the bridge over the river we found it was impassable, but we managed to get across on stepping stones, and the jeeps negotiated a ford. About a quarter of a mile up we met six bullock carts coming down. However, the jeeps held their ground and when the bullock carts had somehow been hauled up the bank out of our way they leapt forward from what seemed an angle of 45 degrees. They really are marvellous cars. Finally we reached a ridge where some Kukis sold us oranges and we walked along to a small plateau whence we had a view of Lake Logtak, and the whole Imphal plain. Bayley gave another of his lucid expositions of the fighting. I looked across to Hampton Hill where the Northamptons and the 8th Gurkhas of Mackenzie's 32nd Brigade fought one of the decisive actions of the Imphal battle.

We drove back down into Bishenpur. It was here that the Japanese mules were obliterated. The place was carpeted with their mutilated bodies and the drivers of the bulldozers which cleared up the rotting carnage had to wear gas-masks; and it was here that the Japs sat in their water-logged trenches, dazed and waiting for death, looking like the crews of a series of sunk racing fours.

We drove on to the two villages of Great and Little Ningthoukhong. Both were entirely destroyed in the fighting, but now unless one looks close there are few signs of the ravages of war. Once upon a time what might be the village green between them was swept by a Jap machine-gun hidden in a culvert and here it was that Sergeant Turner of the West Yorks saved what was left of his platoon at the cost of his own life. Four V.C.s were given to heroes of this square mile (if as much) of earth in the month of June 1944. Can any square mile in the world except Cape Helles claim as many?

The two tanks in Ningthoukhong which Rifleman Gungi Ram of the 7th Gurkhas destroyed single-handed with his PIAT still stand where the wounded hero left them after crawling forward, with wounds in his right hand and leg and his left wrist broken, to wipe out their crews with grenades. In one of them a hen with chickens was scratching about, and the village children stood round wondering why we were interested in this to them familiar object.

We saw this morning several other sites of action, and I am grateful to the clarity with which Bayley expounded their significance. Not for nothing was he known affectionately as the Professor when he was B.G.S. to 4th Corps. On our way back to the Residency we passed the Gunners' Box, a lightly wooded green ridge such as one sees rising beside the road in Dorset; and we stopped for a moment at 14 Milestone where the road was shot up by 300 Japs who had struggled for miles over the hills with an anti-tank gun. 14 Milestone is on the road to Tiddim, and it was exasperating to reflect that this road was now impassable and that we should not see the terrain there.

At 19.30 Pearson, the President of the Durbar, and Lt.-Colonel Burrell commanding the 4th Assam Rifles came in for drinks. Burrell has been here since 1940 and saw the refugees arriving by three roads; he saw, too, the remnants of Alexander's Army in retreat reach Imphal. One notable exception to the shattered appearance of a defeated army was the 4th Gurkhas who marched in, C.O. and Adjutant at the head and Second-in-command in the rear, as if they were on parade. That's the kind of story that gives me a lump in the throat which one gratefully washes down with another pink gin. 7th Armoured Brigade who had had to abandon their tanks at the Chindwin crossing marched into Imphal with the same pride of soldierly bearing.

January 13th. IMPHAL

We set off about 9.30 along the Ukrul Road. The dust was terrific. After about 15 miles we had to transfer from the staff-car to jeeps in order to get up a steep rutted hill for a useful view. Alas, when we arrived at the top the grass was too high to get the view we were after, and scrub typhus communicated by mites makes it inadvisable to walk through such grass. Elsewhere round here the country was in most regards almost as austere as the Highlands, but in the monsoon it would have been a vivid green instead of the hue of dead bracken which it is now. While we were resting, Brigadier Bayley related and discussed a variety of military operations, from which I extract for the published diary what he told me about the 1st Patialas who were in 1st Indian Brigade. This battalion of State Forces without any British officers did magnificently all through. It was commanded by Lt.-Colonel Balwant Singh who was over fifty years of age. Whenever a Medical Board came up to test him, he used to take them out on such a fearful tramp that they had to be brought back on the stretchers he always provided for them. Whenever he was asked if he wanted anything he always used to reply, "More rum, more milk and more Vitamin B tablets." On our way back we turned off at Nunshigum which was where Gracey had his H.Q., to see Runaway Hill where Jemadar Abdul Hafiz of the 3/9 Jats gained his posthumous V.C. in April 1944, being the first Muslim to gain a V.C. in the Second World War. The track through the valley of the Iril was appalling, but it ran through a most lovely stretch of Arcadian country. Part of the way was along a river bank where magnificent peepul trees overhung the moss-green water of the Iril. Finally even the jeeps were defeated by the vegetation closing in on the track and regretfully we had to turn round and make our way back to the Residency, which we reached about 15 o'clock.

After tea we went along to the Naga village to see the dancing on the last day of the harvest festival. The men were wearing horns tipped with a bunch of white bunting and a bunch of peacock feathers at the back of the head. They had sashes in the style of a sergeant-major sewn with large sequins and most of them wore a sort of crimson kilt, though some were wearing shorts and gym shoes. There were many women and girls dancing, and there were boys down to a child of about five in a yellow shirt. They were dancing round a maypole decked with banana leaves and bougainvillea. At the moment of our arrival they were all seated and beating time with knives to a lament for members of the tribe who had died during the past year. All the men, and even the smallest of the boys, carried knives. There was one dance in which the performers were presented with rice balls and oranges by women in the audience. There was also a band which from time to time played *For He's a Jolly Good Fel-*

low, regardless of the ceremonial chanting and the two ceremonial drummers. We sat there sipping our *zyu* until it was dark.

About 20.15 Wyndham Robinson who has been sketching his way up from Rangoon came in with Major Hulme (1/7 Gurkhas) and Major Holt R.E. I had seen them arrive the day before looking much travel-stained and was rather worried about the prospect for ourselves as we are to go back with Hulme to Kalewa and Shwebo. The roads sound pretty bad, and there will have to be at least one night's camping in the jungle. Wyndham Robinson and Hulme insisted that it would be madness for me to miss seeing the Chin Hills and Tiddim which *can* be reached from Kalewa. So, after a debate with our two Brigadiers and our kind hosts, it has been decided that C. shall stay on here for three days and join us at Kalewa, escorted there by Major Cassels, while Bayley, Thomson and myself tackle the Chin Hills. Burma Command will be notified of the change in the time table.

Once a Chin tribesman came down from the hills with a bag in his hand, and asked for his reward. The British officer said "what for?" So the tribesman offered him the bag into which the officer dipped his hand and hastily had to extricate it from six decomposing Japanese heads.

January 15*th*. *IMPHAL*

I left at 9.30 with Roberts, Bayley and Cassels to see the sites of the fighting on the Shenam Saddle. The splendid road was made by our Sappers. Not far outside Imphal a great peepul tree stands in the middle of the road and traffic has to pass on either side. A peepul tree is sacred both for Hindus and Buddhists and must never be cut down. A large aloe beside the road was covered with a silver network of dewy gossamer, and the telegraph lines at intervals were festooned with it. Brigadier Roberts told us that one of the most shuddery experiences in the Arakan jungle was to walk in the dark right into the cobweb of a very large black, white and green spider.

The scenery when we left the plain behind and went sweeping up toward the Shenam Saddle was sublime. There was one point where the road ran into the cold shadow of a northerly aspect when I had to alight from the car and gaze entranced at the view of wooded gorges and ravines and jagged ridges, beyond which the plain of Imphal lay like a pale green lake in the sunlight bounded along the horizon by grey-blue mountains. This view was framed by a couple of 20-ft. high peach trees in full rosy blossom; they were growing above the 2,000-ft. wooded precipice along which the road had been driven. Behind, the same wooded precipice towered above and cut off the sun, so that the peach blossom seemed a frozen blush, the beauty of which almost hurt.

Some of the features of the Shenam Saddle went to the Mediterranean for their nomenclature. I suppose it started with the hill Gibraltar which really did resemble the original. The Japs captured and held it once for 24 hours and left behind them the flag they had flown on the top. Malta, Crete and Cyprus were less happy comparisons than Gibraltar, and finally the realism of Scraggy and Nippon Ridge was resorted to. The blasted trees on Scraggy, which the Japs held for a full month, reminded me of landscapes of Flanders in World War I. 20th Indian Division had perhaps its hardest fighting on the Shenam Saddle. We wandered round to visit Brigade Hill where the Staff were dug in, and to look at another wooded hill which was the H.Q. of Sam Greeves and 100th Indian Brigade—it was with Sam Greeves I spent the day at the Avadi Base. Presently the crackle of a fire, where the hillmen were burning the jungle to clear a space for cultivation, sounded like small arms, and one could have fancied it was an echo of the desperate battle of about three years ago. The holding of this vital bastion by Douglas Gracey and his men plucked many petals from the chrysanthemum.

Lurching over the side of the road below Crete we saw a medium tank which had been knocked out by one of our twenty-five pounders. I cut from it a piece of rubber for an eraser. A little farther along there was a superb view of the country southward—green mountains turning to blue mountains on the horizon and down below the old road along which Alexander's men came wearily out of Burma in '42. This terrace was ablaze with what we call African marigolds, and I was told that these maroon and golden flowers are always found where Gurkhas have been. I was also told that the Japs used to fling their dead over the precipices of Gibraltar and the other heights from which they fought in order that as much as a finger could be burnt and the ashes sent home to Japan. In the troopships the Japs used to keep the trimmings from their fingernails and burn these to send home in advance for burial when news of their death should reach home.

When we got back to the Residency I found C. pretty poorly, and arranged with Brigadier Roberts to have her taken to hospital in Shillong if she grew worse.

BURMA

January 16th. IMPHAL TO HTINZIN

C. seemed a little better in spite of a bad night and Thomson felt fairly sure that it was not jaundice, which we had feared it was yesterday evening. It is hoped that she can come on with Cassels on January 19th and pick us up at Kalewa on January 21st. If she can't she will have to stay in Assam until she can meet me at Chittagong on February 16th.

Bayley, Thomson and I said good-bye to our kind hosts and left Imphal at 9.30 with Major Hulme, two jeeps, two 15-cwt. trucks, and a small Gurkha escort. The Dodge had got into trouble just before reaching Imphal with Wyndham Robinson and Hulme, and was now in hospital in the hope of coming on with C. and Cassels later. Brigadier Roberts who had arranged everything so splendidly for our Assam trip kindly lent his staff car to take us as far as the road was likely to be tolerably good, i.e. four miles north of Tamu.

We took the road to Palel and went back over the country I had seen the day before. From the Shenam Saddle the road ran down in great sweeps through majestic scenery and glorious vegetation. It has worn wonderfully well and is a noble monument to the work of G.R.E.F. (General Reserve Engineer Force), even although it is used now only for black market smuggling between India and Burma. Still, it cannot last indefinitely without maintenance, and of that there is no sign. We rounded Tarpaulin Corner, so called because, in order to keep the soil from slipping in the heavy rains after it was first made, it was covered with tarpaulins. We passed Typhus Hill which had once seemed to offer a pleasant bivouack for a hundred of the Devons among the vivid green of bamboos shooting up again after being cut. Unfortunately it was infested with the mites that carry scrub typhus, and seventy out of the hundred got typhus, fifteen of them dying from the fever. As we came round one of the curves a troop of rhesus monkeys crossed the road in front of the car, a baby monkey bringing up the rear. Later on they must have crossed the road back to the other side, for the baby monkey was killed by a lorryful of Manipuri black-marketeers just behind us. One of our jeeps found it.

About two miles before Tamu we sent back the staff car and ate an agreeable lunch beside a dry waterfall. We were lightly shaded by slim trees growing up the bank, and when the faint breeze blew, their leaves came whirling down as upon an autumn day at home, but instead of reaching the ground silently their fall was as audible as a sliver of tin. Thomson and I rode and Bayley now took the wheel of one jeep. Hulme was our vanguard in the other. Hence onward the thirty miles to Htinzin ran over an almost steadily atrocious road except that here and there for fifty yards it would be as good as Western Avenue and testify to what it was when our Sappers, British and Indian, made it for the Fourteenth Army to throw the Japs out of Burma. Our rate of progress never exceeded ten miles an hour. At intervals strips of P.S.P. (Perforated Steel Planking) had been laid over the Bithess or Bitumenized Hessian, which with the traffic of the Manipuri lorries were by now almost all crumpled and made a noise like a train clanging through a tunnel as we drove over them. The road was wide, straight and, apart from the surface, level, running between light jungle on either side in which the trees were mostly poor specimens of teak. Bird life except for the ubiquitous wagtail was scarce, but I saw an animal which looked to me like a rich brown Belgian hare. This was identified as one of the six varieties of civet cat round here, but I was not convinced. Hulme, ahead of us, tried to run over a five-foot snake which crossed the road but missed it.

Just past milestone 28 from Tamu we turned left along a track through the jungle by a notice-board with 'H.Q. Elephant Company' on it. This was a relic of Lt.-Col. W. Williams known as Elephant Bill who is probably the greatest living expert in the Burma country. After a mile or so of jungle we came to the bungalow of the Bombay Burma Trading Corporation. It is built on piles with a teak frame, unceiled rooms and walls of split bamboo. The roof is shingled with teak tiles. Sam Cope the boss gave us a warm welcome. He had a remarkable war career, having spent much of his time with Force 136 which was the organization for dropping men behind the Japanese lines, where indeed Cope spent a long time. I found he was a devotee of my comic books. It's extraordinarily gratifying to be told that one's work has diverted somebody like Sam Cope. I never expect to hear it, and that makes it all the more pleasant to hear.

The view at twilight across the Kabaw valley to the blue misty bluffs of the Chindwin seemed rather sinister, probably because I had been told about the blackwater fever for which this hollow land is notorious. However, the melancholy dusk was brief. A huge log fire had been lighted outside the bungalow—one could not have a fire inside such an inflammable structure—and we sat down to dinner beside it. We had some beautifully tender jungle-fowl and a kind of whitebait, netted in the pools round about. This was more chips than fish but good eating nevertheless. After dinner we sat round the fire, and it was 2 a.m. before I went to the camp-bed Hulme had kindly lent me after an absolutely grand evening. We were told that a thick mist would rise and envelop us before dawn, but although it was very damp the mist was not too formidable. As there is no glass in the windows of these Burmese bungalows and the walls admit as much light and air as they exclude, the mist penetrates everywhere. I had had rheumatism in Imphal, but in this damp place I was without a twinge and slept soundly.

The teak trunks—a teak tree is in prime condition when 150 years old—are dragged by elephants to the Yu whence they float down into the Chindwin. They are then collected into rafts and by way of the Irrawaddy finally reach Rangoon, at least 600 miles away. I can imagine nothing more remote than this bungalow. The last papers they had had from Calcutta were just after Christmas.

January 17th. HTINZIN TO KALEWA

Hulme gave me a bamboo pipe from Moulmein as a present for my 64th birthday. The bowl has two small excrescences which look like ears and are excellent guards for the fingers against a hot bowl. We left Htinzin just before ten, the hour at which I was born, for the 72-mile journey to Kalewa. This may not sound far, but as our average progress was 12 miles an hour it was a tiring trip. Once again 50 yards of Western Avenue and then 200 yards of ruts, bent P.S.P. and pot holes. We crossed 150 bridges between Tamu and Kalewa, each one over a stream which, shallow enough now, can be 12 feet deep and more in the monsoon. I hope this suggests the kind of country through which the Fourteenth Army had to fight its way. The girders of some of the bridges are now festooned with creepers. On one of them was painted 'Battersea Bridge'. Bird life was scarce again and one tired of the teak trees as one drove over mile after mile of atrocious surface between light jungle. We passed one of the dropping places for supplies where Bayley remembered standing once at dusk and seeing the trees all round hung with parachutes like ghosts.

At last we emerged from the jungle and had a view of the Chin Hills we shall be tackling to-morrow. The last 14 miles to Kalewa ran through a gorge of the Myittha, a noble stream the water of which was a dark leafy green in the afternoon light. Birds were now more frequent. A large kingfisher was perched on the rail of one bridge and we stopped to admire its azure-flashing plumage. It did not fly away till we moved on again. Doves kept fluttering in front of the jeep. The people on the road were unresponsive in contrast to the jolly Nagas. Just before Kalewa I saw my first pagoda, on a bluff above the river.

It seems to me that we annexed Burma too late to make a good job of it. It was for long administered by the throw-outs of the Indian Civil Service. My immediate impression is that we have failed completely to win the people and should get out. Churchill's attitude about the Empire is doing harm out here because many both in India and Burma think he will come back to power and dash the cup of freedom from their lips. I assure everybody that the old Conservative Party is as dead as the Liberal Party, but they are incredulous and determined to hustle with the quitting of India and Burma before the next General Election, of which they are frightened.

We reached Kalewa at 16.30 and found that the rest house was without furniture except for four chairs and a table lent by U Ba Tun the S.D.O. (Sub-Divisional Officer). The only decoration is a parachute which drapes the inside of the roof. Every plank in the floor is loose and one can see through to the ground. We have only one lamp—a dim and dirty hurricane.

There was a moment of great beauty after sunset when I went out on the west balcony and saw a tree in the foreground such as you see in Chinese paintings black against a luminous green sky in the dip between two ranges of hills.

I had started to write up my diary, when I was interrupted by a visit from Mr. L. Kwan Lone, the District Supply Officer, a Chinese speaking perfect English. He had been taken by the Japs and tortured, but on the day he was to be executed he "played a trump card" by appealing to a Japanese professor he had known and instead of being executed was released, after which he spent two years in a hill village. He vowed he had read many of my books, but I don't think he had. He said his memory had been affected by the hammering the Japs had given his head.

By good luck a troupe of strolling players had reached Kalewa, and at 21 o'clock Hulme, Thomson and myself went along to the theatre with Kwan Lone who had set a bench for us at the back of the audience. There were well over six hundred spectators, all sitting on the sloping ground, men, women, and children, most of them (children included) smoking what looked like Roman candles but were in fact tobacco wrapped in maize. Kwan Lone presented me with 50 cheroots called Moonriders which are really excellent. They are strong, and each one lasts over an hour in a jeep.

The performers consisted of four 'clowns' and three women in long tight pink skirts and what looked like white boleros. They danced beautifully, sometimes turning deliciously discreet somersaults, and when a whistle blew they instantly remained motionless in a stylised pose like figures on a Chinese screen. Their faces were white with rice-powder, and how they managed that acrobatic dancing in those tight long skirts I do not know. The orchestra was a medley of queer instruments, but I could not get near enough to see what they were. For our benefit there were several gags in English. We left at 22 o'clock after which there was to be a play, the performance of which would last till dawn. Outside the theatre vendors of food were sitting at their candlelit stalls, ready to sustain the audience during the nine hours' show.

I slept wonderfully and only woke once to hear the distant sound of singing and a cock crowing at 3 a.m. At dawn there was an outburst from at least forty roosters, all of them perched on the top of the thatched roofs and crowing one against another.

A good birthday, and it was a relief to hear from Imphal that C. was better. She should arrive at Kalewa on the date fixed.

January 18th. KALEWA TO TIDDIM

We had hoped to get away from Kalewa by 8, but the complication of food and packing made it 8.45. I decided to leave Gulaba to help C. and Cassels when they arrive on Tuesday and commended both to the good services of Kwan Lone. We had to drive back about 14 miles through the Myittha Gorge to take the turning to Kalemyo. The river was beautiful in the glitter of the morning and I had the thrill of seeing the flight of a scarlet minivet dipping bright as a firework against the jungle. Just after that we met a Dodge truck with a solemn white man under an outsize topee beside the driver. We decided he must be an American Baptist missionary. Later, we found this was a good guess. These American Baptists have a strong hold on the hill tribes, and their influence over their way of life is not always beneficial. One would have thought that they would all have stuck to their posts when war came to Burma and Assam. I am informed that most of them cleared off.

The road to Kalemyo ran for a while through level country between what Bayley said was the true elephant grass. What we had been calling elephant grass looked like the pampas grass of gardens. This was plumeless. Some thousands of acres of land round here must have been cultivated before the Japanese invasion.

After several miles of rough but agreeable progress we reached the Neyinzaya river, the bridge over which has been destroyed by the Japs. We crossed over by a wobbly improvised bridge on one side of which in the water lay a Jap tank. From Kalemyo where the villagers stared at us with obvious dislike we drove along an avenue of various trees which must have been left when the ground on either side was cleared for cultivation. Most avenues have only one or at most two varieties of trees and this procession on either side of at least twenty kinds was exciting. We admired particularly a tall acacia-like tree with large glittering pods the colour of rose-madder. We stopped to look at a minute cemetery on the left of the road. There were four white crosses without names and a wooden headstone inscribed Sapper Iruchan, Q.V.O.M.S.M. (Queen Victoria's Own Madras Sappers and Miners) 5.12.44. I recalled the Mess in Bangalore and the silver mule upon the table and the dark merry faces of the boys training for what might be a lonely grave like this.

The avenue now entered a grove of magnificent trees and began to climb, narrowing to barely enough width for one way traffic by trucks. The surface was slimy and damp and often fairly deep in mud, which made the turns tricky for a jeep with a trailer. I was driving beside Bayley with Thomson at the back.

Up and up through a gothic landscape of craggy watercourses and huge trees, the land rising steeply to the left of us and dipping down on the other side to a green sea of jungle below. Up and up, occasionally passing parties of Chins who with their heavy packs looked like gnomes. We reached a superb punchbowl of foliage. Up and up until we were in the clouds, which, however, were never dense enough to create an awkward fog. Sometimes the sun, striking the mist aslant, turned it into a ladder with silver rungs. Up and up, until we were above the clouds, which now became a sea of milky billows in which was set an archipelago of mountain tops like dark pyramids. Up and up, corkscrewing up the slimy ochreous road, I suddenly saw my first *rhododendron arboreum* and nearly bounced out of the jeep. They became more plentiful, some of them with hoary trunks at least a yard round and thirty feet of blossoming rubies, but mostly they did not exceed fifteen feet. Up and up. We turned left to run along a level ridge. A foot or two beyond the jeep on the left there was an almost sheer drop of 3,000 feet to a wild glen, but the sides being covered with trees it was easy to gaze down unperturbed. From time to time we passed an abandoned lorry rusting away, and once we saw a Jap tank. Two golden orioles swam down into the abyss. It was down this road that 5th Indian Division marched through the monsoon to victory; but I do not suppose that they admired the sublime landscape.

The air began to be really cold as we came to a country of what looked like dark holm-oaks. Birds of every kind were now numerous, but for the first time the ubiquitous wagtail did not go dipping along the road ahead of us. We saw two or three large trees with silver trunks and a spreading head of grey-green poplar-like leaves. We passed the Third Stockade, which our forces held in about 1890, and reached Fort White, where down below the small village we could see the cemetery of those who fell then. Presently Hill 52 (8,198 ft.) rolled up skyward before us—an eagle soaring above its bald top. We found a spot where the wind was not too shrewd and settled down to tiffin at 13.45. The lower slopes of Hill 52 were sprinkled with the débris of war—the quick release buckles of parachute containers and many empty cartridges. I saw to my joy my first primula. It was the colour of P. denticulata, but grew with a looser head of flowers and was perhaps a shade rosier. I ache for a Flora. With the primulas were growing what resembled an androsace of exactly the same shade of rosy-mauve. They both sprung from the short brownish grass on which the cattle of the Chins seem to thrive. These were being driven to their grazing—bells tinkling from their tawny necks.

After lunch we drove on round to Kennedy Peak (8,876) on the forward slope of which Hulme says he and his Seventh Gurkhas used to watch with mixed feelings a bunch of red tabs observing their bitter and bloody struggle for Hill 52. The road ran into light jungle. We saw a large civet cat with a dark bristling tail as bushy as a fox's go bounding along a tree-trunk above the road. A new tree with blossoms like a small white magnolia was in evidence. The foliage was like a rhododendron. After rounding Kennedy Peak we passed Vital Corner after which the road ran gradually down into a country full of pines and about 16.30 we reached Tiddim (5,500 ft.) at the end of the most wonderful drive I have had in all my life, the beauty and grandeur of which evaporates in these feeble words of mine.

Tiddim was completely destroyed, but the village has been rebuilt with corrugated iron. We are being housed by Lt.-Colonel T. T. West of the 1st Chin Battalion, Burmese Frontier Force. Unfortunately he is away on a month's tour of his 3,000-odd square miles of territory. The walls of the Assistant Resident's house remain and a new roof has been made, covered with corrugated iron which is like a starry sky from within on account of the many holes. I am sleeping in his room, the furniture of which consists of a wire-bed without a mattress, a mosquito net held up by four slivers of split saplings, an improvised low wardrobe with two shelves and no doors, a rough table, and a deep low cupboard with a small battered mirror. The planks of the floor clatter and are sometimes an inch apart. There is no glass in any of the windows, which are closed with wooden shutters at night. There is another bedroom on the other side in which Bayley, Hulme and Thomson will sleep. Between them is the living-room which has a splendid fireplace for logs, a coconut-fibre mat, two wooden-seated chairs and two canvas-seated chairs both shrinking fast and one without a back. In a corner stands a wireless set with signal batteries, on which we listened to Australia. In the whitewashed stone walls is a niche for the board which used to give the tariff of what was once the Inspection Bungalow. The former bungalow of the Assistant Resident was destroyed and for his present palace West is charged 90 rupees a month by the Government. I will add that the privy follows the Burmese fashion of an inverted ace of spades for the seat and is covered by tattered tenting.

West has already made quite a garden. Hemerocallis is in bloom, peas are podding, and a bed of strawberries show promise of fruit. There were also some pink Wichuriana roses, a young bougainvillea, nasturtiums, a small plum-tree, a sizable lemon-tree and two clumps of hippeastrum, pale pink with a pale green stripe—an attractive medley.

I went to bed at 22.45 after a supper of tinned salmon and soup, and read a chapter of a tattered Western blood called *Singing Guns*. which I found in the bungalow. By the way, an earthenware pot of the local *zyu* was brought in by a Chin boy. This was filled with fermenting millet in water and everybody is supposed to suck through a bamboo in turn. However, Hulme syphoned some into bottles. Bayley and I demanded the strong stuff at 2 rupees a bottle, but it was not nearly as good as the Kohima brew from rice. It tasted like methylated spirits which had been filtered through mildew.

I slept well and was not too stiff after an arduous drive. An agreeable feature of the night was the striking of the hour on a sweet-sounding bell at the Police Station.

January 19th. TIDDIM

We started off at 10 in two jeeps without trailers, Bayley driving me and Hulme driving Thomson, to see the Tuitum Saddle close to the village of Tongzang.

It was 20.40 o'clock of March 13th, 1944 when 4th Corps H.Q. gave the signal to 17th Division at Tiddim to withdraw. The only word said was *Moccasin*, the code word for the operation. The reason was that 2,000 Japs with four mountain guns on elephants were moving toward the ridge west of the Manipur River valley and a longer delay would have meant that the troops would not get through. As it was, this force cut the road at Milestone 109 from Imphal beyond the Tuitum Saddle. 63rd Brigade marched that night and were between Milestone 140-142 by the following morning. Tiddim is 163. 48th Brigade moved back from between Kennedy Peak and Vital Corner on the night of March 14th and after a grilling march of 31 miles reached Milestone 144 by the early morning of March 15th.

Soon after leaving Tiddim we descended the Chocolate Staircase which zigzagged down from 5,500 ft. to the Beltang Lui (2,500 ft.), a swift-flowing mountain stream, glaucous but clear. The Chocolate Staircase still looks like chocolate here and there, but mostly the rich brown soil down through which it was cut is green again. We crossed the wide stream by an improvised bridge and ascended the opposite slope through groves of large-leaved trees as fine a crimson for this brief autumn of theirs as the vegetation along the Palisades of the Hudson seen from Riverside Drive in October. Here and there among the prevailing crimson were trees with foliage turned to gold or amber. We emerged from the woodland, and the road narrowed to run parallel with the Manipur River flowing at the bottom of a shaly precipice, without a tree to break one's fall. One bridge over a deep burn was tricky. Only two of the girders were left, luckily at the right interval to take the wheels of a jeep. The Chauffeur Brigadier and the Chauffeur Major both did their stuff well. We went up a steep rise as far as Milestone 139 and looked at the Tuitum Saddle which was finally captured by 48th Brigade after severe fighting. We could go no farther because the headman of Tongzang had diverted the road into his own village and put up a barrier. While we were looking across at the Saddle we heard, far above, the drone of a Dakota. I could have fancied it was the ghost of those Dakotas whose ability to supply our troops during those critical months was a major factor in the defeat of the Japanese.

In an angle of the road where we got out to study the terrain a large group of Chins were sitting round a memorial stone to a Subedar-Major of the Burma Rifles who was a native of Tongzang. When we examined it we found a superbly executed bas relief on a plaque of reddish slate. If Cyril Connolly could secure a good reproduction of this for *Horizon* it would create a sensation in advanced aesthetic circles. It was done by a Chin artist and measures 24 inches by 18. The upper half commemorates events in the life of Subedar-Major Pau Za Gin and his father. The lower half depicts the animals he had killed during his life—monkeys, a hornbill, an owl, three other birds, a sambur, a porcupine, a bear savaging a wild pig, a rhinoceros, a tiger on top of a buffalo, and an elephant. The killing of that elephant called for a big feast, and the lower half shows Pau Za Gin with a glass of *zyu* in his hand and his wife handing the jar round to the assembled guests. One would say it was of ancient Egyptian or Assyrian workmanship. It is a unique work of art perfect in composition and execution. Hulme had already photographed it, and I hope the negative was successful. Wyndham Robinson took a rubbing of it.

The inscription above says:

PA THUAL KHAM A KHAN LAM A GALL MAT VAI TUN
LIM MI
Sub.-Maj. PAU ZA GIN
Burma Rifles.
1.8.45.

He was killed in South Burma far from his native village. There is a longer inscription above, but as there was nobody, West being away, to translate it at Tiddim I did not copy that out. Most of the Chins are primitive animists and how such an artist could be found among them is a mystery, but I am informed that he belongs to a family of hereditary gravers.

We drove back to Milestone 144 and ate tiffin beside a brawling stream that leapt down to join the greenish-yellow Manipur which had already been joined by the glaucous Beltang Lui. It was a perfect site for a picnic. We raced some twigs and bits of bamboo down the little waterfalls. A bird of wagtail size with white cap, dark back, and a ruddy chestnut breast flitted from stone to stone. I found out later that this was a redstart of sorts.

I was tired by the time we got back to Tiddim after sneezing my way up the Chocolate Staircase with a sudden cold in the head. Three hot whiskies and orange juice brewed by Jim Thomson revived me and I was asleep by 23 o'clock.

January 20th. TIDDIM

Bayley drove me to the cemetery which lies a few paces below the road. It is almost an exact square surrounded on two sides by pines and looks up a slope covered with a shrub with bunchy scarlet tubular flowers round the branches. Three bushes of cherry-red roses are growing among the graves, and these are the only flowers. 74 British soldiers, many of them Borders, lie here. On one side of the square are seven unpainted crosses to eight "unidentified R.A.F.

Soldiers (sic) who crashed near here 12.9.45". In the other half of the square lie 66 Mussulman soldiers. There are the graves of an Unknown British Major and Unknown British Captain, and in the Mussulman half the grave of an Unknown Major. I cannot understand how any of these could be unknown if their rank was ascertainable. The bodies in this cemetery are to be taken to Imphal so that the graves may be better cared for, but surely with a little trouble the War Graves Commission could secure their being cared for in the beautiful spot where they now lie.

When I was walking up through the A.R.'s garden a little Gurkha girl with a ring through her nose smiled at me and I presented her with an orange sweet with which she walked away in her cupped hands as if it were a precious stone. After the annexation the British Government settled a number of Gurkhas in north-east Burma like the military colonists of Greece and Rome. Finally the Maharaja of Nepal objected and insisted that all Gurkhas must receive their pensions in Nepal. Neverthelesss many of these Gurkha colonists remain.

Hulme told me a story after tea about the concert party of six called the Roosters which was the only one to reach up here. One night at a concert on Kennedy Peak, a Rooster was singing 'You'll never know just how much I love you', when a gunner officer put his head in and shouted 'all men to the guns'. 63rd Brigade had asked for a 'crump'. Seven-eighths of the audience vanished, but the singer (a Blackpool Folly) stuck to the stage and tried to make his voice heard above the noise of the guns. When the crump was finished the audience came back to hear the rest of the performance. Hulme spoke highly of the work this concert party did. He also paid a tribute to Noel Coward for giving a show in Bishenpur when the Japs were still in Potsangbum two miles away.

While writing this I was watching crows in a tree opposite with red magnolia-like flowers and no leaves into which they were dipping their beaks and apparently drinking. Bayley says that bears in the Central Provinces eat these flowers morning and evening.

January 21*st*. *TIDDIM TO KALEWA*

We were hopeful that the rain would hold off when we left Tiddim at 8.20. This was going down day according to schedule, but just before we started the head of the police in Tiddim told Hulme that the order had been changed. He probably had a friend who wanted to come up from Kalewa. We were now faced with the problem of twelve lorries coming up a road where passing places are scarce, for it is not easy to back up a greasy corkscrew. Bayley drove one jeep and trailer with Thomson and myself. Hulme and his Gurkhas were in the other, and the two 15-cwts followed with the baggage and rations. Two golden orioles flew across a background of dark oaks just before we stopped for a while to discuss the importance of Vital Corner. Our road ran on round Kennedy Peak where Hulme pointed out Bare Patch, the scene of such bitter fighting east of Hill 52. We stopped where we had lunched on our way up, and jeeped up the hillside in a perishing wind from the west. The brownish herbage was starred with primulas and a small aster which would be a cinch in rock gardens. We dug up some primulas and asters with notion of sending them up to West to plant them in his garden for seed, but I doubt if they ever reached him from Kalewa.

In a hollow just below a strong Jap bunker we saw the bones of the 1/7th Gurkhas who had advanced to within a few yards of it. A dozen tin helmets lay around, most of them pierced by bullets. There were boots with shinbones sticking out of them from decayed clothing. Thigh bones, skulls, and vertebrae were scattered all around. Only the primulas spoke of life in that haunted hollow above which a grove of blasted trees wrote their grim hieroglyphics on the grey skyline. Some of the bones were charred as if an attempt had been made to cremate them, but Hulme thought this was probably the result of a scrub fire. The three Gurkhas of our escort wandered about among these relics of their comrades while the icy wind swirled among the white bones like the wings of Death himself. The very bells of the cows grazing at the foot of the hill were made out of shell cases. We were glad to leave this stricken spot and escape from that wind.

Soon afterwards we reached Fort White, but we did not get out to go down and look closer at the little cemetery which held the remains of those who were killed fighting in these hills after the annexation. We could see from the road that it was in good order; and if this cemetery can be cared for, why cannot the cemetery at Tiddim be cared for equally well instead of moving the remains down to Imphal?

Hulme had gone ahead to intercept the ascending lorries and presently we found three of them waiting for us by a wider stretch of road. We heard that one of the twelve had not left Kalewa and that two had broken down on the way up. Hulme went on again, and we passed two more. There were only four ahead of us now. The 3,000-ft. drop was an immense cauldron of seething grey cloud beyond which the sun was shining on the low land. In spite of the clouds the actual road was free of mist the whole way. We reached

Number Three Stockade of 1890 and passed two more lorries decked with rhododendron flowers, and then to our great relief the last of them was met and safely passed, this too garlanded with rhododendrons by the passengers.

Down and down, with the sun behind us painting the vegetation in the punchbowls and gorges with every shade of green imaginable, while the shadows of the clouds in dragon shapes or like fantastic sea-monsters moved slowly across the shapes of the mountains. Down and down round hairpin after hairpin. A lilac creeper festooned some of the trees. It was exasperating not to be able to name it.* A pigeon with iridescent emerald back and dark breast flew over. At last at 14.15 we came to level ground below Number Two Stockade where beside the rapids of the Kwe (?) Lui we sat down at 14.15 to eat our lunch to the accompaniment of the river's music. A P.W.D. (Public Works Department) chokidar with hardly a tooth left came out from the bamboo basha where he lived to show us a battered Jap rifle and a clip of cartridges. It was idyllic here in the afternoon, but dusk could be lethal, for this is one of the worst spots of all for blackwater fever.

When we reached Kalewa at 17.30 o'clock C. was having a bath, having arrived an hour earlier and seeming well again, though she had had a pretty poor time. The immediate problem was light. We had only the glimmer of one battered hurricane-lantern. So we hired for five rupees a Petromax which lasted only two hours in spite of repeated pumping. Gulaba had made a dressing table for me of the two green trunks and Bayley generously sacrificed his own comfort by lending me his camp-bed. I slept well in spite of the noise of chattering from the village, and the crowing of the cocks at dawn.

January 22*nd*. *KALEWA*

I woke quite rested after the arduous driving of the last three days out of four. It's amazing what one can stand when one is interested. I am writing this on the balcony while C. tried to catch up with the typing of the 17 pages I wrote during the Tiddim expedition. Opposite is a long low thatched bamboo building, the only light in which enters by the door. This is a school, and the lessons are being rhythmically chanted by the scholars. The bazaar is beyond and 300 yards away there is a small hill with a monastery on top. The farther horizon is a switchback of low hills above the Chindwin. Small pagodas stand on either side of the road running round the monastery hill. A little procession passes immediately below the rest

*Congea tomentosa.

house. A boy is beating a triangular gong, two boys are bearing pots like tripod scuttles, two pairs of boys are carrying a sort of tray suspended from a pole and shaded by what appears to be a green Burmese hat. On the trays are various small pans with oranges. This is a procession of food offerings to the monastery or *hpoongyi kyaung*. Every boy wears a differently coloured *loongyi*, the narrow Burmese skirt which reaches to the feet.

The clerk of U Ba Tun the S.D.O. arrives with a tray on which are eleven eggs, two cauliflowers, and twenty-one oranges. This is a present to me and heralds a visit from the S.D.O. himself later on. At 13 o'clock the children come fluttering out of school like gay particoloured butterflies. One boy in pale blue shorts is wearing a topee painted a vivid orange which the other children keep knocking off. Ten Tibetan pedlars dressed apparently in rag mats are hawking a collection of dull stones. Kwan Lone arrives with a note-book in which I have to inscribe my name.

After lunch Thomson and I walked down to see the two trucks and one of the jeeps taken on board old landing craft of ours to make the 8-mile crossing of the Chindwin to Shwegyin. The longest Bailey bridge ever put up to span a river was put up here about half a mile above the ferry, but there is a gap in the middle now. It was a tricky job backing the transport down the steep sandy bank, and the jeep had a loaded trailer. However, Hulme in charge of the operation was in dashing form. Bayley and Cassels decided to take the trip now as they would not be with us to-morrow.

When we got back to the rest house L. Kwan Lone appeared, to remind me reproachfully that I had not been to see him as I had suggested. So I went round with him to have three of the best cups of coffee I had had for a long time. Generally, much to my surprise, coffee has been a complete failure in the East. This coffee was made by his charming little Burman wife, who did not speak English. Kwan Lone told me a strange story. The image of Buddha in the monastery on the little hill is of great antiquity. When the British were trying to subdue the Chins and finding it a bit of a job, one of the monks told a British Major to carry the image before him, when resistance would cease. In due course resistance did cease, and the Major took the Buddha back with him to England. In 1939 some Burman students asked the officials (of the British Museum) to be allowed on religious grounds to take it back. This request was granted. When its Buddha came back to Kalewa an ancient monk said that this return would bring bad luck to the British and by astrology he calculated that they would be out of Burma within three years. The Buddha had been a free gift, and they should have kept it in England. When the Japanese arrived, the Buddha was hidden and Kwan Lone discovered it finally in a small jungle village on the other side of the Myittha. He brought it back to Kalewa where it now stands in its immemorial place. It is inscribed *Bilat Pyan Paya*—the God that came back from the British. Kwan Lone could not remember the name of the British officer. He reiterated that his memory had been affected by the hammering the Japs had given his head. It was actually done with a hammer.

U Ba Tun came to see us and went out of his way to help. He was a little anxious about January 31st which is the date for Burma to rise and declare its freedom, but he consoled himself with the reflection that he had a Sten gun, rifles, and plenty of ammunition in his house, and that his house is strategically situated to command the village. When he had gone his clerk came down with a present of three books about Burma.

January 23rd. KALEWA TO PYINGAING

A noisy night again with cocks and coughing and a good deal of singing. Bayley left at 7 for the journey back to his Brigade in Meerut. We shall all miss the Professor. Besides being a perfect exponent of military matters he has been an ideal travelling companion, and I am truly grateful to Scoones for suggesting him. By the way, Bayley showed me a copy of Scoones' appreciation of the situation written in February 1944 which was uncanny in its forecast of what the Japs would probably do. I've asked for permission to print it in the book. Cassels who had been another good companion went off with Bayley.

We walked down to the ferry at 9.30 of a misty morning. U Ba Tun came along to say farewell and brought with him twelve ducks' eggs. Kwan Lone was at the ferry. He shook me warmly by the hand and wished Heaven would grant us a safe journey. He was nervous about dacoits past Pyingaing (Pink Gin to the troops) and begged us to cut the linesman's wire there which was a source of communication with them. X—, a former British officer with a lorryload of smuggled goods, had been murdered only three weeks ago some miles past P.G. I heard later that he himself was not murdered, but that some of those with him were.

By 10 o'clock the mist was lifting and the ferry started. It was delicious gliding along for eight miles farther down this stately river. I noticed an abandoned river steamer with broken back. Fishermen in dug outs were pulling up the long lines set from bamboo poles in mid stream. The morning light emerging from the now fast-fading mist had a kind of virginal quality. The sun scattered diamonds upon the water ahead. Our progress was strangely serene. It was hard to evoke the confusion of that army crossing in retreat not yet five years ago. Above the ferry at Shwegyin we saw remains of the motor transport. It could not be got across because the Japs were already on a hill overlooking the river, luckily without enough guns to wreak destruction on the troops scrambling over in every kind of craft and plunging into the jungle on the other side to find the road north to Assam. All the M.T. and guns were destroyed. One Stewart tank got across—God knows how—and reached Imphal. Not only that, but it actually went back to Rangoon in 1945. Its name was 'The Curse of Scotland'.

Thomson, C. and I walked along the road for a bit while Hulme was getting our M.T. in order. To the right is a large semicircle of scrub with a few trees surrounded by a line of switchback cliffs. This is the Basin. Here we saw the mass of tanks, trucks, armoured cars and guns left behind on that sweltering day just before the monsoon broke, and the slit trench dug to protect from Japanese bombing those who were putting them out of action. I thought what a fine subject for a sonnet the Shwegyin Basin would have given Wordsworth if we had had the old gentleman with us. It was indeed a chastening spectacle.

When we were on the move again, Thomson driving me in one of the jeeps and Hulme driving C. in the Dodge, we passed vehicle after vehicle on either side of the road, the bonnets of them all pointing north. There was one group of six tanks in perfect alignment which recalled the 7th Armoured Brigade, who had brought them all the way up through Burma, marching into Imphal, themselves in perfect alignment with arms swinging. These tanks were painted yellow; they had been intended for the desert not the jungle. Then about eight miles along the road I noticed an abandoned staff car the bonnet of which was pointed south. I realised with a thrill that this was an early casualty of the advance of the Fourteenth Army in January, 1945. I felt inclined to dejeep and pat that bonnet, but enjeeping and dejeeping are a strain on the legs and I sacrificed sentimental elation to sciatic prudence.

The road to Pyingaing lay through extremely beautiful jungle. We crossed one or two streams with water in them, but mostly the beds were dry—stretches of what looked like sea sand above high water mark. An extravagant zigzag of sheer sandstone cliffs suddenly slashed the jungle, in one of which the water of a stream had gouged out a great round dark cave. I saw giant anthills for the first time since the jungle of Mysore, and tall trees smeared with mud for some way up which was a sign that the termites were at their deadly work. Green parakeets were frequent. Cycads occurred from time to time. Those primeval palms look ugly and artificial in a suburban front garden, but here they had a tree-fern effect. A small animal like a walnut-brown squirrel puzzled us to name it.

We lunched under the shade of high trees. I fired at the bone-grey trunk of one fifty yards away with a carbine and to my satisfaction hit it. We had eleven rifles in the party.

When we were driving on after lunch I was on the point of telling Jim Thomson about a wild cat in Glen Affric I had once seen cross in front of the car and go bounding up the brae beside the road when a leopardess with her cub crossed the road and plunged up the slope of the jungle on the right. I did not see the cub, but Thomson did. It was a rare piece of luck to see a leopard in daytime.

We reached Pyingaing at 16 o'clock and found that the rest house was just a large wastepaper-basket on bamboo piles. The floor was bamboo slivers and one was liable to put a foot through it if one stepped off the rush mats. It was like walking about on a wire mattress. There were three rooms. C. had a door to hers. One reached the ground from the balcony by steps of single bamboo canes. C. put her foot through the balcony.

Just before dusk, Thomson, C. and I explored the abandoned temple near by. The pagoda had been badly knocked about, but the gilded Buddha in the small dark sanctuary below was not much damaged. Three alabaster Buddhas had had their heads knocked off by the Japanese. A gilded papier mâché Buddha had nothing left but the trunk. The guardian chinthis—lions with a bit of griffin about them—on either side of the sanctuary were undamaged. From the wall of the roofless fane a clump of cockscomb was glowing red above the painted blue and pink of the decoration. The drooping white bells of a datura clinging round a slim tree scented the evening air. A wrecked Bofors gun was standing beside the entrance. In the gloom beyond was the ruined monastic dormitory on high teak poles. A large red and green woodpecker flew chuckling to a tall palm and played peep-bo with us from the other side of the bare trunk. The scene was a symbolic picture of *Burma 1942-45*. The plaster walls inside were scribbled over with the names of Indian and British troops. H. Brace of Ynyshir, Rhondda, Glamorgan, Murdo MacS., Abraham Nathan, and many other names. Some months later Lieut.-General Treffry Thompson, who was D.D.M.S. in Burma in the spring of 1942, told me how during the retreat the I.A.M.C. doctors marched all day along what was then a mere track through the jungle and within a few minutes of arriving at

Pyingaing performed five major operations in this fane, then already abandoned but not yet ruined.

A log fire had been kindled when we returned to the basha, a noble fire which lasted all night in spite of showers of rain. We sat round our dining table which was a drum of wire—no wire left of course—I in a crazy deckchair, the others in two wooden chairs and a stool. We retired to bed early. I heard a rat exploring the basha and one of our fowls for to-morrow's lunch clucking uneasily on the ground underneath. In the morning we found the rat had nibbled a hole in C.'s slacks, gnawed my bananas, and gone off with Hulme's toothbrush.

January 24th. PYINGAING TO SHWEBO

When I woke at 7 I saw a large black and chestnut shrike sitting on a pole opposite the window-door. I don't know whether this bird is usually a harbinger of a tough time for travellers, but this one certainly was. The sky was grey and a drizzle of rain was falling when we left our paper-basket lodging just after 9. Thomson and I with Gulaba led the convoy. Hulme and C. were in the Dodge. The two 15-cwts followed, and the other jeep brought up the rear.

The rain became heavier, but I was glad to see the jungle in rain. Not having to make my way through it on foot, I could admire the heightened colour of the various greens. At about 10.15 our jeep, which had been making a noise like an outboard motor puffing along on one cylinder, conked out just before it reached a bridge over a wide sandy chaung (watercourse) bounded on the opposite side by a 50-ft. cliff of sandstone. Thomson and Gulaba tried to start it by pushing it downhill, but to no purpose for when it reached the bridge it stuck there. We expected every minute to hear the rest of the transport, because we had not been driving fast. However, there was no sign of the others. The silence was eerie. There was nothing but the whisper of a fine rain and the occasional husky rattle of a big dead leaf as it reached the ground from one of the tall trees that enclosed us. After waiting half an hour Thomson and I began to wonder if we could possibly have taken the wrong road, but we decided against the possibility of error because Milestone 60 of the Fourteenth Army's advance was visible on the tawny slope up from the dry watercourse. We were about eight miles from Pyingaing—in fact just about where the people had been murdered by dacoits three weeks ago. An hour passed. Neither Thomson nor I was armed. We walked back round the next bend. There was still nothing except the whisper of the rain and the fall of leaves. At last we told Gulaba to walk back for half an hour in the hope of finding the rest of the transport. Thomson strolled up the road ahead to see if he could get a view. I settled down in the jeep to finish my diary of January 22nd.

After about half an hour the other jeep arrived with C., one of the Gurkhas, and an R.I.A.S.C. driver. Some five miles back the Dodge had seized. It had been towed by one of the 15-cwts, but the latter had skidded on a slope and gone off the road, mercifully being stopped from plunging down into a deep gully by a fallen tree.

Thomson now superintended the clearing of three of the plugs of our jeep, working himself twice as hard as the driver. One plug was broken. C. wandered off along the chaung and discovered a Japanese inscription cut in the sandstone cliff. At last Thomson got the jeep going, and we all returned to the scene of the Dodge disaster. We found Hulme on his back under the 15-cwt lorry, which was hanging over the gully, and finally by some miracle of determination he managed to get it back on the road. At first we considered turning back to Pyingaing, for by now it was a quarter past thirteen. However, after weighing up the pros and cons, it was decided to go on.

At 14 o'clock we lunched where the ground on either side of the road was clear of dense jungle for two hundred yards and dacoits would have difficulty in making a surprise attack. This was the site of the camp of the Sappers who were building the bridges for the Fourteenth Army. The only relic of that once busy scene was a mouldering khaki shirt in a slit trench. Just as we finished lunch at 14.30 Hulme arrived with his M.T. A quarter of an hour later the jeeps went on. The jungle turned to thinnish teak forest. A hoopoe kept flying in front of the jeeps and alighting on the road from time to time, until it tired of this fidgety progress and disappeared in the woodland. About a mile outside a village called Karduma we saw a dozen figures strung across the road ahead of us. My mind went back to January 1902 when Harry Pirie-Gordon and I rode from Tangier to Tetuan with a Moorish soldier for escort. As we drew near the city after dusk we saw Riffs with muzzle-loaders and top-knots silhouetted against the fading sky, and the gates of Tetuan were shut. After an argument with the janitor, in the course of which our dragoman demanded entry for us on the grounds of our personal friendship with Queen Victoria, he came down from the gate tower and pulled back the bolts. With the same sense of relief as when I rode through the archway into Tetuan I perceived that the dozen dacoits in the road were road menders.

We reached Milestone 90 after thirty miles of fairly good road or rather not *very* bad road about 17 o'clock and were puzzled which turning to take. We had just decided to turn left, when Hulme and his convoy overtook us, having made wonderful time in the circumstances.

The next fifteen miles were terrible. Heavy rain had fallen and the road was a quagmire in which the jeeps seemed to be on roller skates. Luckily the road was wide and there was plenty of room to skate from side to side, but the bridges were nasty. Thomson and I reached the outskirts of Ye-U at last, and there we had to wait anxiously for Jeep Two which we had last seen successfully crossing a brute of a bridge. Dusk was falling fast when Jeep Two reached us with the news that it could go no farther without oil. We managed to get some oil from a near by rice mill; but it was too late to repair the damage, and Jeep Two conked out. Meanwhile, Jeep One had also conked out. We were on the extreme outskirts of Ye-U, a mile from any telephone, and at least 25 miles from Shwebo. Even if we could start Jeep One to which C. had been transferred we had no lights because the battery had run out, and the prospect of walking into Ye-U in the dark through mud above the ankles was grim. At that moment, when I was wondering if we should have to spend the night in a jeep, I saw the new moon above a dull red scar in the clouds where the sun had set. I felt completely at ease and began to meditate on the beauty of the drive.

Even when slithering about during those last nightmare fifteen miles we had been enchanted by the pagodas along the road. I don't know why people call pagodas monotonous. They are all different and not a bit more monotonous than the towers or steeples of our own village churches. Apropos of steeples and towers, we passed a large Catholic church with a steeple on a tower. It had been burnt out by the Japs, but we were told later that some ten miles away at the end of a bullock track there is another church completely undamaged, with French and Karen priests, an English Mother Superior, and nuns of various nationalities. The Japs interned them. They suffered much, and six died; but the rest of the Community is back. It is to be noted that with very rare exceptions Catholic missions flourish where Buddhism prevails.

At last one of the 15-cwt trucks arrived, and with it Hulme. The battery was transferred from Jeep Two to Jeep One, and Jeep Two was taken in tow by the truck. We started on again, everybody and everything caked in mud, at about 19.30. In Ye-U Thomson went along to the police station to telephone to Shwebo for a truck to be sent to meet us in case we broke down on the 25 miles that still lay between us and Shwebo. While we were waiting for him to come back a train of 50 bullock-carts passed, every wheel squeaking. It sounded like a movement from a contemporary symphony. It was close on 20 o'clock when we moved on again. The R.I.A.S.C. havildar in the 15-cwt truck towing Jeep Two wanted to wait and cook a meal in Ye-U. He was a thin bearded mullah of somewhat ostentatious piety, and was probably worried by missing his evening devotions and the prostrations westward to Mecca.

We had a tricky bamboo bridge over the Mu to negotiate and the roads out of Ye-U seemed alarmingly complicated in the darkness. At last, some two miles out, we reached the metalled road to Shwebo, along which we were able to drive at 15 miles an hour, which seemed a breakneck speed after what we had been doing. Apart from taking the wrong turning at Kin-U the rest of the drive was unadventurous. We were all very tired, and kept ourselves amused by arguing which furlong it was on the milestones. There was nothing to be seen except the procession of wayside trees and sometimes below the road a group sitting round a log-fire. About 7 miles from Shwebo a lorry appeared, but we told the driver to pass us and when he could find a turning place to follow us in case we broke down again.

Finally just after 21-30 we reached the Mess of the Assam Rifles where the 1st Chin Regiment was stationed. Lt.-Colonel Sullivan gave us a cordial welcome. They had been telephoning along the road without getting any news and had expected us by 16.30. A farewell party to the Chins, who have been transferred to Rangoon, was in progress, and fortified by strong whiskies we joined it. Our host and hostess, Mr. and Mrs. V. T. C. Hay were so kind. After a buffet supper Mrs. Hay drove C. round to their house, and she was in bed by 23 o'clock. I sat on at the party, watching an amusing substitute for musical chairs in which the couples had to reach and then hook their arms round the poles of the tent. As there were only three poles the process of elimination was much more rapid than at musical chairs. Hulme arrived after a hot bath and performed doughtily for a man who had had such a harrowing day. Dear Hulme, I shall never forget his coming up to me, that chin of his jutting out like a cow-catcher, and inviting me in deep solemn tones to shake hands.

A merry evening broke up an hour after midnight and I slept well after what had been rather a strenuous day.

January 25th. SHWEBO

St. Paul's Day, and a flawless and serene morning, which is a good omen for 1947. I sat talking to our hostess who is a niece of David Seth-Smith, sometime Curator of the Mammals and Birds at the Zoo, and beloved by innumerable children (and grown ups) as the Zoo Man of the B.B.C. Trevor Hay himself is a New Zealander, and he is in charge of the Irrigation Department. The Hays were lucky to find their own house not too badly damaged by the Jap occupation, but of course they lost most of their furniture and personal belongings. The only visible sign of the departed enemy is an inscription in Japanese on one of the bricks and the Hays are hoping to find somebody soon who can read it for them. They have been most ingenious at improvising domestic necessities. For instance, cocktail glasses have been made by cutting off the tops of beer bottles with oil and a red hot poker. Then the top is re-corked and after being fixed with sealing-wax is set in the upturned lid of a cigarette-tin covered with aluminium paint, and Mrs. Hay paints little decorations on the glass. Tumblers are cut from the bottom halves of the bottles.

At noon we went over to the Hines' bungalow where Mrs. Hines gave us all a superb curry lunch which was one of the notable meals of our tour. A Burmese curry can compete in variety with the best Madras curry, and personally I rather like the rotten fish which is one of the many side dishes served with it. At 15 o'clock gloriously replete we went back to the Hays' bungalow and I slept till 16.30, when I got up and wrote diary till 19.45.

The sunset was exquisite—a luminous pale blue-green sky deepening to orange-gold behind a filigree of small trees and in the level distance a pagoda dark against one slim rosy cloud, above which the young moon was sailing on her back like a boat. There was only one electric light bulb and that was inclined to fade out. So my host brought up a couple of candle-bottles painted with aluminium. I was writing by the toilet table and, looking up, suddenly saw a gecko in search of flies eyeing me from the wall framed by the glassless mirror. I whistled and it listened, its neck askew. Presently the house-lizard came down on the toilet-table, but when I moved jumped back on to the wall all four feet adhering at once. The geckos in the East utter a loud trill of surprising volume for the size of the creatures. The house-lizards of Southern Europe are silent in my experience.

Lt.-Colonel C. C. Dykes of the 1/6th Gurkhas, known as Sailor Dykes because he was a Marine for nine years before he became a Gurkha, came round before dinner. He is to conduct us as far as Mandalay and went over with me on a map the country round 19th Indian Division's bridgehead for the first crossing of the Irrawaddy, which we are to see to-morrow. We persuaded Mrs. Hay to come with us, but Trevor Hay insisted on staying behind to superintend the erection of a theatre in the garden for the puppet-show they have planned for our entertainment to-morrow evening. Lt.-Colonel

Sullivan came to dinner, which brought to a close a restful St. Paul's Day spent in delightful company.

January 26th. SHWEBO

We set off about 9 o'clock in two jeeps for Kyaukmyaung (pronounced "Chawk". "Ky" is always "Ch"). Dykes drove me and Mrs. Hay in his jeep, and Jim Thomson drove C. We had one Gurkha and a couple of police with us. The D.C. had obligingly put his motor-boat at our disposal. It was a drive of about 20 miles along a tolerably good road which allowed a speed of 30 miles an hour most of the way. The country was completely flat on both sides of the road, and the only birds we saw were magpie-robins and one pheasant-crow. The former are black and white with perky tails and a sweet song. The pheasant-crow is also called the subaltern's pheasant because so many novices have shot it in mistake for the real thing. It is mostly bronzed like a pheasant with the head, rump and tail of a crow.

Kyaukmyaung is a fascinating riverside village with a good pagoda destroyed by an earthquake last September and now being repaired. We had plenty of time to look around because the motor-boat was behaving in a Hebridean way and could not be found.

A pole with white flags had just been put up in front of a big bamboo basha. Mrs. Hay thought it was probably for the funeral feast of a *hpoongyi* (priest). Apparently when a *hpoongyi* dies it is customary to pickle the body in honey until the feast is over, at which the dead man presides. It is another aspect of the wake. The dead are carried round the village on the beds in which they died, and these are always gaily decorated. The shops were rich studies in still life with lovely coloured patterns of fruit and grain and other comestibles. We bought for 2 annas a hollow bamboo segment in which rice had been baked, but nobody would eat it because it was so sticky and a curious dark mauve at one end.

At last the boat, which was a pontoon with an outboard motor, was found. Deck chairs were put in and we set off up the noble river to see the cove two miles from Kyaukmyaung where the first crossing was made by 4/15th Punjabis. The main bridgehead was at Kyaukmyaung. The cove was a sandy bank among dense bamboos, which at this season here are as golden as autumnal birches in a glen of the Highlands. The bamboos we saw in the jungle showed no sign of changing their green. I noticed two white marble Buddhas on rocks by the river's edge at Yedaw, a village above Kyaukmyaung on the same side of the Irrawaddy.

We turned back downstream, passing Ngapyin and the long strand which received the greater part of 19th Division. At first the mules had to be swum across six on a stick and the least vigorous of them were drowned. Here and there the land had been cleared of bamboos for a space and was green with Indian corn, with ground nuts by the river's edge. A net, full of small glittering fish, was being lifted from the shore just before we stopped below Pear Hill, the scene of much desperate fighting when held by the 5/10th Baluches against suicide Japanese attacks. The last time Dykes had seen it the supply parachutes made it look like a laundry's drying ground. We landed below a steep stairway of 302 wide steps and walked to the top where an ancient *hpoongyi* was sitting under a tree and superintending the rebuilding of a small pagoda shattered by shell-fire. We offered him alms for his pious work and went on through speargrass and scrub to what had once been a Japanese Observation Post made from the brick base of another pagoda. From here I had a wide view of the surrounding country—and was able to follow all the details of the fighting. Dykes made every operation perfectly clear. He himself commanded the 1/6th Gurkhas on the Monban Taung ridge, the capture and defence of which and Pear Hill against repeated Japanese attacks was decisive. The story of the crossing of the Irrawaddy by Major-General 'Pete' Rees and the 19th Indian Division is a highlight even in the bright epic of the Indian Army's defeat of Nippon.

We came down the 302 steps of Pear Hill to picnic under a tree beside the silver river. C. sat on the abode of some red ants, and for two or three minutes gave a realistic performance of ants in pants. I ate five hard-boiled eggs. Thomson contributed a firework display with the sun-stimulated bottles of beer. The weather was like a perfect midsummer's day at home. The Irrawaddy varies from half-a-mile in width here to nearly a mile, and everybody is unmistakably aware of its being one of the great rivers of the world.

After tiffin we went downstream as far as Singu, a steamer-station at the head of the road to Mandalay. We saw a porpoise leap from the silver water, and then turned round to return to Kyaukmyaung which we reached by 15 o'clock. While we were waiting on the bank for the jeeps, a woman was swimming about fully dressed and her husband was washing the pans in the river. A party of Bombay-Burma Trading Corporation people were hoping to get river-transport, having had to evacuate their particular stretch of teak forest on account of dacoity.

We were back in Shwebo an hour after landing at Kyaukmyaung. Ba Kyi (Ba Chee) a charming Burman with a scholar's distinction, who keeps the records, came along to take us over the great Pagoda, but first to see in a stone alcove beside the road statues of the three contractors and the works manager who built it about 400 years ago. These long vanished worthies of the building trade had slipped from their pedestals and were lolling against one another with ludicrous effect. I commend this reward for valour with bricks to Aneurin Bevan.

The Pagoda itself was covered with scaffolding. We drove round it, and heard the nuns chanting their evening prayers. Then we went to see a modern stucco tomb commemorating some king, which I thought was almost as ugly as the Albert Memorial. Wyndham Robinson's water-colour of it was a great deal more pleasant than the original; but I cannot think why he liked it.

When we got back to the Hays' bungalow I sat reading Sailor Dykes' copy of the history of the 1/6th Gurkhas in the war while the orchestra rehearsed the music for the puppet-show on their strange instruments. There was a set of gongs in a circle in the centre of which sat the player. There was a kind of low pulpit in which sat the player of what looked like a set of tabors all round him. These were tuned with wet mud. This instrument is called a *saing*. Time is beaten with a clapper made of the two halves of a large bamboo stained black. There were cymbals, too, and bass drums which were also tuned with mud. There was a kind of flageolet called a *hne*, which exactly expressed the sound of the reed. Finally, there were small cymbals which regulated the pace of the music.

Normally the puppet-play would have lasted all night, but we were only to see the dancing items. Even these lasted two hours because there was a lot of dialogue. The back cloth was painted in four panels—a throne room with a vermilion rug, a house and garden, a moat with a red wall and mountain in the distance, and a woodland lake.

The performance began with the entrance of a marionette dressed in rose du Barri who offered bananas to the *nat* or spirit who presides over the play. Then a monkey did a dance while two parakeets flew round him all the time. A hermit followed this with a lively dance for his age, the only evidence of which was the stick he held over his head. The hermit vanished. A white horse pranced about the stage. Then a golden throne was brought on and put against the throne-room panel, after which the Queen, with white face and silver dress, entered and sat on the step of the throne to hear the reports of three ministers and a provincial governor. The handling of these puppets was astonishing. They were utterly alive; their painted faces seemed to change expression to suit the dialogue.

After this the throne was removed, and a Prince and a Princess danced, supported by two clowns who cracked jokes and did some good slapstick.

A red throne was now put against the throne-room panel on which the King sat in majestic tranquillity while a fantastic dance was given by nine dancers, a dragon-spirit like a scarlet snake, and a white rabbit. In the end the fast and furious dancing became too much for the King's composure, and he began to dance upon his throne. With this finale the curtain came down.

The dolls were brought out to show me, and not one of them was much more than eighteen inches high. Yet on the stage they seemed lifesize. The greatest compliment one can pay a live Burman dancer is to say that he or she dances as well as a marionette. I asked our host, who had taken so much trouble for our enjoyment, to thank the performers, and we went indoors.

January 27th. SHWEBO TO MANDALAY

We went forward on our travels at 9 o'clock after most regretfully taking leave of our host and hostess whose kindness has been outstanding even on this tour when everybody has been so kind. C. was with Thomson in Jeep One. I was with Dykes. Hulme followed with the lorries. The road was dull and much corrugated, running through paddy-fields at first and later through a dry belt where cactuses appeared again. "We killed a lot of Japs here," said Sailor Dykes in the tone of a village blacksmith who had earned a night's repose. This contented ejaculation was uttered as we were crossing a small bridge.

About ten miles this side of Sagaing the road was transformed into Western Avenue and we spun along without a bump. Before reaching Sagaing itself we stopped to turn aside and look at the great Pagoda which is different in design from any other. Legend says that the Queen who built it was approached to find out what design she wanted. Pulling open her dress she asked what better design than her own breast. Certainly the pagoda is exactly the shape of a woman's breast. It is solid. I could not calculate the height of the huge dome, but it is 360 paces in circumference. There are 120 Buddhas in niches all round the base and well over 1,000 carved posts making a fence round the circular paved promenade.*

Plants are growing from the great dome, which was not much damaged by shell fire. I noticed the half-thistle, half-yellow poppy,

* Since writing that I have seen the stupas of the N.W. Frontier and Nepal, and I cannot help thinking that the architect must have come from India, for the Sagaing Pagoda is a typical stupa.

we grow as an annual at home. The name eludes me. I noticed also what looked like a tormentil. The precincts of the Pagoda are covered with temples, pagodas and shrines, many of them badly knocked about. In one a magnificent gilded Buddha surveys with sublime indifference the scrabble of names and crude drawings made by British and Indian troops. Another shrine contains a beautiful reclining Buddha.

We drove on in to Sagaing, which is entered by an avenue of ancient tamarinds. Just before that we passed a modern pagoda guarded by elephants instead of the usual chinthis. We had to wait for a while at the ferry and sat under a tent drinking tea, which was so sweet that I was able to believe it was another kind of beverage and drink it.

As we crossed the Irrawaddy past the great Ava bridge, the two central spans of which were blown up by us in the retreat, I saw a wonderful composition. The pillars of the bridge are terra-cotta and grey-brown. The girders are red. Framed in the gap was the grey-brown hill on which Sagaing is built. Red brick and white pagodas were everywhere. An unforgettable picture. Just before we reached the opposite bank a Catholic nun surrounded by singing children under bright parasols in one of the small gondolier-like craft glided past the ferry-boat.

The twelve miles to Mandalay, whose hill had been visible from the ferry engraved upon the sky like an aquatint, were full of bustle and traffic. We reached Mandalay in time to enjoy a good lunch at the club run by Naafi, which was formerly a Catholic girls' school. Here Lt.-Colonel "Tubby" Templeton welcomed us. Naafi deserves the greatest credit for what it does down here in Burma. It could not function in India on account of previous contracts.

I wrote some diary in the afternoon, and then we sat on the balcony, talking and drinking Black and White at 7s. 6d. a bottle; such is Naafi supported by a benevolent excise of which one can say with Shelley, 'rarely rarely comest thou, spirit of delight'. In India whisky costs as much as at home. Everything outside Naafi is wildly expensive. Poor Gulaba was charged two rupees for a haircut. There are 6,000 Jap prisoners in Mandalay, none of whom has heard a word from Japan since the surrender. The city itself has been terribly knocked about.

January 28th. MANDALAY

This confounded diary takes up a lot of time, but I must go on with it. I never wrote one before. After lunch (curried prawns from the Irrawaddy rather like Dublin Bay prawns) we drove round with U Lu Pe Win, the superintendent of the Archaeological Department of the Burma Government in Mandalay, to be shown what is left of worthwhile buildings, and that is almost nothing. The King's palace of teak was burnt out by an incendiary; nothing of it is left except the steps up and the two old guns on either side. Afterwards we went to see the Arakan Pagoda which lying away on the extreme outskirts of the city has escaped damage. This pagoda, reputed to be 1,500 years old, was originally in Arakan whence it was removed by some King to Mandalay and there re-erected. The task of transporting it over the mountains, through the jungle, and down the river must have been formidable indeed.

In the middle of the Pagoda is a large Buddha with golden gates round the four aspects. These are sometimes opened to give the faithful a better view. The Buddha itself faces East, and here worshippers were kneeling in prayer, some holding bunches of blue lotus flowers. Although the arcade leading to the shrine is used as a bazaar, the ground is too sacred for shoes. So Dykes, Thomson and myself ambled along between the shops in our socks. I bought two teak elephants and an ivory comb. In one of the courtyards was a three-headed elephant in bronze and a bronze statue of a warrior with a hole in his navel which I am told is illuminated occasionally and with the help of contemplation will cure anything. The whole place was full of Eastern magic. In some of the shops drums were being sold, at others toys, among which I recognized the prancing white horse of the puppet-show. There were quite a few books beautifully bound.

On the way back into the town we passed Father Lafont's very ornate Gothic church, St. Joseph's, with as many saints in niches as at Chartres. This ambitious Gothic architecture is out of place here. I went inside for a few minutes. There were a lot of children and women chanting the responses to a bearded mission priest in a white soutane, but I could not make out what the service was.

Mandalay in the dusk looked woefully ravaged. The people, however, are cheerful. There are plenty of bicycles and bicycle-rickshaws; there are also horse-drawn four-wheelers like the vehicles one sees in old American prints of the South.

January 29th. MANDALAY TO MAYMYO

We drove off at nine to the far side of Mandalay Hill in order to make the ascent from the northern side. U Hla-Aung, the Secretary of His Holiness the Venerable U Khanti, was waiting for us. There are 737 steps to the top. The shrines on Mandalay Hill were built through the efforts of a humble village priest, who in the year 1907 at the age of forty was inspired to begin collecting money to fulfil his dream. He is now eighty, and he has collected over a million pounds. Age treats humanity less mildly in the East, but U Khanti in his sixties was still walking up to the top of Mandalay Hill two or three times every day.

They have had a passion for corrugated iron in Burma ever since it first appeared, so I was not surprised to find the covered way up roofed with it. The names of the donors are painted above the sets of steps to which they subscribed. Two great cobras stand on either side of the first flight. I asked their significance, but our guide told us that they had none. I suppose they are on guard like a pair of chinthis. All the other representations signify something in the life of the Buddha. A stag, a massive quail, an elephant and a lion commemorate some of his incarnations. There are two standing gilded Buddhas, each thirty feet high. There is a green cage in which the figure of Buddha is seen taking farewell of his sleeping wife and child. In the wife's leg there is now a fragment of shell. Then he is beheld at peace, having achieved Nirvana. Doves are perched upon his prostrate form, and at his feet stand the two figures, wonderfully carved and painted, of Pain and Starvation, from which he is now for ever free.

The various Buddhas all attracted their own particular devotees. One was famous for granting people's prayers, and near this asters, blue lotuses and small coloured candles were on sale as offerings.

Another courtyard shows the female Beeloo or ogress who used to live on the hill and who was so much impressed by the shining face of Buddha that she cut off one of her breasts and placed it at his feet. Four fearsome male Beeloos are seated in each corner and every one of them has about a hundred tiny Beeloos behind him. The heads of many of these were knocked off by the Japanese as souvenirs.

At the very summit of the 954-ft. hill is a great arcade with pillars of red brick and a plaster roof. The arches give a wide view on every side. Four red and golden Buddhas sit on the square pediment of the central pagoda. A framed inscription at the entrance records that Mandalay Hill was captured by the 4/4th Gurkhas on the night of March 8th-9th, 1945. This was put up by U Khanti, not by us.

Dykes gave me an account of this fight and of the combatants throwing grenades at one another round the pillars. Then we sat in one of the arcades, and he described most lucidly the whole operation by which Mandalay was captured, the country below being spread before us like an immense map.

The capture of this arcade did not mean the capture of the whole hill. The next position taken was an immense concrete roof, but unfortunately the Japs were underneath it and for some days they could not be got out. We went down to where they had been and found a great open hall, the roof being supported by iron girders used as posts. This is the audience room of U Khanti, his throne being placed against a background of glass mosaic. Below the audience room are tables where refreshments are served to the pilgrims. We were given coffee and a dozen raw eggs on a plate. Dykes pointed out the difficulties of getting the Japs out without destroying the place. One could wish that the Americans had always been as scrupulous in Italy. A bunch of twenty Japs were burnt out of an arched tunnel that ran east and west behind the audience chamber. The Japs were finally driven from here by two companies of the 2nd Royal Berkshires and a memorial had been erected to commemorate the fierce fighting in the clearance and final capture of Mandalay Hill by the Second Royal Berkshire Regiment, March 10th-12th 1945.

We descended by the 737 steps of the western covered way. The original approach from the south has 903 steps. A reproduction of the Buddha's footprint on Adam's Peak in Ceylon was impressive. So, too, was a forest of scorched infoliated columns beyond which was the printing press. This was burnt out by the Chinese in 1942 to prevent its falling into the hands of the Japs. It is to be regretted that the Chinese did not fight as well as they looted and burnt; but they were badly led, and any chance of their being effectively used was destroyed by the boneheaded anti-British attitude of "Vinegar Joe" Stilwell. On the whole, however, considering the fierceness of the fighting the damage has been slight. I could not help contrasting the lot of Mandalay Hill with that of Cassino.

As we walked down I noticed many *hpoongyis* in orange robes who were telling their beads beside the stairway. Merry family parties and bands of pilgrims were on their way up all the time. The whole place breathed happiness and peace.

U Khanti himself lives beside the south entrance. He received us, supported by five young novices, for now in his 81st year he is frail and palsied. He shook hands with the men and offered a piece of his robe to C. He blessed us all in a quavering voice, and then sat back while we sipped coffee. I wrote my name in the venerable man's book, with the usual lame remarks about this astonishing place built by the faith and ardour of one man.

We drove past the north gate of the red-walled fort, the attack on which by the 8/12th Frontier Force Regiment cost such heavy casualties. The Japs manned the embrasures with machine guns, but with great gallantry the 8/12th recovered their dead and rescued the wounded from the bridge over the 75-yard wide moat.

I went to a cheroot-maker's shop and ordered 50 cheroots for the next day. Four chips (six shillings) was the price asked by the bright-eyed woman who seemed to run the place with her daughters. A great bowl of ripened tobacco leaf stood in a corner, and from this my cheroots would be rolled to the size I ordered. For a shilling I can smoke pure tobacco for most of the day. Compare that with the ten shillings it now costs to swallow all day the pestilential fumes of doctored American tobacco. The spread of the 'gasper' has been a major disaster to the economy, health and amenity of the world.

Dykes, Thomson, Hulme, C. and I left for Maymyo at 16 o'clock. A 10 h.p. Austin had been provided for me which was a relief after so much jeeping, though one misses the free view from a jeep.

Maymyo lies about 3,500 feet up in the hills 42 miles from Mandalay. It was a pleasant drive in the afternoon light. I noticed that the bamboos before we began to climb were straw-coloured and that the ground was thick with fallen leaves. I suspect this means that they have seeded and will therefore die. The soldiers agree that a canebrake of dead bamboos is the most damnable thing of all to get through. Couch-grass, the gardener's and farmer's foe, is the British representative of the bamboo family; but that never seeds. Some thirty years ago the bamboos in Cornwall started seeding and dying off, a severe blow to the eclectic gardeners of the Duchy.

There were hardly any birds on the way up. I saw a great peepul tree growing out of a white pediment, and a marble Buddha with his back to the road contemplating it. We passed another tree superbly covered with an orange blaze of *bignonia venusta*, and some fine daturas. We are staying in a hostel run by the W.V.S., and there I wrote the diary up to the moment of our arriving at 17.40.

I was to dine with Lt.-Colonel Dykes at the Mess of the 1/6th Gurkhas. C. was dining in the hostel at 19 o'clock, a remarkably early hour for this part of the world.

Hulme and Thomson fetched me in the Austin at 20 o'clock. The Gurkhas are in tents, but the anteroom of the mess has a stone fireplace and chimney which allows for a splendid log fire. We had some grand piping during dinner—the Road to the Isles, Kelly McCallum Esq., Captain Richardson, The Ball that was in Oban, the Nut-brown Maid, and afterwards Over the Sea to Skye, Blue Bonnets, A Thousand Pipers, the Cock o' the North and other Scots airs. I was taught a sentence in Gurkhali with which to thank Pipe-Major Shem S. Thappe and congratulate him on the programme.

It was nearly 2 a.m. before the party broke up. A feature of a great evening was some capital Cointreau, of which I'd almost forgotten the taste during the years since I sat next Madame Cointreau herself at a dinner in Paris given by the Club de Cent to the Saintsbury Club in the summer of 1938.

January 30*th. MAYMYO TO MEIKTILA*

Lt.-Colonel Dykes and Major Patterson drove us about Maymyo in a couple of jeeps. We saw the charming artificial lake, round which wild peaches were in blossom—very large trees some of them. I don't believe this is to be found in any gardening catalogue at home and it should do well in the West. It seems to grow normally at about 5,000 feet. *Bignonia venusta* was magnificent everywhere, and I saw one superb magenta bougainvillea. In the bazaar we visited a merchant of precious stones. The rubies were very expensive. They were asking 600 rupees for a stone not worth half. Finally I bought a beautiful spinel for 55 chips. There were a good many white sapphires, but they are too glassy. We tried to buy some silk, but the only kind available was a frail white silk of inferior quality smuggled in from China.

At 11 we started back on the 42 miles down to Mandalay, driven there by a somewhat reckless R.I.A.S.C. driver in 90 minutes. This may not sound excessive speed, but the road down is a series of hairpin bends, and the upward traffic was heavy. It was sad to part with Sailor Dykes. He has been a great help as an exponent of the fighting, and a delightful companion.

Genial Colonel Templeton was waiting for us. We had taken him back some strawberries from Maymyo, which he insisted on putting on the table for lunch.

Our own transport was still in hospital, but Templeton promised to send Gulaba and our baggage in one of his own lorries if it was not ready by 15.30. It was not. Poor Hulme was having a thin time of it. Thomson, C. and I left Mandalay at 14.30 in the Austin. The first part of the drive ran through fertile country between big banana plantations and pleasant trees. After Kyaukse we ran into a country rather like pictures of Mexico with several varieties of cactus and small dry shrubs. It was flat for miles on either side of the road. The surface was good enough for our driver to reach a speed of 65 m.p.h. once or twice, until Thomson forbade him to go more than 40, after which he sulked and drove at 30. The road was too narrow to pass the heavy lorries that met us all the while without going off the tarmac into thick dust. At one point I saw what I thought at first were great red square carpets spread out upon the brown earth. They were chillis being dried; I never saw a more brilliant effect in red.

We reached A Mess of H.Q. North Burma at Meiktila in three hours from Mandalay—pretty good going for 98 miles. Major-General W. A. Crowther, commanding the 17th Indian Division, made us welcome, though I think he was a little shaken by the prospect of putting up C. No woman has ever stayed in this Mess. It faces the lake, and there was a beautiful sunset, the lake a luminous green, the sky orange turning to yellow and blue-green. Our baggage arrived just in time to change for dinner. Poor Hulme did not get away from Mandalay with the M.T.

January 31*st*. *MEIKTILA TO MYITKYINA*

I was up at 6.45 for the 360-mile flight to Myitkyina. The dawn was as lovely as the sunset, of which it was a more delicate replica. My room has a continuous series of windows all round except on the south side. Thomson and myself were airborne by 8.15. The Dakota was comfortable, having been adapted to carry six passengers in armchairs, but smoking was forbidden. We heard with disappointment that we had to leave Myitkyina by 13 o'clock. When we reached Myitkyina I found that the start of the Ledo Road was 14 miles away on a pretty bumpy road and that we shouldn't be able to leave before 14 o'clock at the earliest. Lt.-Colonel H. Chappell of the 2nd Burma Regiment met us on the northern air strip. He was depressed to hear we had so absurdly short a time. He had gathered three or four officers who had been with 136 Force to give me some stories and had expected we should stay the night. We started at once for the Ledo Road, passing a group of wives from the Kackin Regiment in attractive black and red dresses. We drove over the southern and western of the 2,000-yards long American airstrips. On one was an abandoned Dakota. Beside another stood a vast hanger. In a sandy bank charcoal burners were living in dugouts.

At last we came to the head of the famous road built through the jungle by 100,000 labourers, mostly Indians. It much resembled the other end of it at Ledo nearly 300 miles away. We drove along for about a mile of them and then had to turn round and go back to the Mess. Major Sohn Singh of the Kachins was with us. I saw the first Chinese notice-board and passed another big notice-board instructing commanders of convoys where to report. The immense expenditure of time, toil and money on this road was a complete waste. It was finished in time for two or three convoys to pass down it with supplies for China, and that was the end of its utility. It will now revert to jungle, although a few lorries of the Indian

Transport Company are still able to make the journey to and from Assam.

Of the thousands of Americans who were once in Myitkyina all that remains are a "Main Street" and "Virginia Avenue", some large tins of tomato juice, and by far the most luxurious thunderbox I have seen. This was in the C.O.'s tent. Those gallon tins of tomato juice were a treat to us in January 1944 when the crew of the Liberty ship *Samuel Dexter*, thinking she was going to break in half abandoned her off the Irish coast, and she went steaming on for some fifty miles to crash on the north of Barra. The old salts of Barra were scathing about such seamanship. However, they had a great time with the luxurious equipment and food of the American crew.

At lunch were Lt.-Colonel P. M. Maddox and Major Francis who had both done some great work with 136 Force, but owing to our having to leave immediately after lunch there was no time to hear about their adventures. It was really exasperating. We were airborne by 14.15 and flew back over some of the clearings made by the Chindits. They appear from above like sandy islands of complete sterility in the great green ocean of jungle. We were not lucky enough to see any elephants, which are seen from the air fairly often. On the clearing known as Piccadilly we could see the craters left when the Japs bombed it five hours after it had been evacuated.

In March 1946, 700 Chinese with two field guns arrived in Myitkyina with the avowed purpose of searching for their deserters but actually to loot the bazaar. One can safely prophesy that if Burma decides to leave the Commonwealth she will have to keep a sharp eye on China when China gives up her civil war.

Brief though my stay was in Myitkyina it was long enough to set me wondering why the American and Chinese force, after seizing the airstrip in May 1944, failed for so many weeks to capture Myitkyina itself, which lies as it were just across the road without any natural defences. The contribution of the United States Air-force to the Indian Army's final expulsion of the Japanese from Burma was of inestimable value; indeed, without the help of the American flyers the Fourteenth Army could not have been supplied. The contribution of General Joseph Stilwell's American and Chinese infantry was comparatively small. Yet owing to pusillanimity in London, where it was feared that the Japs were going to break through at Imphal, the vital importance of the long drawn out battle there was deliberately played down for fear of the effect on public morale if a disaster occurred. Simultaneously Myitkyina was played up to distract attention from Imphal. The B.B.C.

announcers were even taught how to pronounce it (Mitchinah), and the public fancy was caught by a word which was pronounced so differently from the way in which it was spelt. The result is that to most people Myitkyina says more than Imphal or Kohima or Meiktila. A book has now been published in America packed with Anglophobe lies and scurrility by the Public Relations Officer of that sour-faced, sour-mouthed, sour-brained fanatic, General Joseph Stilwell. When the true story of Myitkyina is written it will be found to contain a certain amount of sheer farce.

February 1st. MEIKTILA

Brigadier Miles Smeeton, now commanding 1st Burma Brigade, drove Thomson and me round in a jeep to explain the battle of Meiktila. He is an exhilarating personality. 6-feet 6-inches tall, as thin as a lath, and with a nose on him like Julius Caesar; he was with Hodson's Horse (4th Lancers) in the Desert and commanded Probyn's Horse (5th Lancers) at the Battle of Meiktila. I was glad to get a view of the fighting from the point of view of a tank commander.

Thomson asked him where our big hospital was. He pointed it out. "I remember the place well. I got a bullet clean through my nose and was inside for three days."

Smeeton told me the story of the Maharaja of Bundi's immediate M.C., and we saw where he had been separated from the rest of his troop and went charging on alone in his tank, shooting up the Japs all round him. He was wounded here. The Japs used to jump on the tanks, but they never seemed to know what to do when they were on them. One fellow went down before a tank to plant a mine, but having made the suicidal gesture he fumbled about uncertain what to do next and was killed before he did anything. In the attack on the Jap hospital area the Jap patients were throwing grenades and the hospital itself was in flames.

Smeeton pointed to the spot where David Anderson, whose tank was between two blazing dumps, said to him, "There doesn't seem much opposition here. May I go forward?" A bullet hit him in the head and he was killed instantaneously. "What wonderful last words for a soldier," Smeeton commented.

We noticed a burnt-out lorry by the road. "That was loaded with red and yellow flares and got a direct hit. I had to get my tanks out pretty quick. You never saw such a display of fireworks."

The last Japs in Meiktila threw themselves into the lake, preferring to drown rather than surrender.

The country round Meiktila would be rather like the Western Desert if it were just a little more bare. The low contours on the skyline are the same contours as there. The picture that the war correspondents have given of the Burma campaign as a kind of vast dripping, green hell is one-sided. It was abominable the way the high ups at home played down these Burma battles. They could not believe that we should defeat the Japs and were afraid to tell the British public what the Fourteenth Army was doing.

February 2nd. MEIKTILA

In a tree on the south side of the Mess were some small blue and yellow birds like tits and a lot of white butterflies grey and orange underneath. They looked like relations of our orange-tips at home but were twice as big. Tree-rats were chasing one another over the roof of my room. Their antics made me laugh aloud once or twice.

At 16 o'clock Thomson and I were driven by Miles Smeeton in his balloon-tyred jeep over to Kindi which was the scene of a tank battle. There were a lot of Jap lorries and bones lying about, and I looked for a skull. Two young *hpoongyis*—very young ones—came up to show us something macabre, as we thought, but when Smeeton walked across with them to see what it was he found it was a mine.

There were two of Smeeton's Shermans which had been knocked out in battle, and we went to look at their names—Captivation and Allegro. They used to call their tanks after the stud horses of Probyn's Horse. "You really got as fond of them as horses." Captivation was almost brought off the field, but had the bad luck to run into a tree when he was turning, and he still lies against the stump of that tree. It was at Kindi that Major Desmond Ryan, one of Smeeton's Squadron Commanders, told him that he was going back to look for his Indian operator. The rest of the crew, mostly wounded, were with the Borders. Smeeton forbade him to go back, but a little later, pistol in hand, he went and was killed. The relations between these British officers and their Indian troops have written some of the finest pages in the long history of war. Smeeton told me that the Indian tank drivers were absolutely first-class.

Unluckily I was seized with acute collywobbles and could not pay as much attention to what was being said as I wanted to, and when I got back to A Mess I was kept so much on the run that I had to cry off dinner and go to bed. I took two of the powders Frances Day gave me before I left London, and they worked like magic.

February 3rd. MEIKTILA

I woke up to a marvellous dawn, turning from orange through pink and yellow to gold. From the west windows of my room one can see against the sunset the volcanic cone of Mount Popa which is infested by hamadryads, not the wood nymphs but king cobras. The inhabitants are reputed to be immune from the bites of these savage reptiles which attack at sight.

The General lent his car for Smeeton, Thomson, C. and myself to visit various places. Just as we were starting, Hulme turned up, having arrived from Mandalay last night with the transport, and very glad we were to see that redoubtable chin again. He should be Colonel of a Chin Regiment. Hulme came with us, and we drove some 25 miles on a good road just beyond Piawbwe. It was good tank country on either side with hardly an undulation. The trees in the distance looked like elms and except for the palms it might have been a midland landscape in a droughty August. Lantana has taken hold here.

I wish I could reproduce Smeeton's own description of the fighting. "This is where we hooked round with Claudcol. It was the greatest fun. Absolutely pirate show. Terrific sport. You see that haystack there? I remember a Nip coming out of a haystack just there and running along down the road. He was hit with a Browning."

We came to the village of Yindaw which is surrounded by a wide moat. This survival of mediaeval warfare defeated the tanks who could not support the 6/7th Rajputs when they had crossed it and were trying to get cover on the other side. The casualties were very heavy, and in the end Yindaw had to be by-passed. 'Punch' Cowan of the 17th Indian Division must have been an inspiring commander in the field. "He never let go of his objective," said Hulme who worshipped him. "He stuck a big cigar in his mouth and went right ahead." When 5th Indian Division was put in to give the Black Cats (17th Division) a let up in the move south after Meiktila, according to Smeeton and Hulme, the pace became slower and the pursuit hung fire. I noticed a tangle of iron beside the road and asked what it was. "That's the remains of a bad show for 5th Division," and the two Black Cats, looking at one another, shook their heads and shed a few crocodile's tears.

The competition between the Indian Divisions in this war was keener than regimental competition used to be once upon a time. They accused one another of stealing the limelight like so many prima donnas. This corporate enthusiasm was of the utmost value to morale. I, a hero worshipper in the audience sitting back and admiring the performance of them all, can only hope that when I have told the tale my readers will find it as difficult as I do to praise one Division more than another. Red Eagle (4th Division), Ball of Fire (5th Division), Golden Arrow (7th Division), Clover Leaves (8th Division), St. Andrew's Cross (10th Division), Black Cat (17th Division), Dagger (19th Division), Silver Sword (20th Division), Fighting Cock (23rd Division), Ace of Spades (25th Division), Tiger Head (26th Division)—where would we have been without them?

Miles Smeeton told a story about Pegu. The Japs used to make a pit on either side of a road covered with a lid in which two Japs sat with a pole between them on which was a mine to put under a tank. An Indian Sapper, looking for mines, prised up the lid of one of these pits with his bayonet, stuck it into the Jap, and then hit him on the head with the butt. A Jemadar rushed along, but unfortunately picked up the pole to knock out the other Jap. The mine exploded; and all four, the two Japs and the two Sappers, were killed.

Just before Pyawbwe we were held up at a level crossing for a jeep on railway wheels to pass. Is there anything a jeep cannot do?

We saw the porch of a large school in which the Japs had one of their 75's with a hollow charge—a fairly deadly weapon for tanks.

"There ought to be a Jap tank we knocked out just beyond here. I shall be most disappointed if I can't find it," said Smeeton.

But there it was!

Before we went back to Meiktila we turned aside for a mile or two to see Ye-we where Hulme and the 1/7th Gurkhas had a bad time. Ye-we was unlike any village I had yet seen in Burma. Two of the pagodas had snakes painted with red hearts coiling round them, the head of the snake taking the place of the usual metal umbrella on the top. Outside one shattered shrine was a gilded Buddha of which only the feet and ankles remained. There was a domed temple carved with strange animals including chinthis with human faces, and a low arcade below in which Gurkhas and Nips chased each other round the columns—a smaller edition of the fight in the arcade on Mandalay Hill. On another pagoda, a bit of broken metal was swinging in the wind with the sound of a tinkling bell. Shells, dead and alive, were scattered all over the place. I nearly trod on a live grenade. The ground was covered with Jap bones. I saw a beautiful solanum with white flowers about the size of a tomato's and green bladders, inside which were seeds like small green peas. I could have spent a long time wandering round Ye-we, but we had to get back to lunch.

I worked on diary till tea-time and then went out with Miles Smeeton for a survey of the fighting with the 18th Jap Division north of Meiktila. When the Japs were driven off the ridge by the tanks they ran down into a nullah full of bamboos, up the other end of which the Baluchs were advancing. The Baluchs, seeing Japs running towards them, thought it was a counter-attack and started firing. Some of the Japs ran so fast that they got behind the Baluchs who made up their minds that they were encircled. It was on this occasion that a remark of Smeeton's was heard on the air and caused a bit of trouble. "The bloody infantry lying down again."

He was feeling a bit sore at the moment, having just been shot through the nose. I was reminded of what Denys Reid said about tanks in the Desert "always hull down" as it sometimes seemed to the infantry. I asked Smeeton the answer to that one, and he said that our armour was outweighted in the Desert, but that our manoeuvring *was* too much hampered by excess of caution. At Meiktila Smeeton refused to let his tank commanders close their turrets. "You can't really see in a periscope what's happening. Five of my tank commanders were shot through the head, but I still think that it's right to risk this for the advantage of manoeuvre."

February 4th. MEIKTILA TO PAGAN

At 8 o'clock Major-General Crowther, Brigadier Miles Smeeton, Michael Wauchope, the General's A.D.C., Thomson and myself set out for Pagan. We had an escort of Frontier Force Rifles as well as Smeeton's Karens and Chins. We were all in jeeps; the kit was in a station wagon.

We took the road to Kyaukpadaung where the Burmese Communists are strong and there had been trouble lately between them and U Aung San's people, but if anybody was looking for trouble this morning the sight of our jeeps bristling with tommy-guns must have made him look again. The road was very dusty and the country grew more arid all the time. The great triangle of Mount Popa was on our right for several miles, rising five thousand feet from the level lowland in isolated majesty. I was reminded of the way Samothrace rises from the Aegean.

In due course we reached the Chauk oilfields, which are the largest in Burma. It was a fantastic sight. Rust-red derricks everywhere, like dead trees among the withered herbage and low scant scrub. I had an impression of there being some hundreds of them. Every well had to be put out of action before the Japanese advance in 1942 and for the first time I appreciated the magnitude of the task performed by the Burma Oil people.

A few miles beyond Chauk we drove downhill to cross a very wide chaung which was a wilderness of loose sand. This was the limit of the advance allowed to Crowther when he was commanding 89th Brigade of 7th Indian Division. On the other side was the zigzag of dry hills about 400 feet high through which we had just driven, and this provided a formidable defensive position for the Nips. We went on through Singu and Myinkapa where the General explained the military operations leading to their capture and finally we reached the outskirts of Pagan.

I had had high hopes of Pagan, but the reality far exceeded anything that fancy had conjured up beforehand. Lots of people tire of pagodas, Wyndham Robinson said he wished he had had a rubber-stamp of a pagoda to save him the trouble of painting one into every picture he made. I never tire of their infinite variety, though I admit that this variety requires a close view to be appreciated. Pagodas on distant slopes are apt to resemble one another. However, the most jaded traveller among pagodas would be wonderstruck by Pagan. It is pronounced Pagán. This was once the capital of Burma, but it was abandoned after being sacked by Khubla Khan at the end of the 13th century. He could have found a thousand models here for the stately pleasure-dome he decreed. A little white pagoda on a hill the other side of the Irrawaddy marks the spot where Buddha is said to have stopped and prophesied a future capital upon the site of Pagan.

The area of Pagan can hardly be less than four square miles, and this is covered in every direction the eye looks with huge pagodas, small pagodas, whole pagodas, ruined pagodas, fragments of pagodas, and many temples as well. One dome at least is larger than the dome of St. Paul's and the architectural influence of India is everywhere apparent. The greatest number are now rose-red brick, the plaster (if they ever were plastered) having worn away in the course of over 800 years, but the dryness of the climate in this part of Burma has preserved the brick in the same way as I imagine Petra, the "rose-red city half as old as time," has been preserved. It would be rash after such a brief glimpse as mine, to claim peculiar beauty for any single one of what are reputed to number 5,000 pagodas in some form or other, but the Nagayon Temple in which General Crowther had his headquarters is certainly one of the most beautiful.

It is surrounded by a red brick wall eight feet high and then within the rectangle by another brick wall four feet high, Within its temple stands one giant Buddha facing north. It is an erect gilded figure, the right hand extended to receive what seems the secret of the world. A huge cobra is coiled at his feet and winds up to show above the Buddha's head its own fearsome countenance with gilded hood. On either side in the alcove are twelve smaller cobras carved in a sort of wreath. At the end of a cloister beyond the central shrine, we scrambled up through a low door with a Gothic arch to where a steep flight of stone steps, none less than eighteen inches high, emerged on the shallow cupolas of the roof, whence by tiers of red brick one could have climbed to the base of the big central dome. I'm giving a feeble description of this lovely shrine. It was impossible to appreciate and note its many beauties in so brief a visit.

Not all the pagodas are rose-red brick. Some are white as wedding cakes. One at least is covered with gold leaf. Others are plastered with stucco now a mellow grey. These abandoned pagodas and the abandoned derricks of the Chauk oilfields provide a strange, indeed a startling contrast.

We reached the Dak bungalow at 13.30 and were received by U Tin, the S.D.O., and the headman of the small modern village of Pagan with one or two dignitaries. A police guard of honour saluted the General. This bungalow was built to accommodate the Prince of Wales and his staff during his tour of Burma, but he did not manage to reach Pagan. On either side of the steps leading up to the verandah vendors of the attractive lacquer ornaments and utensils made locally were gathered with their wares spread in front of them. U Tin had gone to much trouble to make us comfortable, and we sat down to an excellent lunch, which included large Irrawaddy prawns fried. They looked like veal cutlets with pink tails instead of bones.

We set off after lunch to see the Ananda Temple. As this is still used for religious rites, we had to discalce. The covered way in, roofed as usual with corrugated iron, was built in 1920. A frieze of paintings illustrates Pleasure on the left, Pain on the right. Tortures of men and women by giant demons were the chief subject of the latter. In one a demon was hitting women on the head with a mallet before they were thrown into a boiling cauldron. We hoped for a comparative frankness in the Pleasure series but were disappointed, most of them representing the insipid picnics of conventional oriental figures in a Christmas card landscape. The Ananda Temple itself is over 800 years old. Four gilded Buddhas, each at least thirty feet high, face the four points of the compass from sombre Gothic-seeming alcoves, the gigantic doors of which are of carved and fretted teak, too heavy to close. Each Buddha is erect and makes a different symbolic gesture with its hands. A cloister runs right round with six-ft. deep windows with pointed arches and various images in recesses and niches. The pavement is peppered with desiccated bats' droppings, which made walking in our socks an Agag promenade.

From the Ananda Temple we drove on to the Golden Pagoda, which is covered with fresh gold leaf and illuminated with electric lamps at night. We had to discalce again here because this is a contemporary centre of pilgrimage and prayer. The "sexton" in attendance enumerated the nine wonders of the Pagoda. The first is a small hole in one of the praying flagstones which when filled with water holds the reflection of the whole Pagoda. Another is that the shadow of the Pagoda never falls outside the sacred precincts. A third is that nobody can ever rise early enough to make the first offering of food in the great jars provided for this. Somebody has always put food there in advance. I can't recall the other wonders. There were some rather tawdry architectural additions all round and the whole place resembled those Catholic churches designed to attract simple faith. The peace of the precincts was disturbed by the yelping of the dogs belonging to the vendors of votive candles and flowers.

At about 16 o'clock we arrived in Nyaungu just beyond Pagan where the 7th Indian Division crossed the Irrawaddy and made it possible for a mobile column of the 17th Indian Division to pass through and reach Meiktila to the complete confusion of Japanese strategy. On the other side of the great river about a mile away stretched the long sandy beaches from which that vital crossing was made. Looking across the mighty river, pale blue in the light of the February afternoon, I heard my two companions evoke again those epic February days of two years ago.

Then we embarked on a patrol launch and crossed to the other side. It was a windless afternoon and therefore the small sampans were moving down the stream. The square-rigged tonkins, which are half barge half viking ship, lay at their moorings in such weather. The chief of the Burma police in Myitche had provided two jeeps and a station wagon in which we drove over the Myitche airstrip from which the Indian Divisions were entirely supplied. In Myitche a jolly good tea had been provided which we enjoyed in a small pavilion after the General had inspected the Police Guard.

The sun was setting behind a range of grey-blue zigzag hills when we embarked to return to Nyaungu, and before we arrived dusk had fallen. The waters of the Irrawaddy were iridescent in the fading colours of the sunset. A great company of swifts was wheeling and swooping among the flies and midges over the river. Then as if to a word of command the swifts rose in a dark cloud and winged their way to roost, abandoning the dusk to a myriad bats. The *ti* or umbrella of the Golden Pagoda was lit up by electric lamps and round it other lamps were shining. The ivory moon, two days from her plenitude, had watched the sun go down, and was now robbing the stars of their silver as she climbed the sky.

When we got back to the Bungalow the vendors of lacquer were still sitting in the porch, their wares shimmering in the light of a Petrolux lamp. We made some purchases and then went upstairs to eat an excellent dinner in the upper porch. A wonderful day.

February 5th. PAGAN TO MEIKTILA

I woke at 6.30 and watched the dawn flush the high ceiling of my room. Outside a chorus of birds was twittering, cheeping, chattering and whistling in the trees round the bungalow, and the more distant air was filled with the crowing of innumerable cocks. We made a few last minute purchases before we left Pagan, accompanied by the kindly and hospitable U Tin as far as the crossroads to Ngathayauk. If Pagan were made comfortably accessible and a really good hotel built Luxor would have to take second place as a winter resort. The climate is absolutely perfect, the surroundings incomparably more impressive than Luxor, and the antiquities much more varied. Moreover, there would be no Egyptians.

Miles Smeeton was in a mood of inspired reminiscence that morning as he drove his balloon-tyred jeep like a Pegasus over the sandy deep-rutted road to Meiktila. The air was champagne and washed down the dust in our throats. On our left as we came up the rise out of Nyaungu we saw the catacombs in the low hills which had been infested with Nips and gave 33rd Brigade so much trouble. In the end the Nips had to be sealed in. It is strange how one can write of burying human beings alive as if one was writing about the extermination of noxious insects.

This part of the country is for tanks what the shires are for horses and hounds. Under the spell of Smeeton's vivid evocation I was able to visualise every hour of those marvellous seven days from the morning of February 21st until, at about 18 o'clock on the evening of February 27th, Probyn's Horse harboured on a ridge looking down over Meiktila, the capture of which decided Nippon's future in Burma.

The infantry of 48th Brigade were moving in M.T. along the

road on which we were driving now, while Probyn's Horse with the 6/7th Rajputs in their tanks kept pace with them over the open country to the right and the Royal Deccan Horse with the Bombay Grenadiers in their tanks ranged off to the left.

At Seywa we stopped to ask which of about half a dozen sandy bullock tracks was the road to Ngathayauk. It took some time for our pronunciation to make it clear where we wanted to go. The villages through which we passed had clustered round water and were like oases in the arid countryside. In all of them great tamarind trees spread shade and they were surrounded by groves and colonnades of tall palms.

In Ngathayauk I noticed an unusual pagoda covered with images, and inside the fence that encircled it were seated a lot of other images looking at the pagoda like spectators at a puppet-show. It was tantalizing not to know what such an arrangement signified.

The next village was Oyin where the most bloody action of the advance was fought. Here the Nips attacked the tanks individually with boxes of picric acid. They held a deep cross road which ran through the village with high hedges, and the trees were full of snipers.

"They came falling down off that large dark tree over there like crows," Smeeton said.

We stopped for lunch just before Eyaa in the place where Probyn's Horse harboured on the night of February 24th. The slit trenches were still there and Smeeton showed us the perimeter inside which the tanks stood, the infantry bivouacked in front of them. He said the crews would sometimes be working till 2 a.m. to keep their tanks in trim for next day's advance. The workshop had been left at Myitche and for a month the crews were dependent on their own energy and ingenuity. Morale was at its peak.

"No one who took part in it will ever forget the excitement of that dash to Meiktila. The tanks moved along, deployed on each side of the road. They lifted their heads and flourished their tails, and took the little cactus hedges like a hunt across country, while the lorries of the infantry crowded down the road between them."

Among some trees on the outskirts of one of the villages we passed before we struck the main road I saw an orange-tawny bird which, as far as I can identify it from the description in a book on the birds of Burma, must have been McClelland's Laughing-thrush. It is rare and there is no picture of it, but it is the only bird whose appearance and habitat fit in with the one I saw.

A mile or so before Taungtha we crossed a wide chaung along which the tanks saw a Jap company marching slowly.

"Extraordinary sight," said Smeeton. "They paid no attention to us, but trudged along, bent low under their heavy packs. Two tanks shot them to pieces, and not a Nip looked round or stopped marching."

Some of the bones which remained from this massacre were still scattered along the opposite bank of the chaung.

We drove on to Taungtha, crossing the railway line. The formidable hill behind Taungtha kept the 7th Division back for a month because the Japs reoccupied it after the dash for Meiktila had swept by.

We drove on through Mahlaing which had been much knocked about. We now had an impressive view of Mount Popa from the other side. It seemed tralucent, a milky blue against the western sky, and what remains of the crater was clearly visible.

We passed the site of the road block at Milestone 9½ and could see the stumps of the trees which had been cut down to make it. Probyn's Horse and the Rajputs were called up from the airfield at Thabutkon to clear this. There is not much to be seen of that old Jap airfield now, but as soon as it was clear two years ago 99th Brigade of 17th Division began to fly in for the assault on Meiktila.

It was about 18 o'clock when we paused on the high ground by Milestone 6 to look down at Meiktila. The wide prospect was golden as a landscape by Claude. I could see that Smeeton was deeply moved by memories of two years ago. It had been about 18 o'clock on the evening of February 27th, 1945, that "Probyn's Horse and the Rajputs harboured on the high ground at Milestone 6 in sight of the Meiktila lake, on the identical piece of ground where they were later to kill many Japanese on March 9/10th, who however made full use of the slit trenches we dug that night. A Beaufighter circled round us in the dusk as if uncertain whether we could really have come so far, so fast."

I have failed to note where I found that quotation and apologize to the author for not giving the source.

February 6th. MEIKTILA

I worked absolutely all day on my diary and caught up with the last two very full days.

Miles Smeeton left at 16 o'clock on his 200-mile drive south to his Brigade H.Q. He is leaving the Army in April and going to his island in British Columbia. His contribution to the task ahead of me has been of priceless value. I never enjoyed any day in my life more than I enjoyed yesterday.

Michael Wauchope came up to my room to say that Rangoon wanted to know if it would suit me all right to stay one more day in

Meiktila because the V.I.P. plane had to come on Saturday with Arthur Bottomley, the Parliamentary Secretary to the Dominions Office, and the Shan States Commission, and we could then go back to Rangoon in it. I was quite glad to get a free day.

February 8th. MEIKTILA TO RANGOON

We left Meiktila at 11 in a V.I.P. Dakota and after an uneventful journey landed on Mingaladon airfield at 13 o'clock. Captain D. Crookes, A.D.C. to Lt.-General H. L. Briggs G.O.C. Burma Command met us. The Adjutant-General, Sir Richard O'Connor, was staying with the General, and J. R. Bingley of the British Council kindly put us up for the night. He is an old Magdalen man, some twenty years junior to myself. Brigadier C. I. Jerrard, who commanded 98th Brigade of 19th Indian Division, came in and was evidently much worried by Toungoo's having been cut out of the tour. So I said if he could get us a plane at Moulmein I *would* fit it in.

Bingley asked if I would mind sitting on a Brains Trust—the first ever held in Burma. Every Saturday night there was a Burmese gathering under British Council auspices. It may seem a bit late in the day to start explaining the British way of life to the Burmans now, but the Council is doing good work wherever I have had a chance to observe it and the senseless nagging by the Press at its expenditure is tiresome.

Lots of young Burmans arrived and the proceedings opened with some rather half-hearted community singing. Then the Brains Trust started—a poet, a journalist, a civil servant, Daw Mya Sen, an extremely intelligent champion of women's rights, and a medical professor at the University, Dr. Burridge, who was formerly at Lucknow. The question master was a young professor of biology. On the whole, the questions were quite good. I found myself in disagreement every time with Dr. Burridge and in agreement every time with Daw Mya Sen. One question, which I should like to hear put to the B.B.C. Brains Trust, was "what is love?" I was amused to see the way the audience sat up and really did listen to the answers to that. Another question was "Shall Burma join the British Commonwealth?" I said that there was a mistake in the phrasing of the question. The wrong verb had been used. It should have been "Can" not "Shall". This seemed to surprise everybody.

After the Brains Trust we had a buffet meal of Burmese food and then watched a film of physical training somewhere in England—young women in gym dress bounding about. I doubt if the young Burman women in their bright *loongyis* and tight white bodices and high flower-decked coiffures envied this display of occidental energy.

The British Council had sent out one of the new Deccola gramophones and we had some music on this beautiful instrument. After the guests had gone we supped, and later Bingley and I sat up talking till two.

February 9th. RANGOON TO THATON

We left Rangoon at 9 and drove fast in one of the G.O.C.'s cars to eight miles beyond Pegu. It was paddy country on either side for most of the way and monotonous. Then we turned off to the right and for 18 miles drove along the dustiest road we've experienced yet. We crossed and recrossed the still derelict railway line, and the dust of the dreary treeless road between paddy fields grew deeper and denser. There were several stretches where the ruts were so deep that it seemed impossible for the wheels to get out of them. We passed through Waw and at last reached a squalid heap of dirty bashas beside the ferry over the Sittang. There stood the bridge with two of the spans gone and a third on the far side sprawling into the river. This was where the 17th Indian Division, with the exception of two battalions, were left behind when the bridge was blown in 1942, and some hundreds were drowned in trying to cross the river. The plan had been that I should fly over the Sittang, but I am glad for the sake of my account of the retreat that I insisted on driving. Flying gives one hardly more atmosphere than a relief map can give. The bridge is to be rebuilt seven miles farther up. The original site was badly chosen because of the 16-ft. tidal bore which always made the life of the bridge doubtful. At present it is a haunted spot, the paint on the metal work the colour of stale blood.

Lt.-Colonel Roper of the Burmese Rifles and his wife met us at the ferry and kindly gave us their lunch bananas, our transport not having arrived and our own lunch becoming more and more of a doubtful occasion. We crossed over to Mokpalin, a jumbled crowded village on the other side with a red laterite road running out of it to the south. Dacoity is rife round here. There had been a hold up by the Mokpalin quarries a few miles beyond the village four days previously. However, we passed through without incident, and reached Bilin, one of the crucial points in the 1942 retreat. I noticed half a dozen small grass-grown pagodas in a walled enclosure rank with weeds. Soon after Bilin we had our first sight of a rubber plantation, rather like an apple orchard except that the ground beneath looked dead. We reached Thaton at dusk and put up at the Dak bungalow, where we found Major Ronald Heath of the 1st Karen Rifles. He was surprised by our arrival because they had had a signal in Moulmein that we should not be coming till the following day. So the Circuit House wasn't ready. However, we had a capital chow from a Chinese restaurant and plenty of whisky. I slept like a log till sunrise, but C. and the others had a bad night owing to the squalls of a baby underneath. I never heard a sound.

February 10th. THATON TO MOULMEIN

We left sharp at 8, having to catch a tricky ferry at Martaban. It was an enchanting drive in the morning light through a long series of small villages with paddy fields stretching far away to the west, and eastward close at hand a range of low hills. Pools of water gleamed beside the road, and all the way the bougainvillea was jewelled by the rays of the eastern sun aslant it.

The ferry raft at Martaban looked too full of vehicles to squeeze another on board, but after a lot of shunting the Humber staff car and Heath's jeep were loaded on. The next problem was Hulme and the transport. This was again behindhand, and if it did not arrive in time for the next crossing it could not get over till evening.

Martaban lies on the estuary of the Salween. Women were washing the dark sand for wolfram and silver. They carried the result of their dredging up to the derelict railway-line in baskets where they sifted it on the sleepers. One could see the glint of the minerals in the dark sand. Presently Hulme arrived, and there was a lot of shouting and grinding of brakes while the trucks were being backed on to the already crowded ferry-raft. In the middle of the clamour Heath came along to say that Commander Fox had sent over his launch from Moulmein. So Thomson, Heath, C. and myself dashed ahead across the glittering ferry and reached Moulmein a full hour before the kit. C. and I were to be the guests of Leo C. Robertson, the Session Judge. Thomson was staying with the Karen Rifles. We drove first to Robertson's house and found him on the point of leaving for the Court House. So we went along to the Mess of the Karen Rifles until we had given our kit time to arrive, after which we called for our host and drove back with him to the Mess for lunch.

Robertson is a Chinese scholar and a lover of literature. His library of 5,000 volumes was destroyed by the Japs. New epithets for hospitality and kindness are becoming difficult to find. In Burma, where it really is a serious problem for hosts and hostesses to find the wherewithal for entertainment, I know that they often made themselves uncomfortable to make us comfortable, and a few words in a diary are quite inadequate to express my gratitude.

We came back from lunch about 15 o'clock and Mr. Lewis, the Anglican chaplain, came in. He had just had an experience of dacoity.

"I was in a Burmese bus near Mudon when I heard what I ıought was the noise of a burst tyre and was just thinking what a ore it was when I saw everybody diving out of the bus into the ıngle and heard two or three more shots. So I dived out too. The acoits took all they found in the bus, but did not bother to search or the passengers in the jungle. Most unfortunately I had with me a ery nice silver Communion set. I know I should have taken it with ıe into the jungle, but in the excitement I left it in the bus, and I'm fraid we shall never see it again."

ebruary 11th. MOULMEIN

At 10.30 Lt.-Colonel Harmon of the Karen Rifles arrived to drive Thomson, C. and myself to see the graveyard at Thanbyuzayat where about 4,000 British, Australian and Dutch soldiers (of the atter about 200) are buried. These are the victims of the railway of leath from Thanbyuzayat to Bangkok, every sleeper of which was estimated to have cost a human life. The cemetery, forty miles south of Moulmein, has been well designed and when the trees grow it will be a restful spot. At present only sunflowers are blossoming there. The wooden memorial cross which was in the original cemetery has been re-erected far back from the road. It says: "In honour of Australian, Dutch, British, and American 3rd and 5th Branch prisoners-of-war who died in Burma during the construction of the Burma-Thai railway." The American bodies have been taken back across he Atlantic since.

It is right that the original memorial should be preserved, but it is not enough. A record in English, Dutch, Burmese, Hindi, Chinese and Japanese of the crime against humanity should be engraved in bronze or carved deep in stone as hard as a Japanese heart and set up near the road. Many thousands of Indian coolies lost their lives on this railway as well as prisoners-of-war. The Pharaohs built the Pyramids with less human blood. Japanese prisoners-of-war, in order to preserve their morale, are being allowed an afternoon a week to meditate on their contribution to the future of Japan. It might be more seemly to allow them that afternoon every week to meditate on their own barbarism. Thus they might learn a little of the morality understood by civilized nations. Their own morale seems comparatively unimportant. And yet when one thinks of the Germans, who by any conventional standard must be called a civilized nation, what nonsense that last observation becomes.

From the cemetery we drove on 15 miles to Amherst, mostly through rubber plantations. Here we picnicked above the point by a signal station which was flying a grubby white ensign. I much doubt if it was lowered at sunset every night. Thomson, full of energ scrambled down the cliff to explore the monastery on the spacio sandy beach, which looked rather like a pier pavilion. He found he among some gilded Buddhas in a heavily barred niche a silv pagoda. This was the missing Pagoda trophy of the Rangoon Law Tennis Club which disappeared in 1942. Little did the annual wi ners whose names are inscribed upon it suppose that they would o day become an object of religious veneration. An Englishman whom I told this story said that he was swimming farther along th beach when he saw a procession of women in mid-Victorian bathin dresses approaching the sea. They were Catholic nuns.

After getting back from Amherst we drove up to the ridge an climbed 60 or 70 steep steps to see the old Moulmein Pagoda. Th bells of the *ti* were being blown about harmoniously in the ligh breeze on the golden edge of dusk. The Buddhas here, wheth seated, standing or reclining, are all of glazed white earthenwar and look modern.

I cannot find any satisfactory explanation of Kipling's mistak about the aspect of the Moulmein Pagoda. If one makes it the Burm girl who is looking eastward to the sea, it is still a geographic impossibility, and in any case the girl who was hoping a Britis soldier would come back to her would be gazing into the wes Presumably the road to Mandalay is the road of a troopship acro the Bay of Bengal. I believe "eastward" was a misprint for "wes ward" and that having obtained currency Kipling decided not correct it in a later edition.

We dined with the Commissioner U Khin Aung Yin and had delicious Burmese curry. His wife and pretty daughter "Sally had called in the morning to invite us. She is still at the Conver school, one of the nuns at which is called Sister Attracta.

February 12*th. MOULMEIN TO TOUNGOO*

We left Moulmein at 7.30 to fly the 200 miles to Toungoo. Th pilot was Squadron-leader Wilson who flew me to Myitkyina. W were sorry to say good-bye to our scholarly bachelor host, and should much have liked to prolong our stay in Moulmein, th individual charm of which not even the destruction wrought in 194 has been able to spoil. This is the only part of Burma where I fe we had not sacrificed the welfare of the people to commercial inte ests. Moulmein and Tenasserim were annexed as long ago as 182 after the First Burmese War, and the prosperity of Lower Burm under British administration compared with the previous state almost continuous warfare was undeniable. There is no doubt tha many Burmans in South Burma will regret to see British rule vanish. In the rest of the country there is a strong and unanimous desire to see the last of us as rulers, but at the same time a lively hope of most cordial relations in the future.

On a sidewalk near the quay at Moulmein there is a statue of Queen Victoria sitting under a stone canopy illuminated by a solitary electric lamp. This was erected in 1897 to commemorate the Diamond Jubilee. The Queen has her back to the quay and now surveys, sceptre and orb in hand, the ruins of bombed Government offices on the other side of the road. There is not a chip to be seen in statue, throne or canopy, and I would hazard a guess that the very bulb above her crown has survived the Japanese occupation. It was asking too much of the fancy not to attach to this statue a symbolic significance. In exactly fifty years the decline and fall of the British Empire has been consummated. Queen Victoria in Moulmein eyes the ruins. The great Commonwealth we optimists hope to see emerge from the ashes, if peace be granted to the world for another fifty years, will have little in common with the British Empire. Nevertheless, the foundation of that Commonwealth will be that old British Empire, and I found in that solitary lamp alight over the head of Queen Victoria an omen of its vitality in the future. This was sentimental self-indulgence, no doubt, but I venture to think that most people would have succumbed to it in the atmosphere of Moulmein.

The airstrip at Toungoo is a bit bumpy, but our pilot made a good landing. Brigadier Jerrard met us with Major Sawal Khan, the second-in-command of the 3rd Rajputana Rifles (Napier's) in whose Mess we were to stay. I was sorry to miss the C.O., Lt.-Colonel Prendergast, who was on leave. The Raj. Rifs. are in bashas, but they have made their Mess extremely comfortable. We had a second breakfast at 9.30, after which Jerrard spent the rest of the morning going through on a map the part played by 98th Brigade of 19th Indian Division in pushing the Nips back from Toungoo and also in the break out battle of July-August 1945.

At 14 o'clock Jerrard, Thomson and myself set out in a jeep to explore Pagoda Ridge. We took a bumpy track to get round behind it, the same track as the 4/4th Gurkhas and 4/12th Frontier Force Regiment took to tackle the Nips on the ridge. Jerrard's driver, a Punjabi Mussulman who had driven him during the fighting here, handled his jeep with great skill.

We had a picnic tea by the monastery at Pyon Kyaung which was the Headquarters of 98th Brigade. Two gigantic stucco Buddhas stood among the trees at the entrance on top of the slope down which the monastery is built. The place is remote from everywhere and lies deep in the jungle, the tracks through which were difficult to follow. We had to turn back once or twice, and a less skilful driver might have found himself in a jam. When we reached the upper entrance of the monastery the only sound to be heard was the cawing of crows and the cooing of doves. The great pagoda at the bottom of the slope was decorative and impressive, being surrounded by lemon-yellow Buddhas and about forty miniature pagodas. We found a bell which had been presented by Edward O'Riley, a District Commissioner of many years ago. A very long covered way ran beside a meadow like the cloister of some English cathedral.

February 13th. TOUNGOO

We left at 9 sharp to drive up the Mawchi Road. C. had a heavy cold and she stayed in the Mess. First of all we drove round Toungoo. This was burnt by the Chinese in 1942 during the retreat, and what was left of it was much knocked about by our bombing. I noticed in the middle of the town an arrangement of large rocks piled one on top of another with a Japanese inscription, and to my amazement was told that this was a memorial erected by the Japs to the horses and mules killed during the war. They really are a baffling people.

The road to Mawchi, of red laterite which from time to time turns to the colour of chocolate exposed too long to the air, is dusty but in reasonably good order, and winds up and down through the finest jungle scenery I have seen. For much of the way the ground on either side sweeps up to about 200 feet and is covered with many kinds of very tall trees. I saw many more butterflies than anywhere else on our drives. There were some that resembled our own white admirals, many black and white swallow-tails, and a sombre beauty the upper wings of which were shot with ultramarine. I saw one very large insect with dark wings and what looked like a thick yellow body. Presumably this was a moth, but it never came near enough to the jeep for a close view. The flowers were beautiful. A blue-mauve creeper with gloxinia-like blossoms, a brimstone-yellow creeper like an allamanda, and a rosy-mauve convolvulus were the most frequent.

On a piece of rusty iron nailed to a tree by the roadside there still remains this painted notice:

Repat down again,
Drive Slowly, Chum.

Repatriation became an obsession with the British troops in Burma, and this might have had serious results if really well trained

Indian troops had not been in a large majority. The prospect of repatriation is apt to make a conscript army fight slowly, and the drafts from home replacing the repatriated British troops were of inferior quality.

We stopped by a tree with spikes up its grey trunk for at least 100 feet. This was the way up to a Jap artillery observation-post. At the foot was a slit trench.

Off the road to the right was a big Jap ammunition dump, and lying about in the jungle we saw cases of ack-ack shells labelled "Malta for Singapore," which were captured from us in Malaya. These relics in the jungle are of all sorts. I noticed the strands of our field telephones looking like gossamer now.

Jerrard pointed out the spot where General Messervy had stepped aside to talk to some of the men during an unexpected visit from the Corps Commander. A six-inch mortar went off close to the jeep from which he had just alighted and when he returned to it another six-inch mortar exploded just where he had been talking. Soon after this we came to a place where the tanks moved into the jungle from the main road and on the trees still hung the waggish notice-board, "Gerrard's Cross." In the defile beyond, the Nips had put a number of 500-lb. bombs which were to be exploded under our tanks, but the gelignite failed to detonate. The Madras and Bombay Sappers did wonderful work along here in repairing the bridges which the Japs had blown.

We had lunch at the start of the narrow track by which 25-pounders were dragged to the only gun position in the area. We went along this track in the jeep after lunch; it was hard going. We looked at the position, close to a village of which nothing now remains except one resplendent purple bougainvillea. Soon after this, when we were back on the road, we passed the spot where twenty Sikhs brewing tea in a small hollow were all killed by a faulty mortar. The American and Indian mortars were apt to be unreliable. The fins would blow off and the charge explode prematurely. A notice board "Go like hell, shelling ahead" had recently fallen down from the tree to which it had been fixed. All the notices left now say "Go Slow" with "Ahista," the Urdu equivalent, underneath. The wooded hill called Nevis loomed ahead. It is the same height and shape as the Ben itself.

The road began to climb and presently ran along above the gorge of the Thaukyegat, a swift-flowing peacock-green river which becomes a raging torrent in the monsoon. The trees on the opposite slope were taller than ever. They obscured the golden sun of late afternoon with a menacing shade. Finally we reached a spot where a bridge spanned the gorge of the Thaukyegat. This was constructed in a fortnight, a miracle of engineering speed. The Indian Sappers made a habit of miracles. One light bridge, 200 feet long and capable of taking everything except tanks, was thrown in four and a half hours across the river lower down. On the other side of the gorge was another "chocolate staircase", but we decided not to ascend it on account of the time and turned back by the road we had come. We had a brief halt for tea and made our way back through the fast gathering dusk to Milestone 15 where we had a rendezvous with Major Sawal Khan for a night exercise he had arranged. I hoped for a glimpse of a leopard or a deer, but there were only pigeons and one scarlet minivet.

We reached the rendezvous at 18.10 and turned off along a track through the jungle to run into a "Jap" ambush from which we were extricated by our escort. One "Jap" who was shot did a superb backfall down a bank and lay in the road with his tongue hanging out, as still as a man veritably dead. Another surrendered, and was prodded along with bayonets. The "Japs" wore authentic caps.

The next excitement was a "Jap" sniper tied to a branch at the top of a tree. When one of these snipers was hit, he did not fall down and therefore our people did not know if he had been hit or not.

It was growing rapidly dark as we made our way into the heart of the position taken up by a Company of the Raj. Rifs. I went round the perimeter to see the men in their trenches and the fire-lanes cut between the foliage. By now it was so black that a torch was necessary to guide us to the Company Commander's head-quarters, a square dugout, with a seat for three excavated on either side and a ridge of earth for a table in the middle. A shelter of corrugated iron camouflaged with foliage would protect us against fragments from the explosions that were to follow. Mugs of extremely sweet tea were sipped while we waited for the fun to begin. Sawal Khan was in telephonic communication with his platoon commanders by buzzer. We spoke in whispers. A few stars glinted in the tree tops. The ratcheting of the cicadas was the only sound.

After about twenty minutes a frog seemed to croak somewhere close at hand and this was answered by the howl of some nocturnal animal. These were "Japs" signalling to one another, and hoping to draw some fire from our trenches in order to disclose our position. There was a long silence and then we heard what sounded like people stealthily making their way toward our position. This was done by dragging along a small branch with string. It failed to evoke so much as a single shot, and presently there were noises all round us. A "Jap" began to shout propaganda, inviting his Indian comrades to come and join him. Snipers fired from the trees at random. A machine-gun stuttered. This sort of thing went on for another twenty minutes, and then the mortars started. The noise was terrific. Fragments kept falling on our roof. I suggested that we should probably find Toungoo evacuated when we got back under the impression that the war had begun all over again. At last our men began to fire back. Then the "Japs" worked themselves up into a frenzy with ghastly yells to make a bayonet charge, which was broken up. Wounded men, groaning realistically, were taken past on stretchers to the first-aid post. Finally the "Jap" prisoners including a "Jap" general of the Chrysanthemum Division, portrayed by a Raj. Rif. subaltern, were brought in and interrogated at the bayonet's point, and the exercise came to an end. About 200 men took part in it, many of whom had actually taken part in the fighting up the Mawchi road in May and June 1945. At that date the monsoon was streaming and one had to imagine this kind of thing in rain and mud.

We reached the Mess just after 20 o'clock after a strenuous but fascinating eleven hours.

February 14th. TOUNGOO TO RANGOON

We left our kind hosts at 8.30. I have enjoyed an invaluable experience and cannot thank the 3rd Rajputana Rifles enough for the trouble they took; and Brigadier Jerrard, whose nickname is "Hindy", has been a real Hindenburg of a tutor. I have learned a lot from him which will be of much service in writing *Indian Epic*.

The drive to Rangoon (190 miles) was through monotonous paddy country. It was valuable as a glimpse of the terrain over which the break out to the Sittang on July 21st-22nd, 1945, was made when over 6,000 Japs were killed for the loss of 95 Indian and British troops. They fell so thick in the sugar cane that bundles of dead bodies were roped together, dragged to the banks of the Sittasy by elephants, and flung into the river, then in spate. Jerrard gave a lucid exposition of the battle, which involved a certain amount of turning aside from the main road. We went round Zeyawadi, where 5,000 of the I.N.A. surrendered, which is an Indian village and the headquarters of the Sinha sugar-refinery. We saw the place where a Jemadar of the 1/7th Gurkhas found a Japanese messenger asleep with the operation orders of the 55th Jap Division on him, which helped to make the massacre of them complete. Another good cop was an American-Japanese prisoner who deserted and gave the date of the break out to the Sittang. According to Jerrard, it was not believed by the High Command. Tales of the retreat were mingled with tales of the advance. We passed through Pegu of gloomy memory, and we saw the white house by the bridge where an advance party of 26th Indian Division, who had captured Rangoon in a combined operation, met an advance party of 17th Indian Division, who still feel sore that they were not given the triumph of entering Rangoon, Hulme, who was driving me in the Humber to which we had transferred from the jeep, shook his head by one bridge.

"I could have crossed here easily and got to Rangoon before 26 Div., but I wasn't allowed to," he sighed.

We reached Command House about 16.30, and were welcomed by Lt.-General H. L. Briggs, with whom I was to have some good talks about Keren and Benghazi, the Admin. Box and Imphal, where he was commanding 5th Indian Division. The General and I went to a cocktail party at which I was introduced to more pretty women in a short time than anywhere else on the tour.

February 15th. RANGOON

I had intended to write up the diary, but I found General Briggs's quiet humour too attractive to deny myself a moment of it. He takes the week-end off as far as possible, which was lucky for me. Besides, I had woken with sharp rheumatism in both knees which doesn't interfere with talking but discourages writing. What I have enjoyed as much as anything during this tour has been the opportunity of studying the diverse personalities of generals and brigadiers. In my youth they were more stereotyped than they are to-day. I haven't attempted to present snapshots of them in this diary, because it seems a breach of manners to enjoy a man's hospitality and then rush into print about him. In fact I find it difficult to write about anybody I have met until ten years later. It's a form of shyness.

The General gave a dinner party that night. Arthur Bottomley, Parliamentary Secretary for the Dominions, was another guest. He is dealing with the frontier tribes problem and had just come back from the Shan States. I found him genial, and, I should say, extremely competent. The more I see of these younger Labour Members the brighter grows my hope of the future. Of course Conservative prejudice among our people in the East is rampant, so rampant that Asians themselves cannot yet believe in the decay and final disappearance of the Conservative Party familiar to them for the last sixty years. 'This awful government' is blamed for throwing away the Empire, and people are genuinely startled when I point out that the Conservatives, being primarily responsible for the unimaginative incompetence which directed our country's course between the two wars, are therefore responsible for throwing away our position in the East, although the muddle-headed Labour advocacy of disarmament involves them in a share of the blame. Winston Churchill, since his return to the Tory fold as a bell-wether, seems to have forgotten his political prime when as an aggressive and wanton young tup he was always lowering his horns and charging head on into the soggy earthworks of middle-class opinion. And the irony of a surrender to party, as complete as Pitt ever made, of 'what was meant for mankind' is that there is nobody out here who any longer believes that his party is capable of producing an Imperial policy which would counteract the policy of 'this awful government'.

ARAKAN, ANDAMAN AND NICOBAR ISLANDS

February 16th. RANGOON TO CHITTAGONG

We left Command House at 9.15 for the airfield at Mingaladon, after a most agreeable visit. One falls into clichés at the end of a day of diary writing, which is a poor way of celebrating the endless hospitality we enjoy everywhere. I never seem to meet anybody who is not perfectly charming.

The V.I.P. plane was out of action and we travelled in a reaper-and-binder Dakota. However, it was much more comfortable than that fiendish reaper-and-binder in which we flew from Habbaniya to Lydda, and they had fixed a deck chair for me in which I wrote my diary during the three hours' flight. I went up forward two or three times to sit with the pilot and look down at the country. Arakan from the air resembles a faded jigsaw set scattered about a greenish-blue oilcloth. We made a good landing on the airstrip at Chittagong at 13.30. Our four Burman fellow-passengers, one a jolly journalist called Htin Gyi bound for Minnesota, went on to Calcutta.

It was grand to see Commander John Dalison R.N. and Brigadier M. Roberts at the airport and we drove off to go on board the R.I.N. sloop *Narbada*, the flagship of the Indian Navy, Commander J. C. Mansell R.I.N. I have a comfortable cabin and working cabin. It must be a bit of a strain even on the Navy to put up such a large party, but the Captain makes light of it and we are all set to enjoy this cruise. In Rangoon we had met again Captain W. H. Bennetton whom we had known at Barra when he was making the road up to the Radar station. He had presented me with bottles of Cointreau and cherry brandy. These with the Van der Humm and Johnnie Jameson which Leo Robertson had insisted on giving me in Moulmein made us feel able to face the Mess.

February 17th. On board H.M.I.S. Narbada. *CHITTAGONG TO ST. MARTIN'S ISLAND*

We sailed at 12.30. I went up on the bridge for an hour while we proceeded down the river, and then after lunch, much against my will, I sat down and wrote diary.

At 19.15 I rise to go and have a well deserved bath. The sky is grey. The air is damp and sticky. I haven't a touch of rheumatism, and nothing except the beginnings of a boil on the coccyx, the result of about 1,500 miles of jeeping, to bother about, and I don't bother about that. I am looking forward to meeting the Queen of the Nicobars for whom Jim Thomson and I have brought bottles of rum. I hear we may get some barracuda fishing at Port Blair. It's all very exciting. I feel like Jim Hawkins when the *Hispaniola* sailed from Bristol. Even the discovery that the bottle of cherry brandy has burst over two boxes of my cheroots can provoke no more than a "tut-tut".

February 18th. On board H.M.I.S. Narbada. *Off St. MARTIN'S ISLAND*

We dropped anchor off St. Martin's Island at 7.30, and an hour later Brigadier Roberts, John Dalison, Thomson, Mehta and myself boarded M.L. 1110, our consort, to go to Maungdaw 14 miles away. The last mile or so was up a creek or chaung of the Naaf river. I noticed several Little Bitterns poking about in the mud.

On the jetty at Maungdaw we were met by Lt.-Commander L. Burness, Burma R.N.V.R., who had helped in the complicated arrangements for revisiting this extremely complicated land of Arakan. The baggage was sent on to Buthidaung, and we enjeeped in the hope of getting a glimpse of the Ngakyedauk Pass from west of the Mayu Range. Most of the gardens in Maungdaw had a beautiful small tree bare of leaves and covered with flower spikes of deepest scarlet which I think must be some variety of erythrina. I noticed also one or two cotton-trees, one of which I described at Tiddim when I did not know what it was called. Birds seem to use the cups of rosy blossom as cocktails. Another beautiful floral effect was the fields of Indian-yellow flax protected against cattle by formidable bamboo fences. Thin spiky canes called pangis, six feet high, stick up every yard, and these are interwoven with thicker horizontal canes. The barrier is effective. The Japs used to put these spiky canes round possible landing places for parachutists, and several of those gallant men in Force 136 who were dropped in Burma were wounded by them.

The level country along the coast, mostly paddy but growing flax and other crops, is bounded on the east by the Mayu Range which writes a zigzag line along the sky and rises practically sheer from the plain to about 2,000 feet. I had seen this range from the air and at the south end of it I had noted the wide elephant track which runs along the top for some way. I heard a grim elephant story. A machine gunner took a shot at an elephant. The elephant charged and knelt on the l.m.g. which being nearly red hot burnt him and made him more mad than ever. The rash machine gunner was picked up in his trunk and smashed to death.

We turned off to the left from the Maungdaw-Buthidaung road on which the P.W.D. (Public Works Department) has scattered a quantity of stones without laying on a steam roller. We were relieved to get off this hellish surface and jeep in comparative comfort through the dust. We got a glimpse of Hill 130 with its fringe of blasted trees along the top. Finally we came to what was known as Piccadilly Circus where the road cut through the Ngakyedauk Pass began. There is a mound in the middle which the traffic used as a roundabout. Unluckily we found that the bridge over the first chaung was down, which put an end to our hope of getting any way along the road from this side.

We had just decided to turn back when we met the Fordson of the District Commissioner, Mr. L. Lees, who was visiting this part of his District for the first time. He had come from Akyab in the dark and rusty fishing-vessel, on which the camouflage of the bridge had faded into a dirty green and grey, we had noticed lying off the entrance of the creek. Lees had invited us to dinner on Thursday February 20th in Akyab where he had arranged a *pwe*. This is the name for a Burmese dancing play. We explained that we were going to see the Admin. Box to-morrow and 114th Brigade's Box on the following day, and that therefore we could not make Akyab till February 21st. Lees at once invited us to the farewell party he and the Akyab Club were giving to the 4th Burma Regiment and extended the invitation to the officers of *Narbada*. He asked if he might join us on the expedition to the Admin. Box, and delighted we were to have his genial company. We sat under a tree, drank beer and gin and ate some cheese sandwiches at 13 o'clock, while Brigadier Roberts gave a clear account of 5th Indian Division's fight on this side of the range. Then we drove back to have a look at the Razabil fortress, which is a huddle of low hills covered with elephant grass and scrub. This was damnably difficult country from which to eject Japs because as soon as they were put off one hill they would get on to another, and when put off that the company working on them would find they were back on the hill from which they had just been put off. I did not walk into the scrub with the others to look at some Jap bunkers, but sat in the jeep making the sensitive plant which covered the ground curl up by touching it with my stick. It's a pastime in which I can always indulge. I find such a display of self-consciousness in the vegetable world a fascinating riddle.

We left Lees to go to one of the teas prepared for him on his progress and noticed another tea waiting for him farther along under an awning the front of which was decorated with the graceful fronds of the *dahni* palm. At the jetty in Maungdaw we embarked in sampans to return to the M.L. which was waiting for us off the creek. The seat and prow of the sampan in which I went were painted orange-red, blue and white, and along the back of the seat some wag had painted two steamboats—one "S.S. Pakistan" and the other "S.S. Burmistan".

There was quite a lively little sea running on the 14 miles back to *Narbada*, and to starboard we saw a fleet of what looked like mediaeval galleons with high poops, their white sails bellying to a soldier's wind. We reached our ship about 16 o'clock. I was too tired to tackle the diary.

February 19*th*. *MAUNGDAW TO BUTHIDAUNG*

We boarded M.L.1110 at 7.30, transferring at Maungdaw to M.L.1304 of the Royal Burma Navy. *Narbada* and M.L.1110 were proceeding to Akyab where *Narbada* could water. C. remained in the ship. M.L. 1304 is commanded by Sub-Lt. Nakoda, Burma R.N.V.R., a charming young Anglo-Burman, on whom would devolve the task of getting us to Akyab and circumventing the spring tides. We were alongside the D.C.'s fishing vessel at 9.30, and he hopped on board with extreme agility, followed by a welcome consignment of beer. We reached the Maungdaw jetty in time to enjeep at 10. Brigadier Roberts drove Lees and myself. Thomson drove John Dalison and Mehta. Our kit was to proceed straight to Buthidaung in a lorry when we turned off toward the Admin. Box. The surface of the road improved as we drew near the Mayu Range. The clumps of wild and quite uneatable pineapple gave way to jungle. We passed a memorial to the 19th Hyderabad Regiment, and another to the York and Lancaster Regiment. The road was originally the permanent way of a light railway built in 1918, but soon abandoned because it did not pay. I find the country most difficult to describe.

We entered a valley between the precipitous hills of the range, full of smaller pointed hills with streams and a very rich vegetation of innumerably various greens. The effect resembled an elaborately laid-out super-landscape-garden. After a few miles we reached the West Tunnel which pierces the steep range for 300 yards. The tunnel was used as a store by the Japs, and there is much evidence of attempts by the R.A.F. to seal it with heavy bombing. The two East Tunnels are much narrower. A stone over the arch of the second records that it was built by J. Martin of Rangoon in 1918

We came down into the wide plain between the Mayu Range anc the Arakan Yomas. The long low hills known as Cain and Abel ris from the plain on either side. Abel was the scene of desperate fight ing in January 1944 when it was taken by 33rd Brigade. The 4/1s Gurkhas held it for six weeks and it was never lost, but Cain remaine in Japanese hands much longer. After passing Cain and Abel w reached a point of the road where a dust track turned off to the lef across the paddy. Here we were met by the S.D.O. and Chief o Police in the taxi that was to lead the way to our destination—th village of Ngakyedauk. The villagers in this part of Arakan did no leave their homes during the fighting. We reached the village o Tatmingyaungwa where we had to cross a deep chaung by a ricket bridge. I don't know how the taxi negotiated it. It had alread jibbed at a much shallower chaung and had to be pushed up by th united efforts of the whole party. When we got to the village ou taxi guide was out of sight and we had some trouble finding th right track.

The landscape became more attractive, bounded by the May Range to the west and level as a billiard-table except for a smal ridge prodigally clothed with trees on which there were more orchid than I had seen anywhere else. Alas, they were not in bloom Michael Roberts told me they were mostly the yellow and brow kind the name of which eludes me. There were also white ones. W stopped for a few minutes to eat some chocolate and to my horror discovered that my glasses were missing. I had put them in m trouser pocket and with the bumping of the jeep they had bee ejected on to the road. Instructions were sent back for the childre of Tatmingyaungwa to search for them, but I was pretty depresse about the prospect because even if they were found it was likel that one of the other jeeps would have driven over them in the thic dust. However, I put it up to St. Anthony, and turned my attentio to watching a water-buffalo enjoying a glorious wallow. How muc women would pay for such a mud-pack! At last we reached a dyk across the paddy and after driving over that we came to an end o any road negotiable even by the most optimistic jeep. Half wa across the dyke Brigadier Roberts pointed out the trees away to th right where General Messervy and his Divisional H.Q. were sud denly overrun by the Japs in February '44.

The villagers of Ngakyedauk had fenced in with bamboo a spac beneath a spreading peepul tree, and there set out deck chairs and table for our reception. Outside the fence they were gathered to th number of about 200—almost all Chittagonian Mussulmans—t 'aze at the rare visitors. A deck chair slung on a bamboo pole had ›een arranged to carry me along the two rough miles from the :astern gate to the western gate of the Admin. Box. I was borne .cross three streams up and down a very rough path, and I felt orry for the four villagers who took turns with the burden. The sun vas blazing down and another villager walked beside the chair, .olding an umbrella over me. From time to time we were refreshed ›y the shade of some really magnificent trees. It was fantastic to hink that along this track only three years ago hundreds of every ind of motor transport were passing.

Sinzweya, in which three years ago there were thousands of 'ehicles and pile upon pile of stores, resembles an expanse of common and in a sylvan area at home and is surrounded by low wooded ills with one higher conical hill to the south-west known as Artillery Iill which was completely blasted by our guns firing at point blank ange, but is now green again with the rapid growth of three monsoons ince that February of 1944. Nothing now remains to recall that lesperate struggle in the Admin. Box except a few tanks and the lit trenches gradually filling up. Cattle are grazing tranquilly. We at beneath a tree and surveyed a scene of Arcadian peace. The local nhabitants have found a use for most of the debris which once overed the place. I was carried as far as a point from which one ould see the road our Sappers had cut through the Ngakyedauk 'ass, but it is rapidly falling to pieces so that even its trace will ardly be discernible after another couple of monsoons.

It was on February 19th 1944 that the Jap attack on Sinzweya egan to weaken, and here three years later to the very day we were tanding on the spot which marked the end of the beginning to lestroy the military power of Japan. This green enclosure in its lecisive influence upon the course of human history may stand eside the mound of the Athenian dead at Marathon. In the middle f the 'Common' we saw where Lord Louis Mountbatten stood on . soap-box and addressed the visitors of the Admin. Box, having been lown there from his H.Q. at Kandy.

I left this inspiring spot, conscious that very few Europeans were ikely to see it again and immensely grateful to the energy and letermination of Brigadier Michael Roberts which had made possible what everybody told me would be an impossible expedition to arry through.

When we reached the pavilion of the peepul tree where we were o eat our lunch we found the bamboo fence surrounded by a throng f villagers prepared to enjoy the spectacle. The officials began to ustle them away, but John Dalison and I intervened and they were

allowed to come back and watch our demonstration of drinkin
gin, lemonade and beer, and the rapidity with which we coul
put away the hard-boiled eggs provided by the headman. Lt
Wellard of the Graves Concentration Unit was with us. He had bee
helpful in making our expedition the complete success it was. W
left Ngakyedauk, grateful for the hospitality of the villagers.

By the way, Lees told me that it is always Arakan never *th*
Arakan. As usual journalists were blamed for the vulgar error, bu
I expect the military must share the blame. It was certainly the
who were responsible for the much more vulgar error of calling th
Near East the Middle East, which I was glad to find Claude Auchin
leck agreed with me in considering prejudicial to the strategi
conceptions of 1942. We are such a nation of nominalists that it i
particularly dangerous for us to get a name wrong.

Just as we were leaving, word came that a child had found m
glasses and I asked for him to be gathered at Tatmingyaungywa fo
the reward. Lees left us here to be entertained at a ceremonial tea

On our way back we missed the track to Tatmingyaungywa an
had some difficulty in picking it up again. Our jeep jibbed at
ridge in the paddy and had to be lifted off it, which for a jeep is
pretty humiliating experience. We reached Buthidaung about tea
time and found M.L. 1304 at the jetty.

Now began a great discussion about the next day. Should we wai
for the top of the tide to get right up the Myan Chaung as far a
Roberts' old H.Q. of 114th Brigade, return to Buthidaung abou
15 o'clock to catch a river steamer, sleep on board, and descend th
Kalapanzin-Mayu River to reach Akyab at 15 o'clock on Februar
21st? Or should we rise at 5.30 and go up before high water in tw
sampans, returning to Buthidaung in time for M.L. 1304 to star
at noon and get us to Akyab by dusk of the 20th? The Navy strongl
favoured the latter plan. The Army felt that this would spoil th
visit to H.Q. 114th Brigade. As usual in any agreement abou
combined operations the Navy won, and finally it was decided t
take the sampans at the crack of dawn and aim at reaching Akya
to-morrow morning. As if to endorse the Navy's plan a Unit Cra
of the Graves Concentration Unit turned up and offered to tak
us up the river next morning as far as the Myan Chaung.

We went up to our basha about 22 o'clock. It was a rat-infested
primitive building, with a mud floor and sanitary arrangements a
which even Adam and Eve might have raised their eyebrows
Certainly Eve.

February 20th. BUTHIDAUNG TO AKYAB

I was awake at 4, watching the morning star winking through the roof of the basha, and through the "walls" the kindling of a fire by the admirable Abdul, John Dalison's bearer, who would serve as a model for Sinbad the Sailor. I had left the equally admirable Gulaba Ram on board *Narbada.*

It was still dark when we left the basha and stumbled down the bank to the water's edge. In the east, Lucifer was showing his incandescent lamp to guide the sun up, and the Great Bear's snout was below the western horizon. The dawn was beginning to break in rose and orange when we boarded the Unit Craft. Wisps of mist were rising from the water like cold smoke, but the shades of the morning dusk were warmer than at home and more like the dusk of evening there. Flights of egrets broke into the patterns of a Chinese painting on rice-paper as they winged their way to the feeding-grounds. The trees on either side of the stream were loud with bird-song.

A unit craft is not designed for comfort but to carry the remains of those dead soldiers which are to be concentrated in certain cemeteries. Those who fought in Arakan will rest in Akyab. The members of the Graves Concentration Unit are all volunteers and the work they are doing in these remote spots deserves a tribute. These men are living hard. They have to explore the remotest parts of the jungle, which on these Arakan hillsides is particularly dense, and their labour is arduous. Lt. D. Gilday of the Royal Welch Fusiliers commands this unit craft, which lacks a name. Brigadier Roberts was able to tell him where he would find some bodies not yet gathered in, and that was to him and his crew a rich reward for their kindness in taking us up the creek and bringing us back to the M.L.

After the sun rose to starboard, the mist gathered more thickly. It was a typical Arakan morning of early spring, Brigadier Roberts told me. We passed Kyaukit where there was much heavy fighting. We passed the funnel of a Jap steamer sunk by one of our Hurricanes. This used to serve as a mark for our patrols. We saw where a Polish officer called Lubeck who was attached to 114th Brigade launched his fireships full of explosives against the bottom of the hill held by the Japs. Lubeck's formula was "You give me a string and explosives. I will arrange". His originality in devising trouble for the Japs was inexhaustible until at last he was killed. Peace to his bones where they rest far from his own tormented country.

Kingfishers flashed through the trees. A couple of monkeys stared at us from the branches. Suddenly a 25-lb. *rohu* was sighted on the mud of the bank, and the craft slowed down to allow one of th sampans we were towing to investigate. The big fish was not deac and the chap who landed to get it sank up to his thighs in th mud. The *rohu* was put in the pot and was to be served for breakfas next day. Later we saw a much smaller one stranded in the same way

After moving up stream for about an hour we reached the mout of the Myan Chaung which runs eastward from the right bank c the Kalapanzin.

At this point we transferred to a couple of sampans and made ou way up a chaung about the size of the Cherwell where it runs alon Addison's Walk in Oxford. A peasant carrying a large bunch c golden pumpkin flowers beamed at us from the bank. The chaun grew narrower and darker and shallower. The sampans whic require only 18 inches of water always seemed on the verge of goin aground. The left bank was fringed with abutilons in flower, thei brick-red bells swinging gently over the black slimy mud. We passe under a crazy bridge consisting of one bamboo cane and a handra across which a party of cultivators were passing in single file. A couple of hundred yards beyond this the sampans went firml aground. Planks were taken out of them and we scrambled up th steep bank without getting much of the mud on our clothes. W walked across a stretch of paddy to a small village called Paledaung John Dalison and I sat down on the outskirts of it, he to sketch, to smoke a cheroot. The sun was blazing. The others walked on fc a mile or more to see Brigadier Roberts' old H.Q. the full exten of 114th Brigade's Box, and the air strip from which casualties wer evacuated. It has been frequently stated that the R.A.F. made lot of these strips in this part of Arakan. In fact this was the firs and only airstrip made for the evacuation of the wounded in th area.

After a while John D. and I were beginning to wonder whethe we should ever get back down the Myan Chaung by sampan an walked over to find out the state of the tide. Both sampans were sti ast aground. So we walked back across the paddy fields, havin left word for the others to follow us when they returned. After laborious trudge of about half a mile we came to one of thos formidable bamboo fences, which, no easy job, we had to brea through to reach the point where the chaung enters the river. W hailed the Unit Craft, which was backed in, and with the help c planks laid along the mud we managed to get aboard. The other arrived soon afterwards, Jim Thomson caked with mud up to th knees.

We were back at the Buthidaung jetty by 11.15. Here Brigadie

Roberts left us to find his way back with the transport to Shillong. I was sad to part with Michael Roberts to whom I owe some of the best times of our tour.

At 11.30 we set out down the Kalapanzin in M.L. 1304. The river was sometimes very wide, sometimes very narrow. To left of us the Arakan Yomas, to right the Mayu Range, slowly turned from green to blue and at last to misty grey. I slept for two hours after lunch and came on deck to find Sub-Lt. Nakoda steering the M.L. through a very tricky stretch. The leadsmen were on both sides of the M.L., crying the soundings, which were frequently shallower than the draft of the M.L. Once or twice the propeller churned up the mud, but thanks to a really skilful and judicious piece of steering we came through without going aground. I recall a *hpoongyi* sampan with an orange sail and three *hpoongyis* in their orange robes crouched amidships when we left them astern. Just after 17.30 we were alongside *Narbada* in the war-shattered harbour of Akyab. I felt rather tired, but it had been another day of days.

February 21st. On board H.M.I.S. Narbada. *Off AKYAB*

John Dalison, Jim Thomson and myself were up at 5.30 to go on board M.L. 1110 which, accompanied by M.L. 1304 with Burness and Nakoda aboard, was to take us to see the beaches of the Myebon peninsula where the landings were made in February 1945. The D.C. had warned us that this part of Arakan was in some disorder under the influence of a turbulent monk called U Senda. We were advised not to land without an escort of at least two sections of the Burma Regiment. In view of their departure from Rangoon in two days we did not feel entitled to put them to this inconvenience and decided that a view of the landing beaches from offshore would be enough. As we drew nearer to Myebon, after six hours steaming through chaungs of various widths and depths, John D. told me I was to lie down on the deck at once if we were fired at from the bank, and our own guns were made ready. However, when we reached Myebon nothing could have seemed less bellicose. We saw the four beaches clearly, and the turret of the tank that was lost in the mud was still sticking out of the water like the top of a submarine's conning tower. Before we reached the main village of Myebon the scene ashore resembled pictures of the Solomon Islands: a narrow stretch of level foreshore below a steep jungle, a grove of coconut palms, and reed-thatched dwellings. Farther round some large sampans were lying at anchor in the harbour. On the other side was a mangrove swamp and a ridge of steep hills. We got a clear idea of the geography, and when the time comes to write the full story I do not think I shall have lost much by not going ashore, although it was tantalizing not to be able to take full advantage of visiting a remote spot like this which one is most unlikely ever to see again. We got back to *Narbada* at 18.15.

February 22nd. On board H.M.I.S. Narbada *in COMBERMERE BAY*

I found we were at anchor when I woke at 9, and at 10.30 John Dalison, Thomson, Commander Mansell, Lt.-Commander Sawhny and myself went aboard M.L. 1306 (Sub.-Lt. Tet Myint, Burma R.N.V.R.) to get as near as we could to the landing at Ru-Ywa. We were advised that for us to land either there or at Kangaw without a heavy escort was not to be thought of. So Kangaw was ruled out.

On the whole it was a monotonous trip, the least uninteresting part of it being a narrow chaung fringed with mangroves and the tall graceful palms that the Burmese call *dahni*. They grow in what must be brackish mud without trunks, rising in lovely fronds sometimes as high as fifteen feet. They are used for roofing. We saw several kingfishers, and a group of monkeys running along the muddy bank beneath the mangroves. Most of the way, however, the chaungs were too wide to get much view of the life ashore, and we were glad to get back to *Narbada* about 17 o'clock. We said goodbye to Lt.-Commander L. R. Burness, who had been so helpful during our exploration of Arakan, and at 17.30 we sailed for Port Blair.

February 23rd. At sea in H.M.I.S. Narbada

I was woken by Gulaba at 7.30 to say that a very big fish was to be seen. Up on deck I found that our bow had hit and impaled a young 35-foot Blue Whale which had crossed it during the night. Its head was lolling to starboard and its body was streaming along close to the ship on the port side. An attempt was made to get the carcass on board, but when the ship slowed down for the difficult operation the whale sank. It was probably killed by the first impact, for its neck was half cut through. It was reckoned that our catch lost us 28 miles during the night.

I spent a grey sticky day, writing up my diary. At 17 o'clock we sighted Preparis Island on the starboard quarter at least 20 miles away and at 18.30 the Coco group were just visible in the dusk. I saw the new moon. Does she always lie on her back in these latitudes?

February 24th. On board H.M.I.S. Narbada *in PORT BLAIR HARBOUR, SOUTH ANDAMAN*

We dropped anchor at 7.30. A grey sky and a grey sea with a bit of a swell. The N.E. Monsoon should have shut up by now. It is warm and very sticky weather. Eng.-Commander J. W. Stephenson R.N. came on board. He is harbour master and general marine boss here. We went ashore in his launch, landing at Alexandra Jetty and after visiting his office were driven up to call on the Chief Commissioner, Iman-Ul Majid, who was educated at the Persse School and Christ's College, Cambridge. He has an English wife and a sixteen-year-old boy. Here we also met the Deputy Commissioner Michael Sullivan, the Cambridge and Olympic runner, and Captain Michael Littlewort, the Superintendent of Police. The D.C. offered to drive Thomson, C. and myself across the island and at 2.30 he met us with his Dodge at Aberdeen Jetty.

It was a glorious drive. The Andaman jungle seems even richer than the Burma jungle in variety of trees, for it has some of the characteristics of the Malay jungle added. Besides the jungle there are many coconut groves and wide valleys of paddy. We visited two Bhantu villages. The Bhantus were transported here as one of the criminal tribes from the U.P. Now they are to be sent back to Lucknow by their own request. Only the older people can remember anything about India and they seem to have drawn a fanciful picture of life there for the younger people. Probably the latter will soon be just as anxious to return to the Andamans and plague the life out of officials in Lucknow as they have plagued the life out of the D.C. here. Sullivan has a splendid way with them and I could see that every one of the extraordinary mixture of people here respected him. And it *is* a mixture. There are Moplah villages to which the rebellious Moplahs of Malabar were transported. There are ex-convict villages which contain every kind of Indian nationality. There are Burmese villages because before the Burmese administration was separated from India Burmese convicts were transported here. The Japs brought in a lot of Indonesians, so there is one Indonesian village too. Then there are the 'local born' Andamanese who are the descendants of convicts. There is a large Anglo-Indian colony. Finally, there are the three kinds of Andamanese aboriginals —the Andamanese proper, now almost extinct, the Jarawas and the Onges. Nobody knows much about the two last. They are stone-age pygmy negritos, and the Jarawas shoot at sight, but not through a blow pipe as Conan Doyle thought in *The Sign of Four*. They use the bow and poisoned arrow. The arrows used to be made of wood, but latterly they have learnt how to pick up and use old iron and their lethal range is about seventy yards. So little is known about these pygmy tribes that estimates of their numbers vary between 500 and 5,000. We had intended to cruise round North Sentinel, a small island about fifty miles from Port Blair, in the hope of catching a glimpse of these mysterious creatures; but everybody assures me we shall see nothing except an empty beach with dense jungle behind, and as to land there might easily mean getting shot by an arrow, we have decided to take a day for Car Nicobar instead.

After we had visited the Bhantu villages called Anna and Kate for the daughters of a former Chief Commissioner, we found a place in the jungle for a picnic tea and while we sat in the Dodge to enjoy it an emerald dove was pecking about in the road just beyond. During this drive I saw pandanus trees for the first time and the variety of bird life was rich.

My mind was too full of the horrors of the Jap occupation which Sullivan had been telling me about to settle down to diary writing when I got back to the ship. Of 20,000 people they managed to exterminate in one way or another over 7,000. The kindest way to account for the Japanese atrocities is to attribute them to panic. They were in a panic throughout the occupation.

When the British and Indian authorities escaped in March 1942, the Indian Government asked for volunteers to remain and look after the local population. Among these volunteers was Major A. J. Bird, the Secretary of the Chief Commissioner, a man in his mid-forties. A Bengali convict called Bagchi, who when manager of a cinema (I think in Calcutta) murdered a man and received a life-sentence, had been employed by Bird and sacked for malingering. So, to revenge himself, after the Japs had appointed him chief Naval Intelligence officer, he forged a letter from Bird which purported to give instructions about the establishment of an espionage service. This letter he hid in a house, which he then urged the Japs to search. The Japs found it. Bird was taken from the internment camp and tortured to make him confess. Finally he was paraded round the Bazaar in Aberdeen and from time to time a huge Jap sergeant would fling him over his shoulder after which the guards would kick him until he rose on his feet again. Every brutality was watched with open glee by Bagchi. At last Bird moaned for water whereupon the executioner, a Jap naval officer, called for water which he poured on his own sword before cutting off Bird's head by the edge of a trench dug to receive his body.

Bagchi is now in jail in Port Blair, but the evidence considered legally necessary to hang him will probably not be forthcoming.

The only hope of being able to make this vile creature pay any kind of penalty is to secure enough evidence to justify sentencing him to a term of imprisonment for forcibly procuring women to enter the Jap brothels. The method used was to drag before Bagchi some wretched woman—often enough a married woman—strip her naked and let a Jap doctor examine her with great brutality for V.D. One woman has testified that the doctor's hand was thrust up her so roughly as to draw blood. If after this she still refused to serve as a prostitute, she was beaten. If beating did not break her will, the guards would put lighted pieces of paper between her thighs. If in the end she still refused to give way she was violated by half a dozen soldiers. Women who suffered this kind of horror are still living in various parts of South Andaman. The right thing to have done with Bagchi was to hand him over to be lynched by the people as soon as the islands were liberated. There are a few exceptions to the rule that mob-law is always reprehensible. As he was left alive and protected by the law, it will be an abortion of justice if this vermin is not hanged for his crimes whether the legal code provides for the penalty or not.

The atrocities committed in the Andaman Islands upon the unhappy people there cannot be dismissed as propaganda. They are all too foully true, and the Indian Nationalists who with patriotic intent allied themselves with the Japanese will stand at the bar of history as the tools of a sub-human nation. It is intelligible that for the freedom of his country a patriot might accept the help of apes, but he should not try to pretend afterwards that the apes were civilized human beings, and whitewash their essential bestiality. If one of those Indians who hoped that his country would be liberated by Japan would come here and question the people himself, he would never again talk of propaganda stories and he would be thankful that India was freed by a people whose civilization was more akin to his own. Subha Chandra Bose did come here, but he was not shown the wing in the jail where the tortures were inflicted, and it is charitable to suppose that he did not know what was going on. I am glad to set on record that Colonel Logonathan of the Indian National Army did his best to help the people in South Andaman.

We reached the jetty at 18.15 and when we returned to the ship found that the Captain and John Dalison had been fishing and that the Captain had caught a barracuda, 4 feet 7 inches long, weighing 30 lbs. 12 ozs. John D. caught two small ones which we had for dinner and jolly good they were. Rather like hake but much richer and firmer.

February 25th. On board H.M.I.S. Narbada *in PORT BLAIR*

Thomson, C. and I went ashore at 9.30 and were driven up to his bungalow by the D.C. He had arranged for some of the victims of Jap barbarism to come up and talk to me. Captain Littlewort and his Number Two, Captain Macleod, gave me a summary of what had happened during the Jap occupation. Then I saw Mr. McMullen, an Anglo-Indian, who had been Chief Jailer in the prison. He described the landing and the funk that the Japs were in. When Luty (?) the wireless man, who volunteered to stay behind and send out signals until the last moment, blew up the station the Japs all fell down on their faces and did not move for twenty minutes. Luty was killed by them later. When they got up they began to scamper around tying little Jap flags to the trees. A Swede called Cato who ran the match factory was allowed to go free at first, but they could not stand his contempt for them and took him away to Ross Island where he was murdered; nobody has been able to find out exactly where or how. In North Andaman there were 400 Karens, mostly Baptists, and the Jap general sent there was also a Baptist of the same American Mission. So until he was removed the people were decently treated. The three I.N.A. officers who arrived later in Port Blair all behaved well while they were there.

The Nips issued pompous proclamations about the mighty Nippon Empire after they landed, in which they promised to give the inhabitants an example of its beneficent rule. They then proceeded to cut down all the fruit trees and plant sweet potatoes and tapioca everywhere. There were four spy scares, and each one cost many lives. Men and women were tortured to make them confess. When they confessed to avoid further torture, they were killed. Many others died in prison of beri-beri due to malnutrition.

A group of seven or eight victims came into the D.C.'s office and the expression in their eyes as they told me what had happened I can never forget. The father of the young man who had fired at a Jap officer with a shot gun and wounded him in the cheek with two pellets (the only shot fired against the Japs) told me the story. They had been looting the bazaar and the young man fired in a sudden burst of rage, after which he escaped. The Japs burnt his father's house and threatened to burn down the whole bazaar if Zulfiqar Ali did not give himself up. His father Akbar told how he had given himself up for the sake of the rest of the community. He was put to death after being tortured in public. He was twenty years old. I said Zulfiqar Ali's was the only shot fired; I had forgotten that a Jarawa on North Sentinel killed a Jap officer on the beach with an arrow.

Another little man, who is one of the D.C.'s clerks, told how during one of the spy scares he and his family had been dragged off to jail in the middle of the night. He had been tortured by having red hot needles pushed half an inch under his nails. He described the water torture which, of course, was a favourite of the Germans, and was much used by the English in the reign of King John to extract money from the Jews. He was still unable to get up in the morning without putting a hot-water-bottle against his back—the result of the beatings he had received.

Another habit of the Japs was to strip a man naked and tie him to a cane-seated chair with a lighted candle under his private parts. If he held out and would not confess to espionage his wife was fetched in and stripped. Then they were tied together face to face and both were burnt in the same place. Several of the island women are now sterile as a result of the treatment they received, the generative organs having been partially burnt away. Pouring boiling water up the nose was used in the hill villages in Burma to extract information about Force 136, but I did not hear of that being used in the Andamans.

Perhaps what will show better than anything what these poor people endured is the tale of an "old man (sic) of forty-five" whose heart the Japs hoped to break by making him stand with his arms outstretched and a green coconut in each palm. A green coconut weighs a great deal more than the coconuts you see on a shy at a fair. When the "old man" let one of the coconuts fall he was beaten. At this story everybody turned round to look at the "old man" and laugh. Compared with the sufferings of others what this "old man of forty-five" had to endure was a joke!

Some of the worst Jap criminals have been hanged, but I fear all too many may have escaped retribution. I asked the people I was interviewing if they could give me one example of Jap decency, and they spoke of a Doctor Kamazo (?) who had been kind. He was soon removed in consequence. They could not mention a single other instance of kindness. The Imperial Nipponese Navy, Army, Police and Civil Service were afraid of being bombed, and they all behaved like hysterical monkeys. This inability to stand up to bombing is an interesting revelation of Jap cowardice because the same barbarians in the field of battle were often, indeed almost always, inspired with an insensate courage.

At noon the interviews finished, and we went up to see the jail, being received by Major M. Sendak, I.M.S. who is simultaneously the Governor of the Jail and the Chief Medical Officer in the Andaman Islands. We sat in his office and heard about the convict settlement before the Japs arrived. Sendak himself was here then. All convicts on arrival spent three months in a cell. I looked at one of these cells on the ground floor. It measured 14-ft. by 7 and did not seem as forbidding as the usual cell in one of our prisons at home. After these three months the convicts were to all intents free to work in different parts of the island.

After seeing all over the prison we went into the courtyard to inspect the present convicts awaiting trial in Port Blair itself. There were half a dozen Bhantu rioters, who no doubt will be sent to Lucknow with the others when the ship arrives for them. There was another dozen convicted of theft. Finally there were the Indian ex-jailers who had taken service under the Japs and made a brave attempt to outdo their masters in brutality. These fellows were all dull of eye, heavy of jowl, and low of forehead—the average human brute the world over.

Then I saw a small young man with the face of a weasel and the eyes of a viper. Sendak told me that this was Bagchi, whereupon a greasy propitiatory smile began to trickle over his face. When I stared at him without response he turned his eyes away. Appeals are being cabled from Bengal to the Chief Commissioner on behalf of Bagchi and I hope that no misguided influence may be brought to bear on his behalf. He deserves to be stamped out like a cockroach. He was a murderer before he was transported to the Andamans. He was given a chance by Bird of doing clerical work until he was sacked by him as a malingerer. Then he framed the case against Bird which led to his execution by the Japs in circumstances of the utmost brutality, over which Bagchi gloated as a spectator. Finally, he helped the Japs to commit these outrages upon women. If this vile creature is alive when these words are printed justice will have been cheated. Yet, what a narcotic time is! Sendak told me that when he first came back and saw the creature responsible for the death of his best friend in Port Blair he could not look at him.

"And now I speak to him as I speak to the other prisoners," he added with a sigh.

People who try to remind the British public of what was done by the Germans and the Japs are already being rebuked as impeders of true peace. I daresay when I reach Japan and see the gardens I shall begin to wonder if what their makers did in war might not have been due to temporary rabies. Then I shall see again with the mind's eye the eyes of those people in the Andamans when they told me their horrifying tales and I shall remind myself that forgiving should no more be the equivalent of forgetting than tolerance should be the equivalent of laziness.

We left the jail at 13 o'clock. I was much impressed by the personality of Major Sendak—a frail-looking man with sensitive eyes and mouth and sympathetic voice. I am told he is of Czechoslovak extraction.

Lunch with the D.C. in his bungalow was most agreeable. John Dalison joined the party. The food was as good as the company. At 14.30 we drove down to the jetty at the shipyard and crossed the harbour to Bamboo Flat Jetty, passing below Mt. Harriet at the foot of which on another jetty Lord Mayo the Viceroy was assassinated some years ago by a Pathan convict with a grievance. Then we drove in a Dodge through some lovely country, past the sanatorium on the slopes of Mt. Harriet, through Moplah villages, until beyond a rubber plantation we reached a Burmese village and turned aside to visit a *hpoongyi's* school beside a small pagoda. The children were delightfully natural, and anxious to show their prowess in reading and writing the Burmese script on slates. The old priest himself in his faded orange robes had the gentlest face. He sat on the edge of a bamboo platform about eighteen inches above his scholars on the bamboo floor. A grandfather brought along his baby grandson who was wearing a gaily embroidered khaki cap and round his neck two fine cords, one with a golden sovereign older than the 1887 jubilee and the other with a silver half-rupee. Perhaps the former was a souvenir of some British soldier who loved a Burma maid before Kipling sang about the road to Mandalay. John Dalison knelt on the floor to photograph the infant who was held up on his feet by the grandfather, whereupon the infant behaved like some infant Cupid on a Renaissance fountain much to everybody's amusement. Even the old *hpoongyi* smiled.

After leaving the school by a path bordered with spider-lilies, in our ears the chanting of the interrupted lesson now resumed, we walked along the trolley-track used by the forestry people to a brook beside which we picnicked. Hunting spiders jumped about on the outspread rug. We saw many racket-tailed drongos which we thought at first were lyre-birds. In flight their long tails look as if two tiny blue-black drongos were flying behind their parent. After the picnic we were pushed back in a trolley to where the road started, and a mile or so farther on we stopped to have whiskies with one of the foresters in his bungalow, now being rebuilt after the mess the Japs had made of it. We got back to the ship about 18.30 and changed to go across the harbour again in a heavy shower of rain after dinner to a dance in the club.

Mr. Grueber the Secretary had taken a great deal of trouble to make our evening pleasant and I was sorry I did not get a chance to have a long talk with him. I met a Sikh Jemadar of Force 136 who had landed on one of the islands (not North Sentinel) where the Jarawas live, and he gave me some information about them. He once saw a small boy shooting arrows at his mother's toes and laughing when she jumped in the air. He would pay no attention to her remonstrances, but at last his father came along in response to his wife's yells and gave the child a sound spanking. The Jarawas move about from kitchen midden to kitchen midden in the way our neolithic forebears did, and they have a communal sleeping hut, the sexes being divided by a spiked wooden paling. He had not seen a Jarawa widow going about wearing her husband's skull suspended by a necklace. This was a custom of the Andamanese aborigines. After the Japanese officer was killed the Japs bombed the Jarawa territory, and they retreated further into the interior. Since the Japs went the Jarawas have been attacking the elephants of the Forestry Department, but only after an elephant beat up one of their villages. The bows they use require much strength, and they kneel to shoot like the long-bowmen of England.

C. and I left the dance with Mansell at midnight. It was the top of the tide and the ship's boat bounced about a good deal.

February 26th. On board H.M.I.S. Narbada *in PORT BLAIR*

At 6.30 the Captain, John Dalison, Thomson and myself went aboard the *Elsa*, a steam tug built in Canada for use on the Great Lakes. Here we found Commander Stephenson, Michael Sullivan the D.C., Michael Littlewort the Policeman, and Robin Drummond the Forester waiting for us. We were going out to the Ritchie Archipelago over twenty miles away. There was a strong swell running under a grey sky and the *Elsa* rolled like the pendulum of a grandfather clock. By about 10 we were off Niell Island, and five rods baited with red and white bunting were hoping for the best. The sport was splendid—barracuda (a couple of 22-pounders among them), yellow-spotted, grey, and blue *khokari*, which is a relation of the tunny, and one *surmi* or horse mackerel, the best fighter of the lot. Sixteen fish in all were caught before we turned back to Port Blair at 15 o'clock.

The coast of Niell Island was beautiful—almost four miles of sandy beach in front of dense jungle and then many great trees rising to yellow cliffs. At one point just before the cliffs began there was a fine natural arch in the sandstone. There was nothing actually in the topography to suggest Treasure Island, and yet somehow it evoked Treasure Island. It had been our intention to land in a cove on the other side of Niell Island and picnic; but the weather was

Queen of the Seas! H.M.I.S. *Narbada*

'Four feet, Sah! Ship drawing 5 ft. 6 in.'

Captain Robinson Kettle

Lovely ladies of Car Nicobar

A war canoe

Interior of a hut

‘No foot rest—no strain—no pain—not to worry!’

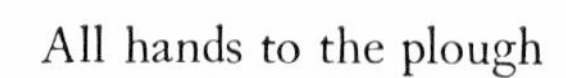

All hands to the plough

Chowrah—Robinson Crusoe alights with magic ring

Local craft

Old packet at Car Nicobar

Chowrah

Chowrah—sunshine above, V.D. 100 % below

Jap fortifications in the Andamans

Canoe with outrigger, Chowrah

nkind, and we lunched on board on dressed horseshoe crabs with range shells and grilled *khokari* fresh caught. Both were delicious.

Beyond Niell Island to the east lies Sir Hugh Rose Island, a perect miniature of a tropical island about half a mile square. To the orth of Niell is Havelock Island, three times as large, the greyishvhite cliffs of which had a menacing and macabre appearance inder the grey sky and above the grey sea. This island was the cene of a Jap outrage only a fortnight before the surrender. Vice-Admiral Hara, the Jap commander at Port Blair, became apprehensive about the food situation and a round-up was made of six or seven hundred men, women and children, who were locked up n the cellular jail. About two hundred of these were released; but he rest, four to five hundred, were herded into boats and thrown nto the sea off Havelock Island. Most of them were drowned or eaten by sharks; those who managed to get ashore perished of tarvation. Rumours of survivors having been seen are always ife in Port Blair, and the D.C. has just sent another search party; out if there *are* any survivors, they do not know that the Japs have been defeated, and so they will probably hide. As late as August 3th, 1945, two days before the surrender, another batch of some hree hundred persons were taken overland to Tarmugli Island and here butchered. It is satisfactory to know that thirty-seven Jap officers, seamen and soldiers were condemned to death after their rial in Singapore. These included Vice-Admiral Hara and Major-General Sato.

February 27th. On board H.M.I.S. Narbada *in PORT BLAIR*

I had a quiet morning working on the diary and after lunch we went ashore to be driven by the Chief Commissioner over to Corbyn's Cove for a picnic tea. This was where the Japs landed on the night of March 22nd-23rd, 1942. It is the only cove in the island sufficiently sheltered for bathers, but even here they have to beware of the current and of sharks. The arc of white beach is strewn with lumps and fragments of coral. Hermit crabs in many kinds of shells are continuously busy; and it is comic to prod what is apparently a lethargic winkle and see it suddenly hare off in a panic. There were other small crabs which moved so fast that they seemed to skim the sand. The beach was backed by a coconut grove and a coconut nursery, in which the young palms sprouting from half-buried nuts looked like very smart aspidistras.

We were back at Aberdeen Jetty by 17 o'clock and said farewell to those who had made our stay at Port Blair so enjoyable. The atmosphere of the place is extraordinarily genial. Everybody likes

the other fellow, and I did not hear a word of criticism by on
official of another. Co-operation is the rule.

I cannot help thinking that it will be a mistake for the India
Government to accept responsibility for these islands, but it doe
not look as if the British are anxious to accept it. I heard a suggestio
that Port Blair should become a sort of Zion for Anglo-Indians
of whom there is already a sizeable colony.

Just after 17.30 the ship weighed anchor, and we steamed awa
from the orange sunset to turn south about five miles out boun
for Car Nicobar. Shortly after we sailed the Captain handed u
the following signal which the Assistant Commissioner of the Nico
bars had sent to Littlewort, the Superintendent of Police.

"Send party. Will endeavour to drown the lot and give his secre
tary the necessary thrill. *Narbada* had better land the party a
Malacca in their motor-boat. Jetty has been repaired and weathe
is good."

February 28th. On board H.M.I.S. Narbada *off CAR NICOBA*

We dropped anchor off Malacca at 7.30, and about 8 o'cloc
Major J. d'Issa-Boomgardt, the Assistant Commissioner, came o
board. He was in the 3rd Mahrattas and fought at Keren. Poo
Boomgardt was rather taken aback to hear that his private joke wit
Littlewort had been passed on with the rest of the message.

We went ashore at 9.30 and landed at the jetty built by the Jap
of concrete walls filled up with sand. It is nearly a hundred yard
long and it had always been declared impossible to build a jett
here before the Japs got busy and did it in three weeks. All th
captains or headmen of the Car Nicobar villages were on the jett
to greet us, and we shook hands with at least thirty people. Th
island is 49 square miles in extent, almost completely flat an
covered with coconut groves and rich jungle. The population i
about 9,000. The natives are passionately British. Every one of then
has taken a British name besides his own Nicobarese name of which
like a small boy in a prep-school with his Christian name, he make
a secret because to know a man's name gives you power over him
Rumpelstiltzkin felt like this, and the same idea occurs somewhere i
the Odyssey. They do not necessarily choose English proper names
One girl is called "Yes please". When Sullivan visited the schoo
of the Anglican mission he asked the names of two boys sitting nex
each other and found that one was called Nelson and the othe
Hardy.

We set out with Boomgardt in his jeep to make a tour of th

island. The sandy roads are in good condition and run in every direction through the coconut groves. The Jap occupation interfered with cultivation and a number of jungle plants have grown up between the palms. It may be bad cultivation, but the effect on the village landscape is enchanting. The girls we met on the road were attractive. Half of them wore only a sarong, but the remainder covered their breasts with the thin white bodice of Burma. The men all greeted us with salutes. I could see that Boomgardt who has been here about a year was already much liked. He told me that it is impossible to get the Nicobarese to settle down to steady and regular work. They are capable of making a tremendous effort, but reaction always succeeds, and the greater the effort the longer the fallow time. As an instance of what they can do in the way of exceptional tasks he told me that he had persuaded a number of them to carry for seven miles a Diesel engine and electrical equipment weighing several tons which the Japs had buried. With his own knowledge as an amateur engineer he had got it working and is now able to provide electric light for many of the houses. This has been a joy to the Nicobarese and it has become the fashion to make up parties to sleep in one of these houses merely for the pleasure of gazing at the electric lamp. And beautiful houses they are, like large beehives thickly thatched with a kind of grass grown in carefully tended clearances in the jungle, which are tabu to other crops. The houses are built on piles with metal guards to keep out the rats, and one climbs up to the living room by a narrow bamboo ladder. The cooking is done on the ground underneath. One third of the floor space in the middle is boarded. On either side the floor is of finely pleached cane. This provides ventilation, for there are no windows. These floors are much better and stronger than the bamboo floor of the ordinary Burmese basha. The houses are built round about a village "brown" of beaten earth on which I did not see so much as the husk of a coconut.

We drove on to visit the store of the only Indian traders now functioning. Before the Japs came the island had been exploited for years by Indian and Chinese traders, who had swindled the inhabitants ruthlessly over their coconuts. They have no system of measures or money, and they never received a fair amount of rice in return for their coconuts. Moreover, the Indian traders had managed to make them appear always in debt. They are much worried by the prospect of being handed over to India. For them that means a return of trading tyranny.

I must add that the existing store is well run and well stocked. I was impressed by the obvious decency and honesty of the Indian manager. Just inside the entrance one may read the followin inscription in white lettering on a painted board:

Always tell the truth.
Give up your bad habits.
Might is right.
God Almighty.
Don't spit here.
R.A.J. and Co.

From the store we drove to the church of the Reverend Joh Richardson, a Nicobarese ordained by the Anglican Bishop c Rangoon. Mr. Richardson is a man of 55 and as fine a specimen c good missionary as one could meet. He has a charming young wif The church is beautifully neat, but the East window was smashe by the Japs and repairs are necessary. In the small side chape stands a dry pomelo, which is a large fruit somewhere between grape-fruit and an orange in flavour. I asked why this pomelo wa kept there and was told the following story.

A young Indian sailor came ashore from H.M.I.S. *Krishna* when she anchored off Car Nicobar at the time of the Jap sur render, and cheated a Nicobarese by paying him for two pomelo the price of one. On returning to the ship he was seized with a kind o paralysis. His conscience tormenting him, he sent back the secon pomelo with a request that it might be put in the church an prayers offered for his recovery. He was immediately cured, and th pomelo is preserved in the side-chapel as a perpetual reminder tha honesty is the best policy.

Close to the church is the school presided over by Mr. Ezekie Joel, who is shortly to be ordained. He is much more High Churc than Mr. Richardson, but the two men are in complete accord In the school we heard some wonderful singing, mostly of hymns but *John Brown's Body* was rendered with much verve and at the en *God Save the King*. One hymn was sung in a Nicobarese translation the rest were in English, sung, it seemed, without any trace of a accent and with complete control of the phrase. Yet not a word o what they were singing was understood by the children. I wish tha a recording could be made of this astonishing choir. Among th brown pupils I noticed three little boys as black as coal, with glit tering pop-eyes. These were Jarawas who with their sister had bee captured during an affray with the police in which their parent were killed. They wore light-blue cotton shorts and shirts and looke like the stock piccaninnies of the picture books. One of them wa wearing a small electric-light bulb on a string round his neck. The were reported to be very naughty, but details of their naughtiness were withheld. Nobody was quite sure how old the eldest was. They suspected that his pygmy size was misleading people into supposing he was only about eleven. After the singing we saw some wrestling between the boys—all very good tempered. The Jarawa boys were thrown by the Nicobarese boys of their own age in every round.

Mr. Richardson's flock is increasing all the time and he does not make the mistake of interfering too much with the old customs. The women of his congregation do not uncover their breasts, but I was told that this was not the missionary's order. It came from the wife of the last Assistant Commissioner who insisted that every woman and girl who came to see her should wear a bodice. I had noticed that occasionally when we had passed girls with bare breasts on the road they had turned their backs and covered them with their hands. It was distressing to see these signs of self-consciousness.

From the school we drove to view the two airstrips made by the Japs. One of them is now quite overgrown, but the other, 1,400 yards long, can be used by planes. The marks of our bombing are visible. In a small fenced-in space by the edge of the strip stands a cross with a Japanese inscription on both sides. This is the grave of a British or American airman, but nobody who can read Japanese has yet seen it, and the date of his death is unknown. There is a story in Car Nicobar that the airman was killed by the Japs when he crashed, which sounds improbable, for in that case why would they have erected this memorial to him. Nevertheless, the Jap mind works so oddly from our point of view that they were quite capable of murdering an airman and erecting a memorial to him afterwards.

About 13.30 we wound up a fascinating morning with lunch at the Assistant Commissioner's house. This had been the H.Q. of the Imperial Nipponese Navy and still bears above its entrance the badge of the anchor and chrysanthemum. With the fish course we had banana chips, which can be made only from green bananas. This was followed by chicken with a hotly spiced stuffing and yams which are like sweet potatoes.

After lunch I went out on the verandah for a pow-pow with some of those who could tell me about the Japanese behaviour. At first the invaders behaved fairly well, but when we started bombing the airstrips they indulged in the same spy scares as on the Andamans. In all 75 Nicobarese were tortured to death. The most moving story was of the captain of Arong, a village in the remotest part of the island and completely animist. The captains of all the villages were ordered to surrender the Union Jacks which they had, and this

was done by all except the captain of Arong. He buried his, an
would not reveal the place under torture. The flag was finally dis
covered by the Japs two years later, and after being tortured agai
the captain of Arong was put to death. This is an authentic story
not a journalist's write-up. If the people of Great Britain are willin
to disclaim responsibility for heroes like the captain of Arong the peo
ple of Great Britain deserve to sink into third-class insignificance.

The tortures used by the Japs on Car Nicobar were the same as i
the Andamans with one exception. That was to make a man clim
a coconut tree and remain all day balanced on a precarious branch
The Nicobarese have a keen sense of the ridiculous. They said th
Japs were comic in their expression of hatred for Britain. If the
found an English picture or an English book they would jump o
it and chatter like infuriated monkeys. After the surrender, while th
Japs were still on the island waiting for orders, the Nicobarese use
to laugh at them continuously. In the end the poor butts would no
appear in public if possible and were well on the way to a nervou
breakdown before they were evacuated.

I was told there were about 15,000 Japs in the Nicobars, but this i
probably an oversestimate. Their habits were filthy. No attempt a
sanitation was made, and the result of this was to bring a plague o
flies to the islands and the accompanying dysentery. From responsi
bility for the venereal disease which is sadly prevalent the Japs ca
be absolved: it was introduced by the traders.

We visited the hospital where Dr. Ram Ratten Lall does his bes
with the miserably inadequate drugs and equipment he has. Th
wards are small and open off a small verandah. One was kept fo
malaria, another for V.D. The complications of childbirth wer
attended to in a third. All the patients were women.

After the pow-pow about Jap atrocities we drove back to Mus
where a representative island team was to play H.M.I.S. *Narbada* a
football. The sailors were a bit inclined to think that the loca
yokels were not quite the stuff for the champions of the Indian Nav
to waste time over. But what a game the local side put up! Th
result—two goals to none in favour of *Narbada*—did not represen
the run of the play, and the game should have ended in a draw. Th
Nicobarese played with bare feet and kicked with great power
if they had been stronger in front of goal they would have defeate
the sailors. The pace was terrific. I was excited and continuall
refreshed myself with coconut milk which was quite delicious—
different matter entirely from the coconut milk we drank on the wa
to Mysore. The match started at 17.30 and it was dusk by the tim
it was finished. The trunks of the coconut palms round the field wer

;ained with rose by the sunset. John Dalison did a charming water-
olour of Sawi Bay close by. I offered to present a challenge shield for
nnual competition by the village league.

From the match we drove to a dance in the village of Perka. Ninety-
ix girls formed a great horseshoe round a bonfire of coconut husks
n the village 'brown', and between the chanting they stamped and
huffled upon the ground. The sound of the shuffle was rather like the
ound of a calm sea running up a steep sandy beach and receding.
'hey moved round very slowly, and the pattern of the dance changed
om time to time. The girls were wearing white bodices, presumably
o save the modesty of the visitors. Round their heads they wore
llets of cellophane. The half-moon was in the zenith. The grove
round was dark. The dancing forms caught the flickering of the
onfire. The beehive houses were mounds of shadows.

Boomgardt had expressed a strong desire to visit the island of
Chowra next day. Rather unwillingly I agreed to go, for it meant
iving up the visit to Nankowrie and a meeting with the Queen of
he Nicobars. She is an old Indian trader who acted as agent for the
Government and received a decoration in the First World War for
rightening away Captain Müller by hoisting the Union Jack when
he *Emden* appeared in the great harbour. He supposed that there
nust be a strong force on the island. When the German raider had
one she sent a canoe to carry the news to the nearest signal station,
nd the *Emden* was caught by H.M.A.S. *Sydney* and destroyed in the
Cocos Islands.

We got back to the ship about midnight after one of the best
lays I ever spent. While we were signalling for the motor-boat, we
ieard chanting over the sea and saw the Chowra canoes coming
n with the big earthenware pots they make. They had left their
sland at 7 that morning and paddled across nearly 50 miles of the
ndian Ocean.

March 1st. On board H.M.I.S. Narbada. *CAR NICOBAR TO CHOWRA AND BACK*

We left the anchorage at 7 and steamed south to Chowra. About 9
ve sighted a Japanese floating mine and after a lively bombardment
asting over half an hour the ship's guns managed to sink her. We
eached Chowra about 11.30. It is a small island hardly more than
wo square miles in extent if as much. At one point from the sea it
ooks like the Dutchman's Cap—one of the Treshnish Islands off
Argyll. At the south end is a square lump of rock, 343 feet high and
erfectly level on top. I should have said it was basalt, but it is not.
The rest of the island is flat, hardly more than a mile across and two

miles long, with a dazzling white beach above which, backed b
jungle and coconuts, stand twenty large beehive houses.

The A.C., John Dalison, Thomson and I with Sinbad the Sailo
embarked in the motor-boat from which we transferred to a ver
narrow canoe with two outriggers. Each of us sat on a couple c
bamboo thwarts no wider than his own behind and tried to keej
his feet out of the water at the bottom of the canoe. Luckily the da
was calm and blue, as perfect a day as one could hope for. We coul
never have landed at Chowra in our Andaman weather. The wate
was clear, but to my disappointment I could not see a single fish. A
Union Jack was flying from a pole above the beach. When we landec
we found that the beehive houses here were guest houses and at th
moment empty. They are used by people who come to buy th
Chowra pottery. Chowra is an island of magic. There are over 50
inhabitants, and their chief occupation is making cooking pots fo
the other islands. The clay on Chowra is now exhausted and it i
obtained from the much larger island of Teressa about five mile
away to the south. The people of Teressa dare not make their ow
pots for fear of coming under one of the potent Chowra spells. I
the same way the Nancowry people fifty miles south have to pay a
commission to Chowra on canoes they build for Car Nicobar a hundred miles away. If they did not their canoes would be bewitchec
by Chowra-conjured devils.

We found the villages of Chowra very different from those of Ca
Nicobar, and the people ugly. The men wore nothing except a rec
cache-sex with a long red string behind representing the tail in
herited by the union between a woman and a dog after the flooc
from which the Nicobarese believe they sprang. On the other hanc
except for a few old hags the women covered their breasts with a
grubby wrap. We asked the headman who had returned with us fron
Car Nicobar if this was done on our account, but it was apparently
the rule. We saw unbaked pots as large as two feet across and mor
than two feet deep fashioned without a potter's wheel in perfec
symmetry. We also saw them being baked on small bonfires anc
banded with black and red. The combination of black and red ha
a discouraging effect on devils; the devil-scarers in every hous
display it.

Chowra was much dirtier than Car Nicobar. The ground rounc
the villages was littered with coconut shells and refuse. The flie
were thick everywhere. There were many dogs. The sun blazec
down. We drank coconut milk, but even that did not taste nearly a
good as the Car Nicobar product. Round the houses broody fowl
in rectangular baskets were hung up out of the way of rats. We saw

various devilish figures presumably intended to scare away other devils.

The most depressing thing about the island is that practically the whole population is infected with venereal disease, not to mention elephantiasis, tuberculosis and malaria. The people have no medicine of any kind, and there is no room for them in the Car Nicobar hospital. The headman of Chowra brought men, women and children for Thomson to look at. Even to be looked at by a doctor was something. Babies with syphilitic sores, small boys with gonorrhea, women eaten away . . . but enough of these horrors.

After this evidence of neglect by the flag flown above the beach I was in no mood to investigate Jap atrocities here. However, there was none to investigate, and I should suppose that the Jap company stationed here must have been too much depressed by these stricken people to commit atrocities. Anyway, they committed none and did not molest the women, which is hardly to be wondered at.

I wished we had not changed our itinerary by visiting Chowra instead of Nancowry, and yet perhaps it is better that we should not have left the Nicobars with only the lovely picture of Car Nicobar in our minds, when a place like Chowra exists. I have not tried to evoke the full horror of this small island where above that dazzling beach and azure sea the Union Jack flies, but the people who fly it with such pathetic pride and trust are phantoms of humanity. I wish that those who so willingly subscribe to missions for the cure of souls would subscribe to a mission here for the cure of bodies. Meanwhile, a grave moral responsibility for allowing such a state of affairs is attached to the British Government.

I forgot to mention that in these Nicobar villages there is always a birth house and a death house. In the one a woman must live for three months after the birth of a child before she is accounted clean. To the other the dying are taken to die. We saw a pomelo tree which had belonged to a man who had recently died. It was now tabu. The fruit was rotting on the ground. It belonged to the dead man's spirit. Not until the ossuary feast held some months after death would the tabu be lifted. Few white men have visited Chowra. I am glad we did take the Assistant Commissioner there, for the Government will no longer be able to claim ignorance of the state of affairs. Who knows when he will be able to pay another visit? He has no boat, and he is confined to an island at the northerly end of a group over a hundred miles long. Great Nicobar, much the largest island, is almost unknown. Boomgardt is a man of immense energy and enthusiasm, and if he were given the facilities he could make a splendid job of these islands. The future of the Nicobars is still doubtful. There is no doubt that the islanders view the prospect of being administered by India with dismay, but unless we are prepared to shoulder the duty we owe to these people in return for using their islands as bases of war we have no moral argument to support our case for holding on to them.

I came away from Chowra, heavy-hearted. At 18.30 we dropped the Assistant Commissioner off Malacca and steamed southward. I should add that the crews of the thirteen canoes which had sailed with the pots to Car Nicobar would have been the pick of the islanders. Still, even most of *them* must be carriers of V.D.

March 2nd. On board H.M.I.S. Narbada *bound for PENANG*

A grey sky, a grey sea, sticky heat, and all day working at the diary. I don't know when I shall have time to write any letters. I feel depressed that to-morrow will be the end of this wonderful cruise. It has been a great privilege to be shipmates with the officers and crew of H.M.I.S. *Narbada.*

MALAYA, SIAM, INDO-CHINA, HONG KONG

March 3rd. PENANG

We dropped anchor at ten o'clock of a grey morning with a heavy threat of rain. Brigadier A. F. Cumming, V.C., who was to be our conducting officer through Malaya, had not arrived. We lunched on board and went ashore at 14.30. The West Yorks had kindly provided a car in which we drove the 46 miles round the island. It was strange to be driving on a perfect road with every bridge intact. Penang was bombed both by us and the Japs and about 800 houses were destroyed; but it is the nearest thing to a pre-war place I have seen for a long time. Indeed, all that is left of the Jap occupation are three concrete blockhouses painted green which are now used as barns, and the stakes in the sea near beaches where they feared a landing by us. There was jungle and rubber all the way, but we saw hardly any birds, and I have bceome a bit hypercritical about jungle. I want the best jungle, and Penang does not provide it. The Penang jungle is neat and sophisticated. On the other hand, the beaches where the road runs past them are delightful. So too, are many of the bungalows. Frangipani trees are in flower everywhere, and we saw really good cannas again.

We arrived at the house of Mr. King, the Resident Commissioner, at 17.30, his Secretary having asked several of those with first-hand experience of Jap behaviour to their prisoners to meet me. Then the R.C. and Mrs. King arrived from a car journey of 250 miles. He had not been warned that we were coming to stay with him, but in spite of the surprise he and Mrs. King managed to give the impression that we were welcome, which was a really conspicuous feat of hospitality at the end of a nine-hour drive.

The Residency is beautifully situated by the sea, with a fine garden. I found out the name of the woolly lilac creeper which has been our companion all the way down through Burma. It is *Congea tomentosa*. I saw my first sealing-wax palm. The trunk turns at the top to sealing-wax red, and the stems of the fronds at the bottom are the same colour.

March 4th. PENANG TO KOTA BAHRU

At noon we drove down to Victoria Jetty and crossed over to Butterworth where a Dakota was waiting to fly us to Kota Bahru.

Brigadier Cumming is still held up at Rangoon. A young Captain of the 1st Gurkhas came from Taiping to fly with us. The pilot was anxious to get off as soon as possible because the weather was piling up. We were airborne by 14.30, after a quarter of an hour's grilling in the plane while they were revving up. We had to fly up to 11,000 feet to get out of the weather. There were wonderful colour effects along the coast.

We landed at Kota Bahru, which means New Castle, at 15.40. Here we were met by Lt.-Colonel Robinson of 3/5th Gurkhas and Mr. Malone, the Secretary of the Resident Commissioner, Mr. A. Churchill, who was in hospital. I found I had been invited to tea by the Sultan of Kelentan, but first of all I paid a call on Churchill who had been having a hernia dealt with. He had been a prisoner in Singapore, and the hernia had been brought on by having to move about heavy tree trunks. The more I hear of the Japs the more unspeakably foul they seem. Churchill told me that what he disliked most were the uplift lectures by the little vermin on such topics as 'unselfishness' to which the captives were compelled to listen.

His Highness does not speak English, but I could see that he understood most of what I was saying. I had an admirable translator, N. Kamil, the son of a former Prime Minister, who was called to the bar at Lincoln's Inn. I was deeply impressed by the brain of this Malay, who is known as the Boss. The Crown Prince was also present, but he did not say much. I had some good sweets. One called golden net, which describes its appearance, tasted as good as it looked. Malone was leaving for the Cameron Highlands that night, so John Matthias, who lives with his wife in the Residency Annexe, took us along to the beach at Kota Bahru.

The Japs put up two obelisks of granite inscribed "To the Fallen" in Japanese. These two have been allowed to remain, but a third farther along the sandy beach has been knocked down. Thomson and I tried to work out what had happened here, but it was exasperating that Brigadier Cumming, who played such a conspicuous part in the action, could not tell us about it. We had found out by now that he had been held up in Rangoon because every plane had been looking for a Dakota which had crashed somewhere on the east coast of Malaya, not far from where we now were. The N.E. monsoon blowing across the South China Sea had cut a miniature cliff in the middle of the sand. A level grove of coconuts backed the beach and behind the coconuts there was creek after creek, the banks thick with those palms which grow along the chaungs of Arakan. I saw no mangroves here.

We wandered about until dusk and then drove round to where

some bathing huts and a restaurant had been put up by Tengku Mahyiddeen. He is a son of the Raja of Patani who was deposed by the Siamese, but has dropped the prefix "Tengku" which indicates royalty. A member of the local corps, he insisted on sticking with the British army as far as Singapore and finally reached India where he did valuable work broadcasting to Malaya. He was wearing a sarong and vest when we arrived, and we sat in his restaurant drinking beer. Then he went off to change for dinner at the Residency and while we waited for him it came on to rain heavily. Thomson went back in the Gurkha wagon. Matthias, Mahyiddeen and myself sat inside a Dodge. We were flung about from side to side all the way, and I felt more physically tired after the 45 minutes of that drive than I had felt yet.

We had a jolly dinner at the Residency. Kamil was there, and I found him one of the most intelligent people I have met in the course of this tour. He and Mahyiddeen are a remarkable pair. I could not get them to talk as much as I wanted because a voluble planter was a guest—one of those people who do know a lot about the East but cannot suppose anybody else can learn anything about it in less than the thirty years' experience of which they are so proud. Moreover, I was feeling tired and by now I was pretty certain that the dysentery I had suspected yesterday was a fact.

March 5th. KOTA BAHRU TO IPOH

At 9.15 I looked in to say good-bye to Churchill who gave me a silver and tortoiseshell paper knife made locally. I wished I could have stayed on talking with him. Matthias went off to get me sulphaguanadine tablets, and Thomson started me with eight. I had to give a miss to flying over Singora and other beaches as intended and make the plane journey as short as possible. The weather was good and we landed at Butterworth in just over an hour. This is much the best managed R.A.F. airfield I have struck yet, and it shows that, given a good commanding officer, the job can be done. Wing-Commander Banthorpe was as kind and patient as he had been yesterday and I parted from Sq.-Leader Taylor and the crew, hoping to be flown by them again sometime. It was my 27th flight of the tour, and C.'s 21st.

Brigadier Cumming was at Butterworth to meet us, much disappointed about Kota Bahru. I can see at once that he will be just the guide I need, and I feel more than ever annoyed that he could not take me over the ground of that crucial first landing by the Japs. He won his V.C. in Malaya—the only one given to a British or

Indian soldier. He commanded the 2/12th Frontier Force Regiment. He is a small man with sharp features and very bright blue eyes.

By noon we were on our way to lunch at Taiping with Major-General Chappell, commanding 23rd Indian Division. It rained most of the way and I was feeling rather groggy. The water hyacinths were beautiful in the dykes beside the road; but their azure flowers are the enemy of the agriculturist. The neat rubber plantations and the wide road with such a good surface seemed absurdly suburban after Burma. The A Mess in Taiping is a delightful bungalow which looks out on a range of hills about 4,400 feet high. In the mist and rain the view was reminding me of Perthshire when one of the officers said, "We had a tiger on the lawn last week." At this moment in those hills is a white rhinoceros with two foals. The white rhinoceros is almost extinct and is carefully protected.

The large circular table round which we lunched had an inner revolving circle about four feet in diameter so that nobody had to pass anything. It was Chinese. I never coveted a piece of furniture more. We drove on after lunch to Ipoh, passing an extraordinary set of limestone cliffs like the Cheddar Gorge. This is the tin district. Ipoh itself is a most attractive town, well laid out with wide streets and good buildings.

Our host the Resident Commissioner, A. V. Aston, was just the tonic I needed. He and his extremely kind and charming wife were hospitality incarnate. He was imprisoned by the Japs, but like everybody else in Malaya does not utter a bleat about it.

March 6th. IPOH

I woke at 4 and had a poor time, with the dysentery going strong. It was decided not to continue our journey till Saturday. This meant missing a visit to the Cameron Highlands, but Thomson was firm about my being sensible. So I stayed in bed and talked to various people for most of the day. Among my visitors was Brigadier F. C. Scott who was B.G.S. of 33 Corps and able to give me a picture of Imphal from their point of view. I am extremely lucky to find myself in a house where my host and hostess manage to make it seem a pleasure to have a guest with dysentery.

The hospital people decided it was bacillary, not amoebic dysentery. Nevertheless, I was threatened with the possibility of at least a week in hospital. I talked to some more people and read *The Cowboy's Revenge* in the intervals. It was very hot in the afternoon but cooled off at dusk and I had a good night, being absolutely determined to keep out of hospital.

March 7th. IPOH

I felt definitely better when I woke and the tiresome symptoms of dysentery began slowly to recede all through the day. Cumming gave me an enthralling account of Kota Bahru, and also of his time commanding 63rd Brigade at Tiddim in the autumn of 1943.

The view from my bedroom window is lovely. A range of granite mountains in the background and in the middle distance those limestone cliffs. I wrote up the diary, but lack the energy to say as much as I should like about this place or the talks I have had here. My Biro pen which was refilled in Cairo dried up here with considerable tact because this is the first place since Cairo I should have had a chance of refilling it. Lt.-Colonel Alasdair Maclean of the Camerons, whom I have met in Lochboisdale early in the 'thirties, came in. He had also written to me from Batavia about *Keep the Home Guard Turning*. He is just back from Japan and "put me in the picture". C. went out to dine at a Chinese restaurant with Brigadier Cumming and Thomson. I had dinner with our charming host and hostess. Jim Thomson whom I feel as if I had known for years suggests no alcohol for a month. Sulphaguanadine is a poor substitute, but it is a miracle-working drug. What a difference it would have made at Gallipoli! There is no doubt that the doctors played a major part in winning the war in the East.

March 8th. IPOH TO KUALA LUMPUR

We left Ipoh at 9 accompanied as far as Kampar by Maclennan who had been with one of the big tin companies when the disaster happened and is now back with them. The limestone caves are even more impressive on this side of Ipoh. I saw a woman in black with a brilliant crimson red handkerchief round her head. She was a *dulang* woman. The *dulang* is a large and deep platter hollowed out from the trunk of a tree with which they wash the biscuit-coloured water of the streams in the tin country for the ore. They wear red round their heads to protect themselves against the sun and they wear long sleeves to protect their hands. We wonder how our redcoats stood up to the Indian sun, but in fact red resists the rays. Maclennan told me that for granite and limestone to meet is always favourable to the prospects of tin. The mines are not unsightly and there are no deep shafts.

We drove on to Bidor, after parting with Maclennan, where we had an appointment at the police station with two more survivors—Major Staley and Mr. Owen Jones. I am growing more and more indignant at the rot that was poured out by the Press at the time of Singapore. I wonder how many of those who sneered at the British officials and planters in Malaya would have stood up to the treatment they received at the hands of the Japanese with such courage at the time and so little complaint now. The blame for Singapore rests upon the electorate of Britain and the politicians who for fear of losing votes lacked the guts to warn them of their imperial responsibilities.

This go of dysentery has made me a little tired and the impressions have not been so sharp as usual. After the talk at Bidor we drove through agreeable country on a good road to the crossing of the Slim River where Cumming explained the military position. From there we went on to lunch in the rest house at Tonjong Malim. I recall from this drive a spot where thousands of small butter-yellow butterflies, akin to our brimstones, were floating in the air and covering the grass verge of the roadside, and were even gathered in a swarm on the road, two or three butterflies deep, looking butter flies indeed. I recall the women and men cutting the grass on those verges with long-handled sickles which they swung above the head with one arm. I recall, too, an electric-blue bird with white on the wings flying across in front of the car. It was not a blue jay: I think it was probably one of the several kinds of kingfishers here.

We reached H.Q. Malaya Command at Kuala Lumpur about 17 o'clock and were greeted by Mrs. Galloway. I did not rest, but sat talking after tea with Major-General Galloway when he came in. He and I strolled out on the lawn to see the flag lowered at dusk and hear the retreat blown by a Gurkha bugler.

March 8th. KUALA LUMPUR TO MALACCA

We drove ahead at 10 without Thomson who was looking round the hospital at K.L. General Galloway had thoughtfully asked Mr. Mohamed Youssif, the Chief Public Relations Officer, to accompany us to Malacca.

He was a grand cicerone. He comes from one of the twelve clans who some three centuries ago migrated to the Peninsula from Sumatra. These clans are strictly exogamous and matriarchal. A husband who misbehaves can be thrown out of his wife's clan back into his own. All property passes through the females. Youssif speaks English beautifully, though he has never been outside Malaya. He hopes to come to London next year and write a thesis on matriarchy. Malays are Muslims, but the stern religion has been much softened by the humid tropics. Fanaticism is non-existent. Even Ramadan is not scrupulously kept. Youssif's father had made the pilgrimage to Mecca and is a devout follower of the Prophet, but there is no attempt to force devotion on anybody else. Purdah has been unknown for centuries.

Youssif told me that without a sea breeze the coconut will grow well only near human habitations and requires smoke. He pointed out a desolate decaying grove of young palms which had ceased to grow since the Japs destroyed the house near which they had been planted. The design of the Malay house came originally from Sumatra. To my gratification he was able to identify various palms for me, and at last I could be sure which was the sago palm, and which the *nipah* palm. They both grow in damp soil, and the latter, with a very long frond rising almost directly from the ground, used for thatching, is what they call the *dahni* in Burma. There was a good deal of tapioca growing along the road, which is a most exhausting crop for the soil. The light green leaves are laciniated, and the long stem looks like a Jersey cabbage stalk.

Malacca was all romance in one too brief afternoon. We lunched at the rest house, and then set out on a rubber-necking tour of the town. Youssif is a native of Malacca State. We saw the gateway which is all that remains of the fort built by Alfonzo d'Albuquerque in 1511 whose coat of arms stands above the gate. Once upon a time it was almost washed by the sea, which is now more than half a mile away. This relic of Imperial Portugal is overhung by two trees of Flame of the Forest, the petals of which stipple the grass around the gateway of the ancient fort and stain with vivid orange the red laterite of the gateway itself. Beyond, upon the sunny grass, a cricket match was being played. The Portuguese were succeeded by the Dutch, and there are many Dutch houses of the seventeenth century in Malacca as solid as those built at home by the burghers of Holland. I thought of the elms in Amsterdam mirrored in the bottle-green canals where ducks and gulls swim side by side—"the ocean-dreaming elms of Amsterdam", to quote a line that ran in my head when I saw them for the first time in 1939.

We went up to look at the shell of the Portuguese cathedral of St. Paul which the pious stalwarts of the Netherlands, who solved the problem of worshipping God and Mammon, turned into a fort. You can see their gun emplacements above the green glacis commanding the grey waters of the Straits. The body of St. Francis Xavier lay here until it was translated to Goa in 1592. The empty tomb with the original grating of wrought iron above it stands in the middle of what was once the chancel of this roofless fane. Pious descendants of the old Portuguese conquerors burn votive candles to the saint still, and the grating is knobbled with spilt grease. Ponderous Dutch tombstones of the 17th and 18th century inscribed with epitaphs in Dutch and heavily carved with cherubs skulls and other emblems of death and eternity are leaning agains the walls all round. I noticed one to the wife of an Englishmar James Barber, who, arriving here pregnant, had been taken to th hospital in Batavia where she had died in childbirth. This tale wa told in the sonorous Latin they knew how to write in 1702. Th English finally obtained Malacca in exchange for land in Sumatra They gave back Java to the Dutch after the Napoleonic wars which was a mistake.

From the Cathedral we drove to Hereen Street in the old Dutcl houses of which the Chinese millionaires have lived for a long time so long that the houses have lost all their Dutch characteristic except solidity. The front doors are lacquered, and inside the room are decorated with exquisite tiles. In these houses the traditiona life of a cycle of Cathay endures, but to appear a match for modernit several of the millionaires have built Riviera bungalows by the sea' edge outside Malacca.

Youssif asked if we might enter one of these Hereen Street houses and a grandmother, with very little of her still black hair left on he head, and three large tufted moles, made us welcome. There wer daughters and granddaughters and grandsons everywhere. Deliciou little girls in flowery pyjama dresses danced around, tinkling witl laughter. On the walls of the first room were hanging ten larg coloured engravings of Chinese landscapes and seascapes about a century old and between them four large framed mezzotints c Farquharson's sheep in Highland snowstorms. There never was a more absurd juxtaposition. Along one side of the next room, whicl was open to the sky, stood six porcelain keg-shaped stools perforate to allow the air to circulate and cool the sedentary behind. Beyon this kind of patio was the altar of the ancestors with joss stick burning, and beyond this at least three more rooms opened out c one another, from the last of which a green-glowing doorway le to the garden. Brigadier Cumming took a snap of as many of th family as we could persuade to pose in front of the house witl Grandmamma in the middle.

From Hereen Street we drove out to the Chinese cemetery, whicl looks like a stretch of the Berkshire downs. Here for two hundre years and more the Chinese of Malacca have been buried. Fo over a mile the grass slopes of the hill are covered on both sides witl large horseshoe-shaped embrasures of stone built into the hillside At the opening of the horseshoe is a stone platform on which stand a slab of stone inscribed with the names of the dead. Childrer were flying large white kites everywhere. I supposed that, white eing the Chinese mourning, coloured kites were forbidden.

We walked up to the summit of the steep grassy slope to look at ıe memorial to a Malay hero who fought the Portuguese. Here ıe Malays still come, bearing votive offerings, and we could see ıe grease of burnt candles—the same kind of candles as St. Francis avier is offered above his empty grave. Youssif told us that when ıe Japs let him out of prison the first thing his mother did, and she a Iuslim, was to come here and make her thanksgiving. Beside this ee-shadowed shrine is a pergola terrace with square columns uch as one sees in Southern Italy. This was erected by the Chinese s a mark of respect to the Malay hero.

At last regretfully we had to shut our ears to the faint breeze hispering of rain and leave this tranquil green down. A grim cloud as darkening the sky and the children's kites were falling when we eached the car.

As we drove through Malacca on the way to A Mess, we passed club at the corner of a street opposite an old Portuguese church edicated to the Holy Angels and still in use.

"Every night passing that club one heard shrieks of agony," said oussif sombrely. "That was the headquarters of the Kempeitai." he Kempeitai were the Jap Secret Police.

A Mess was four miles out and we arrived there in a tropical ownpour. It is a house built beside the sea with as much modernity s possible by a rich Chinese merchant, but the result is not happy rchitecturally. The Commandant, Colonel Guille of Mullingar, Vest Meath, made us welcome, and as usual we enjoyed a prodigal ospitality and a jolly dinner party. Jim Thomson rejoined us here fter his medical researches at Kuala Lumpur and I notified him ıat his ban on alcohol had been withdrawn.

Iarch 10th. MALACCA TO SINGAPORE

With 170 miles to go we left A Mess at 9 sharp. At the rest house e said good-bye to Mohammed Youssif whom I hope to see again ı England. His Number Two in Malacca, Syed Osman ben Ali, a ear little man with remote Arab blood, took on the job of guiding s to Singapore.

About four miles out of Malacca the truck broke down and after delay of 2½ hours we had to go on without it, after transferring the aggage to Syed Osman's jeep and Thomson's jeep with a prayer hat it would escape a downpour. We crossed the Sarong Buaya or rocodile's Nest, the narrow stream which divides Johore from Ialacca. The landscape was less interesting than the previous day. Rubber estate after rubber estate. Well-kept rubber plantations are

avoided by birds, butterflies and flowers. We reached the Mua
a wide river behind which the Australians took up their positions.

Half the ill-equipped, partially-trained 45th Brigade of 9th India Division were stationed by the Australian General on the nort bank in a swamp of nipah palms, and these units were overrun a once by the powerful Japanese drive. Then the Australians pulle out and the Japs swarmed over the river, using among other cra the ferry boat in which we now had to cross. Twenty miles or s farther on we had to cross another ferry to Batu Pahat where we wer due to lunch with the Dorsets, who are back from Japan and no quartered at Batu Pahat (stone chisel). Lt.-Colonel Day and Majo Brown met us and in spite of priority we did not reach the other sid until 13.45—nearly three hours late. On the way through the tow to the Mess I noticed the Gum Chuan Hotel.

Colonel Day had asked the Deputy Resident Commissione Sjovald Cunyngham-Brown, a Shetlander, to meet me. He is grandson of Clunies-Ross of Cocos-Keeling, and is worried abou the proposal to settle some of the islanders in Malaya. The turnin of West Island into a large aerodrome and evacuation of the 7,00 inhabitants here led to overcrowding elsewhere and a serious foo problem. C.-B. thinks, and I cordially agree with him, that th Nicobars would be a much more satisfactory move. There is plent of room on Great and Little Nicobar, and also on Teressa, and th islanders who are ignorant of money and measures would fin themselves at home in the Nicobars.

Owing to our late arrival through the breakdown of the truck w had no time to drive out with Cunyngham-Brown to have a look a the terrain of the fighting at Bachi. C.-B. told me a story about th fight the Madras Sappers and Miners put up there. When thei ammunition was exhausted and the survivors had to surrender, th Japs made them kneel in front of a trench and beheaded them on by one. One eighteen-year-old Sapper, John Benedict, escaped int the jungle and then stealing back hid himself among the dead bodies He looked up to see a friend of his about to be executed and whis pered to him to jump as the Jap raised his sword. The friend jumpe and landed in the trench with his head only half severed. That nigh Benedict carried him out of the trench and swam the river with him They were both captured at Singapore later, but the friend survive and worked beside Cunyngham-Brown on the railway in Sumatra He could no longer move his neck; otherwise he was all right.

We had to leave the Mess at 15.30 in order to make Singapor before dusk. I should have liked to stay longer. The Dorsets enjoye themselves in Japan.

We drove over the causeway at Johore Bahru at 18 o'clock, aving done the last 96 miles in 2½ hours. Our host at Singapore is Iajor-General L. H. Cox, G.O.C.-in-C., Singapore Command, ·ho commanded the garrison of Malta during the siege. He has a harming wife and two enchanting little daughters of five and two, lizabeth the elder having been born in Malta during the siege. Iere at Draycot House is the only half-bred Siamese with almost erfect Siamese points I have seen. A white blotch on her nose and vo white paws with a black spot are all that mark the mésailliance. find that the Malay cats have kinked or club tails and I am satisfied ıat the Siamese cat is an inbred semi-albino from the Malay cat. 'he cattle of the Channel Islands are inbred semi-albinos, and it is) be noted that the Jersey cattle have the same scheme of colour as iamese cats without the blue eyes.

We had a jolly dinner. Our host tells and enjoys a good story, nd he has a capital A.D.C. in Captain Peter Hoskins of the Green Iowards. News that the Kuantan airstrip is no longer usable means ıat Cumming won't be able to show me where he won his V.C. . disappointment to both of us. He has told me the story, which is ɜrrific, and also the story of his escape from Singapore, which is a hapter out of Defoe at his best. Another disappointment is that the o-day tour of the Java and Sumatra fighting is off because the ndonesians shoot at planes, but we shall be able to fly to Batavia.

A cable from the Governor of Hong Kong, Sir Mark Young, indly invites us to stay with him and Lady Young when we are ı Hong Kong.

Iarch 11th. SINGAPORE

Off at 9 with Cumming and Thomson to drive round the island. t is almost exactly the same shape as the Isle of Wight, but larger, eing 24 miles by 16. We drove over to the N.E. point where the aps who came down from the east coast landed. It was a dull rive. There is nothing to look at except rubber plantations and ınumerable administrative offices. We drove through the Naval 'ard to the gate of the Causeway, and on to the jetty in Johore Bahru. The Sultan's big green new palace stands on a hill, but it vas only just finished building when the Japs arrived, and he has ıot lived in it yet. At the jetty, where Jap prisoners were loading a raft with shells, running them along a narrow bridge on rollers, ve crossed over the shell ship and boarded a launch to go to Pasir ,aba and see where the Japs landed from the N.W. By mistake the *Blackwater* put us off at Baja, four miles short of our destination. Ve landed and could find no sign of the motor road marked on the map. There was nothing except a couple of fisherman's hut coconuts, bananas, goslings, ducks, and a tortoiseshell cat with club tail. At last after a great deal of gesticulation we discovere that Pasir Laba was farther on.

So getting back into the dinghy we were towed behind th launch to the real Pasir Paba. They had been looking out for us i what is to be a rest camp. Once upon a time this was the barracks those who served the big guns placed on almost the only hill in th island above 200 feet. They were rather anxious about us becau they thought we were steering into the bombing area for practisin planes. As a matter of fact three planes did go over. We just manage to get ashore before the tide turned and walked up a very stee cliff to where the cars were waiting. Then we drove back to Drayc House by the Jurong Road and the village of Bukit Timah whe Cumming had a lot of fierce fighting. We passed the Ford Factor where the formal surrender was made.

I was too tired to tackle the diary when I came back abou 16 o'clock and after tea I sat talking with 'Bouncer' Cox. Majo Sandeman-Allen who is arranging the tour onward came for som necessary information about our passports. There is a great deal red tape in Japan manufactured by the Americans who in spite individualism turn out more of it than any other nation, excep Russia. But tape is not the word for the Russian variety. That is re hot barbed-wire.

March 12th. SINGAPORE

Cumming came round in the morning and told me some mor of his adventures. They really beat any I have heard. I worked a the diary till 12.30 and then went off with the General, Cummin and Peter Hoskins to a Rotary lunch. Sir Franklin Gimson, th Governor of Singapore, was there and I sat between him and M Peek the President, whose boy lost a leg on the death railway i Siam. Gimson has an agreeable sense of humour. There is a gaggle o Governors and Commissioners in this part of the world. Sir Edwar Gent of Malaya, Sir Franklin Gimson of Singapore, Malcol MacDonald, the Governor-General of our part of S.E. Asia, an Lord Killearn, the Special Commissioner. Generals, too, ar numerous, Major-General Galloway, G.O.C.-in-C. Malaya, Majo General Cox, G.O.C.-in-C. Singapore and Lt.-General Sir Ne Ritchie, G.O.C.-in-C. S.E. Asia. Also Major-General Chappe commanding 23rd Indian Division. One Governor and two Genera manage Burma.

I spoke for twenty minutes to the second and took the opportunit ɔ pay a tribute to the outstanding dignity with which the civil opulation here endured the horrors of internment by those missing nks, the Japs.

On our way down to the hotel where the Rotary Lunches are eld we passed the Y.M.C.A. building in which the Kempeitai did ıeir foul work. In eight cells at the back as many as twelve men and omen were shut up together with nothing but a latrine pail from hich the only water they could get had to be taken. The Bishop of ingapore was confined in these conditions in a vain attempt to ıake him admit having helped his fellow sufferers to escape. One rute got off at the trials because he was a native of Singapore and herefore as a British subject could not be tried by a military tribunal. Ie has been free now for a year, the Civil people being apparently nwilling to indict him for treason.

Aarch 13th. SINGAPORE

Cumming and I drove round the island in the morning. We ɔoked at Hill 95, Tengah airfield, and the reservoirs, the last vell arranged from the point of view of landscape. We went into he Ford Factory and saw the inner office room in which the surren- er was signed. The table is still there and on the floor where they at have been inscribed the names of the Jap officers. It was a uitably ugly room for the ugly business.

Then we drove down to the port, noted a good deal of shipping, nd visited Raffles Hotel for a beer. It is quieter than the ineffable hepheard's in Cairo, but has lost the authentic stamp of a great ıotel. Too much chromium plate and too many squiggles in the ecorations in an attempt to be modern. The result is hopelessly uburban.

Aarch 14th. SINGAPORE

The Brigadier and I were to have flown over the island this ıorning, but the rain was so heavy and the prospect so cloudy that t was decided to abandon the flight. About 16 o'clock I was rung ıp by Michael Wright, the Special Commissioner's Number Two, to ısk if I could come along and see him. Sandeman-Allen turned up nd we went down to Cathay Mansions where the Special Commis- ioner's staff was housed. Cathay Mansions is a sky-scraper which was lats once upon a time. When the Japs invested Singapore one of heir agents used it as an O.P. and wirelessed information to them ll the while. It now holds Radio Malaya, the Governor-General's ffice staff, and the Special Commissioner's staff. Wright was ordial but obviously worried about my going to Batavia. I thought

at first it was the Dutch who were objecting, but finally I suspecte
that it was our Consul-General there. I saw it would be useless to g
to Batavia in the teeth of such opposition and said I would give up th
project. Wright was evidently much relieved, I think if there had nc
been the possibility of flying to Jogjakarta I should have tried t
insist. The idea is that I shall go over in the plane chartered by th
Indonesians and return with the members of the Indonesian Cabin
who are going to India for the Asian Conference. If I do not go t
Indonesia there is a possibility of accompanying the Governo
General to Borneo, but that will depend on the length of his pr
posed visit. I came back to tea with Lt.-Colonel Crookshank an
another Mahratta officer who gave me a vivid picture of the fightin
round Sourabaya. The Mahratta Captain whose name I have stupidl
written illegibly in my notebook was with Brigadier Mallaby whe
he was killed*. At the time Tom Driberg asked in the House whethe
the story that Mallaby had been shot by his own men was true. Th
vicious story is very strongly resented by the battalions in Mallaby
Brigade and is so completely destitute of any foundation that I car
not understand how Tom Driberg let himself be fooled by wha
must have been a pretty poor specimen of an informant.

We went on to dine with Lt.-General Sir Neil Ritchie at th
Chinese restaurant in the Great World, which is a combination c
market and fun-fair. The Happy World and The New World ar
two others. We began with shark's fin soup, then prawns and ginge
then pork crackling, then crab omelette, then pork, then bird
nest soup, and wound up with vermicelli. Hot towels were hande
round from time to time, and a small bowl of soya and ginger stoo
in front of each plate. I could not manage the chopsticks, and th
waiter gave me a spoon and fork. C. managed her chopsticks wel

We are lucky indeed to be staying with such tolerant hosts. Th
sudden prospect of having guests for an extra eleven days is not on
that makes for equanimity. The best news is that Jim Thomson
to go with us to Japan. He has been a very great help throughou
the tour, and my inside is not really right yet.

March 15th. SINGAPORE

Thomson, C. and I visited the Botanical Garden this mornin
No doubt the Jap occupation set it back, but it was badly planne
from the start. The best part is a large dell with various palms an
some entertaining monkeys. I find the prospect of getting to kno
the palm family pretty formidable. There was a good specimen c
Milletia atropurpurea, the seeds like large bean-shaped chestnu

*I have since learned that he was Captain T. L. Laughland.

strewing the ground beneath. The *Gustavias* from Venezuela were attractive, and there was a remarkable hybrid between *Brownea coccinea* and *B. Ariza* called *B. Crawfordi* with a great orange-scarlet cockscomb head of bloom the size of a football. *Cassia multijuga* looked well, and there were a few white and pink water-lilies out, but as a whole the Garden was a sad disappointment.

In the evening we met Air Vice-Marshal Breakey and his wife. Mrs. Breakey gave me a glimpse of Lawrence when as T. E. Shaw he worked as an A.C.2 clerk under her husband. I have two letters from "T.E. Shaw" at that date. In one he says he has just picked up a signed copy of *Guy and Pauline* in a Southampton bookshop which he will send me if I want it but which he hopes I won't want because it is one of his favourite books. In the other he writes to say that he has just been telling the people of M.I.5 (whom he mentions by name) what duffers they were making of themselves by getting me prosecuted under the Official Secrets Act.

Later I went to tea with General Ritchie and had a good talk. He was generous in his criticisms of other people and blamed himself where he thought he had made mistakes. He was illuminating on the subject of our inferiority with tanks. Some of the new anti-tank six-pounders arrived only the night before the Knightsbridge business, and there was no time to give the gunners any practice with them. The Grants were useless against the German Mark 3 and Mark 4. He attributed the original muddle made with tanks to the failure of the R.A.C. after the old war to grasp that tanks were not just mobile steam-rollers armed with machine-guns. Our horse-power per ton was always too low. The Germans had 30 h.p. We had 16 h.p. Stepping up the armament was like overbodying a car.

In the course of our long talk I was impressed by General Ritchie's objective view.

March 17th. SINGAPORE

Colonel Jones who was Brigade Major of 45th Indian Brigade came round in the afternoon and told me a lot about the Muar River fighting. The Brigade was trained in India for desert fighting, but on the voyage from India when presumably outward bound for Suez the troopship turned to port and ultimately they were disembarked at Singapore.

Most of the troops had hardly seen a tree. Every British officer except two were killed or wounded. Jones himself was wounded and had the luck to be evacuated from hospital before the surrender.

The Brigade had no wireless, hardly any artillery, and in fact were flung into action under the command of General Gordon Bennett, badly equipped and completely untrained for the kind of fighting they had to face. He paid a tribute to the fight the Madras Sappers and Miners put up against overwhelming odds. The ferry boats on the Muar had been put out of action by the ferrymen, who all bolted. They got the Indian troops across on a private yacht, going very slowly because none of them had ever steered a boat before. Then some Naval ratings arrived and handled the boat in Navy style, the unfortunate end of which was that it was smashed up.

March 18th. SINGAPORE

Major-General D. Cowan, who commanded 17th Indian Division out of Burma and back into it again, spent the night in Singapore on his way back from Japan where he was commanding the British and Indian troops of occupation.

I went round to see him at General Ritchie's house at 9. It was an agreeable surprise to find somebody who smoked a cigar after breakfast. I am sure that historians of the far future will discern in the gasper a contributory cause to the break up of the British Empire.

'Punch' Cowan's personality was exactly what I thought it would be. A tight-lipped damned determined fellow. He told me he had laid on everything for me in Japan. All the same, it was a disappointment just to miss him there because there was a good deal I wanted to ask him about Burma. Moreover, I wasn't feeling too fit that morning. In fact, I spent most of the day lying down and reading third-rate thrillers. How dull detective stories can be!

Indonesia is off. The chartered plane has broken down.

March 19th. SINGAPORE

Complicated and fussy discussions about the journey on to Hong Kong and Japan. Luckily General Cox took a hand and insisted on the S.E.A.L.F. (South-East Asia Land Forces) people sending a telegram to know if our return to Delhi by April 11th could be guaranteed. I do not want to take any risk of upsetting our visit to Nepal.

I went to tea with Malcolm MacDonald, the Governor-General, and had a most agreeable tête-à-tête. His house belongs to the Sultan of Johore and is pleasantly situated beyond the Botanic

Garden, but it is not so cool as Draycot House where we are staying and the trees encroach upon the air. Mrs. MacDonald is still in Penang, and H.E. goes off to-morrow morning at 5.30 for a fortnight in the interior of Borneo. He enjoys sitting on the floor in the long houses talking to the old head-hunters, and every evening there is wonderful dancing. I did wish I could have gone with him. He spoke highly of Lord Killearn's work.

M.M. has great charm, is a demon for work, and everybody here pays a tribute to the skill with which he is carrying out his duties. He has admiration and affection for De Valera; he agreed about the remarkable way in which he has steered Eire through these years of war, and that his neutrality has been consistently benevolent.

M.M. asked my opinion of Nehru and I said I thought he had the same kind of moral integrity as De Valera. The question was whether he could achieve for India what De Valera had achieved for Ireland, the vast difference in size and population making his task a thousand times more difficult. There is a disquieting parallel between the way certain elements in the Conservative Party are playing with the notion of exploiting the Indian Muslims as they have exploited the Irish Protestants.*

I raised the question of the proposed resettlement of several thousand Cocos-Keeling islanders in Malaya, and M.M. said he had already had his doubts about the advisableness of this on account of their ignorance of money and measures. I pointed out the suitability of the Nicobar Islands for the experiment, and he said he would go into the question. I left about 17.45 after as good an hour's talk as I've had since the tour began.

March 20th. SINGAPORE

After lunch we went to hear a bit of one of the war crimes trials in the Victoria Hall. It was a queer scene. There was a concert platform, backed by an organ at the north end of the hall, with a battered-looking grand piano on it. At a table in front of the platform are seated the five members of the military court under the

* *September 8th. Simla.* The Muslims here are now blaming the Labour Government for the state of affairs in Eastern Punjab. A Kashmiri coolie was killed outside our gate just before lunch and as I write this another coolie has been brought in with his hand almost cut off. This is the work of Sikh refugees from Western Punjab who have themselves escaped from death there. These are horrors and much worse horrors are going on, but they should not be exploited in the interest of party politics.

presidency of Lt.-Colonel Forsythe. Below them on the floor sits the interpreter, a Japanese with a foghorn American accent. To the left on a sort of village-inn settle with a high back sit the seven accused. They are all dressed in breeches, high leggings, and Kate Greenaway short brown tunics, the white collars worn outside adding to the Kate Greenaway effect. A number on a square of cardboard hangs round each neck. At a raised table opposite the table of the Court sit the defending Counsel—one of them an English officer, Captain Wait, with an advisory brief for the Defence —and on the left is a female stenographer wearing very glassy glasses. Beyond them half the hall is filled with the public. We sit at right angles to the platform behind the witness box. The walls of the hall are hung with large portraits in oils of the civic and military fathers of Singapore, at least one Chinese among them. One of the former Governors in uniform sits against the background of a blue and white April sky at home. Fifteen fans whiz round above. The big south doors are wide open.

As we came in Lt.-General Kashimura Takuma, the commander of the Imperial Guards Division, was answering his last question and on leaving the box was conducted back to the village-inn settle by two kilted Seaforths. The 1st Seaforths have provided the military guards for the proceedings. Takuma's place is taken by another Lt.-General whose name I did not catch. He salutes the Court and stands in the box at attention. The Japanese Counsel for the Defence reads the questions from a sheet of paper, and these are translated into English by the interpreter. The seven men are accused of the massacre of at least 25,000 Chinese after the surrender. It is the usual tale of Jap savagery, and I cannot help thinking it is a mistake to allow a British officer to play any part in defending them. He is bound to plead that the massacre was perpetrated under military necessity, for that is the defence, and surely military necessity is not a plea that any British officer should make for an indiscriminate massacre. It allows the Japs to suppose that some Britons consider their behaviour excusable. They admit the massacre, and that being so should all be hanged without further argument. All this legal pomp and circumstance is wasted on them. The Jap defending counsel congratulated the Chinese defending counsel on his presence as a sign of the fundamental understanding between the two Oriental races. I find it all a nauseating prostitution of fundamental morality to conventional justice.

Japanese spoken thus in formal question and answer, with the microphone helping, sounds like nasal Russian. We remained till the clock struck three when the Court rose for a breather and a cigarette and we left the proceedings. It is fantastic to think that these sub-human creatures were once our allies.

Kingfishers are screaming in the garden as I write this.

Many years ago Mr. A., a wealthy Singapore Chinese, had to go abroad on business and left his friend Mr. B. with power of attorney for his affairs while he was away. When he returned he read with some surprise of his renown as a public benefactor and on enquiry found that Mr. B. had presented various charities with large sums in his name. In due course Mr. B. had to go abroad on business and left his affairs in the hands of Mr. A. When Mr. B. returned to Singapore he was surprised to find his Number One (head servant) calling down blessings upon his head, and on enquiry he found that Mr. A. had endowed him with enough money to send his son to the University and live himself in modest comfort for the remainder of his life.

To-day the boy educated by Mr. A.'s vicarious benevolence acting for Mr. B. is one of the wealthiest of Singapore's Chinese citizens, and we dined with him to-night. We ate a stew of shark's fin, the crackling of roast sucking pig, roast chicken, prawn and ham jelly, a turtle stew, special frog soup (the Chinese call the frog the paddy chicken), a stew of edible bird's nest, steamed fish, crab dumpling, mixed soup and prune pudding. Before this feast began we were served with a special hors d'oeuvre called Makan Kechil. We rose at 23.30. There were longish intervals between the courses and we were given as much champagne as we could drink. The chief criticism I have to make of Chinese food is the similarity between every dish. So much exotic variety does not produce the effect it should.

March 21st. SINGAPORE TO BATU PAHAT

When Indonesia fell through I telegraphed to ask Cunyngham-Brown at Batu Pahat if the invitation to spend a week-end with him held good. It did. C. and I left Draycot House at 10 and arrived at the Residency in good time for lunch. The Deputy Resident Commissioner and his delightful old mother made us welcome.

We drove that afternoon to Parit Salong where the bridge is still mined. The country was agreeably diversified and we saw and followed the track which the Japs took when as usual they landed, as they regularly did, above our forces on the west coast. The road was not marked in our maps, but it is good enough for a sizable car. A terrific shower caught us when we were crossing by ferry on a narrow upper reach of the Batu Pahat river. The stream was running strongly and a bridge which the Japs built had been condemned as unsafe. Bicyclists and pedestrians cross at their own risk. Seeing that half the piles are waving about in the stream, the warning is not unreasonable.

The fighting was grim all round here, and the Japs knew the country much better than we did. They owned several rubber estates in the near neighbourhood, and a large iron mine which is now closed down.

March 22nd. BATU PAHAT

Cunyngham-Brown, C. and myself set out for Malacca about 10. The road was made more interesting by C.B.'s ability to tell us the why and wherefore of everything. We were lucky at both the big ferries over the Batu Pahat and Muar, and were not long delayed. At one point we got out of the car to see a trained monkey climb a coconut tree and throw down the right coconuts. He was in rather a bad temper because he had already done the regulation 500-feet of climbing that morning, and he thought that was quite enough. He carried the end of the rope over his arm, as once upon a time when dancing a woman carried her train, so that it did not drag too much on his collar. When he had twisted off and thrown down the three coconuts pointed out to him he was told to jump to the next tree, but this he declined to do and grumpily descended. These trained monkeys work for many years and are paid by being given a percentage of the coconuts they gather in the day's work to eat. The monkey we saw was nearly twenty years old and was due to retire shortly. They are fed if they wish to remain around the plantation, but most of them go back to the jungle.

While we were watching the monkey a flying lizard flew a full ten yards from one coconut trunk to another whence we tried to make him fly again but without success. These lizards are engaging creatures with ruffs round their necks.

We reached Malacca at lunch time and went to the same rest house as when we passed through southward some days ago. We had a good lunch under the eyes of Attlee and Bevin gazing at us from large framed photographs on the wall. After lunch we went to the shop of T. K. Kutty Brothers, 37 Jonker Street, full of a collection of extraordinary junk, much of it English mid-Victorian and late Victorian stuff. I bought a good deal of porcelain, four Chinese chairs, five picture frames, a Malay sewing-box, a magenta processional umbrella, an ancient Chinese lantern, six black lacquered planks with gilded lettering from a Chinese temple and two green ones, a lacquered red wooden bowl, an opium table and a Malay bull's head carved of wood with real horns after bargaining that lasted from 14 o'clock to 17.30. C. evoked such admiration from the proprietors by her ruthless knocking down of the prices asked that she was presented with a silver Siamese ring. There were some lovely red lacquer Chinese beds, but being still uncertain about the problem of transport I regretfully did not buy any. C.B. bought a very large 18th century Dutch armoire with a kind of bureau inset for 80 dollars (£5)—a great bargain.

On the way back we got out of the car to look at a rubber tree being tapped. C.B. says the big planters are trying to knock out these 2-acre plantations owned by Malays because they plant the trees much closer and tap them much more severely, producing proportionately at least twice as much rubber as the elaborately cultivated and selected trees in the plantations.

We had hoped we might find one durian or mangosteen, but we were unsuccessful. Somebody described the taste of durian as strawberries and paraffin, another as rancid butter. Nobody seemed able to think of anything to express the smell. I wish I could taste one.* The Malays think our liking for pineapple odd. None of them will eat it.

We had a hold-up at the Batu Pahat ferry and did not get home till nearly 21 hours after a most delightful day.

March 23rd. BATU PAHAT

C. stayed at home with Mrs. Cunyngham-Brown. C.B. and myself went to Muar to look at the battle country. Tengku Hassan ben Omar, a descendant of the last Sultan of Malacca and now in charge of the Land Registry, arranged for people who had had direct experience of the Japanese advance to accompany us. We drove to Bakri and other villages. At the last one, the name of which I can't remember, we met a headman aged seventy-five, who was a very lively specimen of old age for the tropics. Yussip invited us into his house to drink a favourite mineral water called orange crush made extensively in Singapore. I should doubt if it contained as much as one orange to the ton.

We took off our shoes, which is the custom on entering a Malay house, although Yussip begged us to keep them on as an Italian host in the south will beg a visitor to keep his hat on in the *salone*. C.B. said that compliance with the custom was always much appreciated.

* This wish was gratified in the Seychelles in March 1948. Dr. Selwyn-Clarke the Governor sent me one after a party at Government House, and the smell of it at the bottom of the stairs up to my room waked me from deep sleep. I found the flavour delicious—a cross between apricots, Irish stew with lots of onions, and cream cheese. The smell dies down when the fruit is cut open.

Inside, I was astonished to see a number of men, mostly elderly, with notebooks in front of them squatting all round a large room with their backs to the walls. In the middle was the teacher, seated in a wicker chair at a small circular table, for this was a sort of Sunday-school class for grown-ups from twenty-five to sixty. The exposition of the Koran was held up for a bit while Yussip, C.B., the teacher, and myself drank orange crush.

On the other side of the road a Chinese school was having a music lesson to the accompaniment of a gramophone; and the contrast between the young voices and these elderly men taking notes on the Koran was piquant. These classes are held about once a week. The desire for education in Malaya is impressive. The Chinese voluntarily tax their own trade to support their schools, which appear to be excellently run. The Malay schools are equally well supported. The sight of the girls on their way to and from school in single file, each one carrying her gay paper unbrella, is quite entrancing.

C.B. addressed the elderly scholars and told them I had written over sixty books, which evidently made a profound impression. After he had finished, our old host asked him where Cunyngham-Brown was nowadays, and on hearing that C.B. was himself almost embraced him. He pleaded his failing eyesight as an excuse for not having recognized him. C.B. has a splendid way with the Malays, young and old. They obviously all love him. He worked on the Sumatra railway of which bad business few have heard. It was nothing like such a large undertaking as the railway from Siam to Burma, but the sufferings of those compelled to work on it were severe enough. Toward the end the Jap guards used to come in every morning and indicate by signs that the prisoners would be put to death that day. The latter expected to be massacred at any moment. That was when the invasion of Malaya was threatened, and there is no doubt that every prisoner would have been put to death when the invasion started. However, the atom bomb changed the whole situation, and any doubts I had about the rightness of dropping the bomb have vanished since my visit to Malaya.

March 24th. BATU PAHAT TO SINGAPORE

We left the Residency at 9, most unwilling to part with our kind host and hostess. As I've said before, I can't keep pace in words with the hospitality we've enjoyed during this tour. We reached Johore Bahru at 11.45 punctually, and went on from the Government Offices, a vast and expansive piece of architecture, to the house of Mr. J. Corry, the Resident Commissioner. Corry told me the story of Subedar-Major Falak Shere, a Punjabi Mussulman, and 150 of the Singapore-Hong Kong heavy battery of the R.I.A. He would not listen to the Japs when they tried to persuade him to join the I.N.A. and he was tortured every day for many days. Every one of his men held out as steadfastly. Finally Subhas Chandra Bose arrived and addressed them all, but his oratory failed. The Commander-in-Chief of the I.N.A. was no more successful as a recruiting officer than the Japs. What is more they laughed at him and after he went away the Japs, impressed by the courage of Subedar-Major Falak Shere, left him alone. This happened at the oilfields in Sumatra where Corry was working as a prisoner.

We went along soon after midday to see the Sultan's Palace, his furniture, his gold plate, his jewelled swords and his crown. The father of the present Sultan was much liked by Queen Victoria, who presented him with the ugliest silver tray imaginable when he left England after a two years' visit in 1886. It is a really ghastly tray with scenes of English rural life engraved upon it. They did very odd things with silver in the early 'eighties. My godfather gave me a large Queen Anne mug on which he had employed some craftsman to emboss the meeting between Robinson Crusoe and Man Friday.

I have seldom seen so many ugly pieces of furniture gathered together in a few large rooms as in the Palace at Johore. Most of the stuff must have been brought back from England by the late Sultan. Queen Victoria persuaded him to dress up in a kilt at Balmoral, and the framed photograph of him thus attired suggests that John Brown lent him his sporran, which is almost as big as a billy goat.

We drove on to Singapore about 15 o'clock and found that Bridadier Cumming had got a plane to Calcutta. He is going back to wind up as Sub-Area Commander at Dehra Dun. Then he leaves for England and is looking forward to having his V.C. pinned on by the King.

We had a quiet evening with the dauntlessly hospitable Coxes, at the end of which Thomson inoculated us for cholera and typhus.

March 25th. SINGAPORE

A very fussy morning solving various problems—the luggage for the freight plane to Calcutta, a laissez-passer for Gulaba, vaccination and a cholera injection, for Gulaba, seats in the flying-boat, on which we find there is room for Thomson and Gulaba who otherwise would have had to fly in the uncomfortable schedule Dakota coming down at Saigon in the evening instead of Bangkok.

At 19 o'clock the Coxes, Thomson, Peter Hoskins, C. and myse went off to the Airport Hotel where one can have oysters, sent ove from Australia by plane. We drank a capital non-vintage Bolling and ate nine dozen oysters between us. They are on the small side bu of really good flavour—not unlike Helford River oysters with touch of the Marenne. This was my party. Then we went back t Draycot House and our host and hostess opened more bottles c champagne. We wound up with records on a portable H.M.V. asked why there was only a bit of an automatic recording of Haydn' Clock Symphony and found that the Singapore habit is only to bu a bit of a symphony or any other long composition. If a music-love wants a complete work he can seldom get it.

The General has to go into hospital at the end of the week becaus his prickly heat has now become a dermatitis. He's in the same kin of purgatory that I was in last year, and I salute his good tempe He and his wife have been wonderful to us.

March 26th. SINGAPORE TO BANGKOK

Sandeman-Allen arrived with the transport at 8.30 and soo afterwards we were on our way to the airport. There was a brie crisis about overweight, but it passed and by 10.30 we were in th Sunderland, churning up the water of the harbour to take off. Th General and Peter Hoskins came down to the launch to say fare well. The protracted stay at Singapore has been an irritating hold up of the programme, but fortunately we were guests in a mos comfortable house and were never allowed to feel for a moment tha we were overstaying our welcome. Nevertheless, it is maddening that the people responsible for our not getting to Java could no have been frank from the start instead of making us hurry down through Malaya, where we missed a lot, and not saying a word till a day or two before we were ready to go.

I am writing this in the air. It is now 15 o'clock and we are nearing Bangkok. Apart from the Sunderland's kicking about like a bronco in great billows of cumulus high above a blue sea it has been an uneventful flight so far. I saw a phenomenon I had not seen before— a rainbow on the sea. Presumably this could only happen near the equator. I saw another one later.

We came down in the grey-green river about 15.30 and had tea while we were waiting for the night luggage to come ashore. A ginger Siamese cat, not of the blood royal, miaowed in authentic Siamese and I gave her milk. At home a ginger female is rare. Her light green eyes were set Siamese fashion, her ears were large and her tail was kinked at the end. After she was fed she crouched beside y chair in typical Siamese attitude. I made friends at the hotel ith a dark grey one. I have nowhere read that the common cats f Siam display all the characteristics of the semi-albino royalties. should much like to introduce them to England, and I have little oubt we can assign the origin of the Manx cat to these Malay or iamese common cats. The cross between a Siamese and Persian at often results in taillessness, even when the Siamese sire or queen as a long unkinked tail. Moreover, this taillessness will persist rough several generations. Probably some sailor brought the cats ack with him from an Eastern voyage.

The drive from the Klong Toi jetty to the Ratanakosindr Hotel ok about twenty minutes, most of it over a wide concrete road ast canal after canal. About three hundred noble geese—both hite and grey—were grazing in the paddy fields.

The hotel is ultra modern in design; but, although the bedrooms re enormous, there are no bathrooms and only a minute basin and hower. Moreover, as there is no running water the shower is useless. tub with a pannikin beside it provides the water. My bedroom vas furnished with two immense beds and a quantity of extremely gly furniture in the most degraded style. As might be expected he mosquitoes were numerous.

Thomson secured a jeep and we drove to the Temple of the Reclining Buddha. Door after door all round the high-walled enlosure was shut and we began to fear that we were too late (it vas 17.30 by now) when we found what must have been about the enth wooden door open. We entered and found ourselves in wonderand. The numerous slim pagodas of graceful design are covered vith porcelain mosaic and the colouring in pastel shades is exquisite. Great stone statues of men with fierce handlebar moustaches and vhat look like top hats guard each arched gateway within. These ateways are encrusted with porcelain depicting various scenes in igh relief—cocks fighting, dragons, warriors, grotesque birds, and osy upon posy of bright porcelain flowers. The shrines were all losed with doors of black and gold lacquer.

The big Temple of the Reclining Buddha was shut. I have no kill in describing architecture, but the design of the exterior seems ustere in contrast with the colour all round. The walls are white vith dark marble rectangles in relief like windows. The roof is teep, nine-tenths of it cinnabar-red tiles with the lowest line of lack tiles. The roofs of other buildings have green and yellow and rey tiles in patterns of oblongs and squares, and at every gable oint a kind of horn protrudes. One could spend hours wandering bout the courts of this enchanted enclosure in which rock gardens

with small shrubs are peopled with the strangest human beings o
occupied by dragons and mythical quadrupeds. Of one of these roc
gardens a golden cock was the only occupant, he and a solitar
baluster of green porcelain. I wish Edith Sitwell would visit Bangko
and write a poem about the Temple of the Reclining Buddha. Onl
she with her lute of amber could melt words to enshrine this wonder
land in literature.

The peace of the place was profound; although there were a lo
of dogs all over it, none of them barked. Now and then the soun
of children's laughter rippled across the evening air, for there ar
schools here as well as dormitories for the monks who in Siam wea
robes of vivid chrome yellow not the more sober orange of th
hpoongyis of Burma. There was a moment of supreme beauty whe
the setting sun lighted the gold and copper so that lamps seemed t
be burning in the decorated gable tops and the gilded tiles on on
of the porches of the shrines blazed.

Farther along we found in the enclosing wall, another door ope
in front of what looked like a small temple, with a placard outsid
to say that donations were welcome. I presented five Malay dollar
equal to twenty-five Siamese ticals to an ancient monk and expresse
a desire to see inside the temple. When the door was opened a blac
and white cat sprang out with loud indignant Siamese miaows t
demand a reason for her incarceration in what seemed to be a cros
between a library and a large box-room presided over by a smal
gilded Buddha. I suppose she had been shut in to deal with the rats
Incidentally I did not notice a single Buddha outside, which is th
reverse of the arrangement of these holy places in Burma wher
Buddhas swarm in the open air.

Dusk was now deepening fast, and it would have been useless t
take advantage of the monk's offer to unlock the Temple of th
Reclining Buddha, for the interior would have been dark. O
signing the book we found that a donation of twenty-five tical
entitled the giver to a souvenir, and this proved to be a silver rin
on which was engraved the Reclining Buddha. The monk blesse
us in English before we said farewell, asking for us a happy life
The previous visitors in the book were six rubber-necks from Utah
How on earth or by air do six tourists from Salt Lake City reac
Bangkok in these days?

After we left the enclosure we drove through the shopping streets
which were much like shopping streets anywhere else, full of nois
and neon lights. We were too late for the famous Temple of th
Jade Buddha. It was exasperating not to have more time.

March 27th. BANGKOK TO HONG KONG

The cicadas were loud in the trees outside the hotel when I woke. In the entrance lounge we were given coffee or tea, and when we left for the airport at 5.15 the dark sky was stained with the dull rose of dawn. People were hurrying along through the morning twilight. Already the market women were displaying their wares on the side-walk. Mist was rising from the muddy canals. Birds were in full chorus, and the trams were crowded. At the airport we had more tea or coffee, and finally we embarked on the good speedbird *Hamilton* about 6.15, the sky now ablaze with rosy gold.

I have been writing up my diary during a comfortable flight. We are due to reach Hong Kong at 14 o'clock. I had my first view of the Pacific Ocean where it was rippling along the beaches of the large island of Hainan. Of course, it is technically the China Sea not the Pacific Ocean; I suppose one cannot call the Irish Sea the Atlantic. All the same, this glittering blue sea was the end of thousands of miles of that mighty ocean, and I saw no reason not to share the emotions of stout Cortez.

Hainan looks a good kind of a place to explore. A range of mountains up to 5,000-ft. runs down the middle of it. The grassy undulations are stained here and there with the bare crimson earth. The beds of the rivers are tawny sand and the level ground is everywhere cultivated. We flew over an airfield, but I am told that the Chinese are all against letting anybody land on Hainan.

I had managed to write as far as this before the speedbird *Hamilton* was over the waters of Hong Kong. Hong Kong means "fragrant waters".

In one of my books I have claimed to recognize immediately an island of the first water as diamond merchants recognize a diamond. Hong Kong is in that class. Singapore in retrospect seems third-rate. This is a Crown Colony of which the Crown can indeed be proud. The peculiar charm of Hong Kong is the result of turning a wilderness of hills surrounded by water into a small paradise by planting trees and cutting roads. It is a pity that so many of the houses built up the hillsides with exquisite views that rival the marine landscapes of Greece and Italy have been built without even a semblance of design—mere boxes with windows.

We landed from a launch at Queen's Pier and drove along to Government House. Sir Mark Young the Governor was presiding over the Legislative Council, and Lady Young welcomed us. Old Government House which had already been condemned was so badly shaken by the bombardment that the Japanese pulled it down and built a new one with a ridiculous concrete tower in the Jap style. I enjoyed a bath in a large rectangular Jap bath into which one climb by marble steps, the bath itself lined with teak.

Thomson and I went along with Captain J. A. Phillimore of Public Relations to G.H.Q. where we had a talk with Lt.-Colon M. L. Reynolds of the Bedfordshire and Hertfordshire Regiment. saw at once that we were going to get full value out of our vis to Hong Kong. The G.O.C., Major-General G. W. E. Erskin who commanded the Desert Rats, is geniality incarnate, and th plans for me to make the most of my visit could not have bee bettered.

Sir Henry Blackall, the Chief Justice, and Lady Blackall came t tea at Government House. She is a Cypriote Greek with the mingle elegance and humour that give Greek women their peculiar cache After tea I walked round the garden with Lady Young. Nobody ca compete with Chinese gardeners in growing flowers for pots. Th snapdragons in pots were the best for purity of colour and fo texture and shape of flower I have ever seen. The Japs made a smal pool beside a big *Magnolia grandiflora*, but without lilies or goldfis it did not have much point in the landscape. One of the depressin results of the barbarians' occupation has been the cutting down o almost all the trees on the island, and when the trees ran out th Chinese looted all the houses for firewood during the interregnum before British troops arrived to take over the island. I noticed on tree with white lily-like flowers on the bare branches which I neve saw before. It was definitely not a magnoliacious tree.

March 28th. HONG KONG

This was a day of concentrated listening. Phillimore first took me up the Peak to get a bird's-eye-view of the island. After that we wen down to the Secretariat where D. M. MacDougall the Colonia Secretary, a Perthshire man, gave me his account of the disaste and answered many questions. He struck me as extremely able an I heard golden opinions of him everywhere in the Island.

From MacDougall's office we went on to see Dr. Selwyn-Clarke who is acting as Honorary Director of Medical Services. He is a outstanding personality. I have rarely been as deeply impressed by the moral force of an individual. He is a barrister as well as a docto and was sentenced by the Japs to rigorous confinement for many months in prison after much torture and brutality. He is permanently lame from Jap kicking. His courage and humanity during the ordeal were continuous. Now he is repaying evil with good and tries al the time to help the Jap prisoners here. I am told that at Easter he will present each of them with a toothbrush at his own expense.

Ie is inspired with a truly Christian faith in the power of good to vercome evil, and he practises what he preaches.*

From Selwyn-Clarke's office we went on to visit Mr. Ruttonjee, ıe owner of the Kowloon brewery, a wealthy and respected Parsee 'ho survived the Jap occupation. His son Mr. D. Ruttonjee was ıken off one night, given the water torture, and badly beaten. Ie told me he could never forget the consolation of Selwyn-Clarke's oice, when he was lying covered with blood on the floor of his cell, idding him to take courage and to realise the ability of the human pirit to endure so much.

Lunch was at Government House and at 14.15 we went down) the G.O.C.'s office to see a relief model of Hong Kong, Kowloon nd the New Territories on the mainland. This was used by the Japs or their attack, and it showed accurately the whole of our defences oth on the Island and in the New Territories. With the help of his ap model, which was captured by us in 1945, Lt.-Colonel Reynolds ave me a lucid demonstration of what happened from December th to December 25th, 1941, so that I might benefit fully from my isit to the New Territories planned for next day. He had taken a reat deal of trouble to prepare his brief, and I record here my ratitude.

From the G.O.C.'s office we went on to visit Lt.-Colonel J. R. Aitchell, who told me about the fighting of the Hong Kong Volun-eer Defence Force which he commanded. Mitchell is President of Rotary here and I promised to talk at the farewell lunch to H.E. he Governor, on Tuesday next.

Finally, just after 17 o'clock, we went to tea at his office with Mr. A. K. Lo, the head of the leading firm of lawyers in Hong Kong. Besides M. K. Lo himself there was Mrs. Lo, Mrs. Stanton, an American resident of long standing, M. N. Lo, his younger brother, who told me he had read *Sinister Street* when he was a 17-year-old tudent at London University in 1913, and Mr. Kan. For the first ime in years I tasted real éclairs, and the China tea was delicious. Mrs. Lo invited us to dinner. It was a delightful tea-party.

We dined that night with the G.O.C. at Flagstaff House. I talked ather a lot under the genial encouragement of our host. He is narried to a daughter of Evelyn de la Rue who was a third year man at Magdalen when I went up. To be the contemporary of a Major-General's father-in-law is a fresh reminder of age. I thought when could brag of remembering an Archbishop of Canterbury as a fat

* I had the pleasure of meeting him often a year later as Governor of the Seychelles and of being beaten by him in a couple of tough games of croquet.

boy in jackets that I was getting on; but this tour has been a lesso
The only high-up I have met who was older than myself was S
Hubert Huddlestone in Khartum. Even the Viceroy is four mont
younger than I am.

March 29*th*. *HONG KONG*

At 9.30 Thomson, Phillimore, C. and myself accompanied b
D. R. Holmes and Lt.-Colonel Ride, now Professor of Physiolog
at the Hong Kong University, set out for the New Territories. Hon
Kong was ceded by China in January 1841, and in 1860 the poi
of the Kowloon peninsula on the mainland was added to th
territory of Hong Kong. Finally in 1898 by an agreement with th
Chinese Government a 99-year lease was acquired of some 20
square miles beyond Kowloon, and this is called the New Terri
tories. D. R. Holmes is the Assistant Colonial Secretary and was i
Z Force operating behind the Japs with Chinese guerillas. He wo
an M.C. for blowing up a park of Jap munition lorries on the nigh
of the surrender. Ride was through the whole business as a voluntee
and afterwards with the B.A.A.G. (British and Allied Aid Group
in China. This helped many prisoners to escape.

The day was perfect—blue sky and a S.E. wind that turned th
air to champagne. We drove through Kowloon until we reache
the market gardens. What cultivation! Everything grown as we
as it could be grown and looking as neat and exact as embroider
I noticed one lovely square of carnations as rich as old velvet. The
we climbed rapidly up the road cut out of the hillside as far a
Grasscutters Pass where we had a magnificent view of the stra
between Hong Kong and the mainland crowded with shippin
From here, too, there was a good view of the fifteen-mile stretc
of defended hills known as the Gindrinkers Line between Gin
drinkers Bay westward and the sea on the other side.

We got out of the car and walked up the grassy slope. There we
white violets faintly tinged with palest blue and very sweet, a tin
Cambridge blue Gentian, a deep lilac linaria, and a particularl
spruce-looking small hawkweed. A grey-green fern, the youn
fronds red as they first uncrumpled, was in every cranny on the shad
side. The soil was an ochreous decomposed granite. Northward th
hills, nowhere higher than 3,000-ft., rolled away in vast green billow
of grass above the indented coast. Beyond the pale azure of the se
the hills of China were melting into the pale azure of the sky.
was loath to leave this spot, knowing that never again should
stand here and survey that vast serene view of land and sea, th
March wind trumpeting in my ears and the air tasting of wine

Hoc erat in votis. This was how in the mind's prayers, which are dreams, I would have wished to gaze at China. And of Car Nicobar, too, I could have said *hoc erat in votis.* This is what I prayed or dreamed that a tropic isle might be.

We turned to descend the flowery slope and get back into the car to drive down toward the Devil's Peak. On the way we passed an immense municipal cemetery where the dead lie for seven years in terrace upon terrace all round several small rounded hills. After that the remains are exhumed and removed to be burnt and preserved in urns at home. We could see people at work here and there, digging up some grave the lease of whose owner's bones had expired. The wealthier Chinese buy plots of ground for their burial and anywhere on the slopes, sometimes miles away in the country, you may see one of the horseshoe tombs like those I described at Malacca.

After studying the lie of the land for the account to be written of those tragic days from December 8th to December 25th, 1941, we drove back through Kowloon. The wire of the two prison camps (Indian and British) on either side of Argyle Street was still in place. The tawdry posters of American films bedizened the walls. A gaunt building calling itself the Pentecostal Tabernacle stood among blocks of modern flats, all windows and bulges and balconies. Ride told me that one evening he had been sent for from the prison camp to watch a Jap officer eating his dinner in one of those flats. Presumably the wretched little creature thought that this was a demonstration of the might of the Nippon Empire.

Paint and enamel seem in good supply here. We met one jeep glossy with vermilion, another luculent with cobalt blue.

Finally we reached the reservoir round which the Japs had planted orange-red azaleas dug up from the hills farther to the north. The great dam 280 feet high was being patched here and there. From an angle in the road some steps lead up the steep hillside and we scrambled and wound our way round a narrow zigzag of path to the saddle into which was built the Shing Mun Redoubt on the defence of which the Gindrinkers Line depended; on the night of December 9th a company of the 2nd Royal Scots lost it to the Japs, and that was the end of the Gindrinkers Line.

We entered the Redoubt through a doorway called Oxford Street and wandered on through a concrete tunnel in the hillside lighted by large square ventilators into which the Japs dropped grenades. I have seen few such examples of wasted effort as the Shing Mun Redoubt. It is typical of the Maginot Line mentality of 1937 when it was constructed. Another entrance was called Regent Street, another Shaftesbury Avenue, with an arrow pointing to the Strand

Palace Hotel. There was little resistance; the garrison was chased around like rabbits in a burrow by active ferrets.

After a picnic lunch, where we were joined by Mr. J. Barrow the District Officer, Ride left us, and we drove on round the south-west side of the New Territories to the ancient walled village of Kam Tin. It lies in a wide and fertile plain girdled by hills, another plain of Imphal on a smaller scale. I was fascinated by the orange-red Cantonese hats and the hakka hats worn by the women with a shallow black veil round the rim and a hole in the middle of the crown. Barrow said we might see a wedding party with everybody dressed in peacock-blue silk, but we were not so lucky.

We went through the chain-iron gates between the grey brick walls of the village and walked along the fly-thick central alley from which at right angles ran other alleys hardly four feet across, all swarming with pigs, fowls, and children. The houses are built of grey brick, and, though its name means the village of happiness, I can't say I should like to live in Kam Tin.

When our troops came in to take possession of the New Territories after the lease, the inhabitants resisted the intruders, who suffered two casualties, both from infuriated water-buffaloes not rifles. As a punishment Sir Henry Blake, the Governor of Hong Kong at that date, removed the gates of the village and took them home with him to Ireland. This was a great grief to the inhabitants because the gates had been there since the thirteenth century. At last Sir Cecil Clementi rescued them from Ireland and gave them back to the village when he was Governor. Barrow spoke with the warmest admiration of Cecil Clementi whose Private Secretary he had been. I remember him, a dark handsome boy, at St. Paul's in the summer term of 1894 when he was a prospective Demy of Magdalen. Another reminder of age. I find it a little sobering to be able to say I was at school with a man who is now 72. His younger brother Lockhart was a great friend of mine, but I have not heard of him for years. Colonel Clementi the father, who was Judge Advocate General, was the perfect Indian officer of the old school. I can see him now walking along Mornington Avenue, an awesome figure to the small boys of Colet Court.

I regretted I could not enjoy more of Barrow's company, for he gave me a great deal of information on Chinese matters. He lived at one time with Stella Benson and her husband, who was in the Customs out here. She must have had a most attractive personality. I asked him what he thought of *Pekin Picnic* by Ann Bridge, and he said the book had been spoilt for him by the author's making four of her characters sing Orlando Gibbons' *Silver Swan* when, as anybody with even the most superficial knowledge of madrigals knew, it was written for five voices. Thus easily may the novelist destroy reality for one reader by a single small inaccuracy.

As we emerged from the squalor of Kam Tin, the voices of the children begging for pengoes were sounding in our ears like the cheeping of sparrows, and a great black butterfly sheened with dark green was sipping honey from the lantana flowers beside the road.

Presently we passed a small concrete tower with a few narrow windows. This is where the local miser, the descendant of a Sung princess of long ago, shuts himself up every night against thieves. He is said to be a grasping and merciless landlord.

We reached the quay at Kowloon about 16.30 and were back in Government House in time for tea after a fascinating day. All agreed we had been lucky to have such sparkling weather at this time of year.

March 30th. HONG KONG

C. came with me to High Mass at the Cathedral at 8. Between the Blessing of the Palms and the Reading of the Passion it was a long service and we were back at Government House only just in time for the drive round the island. The Cathedral which has been knocked about a bit is very ugly, with some ghastly windows filled with panes of coloured glass and an excess of debased Gothic. There was a large congregation of Chinese and Portuguese whose devotion made one forget the dreadful architecture.

We left Government House at 9.45 and drove first to the Wong Nei Chong Gap by the capture of which the Japs cut the defending forces in two and made surrender only a matter of time. Lt.-Colonel J. A. Bailey, a former Winnipeg Grenadier, who had been through the whole melancholy business was with us. We visited Brigade H.Q. More concrete and excavation. Here Brigadier J. C. Lawson who commanded the Canadians was killed and buried. The cross at the head of the grave was taken by the Chinese for firewood during the interregnum, but the spot was identified and the remains were buried in the cemetery at Stanley.

That cemetery, which we drove on to visit next, must hold more various memorials of human misery in a small space than any similar plot of earth in the whole world. Stanley, which is a peninsula on the S.E. side of the island, housed the original garrison when Hong Kong was ceded after the China War of 1840. During the recent war it was the internment camp of the civilian population and close by stands the prison, the wire fence round which is just below the cemetery. This lies on a slope overlooking blue waters and precipitous green coasts that reminded me of views along the Salernian Gulf and in various Aegean islands.

The oldest graves have solid tombstones with large headstones. These commemorate men of the 98th Regiment who were killed in an affray with pirates in 1844. There are some large gravestones from 1860 of the victims of plague, and then from 1864 there are about a dozen high large tombs with rounded tops. These cover the dust of children who died from the water of a well poisoned by the Chinese. The well may still be seen beside the road, sealed now with a slab of stone. The largest of these large tombs was raised as "The Last Tribute of Affection" to an infant of 10 months.

And now the little cemetery is thronged with the white wooden crosses that mark the victims of the last war. Here are graves of the internees, some in their seventies, who were too old or weak to hold out against the Jap treatment. Here is the grave of Captain Ansari of the Rajputs who endured fearful tortures rather than give away the names of the Chinese in the B.A.A.G. associated with him. With him are buried twenty of those he tried to save by his own death. Captain Ansari was awarded the George Cross posthumously. Before he was taken prisoner he had been recommended for the Victoria Cross for valour in the field. Here lie others tortured to death by the Japs. Here lie the remains of about a dozen unfortunate internees killed by an American air raid in January 1945. Here lie the remains of the nurses raped and murdered at St. Stephen's hospital on December 25th, 1941 together with the remains of their murdered patients. I went afterwards to visit St. Stephen's School—it was only a temporary hospital—and looked at the hall into which the Japs threw grenades among the sick and wounded before bursting in to bayonet them. On either side of the doorway into the hall, now full of desks again, is a huge thermometer advertising Stephens' Ink. These thermometers were there on that Christmas Day of horror.

A short narrow rocky promontory like a horn of the hill above it was pointed out to me as the place used for the executions, from which the headless bodies pitched forward into the sea. Some time ago a soldier bathing from here had his leg nearly bitten off by a barracuda. Barracudas seldom attack bathers, and it was supposed that the barracudas round here had been accustomed to prey upon the bodies.

I left the cemetery at Stanley, chastened by the thought of what sorrow and suffering were enshrined on that slope above the sea lightly shaded by blue-green casuarina trees and aglow with crimson hibiscus flowers. So far, I have seen sixteen war cemeteries in the course of my travels. Most of them are too far away for the graves to be tended with flowers from the hands of those that loved the dead within them. The hundreds of crosses white as bones look desolate. Here at Stanley many of the graves are decked with flowers from the hands of those who suffered with the dead and are still living close to where they suffered so much.

I sat in the car for about a quarter of an hour to recover from the emotional effect of the Stanley cemetery, and then we drove on to lunch with Lt.-Colonel Borrodaile, the C.O. of the 1st Devons. The anteroom was full of people coming in for the Sunday cocktail before lunch. Here I met Mr. Norman, the Governor of the Prison, who had been shut up in it himself—a salutary experience for a prison governor, he assured me.

The Battalion's silver was on show at lunch. The four silver drums presented by the City of Exeter to commemorate the relief of one battalion of the Devons in Ladysmith by the other battalion were particularly impressive. There was also a large centrepiece of silver with kangaroos, presented by the people of Australia because the battalion had not rushed away to Ballarat after gold but stayed soberly on guard.

After lunch we drove to Showson Hill and from there down into Aberdeen, so called not because of its slight resemblance to old Aberdeen but after the Victorian politician. We were expecting to meet Father T. J. Ryan S.J., but the Chinese messenger got it wrong and after waiting for some time we drove back to meet him at Wah Yan College and go to tea at the Catholic Hostel in the University.

It was hot waiting in the car, but the street scene was so lively and so crowded with interest that we could have waited another hour without noticing the time.

Tea at the hostel was pleasant. Father Ryan was amusing about the perplexity of the Japs over Irish neutrality. He was at length released from internment and spent several months on the island before he got away to China. There appears to be nothing, absolutely nothing, to be said for the Japs. The testimony against them is unanimous. Their bravery is the bravery of the unimaginative brute. They display no more courage under aerial bombardment than a dog trained to the gun will show in a thunderstorm. In the hostel as elsewhere, the books had nearly all been taken for fuel.

We had been invited to dine with Mr. and Mrs. M. K. Lo, and just before 20 o'clock Thomson, Phillimore, C. and myself drove up to Robinson Road. Mr. M. W. Lo, the younger brother of our host,

was there and Mrs. Irene Ho Cheng, the widowed daughter c
Sir Robert Ho Tung, the doyen of the Chinese community in Hon
Kong, who is sister of Mrs. M. K. Lo. Mr. Kan was also there, an
a most charming daughter of the house, Phoebe, who has jus
graduated at the Chinese University of Ling Sen (?)—I'm sure thi
is wrong—and is soon to go on to an American University for
post-graduate course. It is a pity that America should now posses
an almost exclusive hold over Chinese education, for it would b
flattery to suggest that the general Americanizing of education ca
be anything but disastrous for the future of mundane culture
However, as even Oxford and Cambridge have succumbed to deal
ing out the snippets of information which is the contemporar
notion of education, what does it matter?

Mrs. Ho Cheng was given a Ph.D. of London University i
recognition of an able thesis on Ancient and Modern Education i
China of which all but two sections were lost during the war, thoug
there may be a complete copy in the Institute of Education a
London University.

I have seldom enjoyed a dinner party as much. We sat round
circular table which allowed the conversation to be general. Th
food was delicious—I recant what I said about Chinese food—an
the dresses of the ladies lovely. Mrs. Lo was the perfect hostess an
her husband an equally admirable host. I would willingly hav
stayed on talking until the dawn, so much was I enjoying thi
highly civilized evening. We left regretfully just before midnight.

March 31st. HONG KONG

Another memorable day. C. had a shopping date with Mrs
Norman. Jim Thomson had business of his own. So it was onl
John Phillimore and myself who set out at 9.45 for the New Terri
tories.

This time we drove by the coast road to Fanling. The whole o
the fifteen miles unfolded themselves in beauty. I recall the patche
of seedling rice in the gleaming paddy fields as the most intense an
lovely green the world can show. Beside it, emeralds and youn
apples, even young beech leaves, would lack verdancy. Presentl
these seedlings will be planted out and then sheets of this radian
green will cover the flats beside the sea.

I recall the Amah Rock on the conical hill above Shatin whic
resembles a woman with a baby on her back gazing seaward. Onc
upon a time, when the last of the Sung Emperors held his court a
Kowloon in the latter half of the 13th century, one of the Emperor'
personal bodyguard brought his mother and his wife to live nea

hatin, which means Fields of Sand, the resort of a few fishermen. fter a while the Emperor's bodyguard left for the attack on Canton hat ended in the annihilation of the Sung Court by the Mongols t Ngaai Moon. The husband was not killed, but he had to hide rom the Mongol troops, and meanwhile his wife bore a child. For hree years she supported herself, her baby son, and her sick mother-n-law by gathering firewood to sell, and every day she would tand beside a stone on a hill, gazing seaward for the ship that would ring her husband home. Then one day the ship came and the young vife standing on the hill, her child upon her back, fainted in her xcitement. The husband carried his wife and child down the hill o the hut where they had been living. Here he tended her; but er heart was broken by sudden joy after the strain of waiting, and he died. And when she died the stone by which she used to stand on he hill suddenly took the shape of her standing there and watching vith the child on her back. The people of Shatin said that her pirit had entered the stone and given to it her own form as a erpetual memorial of her devotion. I can testify that the stone on op of the hill is much more than rather like a woman with a child n her back.

Today the sea no longer washes the foot of the hill. The soil rought down by the mountain streams has silted up the head of he bay, which is now a stretch of paddy fields. Still, the fishermen re not far away. Their black nets are drying in the sun hardly mile from the Amah Stone; and beside the road are great bushes f white roses in prodigal bloom. This must be *Rosa Sinica* of which he shell-pink garden variety, Anemone, flowers in May against a varm wall at home. There is no second blooming, but the lustrous ark green leaves are themselves beautiful enough to demand space or themselves upon a garden wall.

We reached T'ai Po, a small port for some time at the mercy of irates on the other side of the bay until the Royal Navy took a and. These are not professional pirates but what are called Peace reservation Units supposed to be engaged in suppressing smugglers. an Leno as a fireman used to argue that the best way to protect ouses against fire was to remove the furniture before the fire occurred. Why not be burglars?" he used to exclaim indignantly. "Because ve're firemen." One of the Peace Preservation junks attacked a eavily laden Macao junk the other day, but found it was equally eavily armed. They shot it out with machine guns for a while, but hen the Macao junk produced a cannon, the first shell from which nissed the Peace Preservation junk by a quarter of a mile but was nough to secure the surrender of the pirates. Two of the latter were killed, and now the Chinese Government is demanding compensation for the lives of what it still claims were amateur excisemen.

Lt.-Colonel D. H. W. Saunders who met us at Fanling by the H.Q. of 42nd Commando is a Marine. The three commandos at present guarding the New Territories are all Marine Commandos. I was lucky to catch them because next week they are moving to Malta and their job on the frontier is being handed over to the police. Saunders drove us in his jeep to the village of Shan Tau Kok through the middle of which runs the frontier. Therefore one side of the street is in China and the other in the New Territories. We walked along this street, which was being patrolled by two commandos and a Chinese gendarme. Before the attack on Hong Kong there were Jap soldiers here. The houses of Shan Tau Kok are all built of grey bricks and the street is full of dogs, children and flies. Gambling is forbidden in the New Territories. So the gamesters play on that side of the street and the money is paid to and from the Chinese side. So far the lawyers have been unable to get round this evasion of the law. The women were dressed in black with a thin coloured fillet round a sort of nun's coif. We watched the handicraftsmen at work including a clockmaker above whose shop hung a large imitation clock with the hands for ever at twenty minutes past ten. Above another shop hung the representation of a denture which would have been too large for the Giant Blunderbore, each tooth measuring at least two square inches.

We drove on by the stream which marks the frontier beyond Shan Tau Kok until we reached a narrow road winding up a fairly steep slope to about a thousand feet. A thin stone track for coolies went winding away into the heart of China and was lost to view round the shoulder of the farthest hill descending to the great plain behind. In 1917 I landed on the coast of Asia Minor to take off an agent and, waiting there on the beach, my ears sharpened for the tramp of a Turkish patrol, I thought with awe of the thousands of miles between me and China, no other beach between. When I saw this thin winding track it seemed to me that I had imagined thirty years ago just such a track running right across Asia from where I had put my foot upon its soil for the first time.

The glen gradually widened to a strath, bounded on the far side by a much lower range of hills. A great concrete tower rose from the middle of a village on the Chinese side of the frontier stream. This was the local pawnshop where people pledged their goods to buy rice and redeemed them when they had sold it at a profit. We passed a brickmaker's yard whose walls of undried bricks the colour of pale café au lait were drying in the sun, the alternate rows being

et lengthways and widthways to allow the air to circulate. The
brickmaker sat on a large beehive of straw, a heap of sand on his
ight, a heap of damp clay on his left. He sprinkled a metal box,
he size of a brick, with sand and then slapped clay into it, slicing
off the excess with wire strung between a small bow. Then the
brick was shaken out and put aside to be carried away by the women
who were stacking them. Saunders wanted to take his photograph,
for which privilege the brickmaker demanded a dollar, much to
he amusement of the women, who were convulsed by laughter.

Finally we reached Chick's Bridge, a Baillie Bridge over the stream
said to have been erected by Lieutenant Chick in eight hours. Beside
it is the bridge blown up to delay the Jap advance over the plain
to invade the New Territories. One mocking tale relates that while
we were blowing the bridge the Japs were busy placing pontoons
beside it to build their own, neither party paying any attention to
the other.

We have a Commando post on our side of Chick's Bridge, the
Chinese a post on theirs. Buses and wayfarers are searched at both.
I saw a Chinese gendarme chasing some women across a field.
The subaltern in command of the past told me these gendarmes
are a brutal lot and think nothing of beating up the women with
their rifles when they catch them with smuggled rice.

The road and railway continue across the plain to Canton a
hundred miles away. There are many villages and the population
teems in every direction. *Hoc erat in votis*. Once again the view was
what I had always pictured China would be.

We drove back to Fanling along the main road by which the
Japanese entered the New Territories on December 8th, 1941. The
village itself does not seem large. Yet there are 6,000 inhabitants,
about ten times as many as one would find in an English village of
the same size. The Commandos have enjoyed their time in the New
Territories. We visited two other posts besides these I have mentioned, at one of which the Mobile Canteen wagon and the Library
wagon of the 'Fannies' were drawing up as we left. These women
are doing a magnificent job. Many of the roads are abominable,
but they were driving about on them all day and every day, and the
men spoke of their devotion with enthusiasm. I am told they are
proud of being the women's Senior Service, dating back to the South
African War, and they have every reason to be proud of the way
they live up to their seniority.

At 14 o'clock Phillimore and I bade farewell to hospitable Commando 42 and drove back along the road by which we had come.
An hour later we got out of the car and Phillimore jeeped me up a

narrow road round a steep hill to reach Tao Fong Shan, the mission of Pastor Hannetz on the top of it. It is a most unusual mission house, having been built on the model of a Buddhist monastery from money raised in Scandinavia by the predecessor of the present pastor. The idea was to receive in familiar surroundings pilgrims searching for the truth. There is a chapel like a Chinese temple, inside which is a Lutheran altar with a crucifix and two candles in what looks the conventional Lutheran style until one sees that the base of the crucifix is a lotus flower and that some mythical Chinese beast is coiled round each candlestick. There is a rest house and dormitory hung with texts from the New Testament in Chinese. There is a hall for teaching, and in this hangs a text chosen by the only Lama who has visited Tao Fong Shan so that if another Lama should arrive he might be gladdened by the sight of the familiar Tibetan script. Under the chapel is a crypt, entered from outside, with wide benches on either side on which the pilgrims may sit cross-legged in meditation and theological argument. A small stained glass window depicts the Good Shepherd under the text "Come unto Me, all ye that are weary" in Chinese.

The garden is well planted. I saw a white buddleia, honeycomb-scented, but most of the larger trees were cut down for firewood during the Jap occupation. The place was not looted because it was never left empty. The summer residence of the Anglican Bishop of Hong Kong on a hilltop beyond is now a mere shell. An air of peace surrounds Tao Fong Shan with its wide view of sky and sea, of hills and gleaming paddy land about which the squares of seedling rice are scattered like gems. A large sum of money must have been raised to build this mission, which was moved here from Central China in the early 'twenties. The road up from the main road must have cost a small fortune to construct.

Pastor Hannertz himself has the dreamy pale blue eyes and soft voice of the devout believer. He has just returned from Sweden and at present there are no pilgrims. We sat in his room, which is furnished like a room in an Ibsen play. By the door a great Swedish bible was laying on a table, open at some page of the prophet Jeremiah. Captain Haggan who was boarding in the mission came in. He had been entrusted with the defence of the Japs accused of atrocities before professional Jap lawyers appeared, and he told me that when his job was done the prisoners collected 2,000 dollars as a testimonial. This, of course, he declined, but it was obvious that he was already somewhat enamoured of the little beasts. The Englishman derives the same kind of satisfaction from winning the esteem of his enemies as he does from being able to manage a vicious dog. I shall never forget the faces of those who told me their tales in the Andamans and Nicobars. When I have heard of one kindly action performed by a Jap I may be able to contemplate without repugnance the spectacle of an Englishman defending them in a court of law.

April 1st. HONG KONG

It was a warm dank morning and I woke feeling tired. At 10 Phillimore, Thomson and I went up to the University where I was received by the Vice-Chancellor, Mr. D. J. Sloss. He was formerly Principal of University College, Rangoon, and is a man of the widest culture. The University has been much damaged by looting and the trees which once surrounded it have all been felled. In the central courtyard the rich red blooms of *Bombax Malabarica* promise that the fire of learning will be kindled once again. Professor Ride and the Professor of English Literature joined us at the Vice-Chancellor's table. Mr. Sloss was interned. I wished I could have had more time for talking to him. There was much I wanted to ask about Burma, which he knew intimately.

After the visit to the University I tried to do some shopping but found the day too exhausting for walking about. At 12.45 I was due at the Gloucester Hotel, having promised to talk at the weekly Rotary lunch. H.E. was the guest of honour and made a brief farewell. I gave a dull talk, for I was feeling absurdly tired.

After lunch I had a talk with Mr. F. P. Franklin, the Editor of the *South China Morning Post*, who showed me a tome from America which claims to give the history of World War Two. The whole of our Burma campaign hardly occupies a page of the 800-odd pages, and the Hong Kong campaign is dismissed in half-a-dozen lines in which there are four misstatements of fact, one of which gives the handling of the guns to Americans. The author is Francis Trevelyan Miller, who once produced a book called "Photographic History of the Great War". Presumably this bowl of broth, in the making of which Mr. Miller has been assisted by too many cooks, will be lapped up by myriads of Americans hungry for "knowledge". Franklin wrote a crushing review of the book in the *Hong Kong Telegraph* last January and received a letter from "Historian General Francis Trevelyan Miller (Litt. D., LLD)" addressed from "Historical Foundations, 15 West 68th St., New York" in the course of which he writes:

"Our chapter on China paid the highest tribute to China and the Chinese people for their heroic struggle. It seems to us that differences in time elements, exact dates, etc., while we desire to have them correct are minor matters in comparison to the principles we establish. The great thing is that the war is won!"

And he then goes on to argue that all our greatest historians are in conflict over the facts. Mr. Miller's letter was accompanied by a letter from Mr. F. A. Barber, the "Executive Director of Historical Foundations", in which he points out that "Dr. Miller's letter is typical of his courtesy and broad-mindedness".

We did some more shopping, and then Phillimore and I went to tea with Sir Robert Ho Tung at Idlewild, 8 Seymour Road. The 84-year old patriarch is a superb figure. Benignity shines from his bright blue eyes. His complexion is rosy, his ample beard has not yet changed from grey to white. He spoke with enthusiasm of Bernard Shaw and H. G. Wells both of whom he had met and showed me photographs of himself with Ramsay MacDonald and Lord Baldwin. The Japs pinched a photograph taken with Lloyd George. We sat down together at a small table and were photographed in what I hope will look like animated conversation. His charming daughter, Mrs. Ho Cheng, was at tea, but the old gentleman wouldn't allow her to talk. I had to tell him all about the tour while his pretty young secretary stood by him and repeated in his ear anything I said which he had not followed. Tea was delicious, and afterwards we looked at wonderful ivories and brocades. The room was hung with greetings from friends on his 80th birthday (on October 2nd, 1941) when he gave a reception to 5,000 guests. He went to Macao to recuperate and while there the Japs invested Hong Kong. So he, luckier than most of his family, escaped the horrors of the invasion. A truly remarkable figure, and I rejoice that I have had the privilege of meeting him. Before we parted he presented me with a pair of gold cuff-links on which four Chinese ideographs had been cut—signifying Happiness, Health, Wealth and Longevity.

At 18.30 we went round to Flagstaff House and had drinks with General Erskine whom I thanked for the splendidly arranged intensive study of Hong Kong, in which he had taken a keen personal interest. Not one moment of my stay here has been wasted.

When we got back to Government House there was a message to say that the weather in Japan was too bad for the plane and so (to my relief, for I was extremely tired) our departure was put off till Thursday.

April 2nd. HONG KONG

I worked at the diary and in the afternoon went round to have another look at the relief map in General Erskine's office. Afterwards we went down 102 steps to the Battle Box from which the operations were conducted. They had a passion in 1937 for making concrete burrows. This is the largest of the lot, and I cannot believe its effect on the direction of the fighting was beneficial.

In the evening H.E. took us to see *The Gold Rush* at the Lee Theatre. I enjoyed it in spite of feeling more and more ill all the while. On the trailer I saw what were presumably intended to be *bonnes bouches* from the recent film of my book *Carnival.* They were worse than even I had ventured to fear. The book has been filmed three times now, and this trailer at Hong Kong is all that I have seen of any of these burlesques.

At midnight I went to bed with the prospect of getting up at 4 to catch the plane for Japan. I grew worse and worse, and after I was dressed I had to say I didn't think I could manage the journey. Thomson was evidently relieved that I did not try to rise superior to my body. It was a typical demonstration of that accursed influenza with bronchitis in the offing. I undressed again and went back to bed. I felt too ill even to be disappointed about missing Japan.

April 5th. HONG KONG

I got up in the afternoon and sat in my dressing-gown to write some diary. The kindness of H.E. and Lady Young has been wonderful. In the evening Mr. Meiklereid, our Consul General in Saigon, came up with his charming French wife to have a talk. A delightful pair, and we are looking forward to meeting them again in Saigon on April 8th.

April 7th. HONG KONG

I woke at 4 a.m. with colic and didn't get any more sleep. I lay up during the day, but dressed for dinner. We said good-bye to our host and hostess as we were to be off early next morning.

April 8th. HONG KONG

We were up at 6 and left Government House just before 7 to go down to the launch. The morning was chilly, and a Scots mist shrouded the harbour. When we reached the aerodrome at Kai Tak we were told that we should not take off before 9. This became 10, and finally 11 when we were told that a belt of bad cunim, i.e. cumulus-nimbus, 200 miles wide, made any flight that day impossible. So back we went to Government House, feeling a dreadful nuisance. However, H.E. and Lady Young managed to make us feel that they were really quite glad we had returned. At 20 o'clock C. and I went off to dinner at Flagstaff House where Major-General C. H. Gairdner and Mrs. Gairdner, held up on their way back to Japan, were staying with Major General Erskine.

Gairdner started off as Winston Churchill's personal representative with General MacArthur, and now he is acting in the same capacity for Attlee. He gets on well with the Americans and is a great admirer of MacArthur. He told some good stories of Patton, old "Blood and Guts", whose fierce appearance surprisingly covered an unusually high voice. It was a good evening. I read in the afternoon of Cecil Clementi's death about whom I had been writing two or three days ago.

April 9th. HONG KONG TO SAIGON

We were up at 6 again, but the weather looked more promising and we were relieved to hear at the aerodrome that we actually should start this time. We were airborne at 9.20 after half an hour's tinkering with the port engine and recharging a battery. Taking off from the Kai Tak airstrip, which is surrounded by hills, is always a nervy business. There have been some bad smashes here. We were told not to unfasten the straps until we had been in the air ten minutes. One could sense the pilot's anxiety. We had to wear Mae Wests while we were over the sea, and I was quite glad of mine because it was cold and draughty in the plane. These transport Dakotas are not luxurious. We came down at Saigon about 14.15. The heat that blazed up at us from the airfield seemed an incredible change of climate to meet in under six hours of flying. Mr. Davies, the Vice-Consul, came to meet us and help with the wearisome form-signing. It really is ridiculous that one cannot make a compulsory stop for one night without so much signing of documents. The world is in chains. While we were hanging about Bernard Newman suddenly appeared on the scene. He's on some lecturing job. I hadn't seen him since a few days before the outbreak of war.

The Meiklereids, although they are on the verge of departure, are kindly putting up C. and myself. Thomson is going to the hotel.

Mrs. Meiklereid was packing hard and therefore unable to come with us when the Consul-General, who was at Dakar before he was posted here, drove C. and myself round Saigon. The *place* is approached by tree-shaded boulevards. In the middle of it a well-designed Romanesque cathedral gets all the room it wants and leaves plenty of open space, round which runs a wide pavement in front of wo or three cafés, a pharmacy, and lots of typical French shops. f it were not for the Annamites one might suppose Saigon was omewhere a few miles of Grenoble. The dress of the women is the nost attractive I have seen out here; white or black trousers with a ind of narrow tunicle of rich colour and design worn over them as ar as the knee.

We went to the Club where I enjoyed two of the nearest thing o Pernods. A Madame Jacquemar joined us. She had been caught y the Annamites in Hanoi and imprisoned for six weeks. A deep veal round each arm marked where she had been tied with rope. The French residents had a pretty bad time and about 150 of them re still held *incommunicado*. An air of menace broods over Saigon. t is unsafe to venture away from the centre of the town, and to ross the river is fatal. There are three battalions of the Foreign egion here—mostly Germans.

The Meiklereids had arranged a dinner party for yesterday vening. Nobody at the Kai Tak aerodrome had thought it necessary o notify Saigon of the hold up of the plane, and the unfortunate Vice-Consul was kept hanging about all day. The casual behaviour of the R.A.F. ground staffs everywhere is a feature of their administration. One of the guests at dinner had been the Crown Prince of Laos who had been disappointed to miss me, but the Meiklereids sked him to come in after dinner to-night. The throne to which he vill ascend sounds as enviable a royal responsibility as the present an provide. Laos seems to be one of the few Arcadias left. The Crown Prince is going soon to Washington for a few months and pressed me to go and stay with him when he returns. He is a disinguished, humorous and intelligent man, speaking most beautiful French. He spoke with appreciation, as indeed did everybody, of he way Douglas Gracey had handled the situation in Indo-China vhen he came here in command of 20th Indian Division after the ap collapse. It was a most enjoyable evening.

April 10th. SAIGON TO RANGOON

We were away from the Consulate-General by 6 and landed at he Mingaladon airfield at 15 o'clock in blistering heat. There is omething wild in having a bronchial cough in such weather, but I am wheezing like an old gentleman with a winter cold in London.

The rest-house for travellers in transit is worse than the worst Dak bungalow. Half a dozen people are crowded into each of the very mall rooms; two lavatory basins and one privy are considered enough for more than twenty travellers. If the service were free it would

still be a disgrace, but the R.A.F. charge as much as B.O.A.C
American travellers must think us mad to put up with such di
regard of obligations. The 'food' in the reception place is served b
the lowest class of grubby and nitwit Burman girls. A distorted radi
blares away all the time. They haven't even a room in which t
lock up the baggage, and somebody pinched C.'s spongebag whic
was in a pocket of the hold-all. The whole of the baggage has t
be driven and unloaded fifty yards from the rest house which itse
is nearly two miles away from the reception place.

We made no attempt to get into touch with people in Rangoo
because some kind of political business was going on and transpo
for the twelve miles or so was unobtainable at the airport. So we sa
in the verandah of the shoddy rest-house and read. I found an A.C.
throwing stones at a house-lizard and asked him what he thought h
was playing at. He said in an injured tone that he was trying to ki
the brute because it was poisonous. I told him that the neare
poisonous lizard was in Arizona. He gave an adenoidal gape an
slouched off.

April 11th. RANGOON TO CALCUTTA

Sheet lightning in the east below the brilliant morning star was nc
really worth watching for so long. When the sleepy driver did arriv
he answered the sergeant's mild protest like a guttersnipe.

We were airborne about 7.30 in a Dakota with side seats, not th
reaper and binder aluminium type but with strap seats and back
I was too glad to see the last of Mingaladon to bother about seats i
any plane which was flying me away from it.

We came down two and a half hours later at Akyab and remaine
there for about an hour for some heavy freight to be unloaded. Th
aerodrome here is being put in order.

It was pretty bumpy as we came down to land on the Dum Du
aerodrome at Calcutta, and when we landed at 13.30 the heat wa
grilling. We found that every signal sent about our arrival had mi
carried. So nothing had been prepared, and we wound up b
staying at the Grand Hotel because the R.A.F. had booked for u
there and the Army had booked for us at the Great Eastern two day
later.

The afternoon had been intolerable because we had had to driv
in a taxi in search of the office where air passages were granted an
then in search of another office to get a warrant for Gulaba to trav
by train to Delhi—a journey of 25 hours. Repeated misdirectio
heat, dust, interminable form-filling, and the need to get the luggag
to the station before dusk on account of the communal riotin

which is starting again, combined to make the whole business quite exhausting.

April 12th. CALCUTTA TO DELHI

We had a staff car to take us to the airport where we were due at 13.30 to take off an hour later. When we reached Dum Dum we were told that we might be late in starting. The non-stop Viking had not arrived yesterday, and in the end it was 17.30 before we at last took off in a Wayfarer. This is a converted freight-plane and none too comfortable, but we were lucky not to have a bumpy flight.

We came down to fuel at Allahabad at dusk, and there Thomson and I drank some beer mulled by the sun. It really was hot—not just warm.

Delhi was reached at 21.30 where we were met by John Booth, the Chief's British A.D.C. and we drove straight to the C.-in-C.'s house, six hours after we were due to arrive.

April 13th. NEW DELHI

Claude Auckinleck is in great form. Lord Ismay, Sir Eric Mieville and Martin Gilliat at dinner. Ismay told me Mountbatten had had no idea quite what a mouthful he had bitten off, as the last Viceroy. I said I would lay 2 to 1 on his bringing it off. Ismay said the right odds were 100 to 30 against. "Still," he added, "I believe he will bring it off."

NORTH-WEST FRONTIER

April 14th. NEW DELHI

There was an invitation for C. and myself to lunch at Viceroy's House with Their Excellencies. It was interesting to see the complete change of atmosphere. The helpful and friendly A.D.C.s with the addition of Lt.-Commander Peter Howes R.N. were the same, but there was much less formality.

H.E. talked to me for twenty minutes after lunch. Among the guests were three governors and the Diwan of Hyderabad. He said that what gave him hope of success with the Indian problem was the memory of the state of affairs when he took over S.E.A.C. There was lowest priority for everything there. It was impossible at first to persuade the people at home to be interested in the Burma Campaign.

It is that lack of interest which has allowed the Americans to put out on the world the story that they drove the Japs out of Burma. Stilwell's part in the whole business was a minor one. The Chinese fought only one action of the faintest importance, which was at Toungoo during the retreat, and even that was without the least effect upon the situation. There was only one American brigade involved, and though they managed to capture the Myitkyina air-strip they were held up for weeks by the Japs in the town itself. The only real help the Americans gave in Burma was in the air, and even that was always liable to be diverted to China. Yet everywhere I go people ask me if I got to Myitkyina as if that was the decisive battleground in Burma. The illusion of an American victory in Burma is helped by the Star on all the transport. Most of the Burmans suppose this to be an American star.

H.E. spoke highly of Nehru who he said had always behaved with complete sincerity and courage. Later I had a longish talk with Lady Mountbatten. She is certainly not sparing herself. This summer will be a heavy ordeal. The thermometer is already over 105, and she is visiting hospitals, etc., in the heat of the day without any let-up. She said she hoped I was going to devote some attention in my book to the great part played by the women of India—Indians as well as Anglo-Indians—in the war.

I came away from lunch feeling that if any two people in the Commonwealth could win the affection and respect of the people of India these two could.

After tea C. and I drove with Bill Condon to see the Qutab Minar—that wonderful monument 228 feet high built of sandstone with an interior staircase of nearly 400 steps. I shirked going up. The top of it is a favourite medium for suicide. I was much interested to see the wrought iron pillar of A.D. 314—one of the mysteries of archaeology of which I first heard when I was getting material in the Black Country for the Brockhouse book. There is nothing like it anywhere in the world. It is about three feet in circumference without a spot of rust after more than 1,600 years *in situ*.

We drove about among the ruins and walls and tombs of Ancient Delhi in the dusty violet of sunset. Parakeets came flying over the road on the way to roost and the crows were homing. Planes too were coming in to the airport from every direction with roosting Governors arriving for the Gubernatorial Meet at Viceroy's House.

April 16th. NEW DELHI

John Shaw arrived. He and I with Condon and C. went round to G.H.Q. in a small hot car. Major Fry of External Affairs gave us some of the gen about Nepal. We are to tour the North-West Frontier before we go there, because an American commercial mission is in possession at the moment. I met Brigadier Thimmaya who was commanding the Indian troops in Japan. I regret more than ever that fatal influenza which prevented my getting there. It grows hotter all the time. People going to Simla are being inoculated against plague which is in some of the villages round Kalka. We heard later that this will not apply to people from Lahore and Delhi. I sat down after lunch and by a great effort of will in this heat brought the diary up to this point. I don't know how anything gets done in Delhi. The effort to concentrate is tremendous. My writing blotter has buckled, and the life of the Biro is oozing away.

April 17th. NEW DELHI

We went to Major Peter Goodwin's colour film of the Sikkim devil dancing and another of the Chief's visit to Nepal last year. P.G. is head of the photographic section at Simla. I've seldom seen anything so good on the films as the devil-dancing. The background of the Himalayas is terrific. The richness of the colour is superb, but it is never garish and never blurred. So many films kill themselves by excess of technique. The effort to achieve something is always evident. Directors must learn *ars est celare artem*, but they are afraid that if they do their efforts will not be appreciated.

April 18th. NEW DELHI TO RAWALPINDI

We were due to leave the Willingdon Airport at 7, but somebody overslept himself and it was after 7.30 before we were airborne Peter Goodwin came along and was helpful with the kit, tickets, etc A charming girl, the daughter of Brigadier Rudra, in white sar bordered with navy blue and shoulder straps with one star for her rank, presided over our departure. The plane was a Wayfarer. The flight was dull. We came down at Lahore to refuel, reaching Pind at lunch-time. Captain Hugh Dalrymple-Hamilton, General Sir Frank Messervy's A.D.C., met us and we drove straight to Command House. It was sad to miss Lady Messervy and Rosemary; a week earlier would have brought us there in time. The jacaranda trees were even better than at Delhi, but the scent of the *nim* trees, like lime-blossom, which was so rich over Delhi, was absent here. The flowers of the jacaranda on the leafless boughs have the same quality of intensity in lilac-blue as the green of young rice in green. Large trees of *grevillea robusta* are frequent. This Australian tree is grown in the tea-gardens of Ceylon for shade. The faded-orange clusters o flowers are attractive in contrast with the ferny foliage. It can be grown in Cornwall, but it does not get beyond a large shrub there

April 19th. RAWALPINDI

Major H. Conroy (15th Punjab Regiment) and I drove to Jhelum —66 miles away—to see the regimental centre of the First Punjabis amid austere country with no colour except a coral-flowered shrub and the ripe wheat. Colonel Fry took me round the centre. I noticed some twice-as-large-as-life decorations in a show case which were presented by the Chief to his old regiment.

After this I watched the drilling of recruits and saw Afghan officers being instructed in a course of musketry. At noon I went round the King George Royal Indian Military School of 378 cadets, which occupied much more space than the one I visited at Jullundur Colonel Stebbing, the Commandant, handed me over to two of the senior boys—a young Gurkha whose father had been a V.C.O. in the Eighth Gurkha Rifles and a young Sikh. They showed Conroy and myself round with perfect aplomb. The heat was sizzling.

After lunch I had a talk with Subedar-Major Falek Khan of the Hong Kong–Singapore Garrison Artillery, of whom Corry, the Resident in Johore Bahru, had spoken to me. They had taken the trouble to fetch him from his village 100 miles away. He had been tied to a tree by the Japs and badly knocked about day by day to 'persuade' him to join the I.N.A. He took off a sock to show me an ankle still black with extravasated blood from the tightness with which he had been tied to the tree. The example he set was followed by the 150 men under his command, not one of whom would join the I.N.A. They were addressed by Subhas Chandra Bose who promised they should be well looked after financially, but his eloquence was unavailing. The Subedar-Major showed me an acknowledgement of his offer to put his land at the service of the Government during the war, and a receipt for the money it brought in, which he had handed over. Words are incapable of paying a worthy enough tribute to men like these, and every battalion in the Indian Army is lucky enough to possess them. I hope when the time comes I shall be able to inspire *Indian Epic* with some of their spirit. And let it be remembered that his magnificent type was the product of British training and the example of British officers.

We left the Mess of the senior infantry regiment in the Indian Army about 15 o'clock to drive the 66 miles back to Rawalpindi. Was it hot? I don't believe I was ever quite so hot, and when we got back to Command House Conroy and I came out of the car like two eggs out of a frying pan. After dinner we all tried our hands, or rather our mouths, on a six-feet long blowpipe used by the Sakai jungle-tribe in Malaya. General Messervy had a powerful blast. I was less successful, but at the second attempt I managed to send what looks like a miniature conductor's baton against the wall at the far end of the passage.

April 20th. RAWALPINDI TO PESHAWAR

Frank Messervy was in great form at breakfast, and extremely amusing about the orotund telegrams Winston used to send to the Auk in Cairo. He must have been a wonderful pick-me-up for his men. The fighting in Keren, Libya, Arakan and Burma all benefited from his presence.

We left Command House at 9.45 to drive the 106 miles to Peshawar. The sun was obscured by haze and we could keep the windows of the car open without having our eyelids seared by what is more like blast than breeze. There is a kind of exhilarating austerity about this road, in which the only colour is in the fields of ripe wheat. The people themselves seldom add coloured stuffs to the prevailing white or faded lavender of their dress. We passed a great monolith to the memory of Nicholson which stands on a crag towering above the road. The background of hills was hardly visible in the dry haze.

The crossing of the Indus by the Attock gorge was as imaginatively nutritious as it could be. One has not a moment's doubt that this is one of the mighty rivers of history. The ghost of Alexander haunts the place, and the great Attock fort round which the road sweeps down to the bridge with armed guards at either end seems rathe to have sprung out of these sun-baked rocks than to have bee deliberately built. I noticed a good many ruined houses and hear later that these were destroyed in an outbreak of violence only a mont ago. The Pathan War Memorial—a monolith in the shape of gigantic cartridge—stands above the gorge of the Indus on the fa side from Pindi.

Soon after Attock we reached Nowshera, the Regimental Centr of the Sikhs, and I went round to the quarters of the Boys' Company Most of them were away, and the dozen left were off next day t visit the C.-in-C. in Delhi—much elated at the prospect. All thes boys' companies are impressive, but this and the Mahratta one a Belgaum are outstanding.

I enquired about a despatch I sent from Gallipoli about the 14t King George's Own Sikhs (now 1/11th) and was told it was a Dehra Dun. The C.O., whose name I could not recall, wrote m toward the end of the 'twenties to tell me that this despatch, whic was printed at the time in the *Westminster Gazette*, about a wonderfu action fought on the Fourth of June, 1915, was read aloud to th Battalion on the anniversary, and as I happened to have the origina despatch with the grime of battle on it dictated to a staff-sergeant i a tent near Lancashire Landing I sent it to the Battalion.*

After Nowshera the road ran between innumerable orchards o pears which must have looked glorious when in blossom some week ago. There were apricot orchards, too, and many oleanders, and arbours of pale pink roses. Cypresses were frequent. The landscapes of Arabia seemed to mingle here with those of India. In the haze the wheatfields were tarnished gold, and during the harvest the trouble along the Frontier may abate. Lots of smart-looking tongas were on the road, and most of the ponies were in reasonably good condition.

We reached Flagstaff House just after 13.30 to find that Major-General Ross McCay was expecting us in a plane from Ambala. However, as a buffet lunch for about a dozen people was going on, our unexpected arrival was not a nuisance.

April 21st. PESHAWAR

I wrote some diary after breakfast and then at 11.30 Mrs. Deakin, C. and myself drove down to the City escorted by Captain Scott of the K.O.S.B. and a pleasant young Assistant Superintendent of

*June 4th, 1948. That C.O. turned out to be Lieut.-General Sir Lewis Heath who when I was his guest at Limoru in Kenya last month asked me if I remembered his writing to me. I told him that no letter had given me more pleasure.

'olice. The bazaars here are more like the suks of Damascus than he usual Indian bazaar. We wandered up and down Arabian Night treets, watching the coppersmiths, silversmiths and goldsmiths at vork. There were myriads of flies, but the heat of the sun was tem- ered by the haze. A police wagon full of arrested demonstrators rove by. They were all chanting jovially their Muslim slogans. 'here is an air of suppressed expectation of bloody events, and he small Hindu minority—only about 15,000 in a city of 200,000— s feeling apprehensive.

C. bought a couple of Swati blankets and I bought a pair of *haplis* (a kind of shoe) decorated with Russian gold. I was asked hirty rupees. I offered twenty and finally tossed the owner whether should pay twenty or twenty-five. I won the toss and got them for wenty, but gave the vendor a two-anna piece which he put in his ar, the first time I've seen the ear used as a purse. We climbed up o the roof of the Police Headquarters, but the haze of dust eclipsed he view of the hills all round.

April 22nd. PESHAWAR TO LANDIKOTAL

We set off about 9.30 on the drive to Landikotal by way of the Mullagori road. The conducting officer was Major Mohammed Yousuf of the 18th K.E.O. Cavalry, to the command of which he vill presently succeed.

The road from Peshawar ran for some miles across the wide plain between avenues of casuarina trees. We were in jeeps again because the Mullagori road is no road for staff-cars. The hills oward which we were travelling loomed in a haze of dust, and we ad no chance of seeing the high snows beyond. We stopped at a police post and walked up on a parapet which ran round the square courtyard in which the charpoys of the men stood in the sun. In a corner a sentry was standing in the shade of what looked like a lying turret, gazing out toward that frontier whence for centuries the invaders of India have come. He does not expect Greeks nor even Russians to-day. The fierce tribesmen are the threat. Peshawar would be well worth looting.

Not long after leaving the police post the road turned into the hills and we began to wind up through as arid and savage a landscape as one could see. A train of camels met us and seemed inclined to turn round and go back the way they had come. There was much shouting and tugging at ropes and at last they consented to pass the jeeps, with an expression of countenance even more supercilious and disagreeable than usual. We were driving through what is called tribal territory, which means that one never goes off the road.

The road itself by a gentleman's agreement is exempt from the active side of a blood feud, and serves as a sort of sanctuary for anybody whose enemy is sniping at him from behind a rock.

The policing is done by khussedars who are the equivalent of special constables provided by the tribesmen themselves. They wear a kind of uniform and are paid by us (one might say bribed) to keep quiet. After a mile or so of this savage road we were met by a khussedar with a big henna-dyed beard. The Prophet's beard was red, and it is the fashion for Muslims to dye their beards with henna when the first grey hairs show and thus proclaim their potency. Punjabi Mussalman V.C.O.s dye their fierce moustaches instead. The khussedar with his rifle got into the jeep that C. was in, and on we drove. Few European women have travelled along this road.

The rocks seem to be schist, slate or marble. The last is said to be better than Carrara marble, but in this wilderness of savage peaks it will be long before it is a commercial proposition. A thousand feet below the road the dark-green Kabul river was winding through a mighty gorge, and along one of its banks we could see tunnels. These were relics of the metre-gauge railway planned by Kitchener and abandoned after a while under pressure from Russia as 'uneconomical'. We should have had a view of the great snow range of the Hindu Kush and the lowlands of Afghanistan, but the haze denied it to us, the limit of visibility being about five miles. In a way the mysterious horizon and shadowy peaks were even more impressive. There was a brisk wind, but the sun crackled in my ears as we took hairpin bend after hairpin bend. We reached a fortified village with adobe walls and watch-towers. The dogs were large and fierce. In the cemetery white flags were fluttering over some tombs, and here and there a red one. White flags blow above the grave of a man killed in action in some tribal blood feud. A red flag marks the grave of a holy man. There were one or two blue flags, but Yousuf could not tell me what these stood for.

About half way to Landikotal we came down to the Arcadian village of Shilman. Along the banks of a stream flowing over round gray stones were oleanders of every shade of rose from carmine to blush. In the fields the wheat and barley glowed with ripeness, and a troop of tawny dogs came charging at the car. The men of the village were all carrying rifles. The strath stretched for several miles and at the end of it we entered the main road leading up the Khyber Pass to Landikotal. On either side were fortified villages surrounded by high adobe walls the colour of café au lait, each with a narrow entrance and a watch-tower. Villages separated by hardly a hundred yards from one another might be enemies.

It is strange to pass from this landscape of the centuries into the tree-shaded Landikotal Lines and see 'Whitehall' on a signpost beside the main entrance. Presently we turned in between iron gates to find ourselves in what seemed like one of the smaller Oxford colleges. We walked through into the 'quad,' three sides of which were bounded by the Mess and officers' quarters of the Khyber Rifles, the fourth by a grey wall overhung by peaches, mulberries and other trees. There were false-peppers, too, the heady scent of whose bunches of greenish blossom brought back to me the boulevards of Athens. The lawn in the middle was as green as an English lawn; the roses were as sweet. The annual larkspurs were taller and brighter than I have seen them in gardens at home. The flag irises were already limp.

Lt.-Colonel J. R. Booth was busy packing in order to go to Wana and take up the command of the Brigade in Waziristan two days later, and Major Sharif Khan who is to succeed him in command of the Khyber Rifles welcomed us. Poor Yousuf had to retire to bed after lunch with fever and a bad throat. So I went off in the jeep with Captain K. Dance, Captain Game, and two exuberant spaniels to visit the Charbagh Post and one of the piquets. The highest of these is Kafir Kot which crowns a hill along the ridge of which runs a wall of immemorial antiquity. The piquet itself is a square tower the iron entrance to which is reached by a steel ladder of twenty rungs. Then one climbs up steep wooden stairs to reach the platform from which but for the haze the panorama would cover a hundred miles. In one corner stands the sentry on guard. In another the Union Jack flutters and will flutter for a few days more than thirteen months.* This piquet was once captured in a surprise attack and the whole guard taken prisoner. They sleep and sit and eat in a dim guard-room lighted by loopholes.

It must be understood that the haze obscured only the more distant mountains and the wide expanse of the plain in which Kabul (pronounce it Kahbul) lies. The panorama of jagged naked hills for five miles all round would have stirred an eighteenth-century traveller to an ecstasy of disgust and a Roman to denounce such a lack of *amoenitas*.

We drove down the rough winding road to visit the Charbagh Post. This fort is built beside a perpetual spring and from time immemorial it has been a key position in frontier fighting. The men of one of Alexander the Great's columns must have watered here. Outside the gate stands an immense chinar (accent on "ar")

* This was being optimistic. Actually it had only a few days more than four months.

tree at least 500 years old beneath whose ample shade one may sit gratefully beside the great stone well filled with crystal water. Next to the chinar stands a large white mulberry-tree, the ground strewn with its fruit like dusty pearls. The figs and mulberries of this part of the world would not have served Adam and Eve, for their leaves are small oblongs and not the sycamore shape we know. The chinar is *platanus orientalis* of which our London plane, *platanus acerifolia* (the maple-leafed plane), is a sub-species. The leaves have sharper points than the London planes, and the trunk and branches do not peel so prodigally. In autumn the foliage turns wine-red.

The spectacle of this grand tree defying the cruel landscape is magnificent; the grey trunk must be twelve feet round. It is nothing like as large as the great plane-tree of Cos, but it has the same classic quality.

We went round the fort, and afterwards the Subedar in command gave us tea. I noticed that the safety matchbox on the table came from Afghanistan; the matches kindled better than some of the Indian brands. I wish I had started a collection of match labels many years ago.

On the outskirts of Landikotal we passed a caravan, 300 camels strong, preparing its camp for the night. It was here that Nehru was received with stones and objurgations by a wild mob of tribesmen and the windows of his car were smashed. These caravans are sometimes over a thousand camels strong, not to mention three times as many small donkeys and numerous goats. Wandering tribes from Afghanistan come down into India every autumn and return in spring. Some of them even have landed property in India.

The women wearing black edged with sombre crimson have a gypsy look. The large dark brown tents are low. I coveted some of the rugs spread within; they glowed in the tented gloom. We stopped outside the great market square which reminded me of the market square in Tetuan when Pirie-Gordon and I were there in January 1902 and our dragoman nearly set all Morocco by the ears because he was charged a penny for a glass of minted tea instead of three farthings, the proper price. Camels, donkeys, goats, children, flies, refuse, dung, dust, and all sorts of eatables for sale. In a corner by the archway stands the jail with two large barred windows through which the prisoners are able to watch the thronged scene. Dance tried to get a snap of me backed by the prisoners, but they were quick to spot what he was doing and drew back. On the way to the Mess we passed the local casino which is housed by the three arches of the railway bridge. Here all day and all night groups of tribesmen gamble.

April 23rd. LANDIKOTAL

This was another thrilling day. Poor Yousuf who had had a bad night had been given an injection of ten grains of quinine for suspected malaria and ordered to stay in bed. So Dance came with us. The staff-car was sent back to Peshawar and we kept the jeeps. It turned out that we ought to have kept the staff-car and sent back the jeeps. However, I'm glad the mistake was made. We left the Mess about 9 and took the great sweep of road to Landikhana, at the head of the Khyber Pass, along which Beverley Nichols and many another tourist has driven. A young camel was lying dead in the middle of the road.

At Landikhana we stood against the big notice-board which proclaims the frontier between India and Afghanistan and were photographed like so many rubber-necked predecessors. C. got too far over to the left and violated the frontier, which much excited the scruffy little Afghan sentry. I thought he was going to stick a bayonet into her. We do not condescend to mount a sentry. The lorries and buses from Kabul are stopped at the Customs house a hundred yards into India.

We wandered up the parched slope following the line of the frontier. This runs parallel with the Afghan part of the road, so that if we had really wanted to violate the frontier nothing could have been easier. The road to Kabul runs straight for about a couple of miles until it disappears over a rise in the ground. The haze spoilt the view of the snowy mountain range of the Hindu Kush along the horizon. I asked about a largish building surrounded by trees and was told it was the headquarters of the American engineers who were re-metalling the road to Kabul. American commercial penetration is in evidence all over the East. Much of the American propaganda against British imperialism is the patter of cheapjacks attracting public attention to their own wares.

The parched slope had lots of interesting little rock-plants still in flower. I noticed a non-climbing convolvulus with silvery-grey leaves and white flowers which much resembles *convolvulus cneorum*, that star of the Capri flora. What excited me most was a miniature *arnebia*, which is known as the Prophet's Flower because the five yellow petals have five large chocolate-brown freckles declared by tradition to be the marks of the Prophet's fingers. These freckles fade away gradually before the yellow flower itself fades. I think the variety we have in our gardens at home comes from Asia Minor; it is larger than this one on the edge of India.* Yet the tradition is the

**Arnebia echioides* from America is a perennial. *A. Griffithii* from N.W. India is an annual.

same here. An old Pathan Jemadar seeing me looking at it, bent down and picked it and then told in Pushtu the story of how the Prophet had one day made his ceremonial ablution and touched the petal with the tips of his fingers and thumb afterwards.

From Landikhana we drove up a hair-raising road to see Big Ben and Little Ben, which were fortified outposts during the war. The trenches and the machine-gun bunkers are still there, but they seem to-day as desolate as Hadrian's Wall. Below the two small plateaus, where stunted poppies and thistles were twitching in the breeze among the sparse herbage, the country surged away into a seeming infinity of jagged peaks and deep remote glens. Immediately below the outpost is a green abyss over which a pair of vultures were hovering and planing—those small light-covered vultures known as Pharaoh's Chickens. I called the road up to this spot hair-raising, and even I who have looked down from a jeep over several precipices hardly a foot from the edge of the road got a new thrill. A great deal of work was done on the frontier from the time war broke out until Hitler burst into Russia, and even afterwards. This is the only part of the world in which we did make a severe effort to prepare for a possible enemy. If as much could have been done in Burma or Malaya, what a different story!

We drove on from Big Ben through some Shinwari villages, passing a piquet which guards the water supply of Landikotal but from which the garrison itself has to walk down a hill and fetch up every pail of water it requires. We also passed an airstrip on which I should not care to land or take off. Then we went on through Landikotal to drive down the Khyber Pass road. A railway has been constructed through the Pass parallel with the road. It cost two and a half million pounds and there are two trains a week. What looks like a doll's house against the mountains is Kata Kushta station, and it was here that Nehru was fired at during his gallant visit to the Frontier. The Khyber Pass is every bit as romantic as its presentation by the most romantic novelist. Sam Browne's Piquet stands on a conical hill. It has been abandoned ever since the sentry from the look-out came down one morning to find the rest of the little garrison inside lying dead, because everybody was convinced that this was the work of evil spirits. The material explanation is that the men were asphyxiated in their sleep by charcoal fumes.

A short way beyond this is the picturesque little mosque of Ali Masjid and we turned aside to drive up the road to the fort above from which we had another impressive view of the mighty pass. Before we came to Sam Browne's Piquet we saw a stupa which was already there when Alexander the Great came this way. This country was the centre of a great Buddhist culture 2,200 years ago, and the stupa which looks like a great beeskep is the origin of the pagoda. The breast-shaped pagoda we saw at Sagaing must be architecturally linked with the stupa of the north. Round this stupa in the Khyber Pass they are continually digging up stucco heads of Buddha which show what an influence the Greek invasion had on the art of N.W. India. These heads of Buddha might be heads of Hermes or Apollo.

Major Penly of the Khyber Rifles met us at Ali Masjid and drove on with us down to Shagai, a large modern fort, where he commands. Here we had lunch with him and the second-in-command, Captain Karamed Ulla. A tasty hors d'oeuvre in the shape of bits of liver roasted on a spit was the perfection of meat-eating.

A sudden wind sprang up after lunch just as we were leaving Shagai, and I was glad to experience what they have to put up with here in the way of whirling dust. These storms are frequent and most unpleasant. This afternoon the dust was abruptly laid by a shower of rain, and we scooted back to Landikotal at many miles above the speed-limit of 25 miles prescribed for the Pass. However, as all the wild Afghan lorries never go down it at less than 40 miles an hour, it is not an effective speed limit. Fortunately the drivers of camels and donkeys pay attention to the double finger-posts, on one of which is painted a motor-car and on the other a camel, and stick to the track provided for them beside the main road.

In the evening a *tikala* was being held by the Subedars and Jemedars, all in mufti, in honour of Colonel Booth who was leaving next day to take up his command in Waziristan. A long table was laid in the open and lighted with standard lamps from the Mess. The British guests were given knives and forks; everybody else ate with his fingers. When we arrived garlands of sweet white banksia roses were hung round our necks. I sat next Haider Khan, one of the Subedars, who was in mufti. He is going to be a schoolmaster and has studied in Damascus of which we talked while we ate a superlative pilau. Alas, when the rain stopped the wind started again and presently blew down all the lamps. So the shades had to be taken off. Haider Khan is a curiously gentle personality for this fierce corner of the earth. He speaks English well and we enjoyed a philosophic talk about religion, deploring the bitterness of rival creeds.

Here is the "Menu for the Dinner Party":

1. A. Polso.
   B. Dahi (curd)
2. Tarkari.
3. Roti.

4. Roast Mutton.
5. Chapli Kabab.
6. Ferni.
7. Fruit.
8. Green Tea.

That is the way the menu was typed out on a small slip of paper. I earned approval by eating two bowls of the sour curd, but was not considered enough of a gourmand over the meat, though I ate more meat at a single meal than I ever ate before in my life. Roast mutton was *roast* mutton, not that wretched baked mutton we have all had to eat since the kitchen-range ousted the spit.

The *roti* or bread was like a large Highland scone. *Ferni* is a sort of very sweet rice pudding covered with edible silver paper, the latter much esteemed as an aphrodisiac.

The farewell address I reproduce from another typed slip:

Farewell Address

1. Lt.-Colonel J. R. Booth distinguished himself among the public in the re-raising of the Khyber Rifles.
2. This is the highest honour that after 27 years the Khyber Rifles was re-raised at his name and he was the first to command it.
3. He worked out so hard in the building of the Khyber Rifles during the Course of one year and completed it in such a short period that it would not have been possible for other officers.
4. He did all this for our sake with the utmost zeal.
5. For all this we feel sorry to see him off.
6. We cannot tolerate his departure from among us.
7. But we are happy to see him raised to rank of Brigadier.
8. We also hope that our time shall pass peacefully with Colonel Sharif Khan.
9. We feel proud to have a Colonel from among our own tribe.
10. We all rank and file of the Khyber Rifles wish both Mem Sahib and your happiness and prosperity.

The Khyber Rifles were disbanded in 1920 because they were not found to be reliable warriors against their own kin in the Frontier and Afghan War of 1919, which was a much more serious affair than people at home realized.

Colonel Booth made a speech of farewell, and then we all adjourned to the parade ground, where we sat in a circle of at least 2,000 spectators to watch dancing by professionals from Peshawar. The boys dressed as girls were hardly recognizable as boys.

The wind still persisted in raising sudden clouds of dust, and the dancers tended to become monotonous. The whirling round and round which is the chief feature must be most exhausting, and yet when we left about 23 o'clock we were told that the dancing would continue till 2 a.m. at the earliest.

I was pretty tired when I turned in after a wonderful day.

April 24th. LANDIKOTAL TO THAL

Yousuf was well enough to come on with us. The Doctor had given him another 10-grain injection of quinine and his arm was sore, but he felt able to carry on with the tour. This news was a pleasure and relief to us, for he was an ideal conducting officer. We left the Mess about 9. Everybody had put himself out to make our visit as fruitful as possible and another bundle of memories has gone into the rich store amassed during this wonderful tour.

I don't think I should ever get tired of driving up and down the Khyber Pass even in dust storms. No place I ever saw for the first time looked less like the picture of it in my mind beforehand and no place looks more exactly like what it ought to look. It is a magnificent composition of crags and peaks and ochreous dwelling places, themselves as fierce as the surroundings out of which they seem to have been cut, and the chiaroscuro which every turn of the road displays is beyond the power of words to paint.

We drove on down beyond Shagai to Jamtud which stands in the plain at the entrance of the Pass. This is an ancient Sikh fort, and we saw the little room, now a machine-gun post, in which the body of Hari Singh was kept pickled in oil for a week so that he appeared to be sitting up in control of the situation and thus the death of their mighty leader would not discourage his men from resisting the onslaught of the tribesmen.

There was a lot of wind and dust during the drive to Kohat, which we reached at lunch time. Our stay there was all too short as we had to be on the road again by 14.30. The escort provided for the drive to Thal looked strong enough to deal with any martial emergency. We drove through fields of golden wheat and hedgerows of pink roses like miniature Dorothy Perkins ramblers. The orange trumpets of the tecoma trees (*tecoma undulata*, I think) and the orange-scarlet of pomegranate blooms took the place of the roses from time to time. Quail nets were frequent. Yousuf and C. saw a flight of small yellow birds, which I missed. They hoped for a rarity, but as far as I can make out they were the Common Iora.

All along the roadside caravans of Afghan nomads returning home from their Indian winter were resting in the midday heat;

but many were still moving along on the road—children, grey
beards, men like gypsies, women in black dresses edged with dul
crimson, camels, dogs, and trains of miniature donkeys. I wa
amused by one train of these donkeys, each of which was eating fron
the load of the donkey in front of it as they pattered along.

We reached the big fort in Thal after about three hours' drivin
and were welcomed by Brigadier Roche and Major Stephen, hi
Brigade-Major. Yousuf and I were put up in the Mess, and C
stayed with Major and Mrs. Grice whose three brindled Grea
Danes were enough to frighten even a marauding party of Pathans
I rested for half an hour, and then Yousuf and I went round th
defences with Brigadier Roche and Major Stephen. The Valley c
the Kurram was considered a likely way in for Russian tanks at firs
and German tanks afterwards, so dragon's teeth had been sown al
over the place. We went up to the Kurram Piquet which stands on
small hill about 300 feet high and overlooks a wide view of the coun
try. Brigadier Roche gave me a clear idea of the proposed defence c
this vital area.

We wound up with a visit to the dairy where a Sikh exper
superintends an attested herd of water-buffaloes which were bein
looked after as carefully as a herd of Guernseys. There is an idea c
crossing these water-buffaloes with Frisians to improve the outpu
of milk in quantity. I doubt if Frisians will improve the quality. I
was dark before we got back to the Mess and when I was dressed
cocktail party was already gathered on the lawn, where thousand
of sparrows, perplexed by the illumination, were fluttering round th
jacaranda trees like moths round a lamp.

The Dogra pipe-band gave a splendid programme of first-clas
piping, and when it was over I had the pleasure of drinking
dram with the drum-major (who was a juggling wizard with hi
staff) and the pipe-major. Hefty drams they were too.

April 25th. THAL

During the night a band of Pathans broke through the wir
of one of the small piquets round the fort, and before the Sikh sentr
could pull out a grenade one of them shot him in the thigh, luckil
missing the bone.

We started off soon after 8 for Parachinar, up the valley of th
Kurram, a wide and fertile strath where the wheat was full golde
at the beginning; but the deeper we penetrated, the less golde
it became, and before we reached Parachinar it was still green.
was surprised by the number and size of the false-pepper tree
(*schinas molle*) along the road, their rose-madder berries competin

with the hot-scented plumes of blossom, the colour of lime-flowers. This is a Peruvian tree. Later I was told they had originally been planted by Colonel Noel, a former political agent, and that they had propagated themselves. They fit in perfectly with the landscape, which all exotic trees do not. For instance, the Australian blue gum within my observation never suits an old world landscape.

At the barrier between the Thal command and the tribal area administered by the Political Agent we were met by Lt.-Colonel W. Leeper and Major McCauseland of the Kurram Militia. The Thal escort handed us over here to an escort of the Kurram Militia. I left the staff-car and drove with Leeper who answered my innumerable questions with much patience. The people here make great economic use of a dwarf palm rather like *Chamaerops humilis* of the Tyrrhenian Sea. Among other things it provides the grey dye that is the characteristic colour of the men's clothes here.

The men of the caravans all had their rifles now. They have to park them at Thal when they come down in autumn for their Indian winter, and these are all numbered and returned to them when they go back to Afghanistan in spring.

About three-quarters of the way to Parachinar we turned off to the right along a dusty track to visit the Badama or Almond Post on the other side of the Kurbana or Apricot River. This lonely outpost stands at the entrance of the Kurram pass which winds up into Tirah, a great tract of fertile country between here and the Khyber which is the home of perhaps as many as a hundred thousand Afridi tribesmen, all armed with rifles.

This small and remote fort is attacked about once a month by the tribesmen in much the same spirit as we might go shooting partridges. War here is essentially a sport. The slopes of the hill at the left of the entrance to the pass are marked with the figures of the range so that the garrison can get some good practice in markmanship. The grassy hill on the other side has a conspicuous tree on the summit round which the tribesmen gather for the attack before they are dispersed by mortar fire. Yet they have never cut down the tree which gives the range. No doubt that would be considered unsporting.

The Subedar in command invited us to have a cup of tea, and then brought in a cold chicken and various other good things to eat. We protested that we could not tackle a chicken at 10.30 a.m. and then set to and picked every bone clean with our fingers, besides eating a lot of eggs and nuts and slabs of bread baked on a large griddle.

It was a pang to leave that little brown fort with the Union Jack fluttering above the rampart and to take a last look at the pass

winding mysteriously into the heart of the brooding mountain
We walked to our cars across the sun-bleached yard in front, alor
which a double line of Persian lilac was in fragrant bloom.
Spitfire was humming high overhead when we turned back into th
main road, and presently we saw the tribal plane tree—the *pa*
chinar which gives the place its name. Alas, the ancient tree lool
like expiring of antiquity in spite of having recently been dosed wi
the bodies of twenty bullocks to revive its vigour.

How can I bring to the printed page Parachinar itself? Th
hexameters of Theocritus are demanded. Leeper's delightful house
surrounded by lawns as green as any in Oxford. Bowers of honey
coloured banksia roses are everywhere. The wistaria racemes hav
not yet fallen on one side of the house and next it the single whi
rose known as the Rose of Mardan is in full perfection. The leaves
the daffodils are turning yellow, and the little tulips in the gra
have set their seeds, but the irises are still in flower. We rested be
neath a spreading chinar where on occasions Leeper dispenses justic
at what resembles our land-courts in the Hebrides. Then we wer
on to lunch at the Mess of the Kurram Militia, the cosiest small Me
imaginable. There is an admirable library of at least a thousan
volumes—the best Mess library I have seen—rich in books of trav
and history. We had a lunch to which I should like to apply a
epithet of my youth and call 'spiffing'. They have so much asparagu
that they even curry it. And spring onions as large and lustrous a
Roman pearls in an enormous bowl! I must have eaten a couple
dozen.

After lunch we drove out to Ali Kot, another Frontier post, bu
I shirked climbing right up to it. We stopped at Ali Mangat an
gazed at the Safed Koh, the range of snowy mountains which pre
sides over the plain round Parachinar as Taygetus, the line of whic
it resembles, presides over the plain of Sparta. On the way we passe
groves of fruit-trees. These were planted long ago by Lord Robert
who intended to build a Residency here. It was Roberts who "an
nexed" Parachinar. The residency was never built, and the garde
is now a wilderness. Cox's Orange Pippin grows well round here
I picked a sprig of mistletoe from a holm or holly oak, and in one c
the villages, famed for its beautiful girls, there was a grove of nobl
walnuts.

After seeing the Pathans I am certain the British Israelites ar
wasting time and money, and what is worse in these days, paper, i
trying to prove that the lost tribes are to be found in Britain. Thes
Pathans seem like Jews unspoilt by urban life. Leeper says it is th
custom to proclaim from the house-top the birth of a male child

ıd significantly they prolong the celebration of the Muslim Friday .rough Saturday with lighted candles. It is much more probable .at the Jewish tribes were dispersed from Palestine by Nebuchad-:zzar eastward, and the Afghan tradition of being descended from ıul may well have a Palestinian origin. Then there is the Yusufzai ibe which definitely claims to be the children of Joseph. Their)ung men wear the side-curls, which are a characteristic of the :ws as far west as the ghettos of Poland.

We drove on from Ali Mangat past another of our posts and could e the large Afghan post a mile away on the other side of the fron-:r. Many of the fields here are given over to artemisia (wormwood) arted by a late Political Agent, which brings in a good profit.

Leeper turned back into Parachinar where the road by Ali Kot ined the road back to Thal. We picked up our escort, which was nsidered unnecessary round Parachinar itself, and we drove home ter a day of absorbing interest, badly recorded by me over three eeks later. I find the word "woodcock" scrawled on a loose page . my block and remember now Leeper's telling me that woodcock ere scarce round Parachinar, so scarce indeed that when one was otted in a village two men were told off to watch where the bird ent while a third hurried post haste to warn the guns. By the time .e bird was shot it cost as much as a profiteer's pheasant.

pril 26th. THAL TO PESHAWAR

When I looked out of the window of my room about 6.30 I saw ıe Dogra drum-major rehearsing twirls with his staff on the lawn ıder the jacaranda trees. Evidently a real artist.

Yousuf and I started off early in a jeep driven by Major Stephen see Fort Lockhart.

I hesitate to call the road up to Fort Lockhart—a 6,000-ft. climb— ıe most dizzy of all those we have tackled, but there is one stretch ` 50 yards where the road is built out on girders over an abyss)out 2,000 feet deep, and that is a bit of a tester for weak heads. /hen we were getting near the top Stephen listened to the jeep, opped, and asked if there was any oil in it. It had just run out and ıe gears would have seized in another moment. Fort Lockhart ands on a ridge overlooking a vast stretch of mountains. I climbed the top of a wooden platform by a rickety ladder and enjoyed a ıblime view. Fort Lockhart will house a battalion comfortably and .ed to be a summer station. Not far away is a memorial to nineteen .en and two cook-boys of the 36th Sikhs (now the 4/11th) who in 397 defended a blockhouse against 7,000 Orakzais and died to a ıan before they could be relieved.

Stephen drove the jeep down as fast as he could because beside
a shortage of oil there was also a shortage of petrol. When we reache
the bottom we transferred to a staff-car and went on to Kohat
Brigadier Parker had thoughtfully invited two Indian officers an
their wives to lunch—Lt.-Colonel H. L. Bhatya of the I.A.M.C. an
Major Inder Jit Rikhye of the 6th Lancers. The two wives, one
Hindu in a delicious sari and the other a Muslim in equally deliciou
trousers of white satin, were both lovely girls and moreover extremel
good talkers, full of humour. I should have liked to stay talking t
them for the rest of the afternoon, but as usual we had to hurry on
Brigadier Parker took us round to H.Q. where we looked down th
board gilded with the names of previous C.O.s at Kohat—Roberts
Birdwood, and other famous Generals among them. The church
which had many memorials was unfortunately destroyed by fire
year or so ago.

The drive on to Peshawar was very hot and dusty. We passed
local rifle-factory which turns out arms for the tribesmen. Yousu
suggested that I should go round it, but I felt too lazy. We reache
Flagstaff House about 16.30; I changed almost immediately afte
tea and we went off to the Retreat of the 2/1st Gurkhas. Som
grand piping, marching, and counter-marching, but alas, one o
the violent duststorms for which Peshawar is noted sprang up suddenly and at the same moment the electric light failed. We went on t
dine with Brigadier Cabitt-Smith and then to a Sergeants' Social, in
the Mess of the 2nd K.O.S.B.s. The oil lamps and motionless fan
made it terrifically hot. I thought I was going to pass out, bu
Colonel Payton Reid asked me to say a few words and I managed t
pull myself together. From the Social we went on to a dance at th
Club, where the electric light was functioning. Just as I was beginning to feel rather tired our host Ross McCay ordered champagn
and I rapidly revived with some generous bumpers. We got home at 2

April 27th. PESHAWAR TO MALAKAND

We left Peshawar at 11 on a blazing hot morning. Buses crowde
with Muslims waving green flags and shouting slogans were comin
into Peshawar from every direction in order to demonstrate to th
Viceroy the solidity and fervour of Pakistan. Sixty thousand ar
expected to muster tomorrow, but serious trouble is not expected
The demonstrators all looked extremely cheerful and the questio
at issue might just as easily have been the victory of a football tear
as the partition of a country. We crossed the Kabul river by the bridg
of boats and reached Risalpur in time for lunch with Brigadier W
Loring.

We passed through Mardan on the way to Malakand. The weather was blazing, and it was a relief to enter the Malakand Gate and start climbing out of the torrid lowland. No car may go through this gate without the authority of the Political Agent. Malakand itself stands on a more or less conical hill with a superb view across a rich river-watered vale to the mountains of Chitral. These are the territories of the Wali of Swat and the Nawab of Dir. The former has 84 fully garrisoned forts.

The house of Lt.-Colonel Evelyn Cobb the P.A. stands on the crown of the hill above the fort at present garrisoned by the 2nd Assam Regiment. Cobb was out fishing when we arrived and came back about 18 o'clock, having been delayed by being called upon to help another fisherman land a 14-lb. mahseer. He is a man with wide interests about which he talks well. He is keen on flowers, and made my mouth water by describing a hillside of white eremurus in March. These would be E. himalaicus, I suppose. The asphodels are a wonderful lot, from the sweet golden bog-asphodel of the Highlands, hardly four inches high, to these twelve-feet fellows defying Everest and Kanchenjunga. Our daffodils were originally 'affodils', which was a variant of 'asphodels'.

Cobb suggested a quick drive to look at the dam which provides the power for the electricity of some of the N.W.F.P. I should need the brush of Corot if I wanted to convey the effect of that long line of poplars beside the canal and the mountains beyond in the evening light. One part of the road ran through an avenue that might have been in Hampshire. It was planted by Godfrey, a former Political Agent here. A pious deed. We crossed over the bridge in the freshness of the dusky breeze. It was of the country behind here that Schomberg wrote in his excellent book *Between the Indus and the Oxus*, and it was from there that he sent me the *choga*. This is a garment of what looks and feels like crotal-dyed brown handwoven Harris tweed with orange braid, and I use it as a dressing-gown.

On the other side of the bridge stands the Chakdara fort, the outpost of *The Broken Road* of A. E. W. Mason. This country is the scene of Winston Churchill's first book, *With the Malakand Field Force*. Major Cassels of the 2nd Assam Regiment was commanding in Chakdara. It was he who brought C. from Imphal to Kalewa, and very glad we were to see him again. Back at the P.A.'s house I found a flower book and identified the Mardan rose as *rugosa*.

April 28th. MALAKAND TO ABBOTTABAD

Cobb took us down in the morning to see the Mogul garden he has made at the bottom of the hill. He planted it ten years ago

when he was here before and now he has returned to enjoy th
reward of his piety—cypresses, flowery borders, lawns and a foun
tain, with an orange grove which produced over 6,000 oranges la
year. He is still planting hard and will leave a fine memorial o
his reign here. We went on from the garden to the Mess of the 2n
Assam Regiment for drinks. I was delighted to meet several Nag
V.C.O.s. There are over 200 Nagas in the battalion. What gran
people they are!

When it was time to leave for Risalpur, Major Ahmad Jan, th
C.O., presented me with a white Chitrali cap—a sort of beret whic
rolls down over the ears and protects them against icy winds. I
will be a splendid bonnet for the Islands. I was also presented with
coin of one of the Greek kings who ruled here after Alexander'
invasion. I am distressingly ignorant of this corner of history.
think it was near Malakand that Alexander won a great victory
Dargai, too, is close by, where Piper Findlater won his V.C. in 1897

The drive to Risalpur was a griller. We stopped for a few minute
to look at the garden of the Guides' Regimental Centre in Marda
and the memorial to the Guides who were murdered in the Legatio
at Kabul. We were rather late for lunch at Yousuf's house where w
met his charming wife and children. We also met his distinguished ol
father Shawbat Khan who had just come back from the Assembly
and the wife of a son of his brother, Major Afridi, who is a grea
malaria expert. She is a daughter of General El-Edroos whom w
met in Hyderabad, and much resembles her father, which mean
she is as handsome a young woman as one could see. She has twi
baby sons. It was an altogether delightful lunch very much *en famille*
Begum Yousuf gave C. a Russian plate.

We left for Nowshera at 15 o'clock where we put Gulaba int
a second-class waiting-room at the station because he had to go o
to Delhi with our luggage. He had a fearful journey. The trai
was swarming with Muslim Leaguers. When asked if he was a Hind
he always vowed he was a Christian, and this possibly saved hi
life. Poor Gulaba, he has had rather a nervous time on the Frontie

We started for Abbottabad at 16.30 and reached it at 19 o'clock
We were put up at the Park Hotel and welcomed by Brigadie
Harrison who told a good story of going to visit an old bearer i
Haripur Gaol which is now full of over 2,000 Muslim demonstrators
The bearer had sent him a chit inviting him to tea in his cell.

In the evening we dined with the V.C.O.s of the Frontier Forc
Rifles at Kukul and enjoyed a *tikala* with superlative mutton. After
wards we saw a real Khotak or Cuttack dance round a grea
bonfire. The sword play was glorious. A cold wind was blowing an

e felt like dancing round the bonfire ourselves. We got back to the otel half an hour after midnight.

pril 29th. ABBOTTABAD

I went off with Yousuf at 10.45 to have a look at the 5th Royal iurkhas' Boys' Company. They are keen on painting. In one hobby oom they were making paper flowers. Two sparrows had built a olychromatic nest in a corner of the ceiling out of the discarded aper. We went outside to watch a class at work on practical roblems. A 'Japanese' arrived with some cock and bull story. Vould the class fall for it? Most of them did and went off with the Japanese' to investigate. This meant they were walking into an mbush. At this moment a Pakistan procession approached along the oad below the parade ground, singing a doubtless patriotic but ex- remely lugubrious song. Just as they were passing the parade round, the class walked into the ambush and there was a volley of lank. The procession stopped dead and the singing died down. It vidently thought it was being fired on, and some minutes passed efore it realized that the shots belonged to another game altogether.

From the Boys' Company we went on to R.I.A.S.C. Headquarters t Kukul where we were met by the Commandant, Colonel H. S. Voods. He told me a lot about the astounding development of the R.I.A.S.C. during the war. They numbered 400,000 by the end. We ooked in at the R.I.A.S.C. Mess and I was introduced to the fficers—all Indians.

At 16.30 we went on to have tea in the Mess of the 5th R. Gurkhas. Colonel Nightingale's father had been one of the great developers of Abbottabad, which was founded nearly a century ago, and built to ook like a village in the Home Counties with a Stoke Poges Church nd all. Now it is a largish place and militantly Muslim.

In the evening I dined with the 6th Gurkhas at their Regimental Centre of which Colonel N. Eustace is Commandant. The Mess is a rand room alive with history. After dinner we adjourned to the ines where we were joined by the ladies and saw some dancing. was much amused to watch the faces of the Regiment's wives vatching their men made up and dressed as women. They are plendid actors. It is strange that one of the most martial races in the vorld should be able to simulate femininity with such success. We at at a long narrow table facing the arena, and the dancing was as ood as the piping at dinner. Before I left, Colonel Eustace on ehalf of the Centre presented me with a kukri with a decorative cabbard. It was another great evening—my second evening with he 6th Gurkhas. The first was at Maymyo.

April 30th. ABBOTTABAD TO NEW DELHI

We left Abbottabad at 9, making a circuit to avoid driving through a Muslim League meeting. In the paper I read of a bomb thrown and several shots fired at Flagstaff House, Peshawar, either on the night after we left or the next night. I was a little disappointed we had missed the excitement.

We were warned that there might be trouble in Haripur where a Muslim house had been burnt. It had obviously been accidental, but of course the Muslims were accusing the Hindus of having done it on the evidence of an empty petrol tin in the vicinity. Just before we reached Haripur the horn of our car after starting to hoot on its own without stopping, refused to hoot at all when checked, and we had to send the station-wagon in front to avoid an accident in the thronged streets. This meant a good deal of dust. Fortunately the horn agreed to behave itself after we left Haripur.

We took the road by Taxila to Rawalpindi in order to see the museum there. It was indeed well worth a visit, for the excavations in the neighbourhood have produced a marvellous collection of domestic, military and religious relics between the 2nd century B.C. and the 4th century A.D. Various stupas have been excavated. We drove along to Sikrup, which was destroyed and sacked in the 7th century A.D. and the foundations of which take up several acres. Yousuf and I wandered round. The only sign of life in street or house or shop was a tiny yellow flower which starred the sun-smitten rubble. The stone slab of a goldsmith's shop is still there, and a good deal remains of what is called the shrine of the double-headed eagle, which was apparently a Greek temple. I really must cure my ignorance of all this history. This Graeco-Buddhist-Hindu civilization is intriguing.

An old Punjabi soldier came along to ask if we would like to buy some coins. I secured half a dozen, but they are poor specimens, and I doubt if even an expert would be able to date them.

The drive in to Rawalpindi was a sizzler and we were glad to reach Command House. The day before Mrs. Conroy* had been entertaining Lady Mountbatten, who had left by plane at 6 that morning. She had been fascinated by Lady M's vitality. And indeed Lady M. has been doing a really tremendous job of work since she came out. She and the Viceroy will indeed deserve the success which I feel they will achieve.

Lunch was a hurried affair as we had to be at the airport by 14.15 to catch the Delhi plane at 14.45. It was a Wayfarer, which I like

* Alas, this warm-hearted and most attractive young woman lost her life five months later when a flying-boat crashed at Bahrein. R.I.P.

east, and I liked it still less when I left a box of cheroots in it and ome cigars Mohamed Yousuf gave me. It was sad to leave dear Yousuf. He has been splendid company and I wish him all the luck he deserves as C.O. of the 18th Cavalry.

At Delhi we were met by John Shaw and Peter Goodwin, who is definitely going with us to Nepal. We dressed as soon as we got to the Chief's house and went to have drinks with Mrs. Rudra, the wife of Brigadier Rudra who is with the mission now visiting Nepal to discuss the future of the Gurkhas. Mrs. Rudra is a fine pianist and broadcasts frequently. The Brigadier enlisted in The Norfolk Regiment in 1914 and became a Sergeant. Then he enlisted as a Sepoy in the Indian Army of which he is now a Brigadier.

After a most agreeable hour and a half of good talk we went back to dine at the Chief's house. I went up to bed about 24.45, and was half undressed when what I thought was a Sherman tank seemed to rumble past. It was an earthquake shock which lasted 20 seconds. The walls of the room vibrated, but I did not feel any rocking. Captain Govind Singh, one of the Chief's A.D.C.s, had just gone to bed after a party and saw his boots slowly walking along a shelf. He blinked, and the three pairs of polo boots on the shelf above began to walk about. This was too much for him, and he went out of his room to seek advice. He was relieved to find that it was only an earthquake shock. C. pointed out that it was like the rumble of a V.2. She was right.

NEPAL

May 2nd. DELHI TO RAXAUL

We were airborne at 9 sharp in the A.O.C.'s comfortable Dakota and flew high to avoid the bumps. I worked at my diary all the way until we landed at Bihta about 12.30—the gentlest landing of any flight I have made during this tour. It is the habit of the people round here to put obstructions on the airstrip and smoke flares are lighted to give the all clear to pilots.

Major-General H. Stable, the Area Commander at Dinapur, was away, and we were met by his G.2, Lt.-Colonel Miles Hoffmann of the Frontier Force Rifles and Colonel Chandler, the A.D.M.S. C. was driven off to lunch with the nursing Sisters. I was entertained by the Chandlers and after lunch had a siesta for an hour. The bungalow is old, a relic of the time when the Dutch occupied this part of India. It was the first time I heard that the Dutch had ever occupied any part of India. The wisdom of age is the realization of one's ignorance. There's a huge granary here built by the Dutch which is still in use. I am glad to have some experience of these stations in the plains during the heat.

We drove on to Patna at 16 o'clock, and there we had our first sight of the Ganges. Patna, the centre of the Bihar Government, is the sprawling seething city where Mahatma Gandhi lives. There was a police strike here recently, but it was dealt with firmly, and the police who had shut themselves up in the magazine did not relish the idea of field guns being turned on them and Gurkhas taking over their duties. In fairness to the police, it must be added that they have had by far the most difficult task of all during these last months.

Two Ducks were waiting to take us across the Ganges and as we went down the sandy bank I was reminded of old lifeboat launchings when the crews were practising during the summer holidays. Ducks make a good deal of noise, but we sat in stately comfort in wicker armchairs. The mighty river stretched in a pale green expanse of water under the burning silver sunshine of the heat-hazed afternoon. Seven bloated vultures sat in a row on the farther bank while terns wheeled and darted and dived about us. They were the extremes of avian ugliness and grace. We saw the burning fires of cremation along the banks on the Patna side. After a while we overtook the ferry-steamer crowded with passengers, and in about half an hour reached the sandy slope below the railway station of Paleza Ghat.

An unbroken stream of people from the train, many of them in vivid sulphur yellow, were toiling across the wide sandy slope to the ferry-steamers, and when we were almost at the top of this slope one of the Ducks jibbed. However, its companion came to the rescue with a kick in the rump and the summit was achieved.

A muddle had been made about our coach. We were supposed to have had the one that was meeting the mission returning from Nepal. The coach we had been given was filthy and swarming with cockroaches. A great block of ice in the middle of the floor was making pools of dirty water. Colonel Hoffmann argued in vain with the station-master that a mistake had been made and that the other coach was for us. Nothing could be done. As it was fast growing dark by now, he had to leave us and get back to the Ducks.

The train crawled along to Muzzaffarpur where our coach was detached and shunted about to be attached to another train. The electric current was cut off, and we had to eat our dinner in darkness. The restaurant deserves credit for serving such a good dinner in the circumstances. At last we were hitched on to the next train; to our relief the light came on and one fan began to whizz round. We were all pretty tired and were glad to get into our berths, even if every time one lifted a pillow a couple of cockroaches ran out. Suddenly C. gave a yell. She had been bitten on the finger by something. It turned out to be a yellow wasp which had got involved with the fan and had been flung on to C.'s hand on which it took revenge. Luckily she found it on the sheet and was able to slay it.

It was a nightmare journey. We hung about being shunted around at Segauli for over two hours. The metre-gauge train vibrated and jolted so much that sleep was out of the question, and when we arrived at Raxaul an hour and a half later at 6 we were exhausted.

May 3rd. RAXAUL

We were met by Mr. Shyan Naraia, the Overseer of the Legation Bungalow, and to our relief he told us that we would not be going to Amlekhganj that day because the mission would not reach there till to-morrow and we should be taking their transport back to Katmandu. We walked along the railway-line for about a mile to the Legation bungalow and lay down to sleep for the rest of the hot morning. C. and I did not move from the wired-in verandah, but Peter Goodwin had to go off and forage for food.

A great golden mohur in full bloom (*poinceana regia*) was a lovely sight, but the heat was relentless until 20 o'clock when it cooled off slightly. It was too hot for writing up the diary and I read a story about that ridiculous Belgian detective of Agatha Christie's, to the accompaniment of a creaking punkah. The jackals howled round the garden a good deal.

May 4th. RAXAUL TO SIRSAGARHI

We set out at 7 for the Nepalese railway-station, which is next to the other one, and found that we would have the state coach which was a welcome contrast to the one in which we had travelled from Paleza Ghat. There were two comfortable armchairs and even a writing bureau, above which was inscribed "Long Live our Maharaja". The train is almost a miniature, drawn by a small engine with a crimson cow-catcher built at Avonside. It was crowded. The Nepal frontier is marked by a small stream just beyond the railway station. We left Raxaul at 7.30 for the journey through the Terai to Amlekhganj. It is only thirty miles, but it takes three and a half hours to accomplish. Just as we were moving out of the station a representative of the United Press of India jumped into our coach and asked me a series of questions until we reached Birbang, the first station inside Nepal. Here he left us. There were many Gurkhas going home. Most of them had umbrellas, which they carried hitched from the back of their battle-blouses, and new hurricane lamps. These are the two gifts that the women at home demand from their warriors. Money-changers with heaps of Nepalese silver coins in front of them were sitting on the platform. The Nepalese rupee is worth slightly more than the Indian rupee. The local band dressed in yellow-frogged tunics and hussar busbies with orange bags was playing *con brio*.

A storm was gathering in the north, and before we reached Parwanipur it was sweeping across the paddy fields in mingled rain and dust. Vivid mauve flashes of lightning at least five miles long rent the livid sky horizontally. Bullock-carts were galloping along the track beside the train rather faster than the train itself.

After Parwanipur the storm showed signs of clearing. The hills appeared ahead of us under a pearly blue stretch of sky beneath a monotonous weight of grey cloud, and by the time we reached the banyan-shaded station of Simra the sun was shining. We ate our lunch here, and presently the little train went jogging deep into the jungle of the Terai at about three miles an hour. From time to time branches touched the windows. This jungle is one of the most noted big-game haunts in all the East. Tigers abound. The Terai and the Assam jungles are the last refuge of the great Indian rhinoceros. It is also one of the most fever-stricken stretches anywhere. The *awa*, a very vicious malaria, makes it impossible for sport from the end of April to the end of October.

When I was in Rome in 1916 Lt.-Colonel E. V. Gabriel*, who had been on special service in Nepal eight years earlier and was Secretary of the Coronation Durbar, told me that the Maharaja of Nepal had had a glade cut through this jungle which was lighted by torch-bearers on either side so that the Nepalese cavalcade returning from the Durbar could ride through at night to the foot of their mountains. It was that picture conjured up by Gabriel over a dinner-table in Rome thirty-one years ago which first fired me with a desire to see Nepal. The railway is only twenty years old. Before that everybody had to ride through the Terai to reach Nepal.

It was close on noon when we reached Amlekhganj. The mail bus was overflowing with passengers and luggage before our luggage was out of the train, and a Havildar of the R.I.A.S.C. who had a lorry for the returning Gurkhas offered us a lift in that. However, that became too full and another lorry was brought up to take ourselves and what were left of the Gurkhas. A Jemedar from the Airborne Division came up beaming to say he had shaken hands with me in Karachi.

It was piping hot in the sun and we retired to find some shade on the balcony of the station. Here we met Major-General Lyne, Brigadier Rudra, and Sir Girja Shankar Bajpai who were on their way back from a mission about the future of the Gurkhas. Lyne said he thought he should be establishing a record by travelling from England to Nepal and back in eight days. I asked Bajpai, who was Agent-General in Washington during most of the war, how he had enjoyed his visit to Nepal. He said he should have enjoyed it more if he had been twenty years younger. So I said that in that case I should have to be thirty years younger to enjoy it.

The 32-miles drive to Bhimpedi was without doubt the bumpiest we had had during this tour, and that's saying a lot. C. and I sat beside the Havildar in front. Peter Goodwin and Gulaba stood, holding on behind. The scenery was superb. The Havildar, who had been through the Burma compaign, kept pointing to the bare precipices towering above the lush vegetation and exclaiming "Burma! Burma!". He was right about the comparison.

The road was climbing slowly all the way up from Amlekhganj and at Churia (2,100-ft.) we came to a tunnel a quarter of a mile long through the rock. About fifty yards before the end it takes a sharp turn and the weight of the rock is supported by 12-inch rafters and posts. We were glad to reach the end of this wild drive

* Colonel Sir Vivian Gabriel, C.S.I.

and get out of the lorry at Bhimpedi (3,650-ft.) where we were followed by a crowd of children in any direction we went. There were no coolies or ponies or dandies, and while Peter Goodwin rushed around trying to find out where they were I meditated on the possibility of obtaining accommodation for the night in this swarming village.

However, presently the transport arrived. It had been waiting at the other end of the village. C. entered a large black dandy with a hood and was hoisted on the shoulders of eight coolies. I entered a smaller dandy the shape of half a canoe and was hoisted on the shoulders of four coolies, with a relay of two. Peter G. mounted a pony and off we went. We crossed the grey rocky bed of a river and ascended a precipitous mountainside 2,000-ft. up in a series of loops four miles in all to the Maharaja's rest house at Sirsagarhi. On the way across the river bed I noticed a sportsman with a shotgun carrying two large yellow flowers which I could not identify. From the distance they might have been sunflowers.

We arrived at the rest house (5,875-ft.) at 17.30 and sat down to a high tea as soon as Gulaba could brew the tea.

The view was magnificent, but I have no epithets left to describe mountain scenery. The electric aerial ropeway from beyond Bhimpedi to Katmandu is a fascinating sight. One plays with the notion of being strapped into what look rather like chairs and making the journey which is made by so many packages. Yet to travel over abysses 2,000 feet deep from ridge to ridge suspended from a couple of small wheels running along a wire might be just a little too exciting.

Near the rest-house was a small Nepalese fort where a lot of bugling was going on; but I was too tired to walk even a couple of hundred yards for a closer view. However, after ten we strolled along the road in the twilight and watched the Gurkah soldiers with their umbrellas and hurricane-lamps going up to their quarters for the night.

Gulaba cooked a chicken capitally. We asked him if he was getting help from the people on the spot, and he said, "No, just looking and looking and sitting and talking." C. said it reminded her of cooking in the Hebrides. We went to bed very early. Peter G. and I shared a room.

May 5th. SIRSAGARHI TO KATMANDU

I woke at 3.45 to hear wind and heavy rain, but by 6 all was clear, and we set out on the last stage of our journey at 7 o'clock of a radiant morning with a cool breeze.

We got out of the dandies and walked for a while but the road became very rough and the descent to Khuli Khani very steep after about a mile.

When we were going along beside the Markhu River clouds were gathering ahead and we feared we were in for heavy rain, but we were lucky and escaped with a few drops. The members of the mission were less fortunate and were drenched on their way back. The cloud effects were grand. All along the valley thousands of what one could call marbled black butterflies were dancing round the pomegranates and white roses and the candelabra cactus which are used down in this warm valley for hedges. The terraced cultivation up the hillsides was extremely neat.

We crossed the river and had a stiff climb up on the other side through the pass of Chisapani Garhi (6,225-ft.) after which we proceeded through rolling downland for several miles, high above a rapid narrow river running through a wooded gorge. The steep slopes on the other side were terraced to the summit and beyond the grassy downland the cultivation was equally widespread. About 13 o'clock we stopped and ate our lunch under a tree I could not name. Soon after we started again I recognized with pleasure some shrubs of *berberis nepalensis* which I used to grow in Cornwall. The leaves are of the mahonia type with yellow lily-of-the-valley-like clusters sweetly scented, and blossoming at home in early February. I noticed also what was probably *buddleia asiatica*. The white roses I had seen in the valley proved to be *rosa moschata* with an exquisite scent. I saw, too, *rosa sericea*, which is a very small white rose whose beauty is in its fruit. A Chinese variety of this called *rosa sericea pteracantha* has large thorns like cornelians which if planted to catch the setting sun shining through them is one of the loveliest sights a garden can show. The grass beside the track was starred with what I was told was a miniature gentian, though the flowers were more like a *lithospermum*, and the shade was the same as that garden favourite 'Heavenly Blue'.

We reached the village of Chitlong at the foot of the Chandragiri Pass where we rested beside a small stream thick with watercress while the coolies got themselves tea. It was now 14.30. We could hardly believe that we could ascend the rampart of mountain in front of us, which rises to 7,000 feet. The track up looked perpendicular. Over to the left a gash down the mountainside was pointed out as the elephant track. Our own track was strewn with small boulders and loose rocks. The strain on the coolies was painful, and I felt ashamed of having to be carried.

The vegetation was beautiful. I noticed *rhododendron arboreum* and *R. Thomsoni*, and I think *R. campylocarpum*. Alas, only a few scattered

rubies still adorned the boughs, for their flowering season was over
We were too early for those lovely lilies, *Nepalensis* and *Wallichianum*
Cassias were in bloom, and another yellow-flowered tree I could no
name. I saw also a tall scraggy hydrangea with rosy-buff flower
of the *paniculata* type i.e. with a cluster of sterile incomplete flower
in the middle. I don't know the technical botanical name for thi
arrangement. Later I looked through a list of Nepalese flora an
found that three hydrangeas are indigenous—*anomala*, *aspera* an
vestiva. I fancy this rosy-buff one must be *anomala*. Many of the tree
were draped with *clematis montana* at the peak of its blossoming—a
exquisite sight. I saw a *viburnum* of sorts and what looked to me lik
cornus capitata. There were ferns in great variety, and plenty of ilex

As far back as Burma I noted a thistlelike plant with greyish
green leaves streaked with white and yellow flowers of the Icelan
poppy type. I spoke of it as a common half-hardy annual at hom
but could not remember the name. I have seen this flower every
where since, the last place being on the road to Chitlong. Half
way up the Chandragiri Pass I suddenly remembered its name—
argemone mexicana, a poppywort. But how has a Mexican flower sprea
all over the East? This can also be asked of *agave Vera Cruz*—th
"aloe" of popular plant lore that blooms once in a hundred years
I saw any amount of agaves on the track across the downland, thei
unopened heads of bloom sticking up like mammoth asparagus.

From the top of Chandragiri we beheld the great valley of Kat
mandu, and Katmandu itself below us, but we were not grante
the view of the Himalaya beyond. The equally precipitous descen
of Chandragiri to Thankot (1,700-ft. below) was of marvellou
beauty. The vegetation was much more luxuriant on this norther
side, and the variety of greens seemed infinite. The golden light o
afternoon was falling slantwise, and the birdsong was continuous
Yet I actually saw only two birds—a tit and a large falcon hoverin
over the great punchbowl of greenery. Just before Thankot w
passed a small stupa. This country, sacred to the memory of th
Gautama Buddha who was born in Nepal, is now predominantl
Hindu in religion, but there are still many Buddhist temples an
the two religions both take something from the other, nor do thei
worshippers quarrel.

At Thankot we got out of our dandies and into the Legation ca
which was waiting to drive us the nine miles from Thankot t
Katmandu, along a road lined on either side with crimson bottlebrus
trees and grevilleas in full faded-orange bloom. Somebody with
taste for the Australian flora must have been influential in Katmand
once upon a time, but I have not been able to find out who it was.

The Chitlong Valley from Chandragiri Pass

The valley of Nepal

Stupa built by Asoka's daughter near Katmandu

Shrines and the burning ghat at Pashpatti

Crossing the Ganges

Climbing the Sirsagarhi Pass

Bangles for sale

Taking firewood to the market

Colonnade, the Singha Durbar

The Singha
Durbar,
Katmandu

A rcception room, Singha Durbar

Throne room,
Singha Durbar

Carpenters at work, Katmandu

With Christina MacSween in Patan

Courtyard of the Swayambhanath Temple

A shrine in the Swayambhanath Temple

A statue in Patan

Kalabhairar—a statue in Katmandu

We reached the Legation about 17 o'clock. Lt.-Colonel George Falconer the Minister welcomed us. Brigadier J. French whom I had met at a Saintsbury lunch was a fellow guest, but was leaving next morning. Mrs. Falconer is a niece of Sir Robert Hart, the famous head of the Chinese customs.

The Legation is a comparatively new building erected recently when the old Legation, which resembled a country vicarage of the Gothic revival period, was pulled down. It is not beautiful and it is difficult to make these modern houses look lived in.

Poor Gulaba's feet were much blistered by the 17-mile tramp. He attributed it to not wearing "shocks". I had tried to make him ride, but he always declined. It transpired later that he had twice been thrown off ponies in the past.

May 6th. KATMANDU

I spent the morning reading Percival Landon's two-volume book about Nepal. He accumulated a mass of valuable information, but he was unable to put it into any kind of shape, and a more difficult book to find one's way about in I have seldom read. The two volumes are extremely heavy, both literally and figuratively, and I was quite worn out by lunch-time in chasing information that ought to have been in Volume 1 in Volume 2 and vice versa.

I wrestled with Landon again after lunch, and after tea Peter Goodwin, C. and myself drove along to the Balajiri Garden where there is a large fishpond full of Asiatic carp which one feeds with some kind of grain. The overflow from the large rectangular pond, which is surrounded by a flagged terrace below a wooded hill, is spouted away through the mouths of about a dozen black and crimson dragon-heads of wood and feeds a shallow pond in a large lawn surrounded by trees and immense clumps of bamboo, some of the stems of which have a diameter of at least eight inches. This lawn is used as a public park.

In another pond on the terrace a large image of Narain—a manifestation of Vishnu—lies on its back in the water. This was put here for the King to visit because for some reason or other he must not visit the much larger Narain at a place near Katmandu, the name of which I have forgotten. The King is a figurehead and takes no active part as a ruler, all power being in the hands of the Prime Minister who has the title of Highness and Maharaja. The Rana family are Rajputs not Gurkhas. His present Highness is Sir Padma Sham Shere Jung Rana Bahadur.

On the way back from Balajiri we were blessed with a view of the high snows of the Himalaya—a most unusual sight at this time of year.

We went round to have drinks before dinner with Colonel Norm: Macleod of the 1st Gurkhas who was Commandant for a long tin of the Regimental Centre at Dharmsala and is now First Secreta. of the Legation with the temporary rank of Lt.-Colonel, which the highest military rank a political officer can attain. The Legatic compound is thirty acres and in it are the Lines of the Nepal Escor The 75 members used to be recruited from Rajputs or Brahmir but the escort has now been disbanded. A gun booms at 22.20 ar 4.20. This is the curfew. None may be abroad in the streets betwe the guns.

May 7th. KATMANDU

Accompanied by Colonel Sin Shere Mohdkher of the Nepale: Army we went to explore Katmandu in the morning. The fir place we visited was the official residence of the Maharaja who do not actually live in it, preferring to remain in the house he ha before he succeeded his cousin. It is a large place with a profusic of tiles and marble, the latter, quarried locally, a pinkish mauve i colour.

The walls of the staircase leading up to the Durbar Hall a covered with paintings of a tiger hunt, and the anteroom is line with a dozen distorting mirrors, each of which transforms the spe tator into a new grotesque shape. So encouraging for courtie taking a last look at their clothes before entering the Presence! crystal fountain plays in the middle of the Hall at the end of whic are two crimson thrones. Beyond it is a pink drawing-room of th late 'nineties with cosy corners and plush and silver photograp frames. The second Durbar Hall in another building is more in pressive. A large gold and crimson carpet stretches in front of th thrones which are guarded by two metal leogryphs which at solem functions are lighted internally and exhale fiery breath. There ar paintings all round of the Rana family, most of them Generals wea ing the robes of the Most Refulgent Order of the Star of Nepa The King's Durbar Hall which we visited next is much smaller tha either of the Maharaja's, but it is surprisingly adorned by two larg Winterhalter portraits of Queen Victoria and the Prince Consort- the Queen beside the throne, Prince Albert beside the door- separated by the usual portraits of previous Maharajas and Genera

Having been shown these three examples of consciously magni cent modernity, we were free to explore the old Durbar Squar most of the buildings in which date from the fifteenth to the seve teenth century. It would take many weeks to explore this phantas magoria thoroughly enough do to even faint justice to it. A hurrie ılk round followed everywhere by a crowd of about two hundred ople does not allow one to contemplate the details of the carved ɔod and ivory with which every house is covered. There are temples erywhere. I recall most vividly the five-storied Temple of Talegu th its gilded Chinese-like roofs. This temple is opened only once year when there is a procession of all the women of the ruling ›use to the shrine of Talegu, who as far as I can gather is another anifestation of the Goddess Kali. No men may enter this temple, ıd up on the balcony of the second story we could see the female ıardian of the place walking round. I recall the great bell in the iddle of the square and near it two enormous kettle-drums—at ast six feet across and six feet high—which once upon a time unded the alarm. They stand now leaning against either side of a m alcove. I recall a house built entirely of the wood of one tree cording to legend, which is said to be the origin of Katmandu and ay be a thousand years old. I recall the image of Hanuman, the imson-faced monkey-god in a crimson robe who stands by an chway leading into the Court of Silence at the back of the old oyal Palace. The Court of Silence is surrounded by the apartments distant relatives of the Royal Family with carved and fretted indows. Gilded towers spring up from the roof on one side and oisters lined with dark wood surround two sides.

At the far end of the square I saw a large peepul (more correctly *bal*) tree the glittering foliage of which I thought at first was ›vered with great white waxen flowers until one of the blossoms oved and I realized that they were white egrets. Besides the Hindu mples there are two Buddhist temples in the square standing back courtyards entered through archways. One of these had a richer ›ncentration of divers smells than we have yet encountered in this ›ur. It is the resort of scholars.

Back at the Legation I found a telegram written on paper made om the bark of a daphne or edgworthia. It is very thin and pale nnamon in colour. The telegram was an enquiry from an American ublisher about the prospect of my being willing to write a life of 'inston Churchill. I will guess that this is the first time such an ıquiry has ever come to Katmandu. Indeed, I can certainly claim › be the first British novelist to visit Nepal, though it may have been isited by an American. Mr. and Mrs. Roy Kilburne came to tea. Ie is in charge of the electric power station and they have lived in 'epal for twenty years. Mrs. Kilburne is a keen gardener, and romised to get me seeds of some of the shrubs and flowers if she ould. I should like to try that rosy-buff hydrangea at home. She erself has found a beautiful delphinium, pale blue with mauve centre.

After tea I went round to see Colonel Macleod and had a lon talk about Gurkhas. He has a clear grasp of their character and learnt a lot from him.

Some butter-coloured orchids were in bloom on one of the tree in his garden.

May 8th. KATMANDU

The morning was devoted to exploring Patan, the second of th three cities in the valley and practically joined to Katmandu. I some ways the Durbar Square is even more impressive than that i Katmandu, but the smells from an open drain running down th street are a pretty tough proposition for the unfamiliar nose. Ther seemed to be more children following us about here than yesterday They enjoyed standing by the car and laughing at the reflection c themselves in the enamel. I admired as much as anything th Machendranath, a temple standing in a grass courtyard and over looked by a row of ancient red brick houses. It dates back to A.D 1400. Here is kept the image which is carried in procession in th Machendra-jitra car to bring rain for the harvest. No building i Patan is allowed to be higher than this car. I thought I caught glimpse of it at the end of a street beyond the temple, but m suggestion to walk along in that direction was discouraged. On th steps of one of the temples we noticed a crowd of people offerin small bottles to be filled. I presumed it was some kind of holy liquid but when we drew near enough to see what the excited throng wa receiving with such excitement we found that it was kerosene A vendor of kerosene had arrived with a tinful and people wer clamouring for even half a gill of it

There are four stupas in Patan over 2,000 years old: but th amount to look at in a brief visit is so overwhelming that I hav managed to record almost nothing. Was it in Patan or Katmandu that below a great carved panel of some fierce black and crimsor god with many arms I saw a group of smiling twittering childrer sitting as close as lovebirds?

May 9th. KATMANDU

We drove first to see Boddhnath which is a gigantic white stupa over a thousand years old. It is at least 400 yards round and on each side of the *toran* or gilded tower which rises from this mass of masonry are two enamelled blue eyes with a note of interrogation to represent the nose; of course, it is not a note of interrogation in any Eastern script. These great eyes have gazed out north, south, east and west for over a thousand years, although no doubt the gilding and the lue enamel have been renewed from time to time. That those eyes hould have been gazing there since the time of Alfred the Great s something for the imagination to ponder. Such eyes can be seen n other Buddhist temples round Katmandu, and one will often see hem painted on the doors of the houses; but these great blue eyes of Boddhnath make all the others appear insignificant. The stupa s surrounded by prayer-wheels, being a much venerated place of ilgrimage for Tibetans who brave the snowy passes of the Hima-aya to reach this holy place. Notices in Tibetan script hang outside he stairway which leads to the lustral path round the tower. The tupa is surrounded by a road and a circle of houses curiously nodern in appearance. One of these is occupied by the Lamasery, vhich we were allowed to enter.

From the stupa of Boddhnath we drove on to Pashpatti. This is ne of the most celebrated Hindu places of pilgrimage. Steps lead lown to the sacred river Bagmatti to which the dying are brought hat the stream may lave their feet in the last agony. Then the orpses are burnt. One was being burnt when we arrived. Only Hindus are allowed in the precincts of the temple, and a part of the teps down the bank is reserved for moribund royalty. We crossed a tone bridge and walked up among the trees of the opposite bank to a terrace which gave a good view of the temple. I was disappointed o find that so many of the roofs were of corrugated iron, but we vere told that this was done as a protection against the sacred nonkeys who enjoyed throwing tiles at the pilgrims. The monkeys vere all over the place, all of them with short tails.

We wound up the morning by visiting the museum, the most nteresting part of which is the arsenal where a remarkable collection of weapons has been collected and is well displayed. The develop-ment of the kukri through the centuries is a triumph of arrangement, and it is most interesting to see the experiments in blade-shaping to achieve the deadly weapon of to-day. I was surprised to find in the museum the jawbones of a whale. Why anybody should have taken the trouble to drag the jawbones of a whale to Katmandu is beyond guessing. As many as a thousand coolies have been employed to drag some of the things now in Katmandu. Every lorry—and there are many—has been carried over the mountains.

One room in the museum is devoted to the clothes of the pre-decessor of the present Maharaja. These include his uniforms, his helmets, the insignia of all his orders, and a pair of dress-shirts. The insignia include the Most Glorious Order of Rajunga, the Most Refulgent Order of the Star of Nepal, the Most Illustrious Order of the Tri-Shakti-Patti and the Most Puissant Order of Gurkha

Right Hand. In a special glass case is the magnificent brocad
cloak of the Chinese Order of the Sacred Tripod. The succession
from brother to brother and then to the eldest son of the olde
brother. It is a bit complicated for a stranger to follow. Anoth
snag is that various members of the Rana house arrange and sp
their names with a slight difference.

After lunch we went to call on General Sir Baber Shum She
Jung Bahadur Rana who commanded the Nepalese contingent
the Victory March. He is a shrewd man with charming manne
His two sons were there, one of whom Mrigenda Shum Shere is
charge of State Education, with obviously a fine brain. He said t
idea that Gurkha soldiers would not serve under Indian officers w
ridiculous. He also said that in Nepal they did not like calling t
proposed Gurkha Division for the British Army Imperial troop
They would prefer them to be called Commonwealth troops. I w
interested to find anti-imperialism already strong with the young
generation in this feudal state.

Half an hour later we drove on to call upon H.E. General S
Mohun Shum Shere Jung Bahadur Rana who is the commande
in-chief of the Nepalese Army and next in succession as Maharaj
Finally at 15.30 we were received by H.H. the Maharaja himse
He is an impressive personality and was interested to find that h
was only three weeks older than myself. He shook his head and sa
that in his country they were always ten years older for their ag
than we were. He asked me many questions about the likelihood
war in the near future, discussed the future of India and said th
we had been too late in giving much to avoid giving all. Then h
talked about the Government at home and was obviously amaze
when I told him that unless there was an economic cataclysm n
only would it certainly last its full period but would probably b
returned again in 1950. By this time General Baber had come int
the room, and turning to him His Highness exclaimed, "This is quit
different from what we have been told." However, he was clear
impressed by my conviction, and said I must meet General S
Kaiser Shumsher who was leaving to take up his diplomatic post i
London in a few days' time.

The conversation with His Highness laster for more than an hou
and a quarter, and by the time it was over the room was full
people sitting round and listening. If ever he was in difficulty wit
one of my replies he turned to his Personal Secretary, a son of Genera
Mohun, who struck me as another acutely intelligent young ma
I thanked H.H. for according me the privilege of visiting Nep
and expressed a wish to come back some day and study the flor

e assured me I should always be welcome and presented me with is photograph as Colonel-in-Chief of a Gurkha regiment and also kukri in a silver-mounted scabbard. By the way, one remark he ıade was that we English had always been too "superior" with the ndians, "though never with us", he added quickly. Oh yes, and he sked me if it was true that somewhere in the Bible the last war ad been prophesied in detail.

I felt rather tired by the end of the afternoon. I had been anxious) clear up misunderstanding about the stability of the Government, nd that meant a certain expenditure of vitality. I wish the Oppotion would grasp how little they gain and how much the country ıay lose by their substituting prejudiced misrepresentation for easonable criticism in the interest of party. Throughout this tour have found a widespread belief that the present Government is a assing phase and that the Conservatives will return to power deterıined to dishonour every agreement. Hence the feverish hurry to ıake the break between East and West irrevocable. My opinion hat Labour will be in power for at least ten years always arouses stonishment.

We had a jolly dinner with Colonel Macleod, which included a vonderful strawberry and cream ice.

May 10th. KATMANDU

At 9.30 we drove out to Swayambhanath, a Buddhist sanctuary n the top of a hill some miles from Katmandu. It was a fairly long valk up, but most of the way was shaded by large trees. I have a ıote to say that the central hemisphere of the stupa is called *garbh*, hat the gilt tower is called *toran* and that the conical gilt canopy on op is called *churamani*. Here the eyes were grey, blue, and black, with gain that note of interrogation instead of a nose. Round the *garbh* vere five shrines of the Buddha, inset, with prayer-wheels in between hem. A man in a red coat was taking round offerings on silver lishes to each shrine in turn, opening the trim lattice door and chanting some prayers. Peter G. took a photograph of him, which seemed to please all the people very much. I was a little nervous at irst how it would be received. Pilgrims were walking round swingng the prayer-wheels, and it is evidently a resort for pious holidaynakers. All the little girls were in their best clothes. One little girl n vivid magenta was made up with lipstick and mascara. Babies ıad their eyes darkened with mascara, and even the cheeks of the ittle boys were rouged. Monkeys were climbing and running around everywhere, and as we left the hilltop we passed a house in which vomen were keening round the body of a man who had just died.

On the way back to lunch we stopped outside a shop in the main street to photograph the famous H.M.V. dog over the door. At 16 o'clock we went to tea with Colonel Macleod and afterwards drove out to the electric power station. We passed through several jolly villages and much admired the cultivation of the Newars which compares with that of the Chinese. The Newars live in the Katmandu valley and were conquered by the Gurkhas. They contribute the largest proportion of troops to the Nepalese army. The dam on the Bagmatti River is not visible from the power station as the reservoir is much higher up. I was surprised to hear that the sacred river could be played about with in the interest of electricity without offending religious opinion. The villagers take advantage of the curfew to pinch the electric current. Some reckon that as much as 50 per cent. of it is diverted into houses without being paid for.

On the way back we stopped by an ancient temple to scramble up the wooded bank and look down into a gorge of the Bagmatti at the edge of the Gaukerna forest. Gaukerna means cow's ear, which is the shape of the forests. The gorge here is hardly twenty feet across and when the river is in spate it must be a noble sight. As we stood on the bridge looking down into the gorge the scent of jasmine was wafted to us from fragrant bowers among the trees. In the courtyard before the temple stood a large wooden trident, but I could not find out what this symbolized.

We turned off to the left before reaching Katmandu and crossed an ancient bridge over another river, the name of which I have forgotten. These bridges were originally paved entirely with brick, but the traffic of the lorries has necessitated laying two tracks of slate-coloured stone across them for the wheels of the lorries. Even so, these old and picturesque brick bridges are continually breaking down. We reached a park surrounded by a brick wall and drove through a gateway along a wide grassy glade between steep wooded slopes covered with the largest rhododendron trees I've seen yet. Macleod told me that the blossom was disappointingly sparse. However, we had come here for the cheetal deer, not rhododendrons, and we were lucky enough to see many of those lovely dappled creatures, the stags with antlers much larger than one would expect on such small and delicate deer. They were not at all alarmed by the car. If we had been on foot they would have been off in a flash.

On our way back to the Legation we passed the elephant stables and went inside to watch two of them having their evening meal. The large courtyard had about eight circular paved floors sloping gently down round a bulky tree-trunk post to which the elephant is tethered by a powerful cable from his front legs which are chained close together. Bundles of coarse grasses were put down in front of the elephants which picked them up with their trunks and after thrashing them against their flanks to get rid of the seeds, masticated them ponderously, swaying slowly the while. The massive creatures were also given roots that looked like swedes, which they chewed up noisily with obvious relish. We who fling buns into the pink gaping mouths of the Zoo elephants do not hear or see this mastication.

When a wild elephant is trapped and proves difficult to tame, one of the syces tortures it for a week or two, brutally enough. Then another syce comes along, drives the elephant's tormentor away and treats it kindly. The elephant in gratitude to its rescuer allows itself to be trained for service by him. But let the syce who tortured it keep out of its way in future. Twenty years later that elephant will remember him, and woe betide him if he come within reach of that avenging trunk. By the way, at the museum I saw an elephant's tusk from which the whole inside had been taken out and the ivory that was left turned by a marvellous piece of fretwork into what looked like a piece of exquisite lace.

May 11th. KATMANDU

We went off to the Zoo in the morning. A military function was in progress on the great green and absolutely level parade ground, which must extend for at least a hundred acres in the middle of Katmandu. These large scale parades are held twice a week. Katmandu has numerous equestrian statues of Maharajas and Generals and there is plenty of room for as many as they like round the many open spaces, so I was surprised to find one equestrian statue in the middle of the Zoo.

In the afternoon Colonel Macleod drove us to Bhatgaon, the third of the cities in the valley, seven or eight miles away from Katmandu. It is a difficult choice, but on the whole perhaps this is the most beautiful of the three. The golden door is unique. One temple—I think it's called Nyat Pola—is reached by a long flight of steps guarded at the bottom by Jaya Malla and Phatta, two local heroes with huge black walrus moustaches. Above them are two elephants ten times as strong as the heroes. Above the elephants are two lions, ten times as strong again. Above the lions are two dragons ten times as strong as the lions. Finally above them are Baghini and Singhini, the tiger-goddess and the lion-goddess, who are ten times as strong as all the others put together. The images are attractively painted. Indeed, the colouring of Bhatgaon is richer everywhere than either of its rivals. We saw, too, some wonderful female dresses of which Peter G. took a coloured movie picture. But I shall not try to describe any more of these Arabian Nights places. They require months of close study because so much of their beauty lies in the pre-Raphaelite detailed decoration. Impressionistic writing does not convey the effect.

On our way back to Katmandu we stopped in the village of Themi at a shop where a man paints clay birds. C. bought a dozen of them and I bought a green mask. We also saw an enormous banyan tree which had grown round a house. The latter looked as if it had been seized by an octopus.

After tea General Sir Kaiser Shumsher Jung Bahadur Rana, the Minister designate, called at the Legation to bid the Falconers good-bye before leaving for his post in London. He is a great collector of modern books, and a man of taste and wide culture. I said I should hope to call upon him at the Nepalese Legation in Kensington Palace Gardens when I was home. He told me he had been in London when *Sinister Street* was first published and had read it then. He also mentioned a story in *Gallipoli Memories* which he had enjoyed. I forget which it was.

May 12th. KATMANDU TO SIRSAGARHI

We left the Legation at 8.45 and started off from Thankot an hour later. We had the same dandies and several of the coolies who brought us to Thankot. The lucent various greens of the wooded heights of Chandragiri were even more lovely in the light of the morning than when we came down a week ago. The birdsong too was equally rich. I could not enjoy the wonderful scene to the full because I was all the while too acutely aware of the strain upon the coolies of this long steep ascent. Some of the bends on the track were almost perpendicular. I noticed what I think was an *enkianthus* and also a *stachyurus*. I saw too a biggish white labiate which may have been *leonotis nepetifolia*. I had missed *piptanthus nepalensis* on the way coming in, but I spotted two smallish trees of it now. This is a tree which finds its way into almost every nurseryman's catalogue at home. The flowers are yellow of the laburnum type and the foliage is a dark lustrous green. It strikes easily and stands up to our climate fairly well. Yet, in spite of its usually being obtainable, one seldom sees it in gardens.

We took our last view of the smiling vale of Katmandu from the top of Chandragiri, and the precipitous descent began. Shall I ever see Katmandu again? During this century only about two hundred Europeans and Americans have visited Nepal.

As we were going down a steep track to the valley of the Markhu we met a large herd of water-buffaloes coming up, and when we had nearly been tilted out of the dandies the coolies took another track across a very lively and narrow suspension bridge, which brought us through the valley on the other side and gave us some fine fresh views. There were several of these suspension bridges, each one more lively than the last. They were built by John Henderson of Aberdeen.

On the way up the last steep ascent at Sirsagarhi we met women coming down with great bundles of foliage—a large shining oval leaf which I could not identify. They looked exactly like bushes walking along, for one could not see the bent woman underneath. Little girls equally invisible under smaller heaps were accompanying their mothers and elder sisters. It was a fascinating picture. Other women passed with white orchids in their hair.

At the top of the pass we got out of the dandies and walked what was supposed to be the last mile to Sirsagarhi; it was a longer and rougher mile than we expected. Dusk was deepening fast. We met Gurkhas coming home, upward bound on the way to their resting place for the night. A Havildar of the 5th Royal Gurkhas stopped and spoke to us in excellent English. He was going home to be a schoolmaster. "We must keep up the name of the 5th Royal Gurkhas," he said.

We reached the rest-house at 19 o'clock. Gulaba prepared our meal. He was not quite so tired as on the way in, Peter Goodwin having given him a pair of his own "shocks" to wear. He had left Katmandu earlier than we did, and so had had more time to rest on the road. He had been much shaken by the food the coolies ate. "Dirty rice cooked a fortnight old, and dirty fingers, Miss Sahib, never can I see such a thing when I am travelling all this time with Master. I am never seeing such food in all my life." And with an expression of utter disgust he shook his head.

May 13th. SIRSAGARHI TO RAXAUL

We were away by 6.45 of an exquisite morning, and the descent through the pines (*excelsa* and *longigolia*) was aromatic. I walked the first mile, but the track is not nearly so steep down to Bhimpedi, and the coolies had had a night's rest. So I could sit back in the dandy and enjoy the scene with a clear conscience. We passed several clumps of terrestrial orchids with small yellow flowers surrounded by pink bracts, the bracts like bougainvillea almost hiding the green leaves. I must find out the name of this interesting orchid, which is common in Nepal.

We reached Bhimpedi at 8.30 and were met there by one of the

R.I.A.S.C. lorries. This time we put Gulaba in front and sat on our bedding rolls, clinging to the side of the lorry. Bhimpedi to Amlekhganj must be the joltiest drive in the world. We nearly had a head-on crash with another lorry which came sweeping round a corner without hooting. I noticed many frangipani trees in flower along the road, and by far the largest *piptanthus nepalensis* I have seen anywhere. It was not in flower, but the great head of lustrous dark green foliage by the roadside was really beautiful.

A quarter of a mile before we reached Amlekhganj we stopped at the R.I.A.S.C. camp. Our Havildar friend Karam Ellahi, a Punjabi Mussulman of Cambellpore, had put clean coverlets on the four charpoys in the tents and clean covers on the pillows worked by his sister in sampler style. He gave us glasses of what was called sherbet but tasted like sugar and water. Havildar Karam Ellahi had fever on him badly. These four R.I.A.S.C. chaps had no mepacrine or quinine, and the civilian doctor would do nothing for them. The Havildar who is only twenty-three was depressed because if he wanted to stay in the army he would have to lose his stripes and become a sepoy again. Round here is as bad a malarious country as anywhere. The heat is intense, and supplies are hard to come by. Nevertheless, the curried chicken cooked under a tarpaulin was excellent. The Havildar wanted to present me with a kukri he had bought from a demobilised Gurkha for five chips, but I said I would only take it if he let me pay what he had given, and this he unwillingly agreed to. Nobody could have been more hospitable than these four Army Service Corps Indians in their arid, sun-stricken, dusty, malarious camp. They had adopted a Nepalese orphan boy who stared at the chip I gave him in recognition of his accomplished waiting at table as Aladdin may have stared at the treasure he discovered.

A lorry bound for Bimphedi stopped and Colonel Eustace who had given us such a grand evening with the 6th Gurkhas in Abbottabad came into the tent. He had had a foul journey with six changes, and sixteen people in the first-class compartment he entered at Lucknow. Travelling across country in India is no joke. However, he evidently thought a visit to Nepal was worth all the discomfort of getting there. Eustace went jolting on the road to Bhimpedi, and soon afterwards we drove along to the railway station. We did not have the Maharaja's coach this time, and the compartment without a fan was hellish hot. We were due to leave at 14.30, but the engine driver had gone away for a siesta and it was 15.15 before we got away. A man died of cholera on the platform while we were waiting. The journey through the jungle was blazing and we were thankful to reach Raxaul at 18.45. Here we were met by Mr. Shyan Narnia, the Legation Overseer, with the glad news that the General Manager of the railway had sent his own coach for us and that we could board it right away and dine there without going along to the Legation bungalow. The coach was completely de luxe. Two bathrooms. All the fans working. Arm-chairs. Plenty of light. The only thing to worry about was whether we would reach Paleza Ghat in time to meet Lt.-General Sir Francis Tuker on the Bihta airstrip, who was to pick us up there in his plane and take us on to Dehra Dun.

I had a brief fainting fit when going to take a bath before we left Raxaul at 22.5 due to airlessness in the bathroom. However, I soon recovered and was smoking a planter's cheroot ten minutes later. Poor Peter Goodwin had a bad night. We were an hour and a half late leaving Segauli, and at every station he got out to send a 'clear the line' telegram, and then went forward and urged the engine-driver to get a move on.

May 14th. RAXAUL TO DEHRA DUN

We were two hours late by the time we reached Muzaffapur, and it began to look as if we should find ourselves stranded at Dinapur and miss Dehra Dun. However, we ate a jolly good breakfast with some capital porridge and watched a bunch of "Red Shirts" chanting slogans under the direction of a babu cheer-leader, until at last the train started. By this time there were about twenty people on the roof of our coach and that of every other coach. No sooner had the train started than somebody pulled the communication cord, either because somebody had fallen off the roof or because a relation had not been able to clamber aboard. This happened twice, and then at last the train started on the last lap to Paleza Ghat where we arrived only a quarter of an hour before we were due to meet General Tuker at Bihta twenty miles away on the other side of the Ganges. However, Major-General H. Stable, who had kindly come to meet us, said he had arranged with the General not to reach Bihta until 10.45 and that we should just be able to make it. The Ducks behaved beautifully and waddled down the sandy bank into the Ganges without a quack.

Just before we reached Patna General Stable pointed out Mahatma Gandhi's little house beside the river, that little house from which such an influence upon the course of history has emanated. The Mahatma himself is not there at the moment.

We landed at Patna. The car drove fast. The station-wagon with the luggage did not lag. We reached the airstrip at Bihta just as General Tuker's Dakota landed. The airstrip was like a gridiron on a fierce fire, but we sat in the shade of the Control Room and drank a welcome cup of tea with the Gurkhas who had just taken over from the North Staffords.

A quarter of an hour later we were airborne and on the way to Lucknow. It was a bumpy flight, but I did not notice it, being absorbed in reading some papers General Tuker gave me. The stuff was so interesting that the two hours passed in a few minutes. Maj.-General Curtis was on the airstrip to meet us, and delighted I was to see him again. He was in great form, and drove General Tuker and myself to lunch at Flagstaff House.

From Lucknow we flew to Saharanpur—a flight of about an hour and a half, and from there we had 42 miles to drive to Dehra Dun which we reached soon after 18 o'clock. General Tuker and I went off as soon as we landed to see the boys of the 2nd Gurkhas (his own regiment) boxing. After this was over I went along to the bungalow where C. and I were staying with Lt.-Colonel R. I. Wall (8th Gurkhas) and his wife. C. stayed to dine with her hostess, and as soon as I was dressed my host drove me along to the 2nd Gurkhas' Mess.

We had a good dinner, and afterwards 'Gertie' Tuker took me round the Mess and showed me a lot of interesting stuff. Much of the Mess silver has already been packed for dispatch to England. There was a discussion about the future resting-place of the trophies, relics, and pictures of the ten Gurkha regiments. What is to be the place for their centre? General opinion favours Winchester, the home of the Greenjackets. I suggested that it might be possible to find a suitable repository in Edinburgh Castle if there was not room for everything in Winchester, or failing that in Inverness. The historical friendships between Gurkha regiments and Highland regiments would thus be preserved.

It was a great evening. I was back in the Walls' bungalow soon after midnight, and then sat up talking till 1.15.

May 15th. DEHRA DUN

I was up at 6.30 and was driven by Lt.-Colonel Wall to the parade ground of the 2nd Gurkhas to see General Tuker give a couple of M.C.s to officers who had won them in the war and also the ceremony of swearing in the recruits. The famous truncheon of the 2nd Gurkhas presented to the Regiment of Queen Victoria is not at Dehra Dun at the moment, and so allegiance was sworn upon the Union Jack. This truncheon has become a sacred emblem, and no 2nd Gurkha will tell a lie before it.

In spite of the absence of the truncheon the ceremony of swearing allegiance was most moving. Indeed, that and the Retreat I saw at Belgaum last October will remain in my memory as the two most moving military ceremonies I have seen during this tour.

After lunch we went to the bungalow of Colonel 'Fish' Armstrong who is Commandant of the 2nd Gurkhas Centre. Here Tuker and I had a very long talk. This was prolonged after tea when he walked back with me to the Walls' bungalow. He took me to several spots which had meant much to him in the past and we walked across the polo ground, once considered the best in India. The warnings to keep off the grass are still in place, but the grass is sadly to seed nowadays. The General was in an elegiac mood. He is an artist as well as a soldier—a writer and a painter—and is admitted by all to have one of the finest stragetic brains in either the Indian or the British Army. My talk with him has been of the utmost value to the book I am to write and I have seldom spent as fruitful a day.

We had a delightful buffet dinner with Lt.-Colonel J. West of the Rajputana Rifles, the Administrative Commandant. I sat on after most of the guests had gone and heard a number of good stories, among others that of the Gurkha Subedar who was asked what had most impressed him on his visit to England. "The laundries and Queen Mary," he replied.

May 16th. DEHRA DUN

It had been intended that we should drive to Simla to-day, but our start was postponed in order that I might visit the Indian Military Academy where I spent a couple of hours in the morning, admiring very much the lines on which it is run.

In the afternoon Lt.-Colonel Barlow Wheeler of the Sikh Light Infantry came to see me on the suggestion of Brigadier Mackenzie and I heard the remarkable story of the way this regiment, once the 34th Pioneers, had established its reputation in the fighting round Meiktila. The battalion was not accepted by the Eleventh Sikhs because it was composed of two classes of a lower caste. Lt.-Colonel Wheeler was extremely modest about his own share, but it was clear that he must have been an outstanding battalion commander.

We had a quiet dinner with our host and hostess who are a most delightful couple, and set the seal on the marvellous hospitality we have enjoyed all these months.

May 17th. DEHRA DUN TO SIMLA

We left at 6.30 in two cars on the 215 mile drive to Simla. It became violently hot before we reached Ambala at 11 to breakfast in the railway-station restaurant. We left Kalka at 13.30 and reached Simla at 16.30. We found on arrival that a muddle had been made and that we *had* been expected yesterday. Poor Mrs. Kirkwood, who is looking after Snowdon for the Chief this summer had sat up till midnight waiting for us. Even the police had been telephoned to.

May 18th. SIMLA

I went to Mass at 10 and gave thanks for the safe end of our Odyssey. I have made 40 flights of over 15,000 miles in all, travelled over 8,000 miles by sea, over 8,000 miles by road and over 2,000 miles by rail. I have slept in 83 different beds and at least 1,200 people have signed my birthday book.

And the Odyssey is not quite over yet because it has now been decided that I shall fly back to England at the beginning of June in order to see several people I have missed out here and if possible visit the battlefields of Italy and Tunis.

For the moment, however, I shall stop my diary which has taken me the best part of a week to write up, and after keeping almost entirely free from sciatica all these months it is annoying to find that it returns as soon as I start writing hard.

The room in which I am writing was Lord Kitchener's library and I sit surrounded by the coats-of-arms of the Commanders-in-Chief in India from Clive to Cassells. Only the arms of F.M. Lord Wavell and F.M. Sir Claude Auchinleck are missing. My bedroom looks out on the Himalayan snows; but they have been hidden since we arrived.

The laundry and the greengrocer's shop

In the square at Katmandu

Boddhnath stupa, near Katmandu

At Patan: the oldest Hindu temple in Nepal

The Editor of *The Gramophone* finds himself at home

A fountain in Katmandu

The effigy of a Newar king beside a temple in Patan

Temple in Patan

Washing at the fountain, Katmandu

Temple in Patan

Statues of Ganesh and Hanuman in Katmandu

A statue of Narain resting on a hydra-headed snake

The washerwoman

A cremation at Pashpatti burning ghat

The money-changers

Shrine in the courtyard of the old palace, Patan

TUNIS AND ITALY

June 2nd. SIMLA TO NEW DELHI

All over the place again. Peter Goodwin and I left Simla about 17 o'clock. A thunderstorm at Kalka mitigated the heat, and we had a reasonably comfortable journey to Delhi.

June 3rd. NEW DELHI

Delhi was an open furnace. Before dinner we listened to the Viceroy's broadcast. The Chief himself, Lt.-Colonel Sir Geoffrey Prior the Governor of Baluchistan, the Prime Minister of Kashmir and myself. Prior who was sitting next to me on the sofa suddenly whispered a quotation from *Extraordinary Women,* which he said he read once a year. Mountbatten broadcast well. Nehru's speech was deeply moving and a beautiful piece of sober rhetoric. Jinnah started off by talking about himself. "I am glad to have been given an opportunity to speak at the microphone . . . I hope I shall now have further opportunities, etc." The rest was a good lawyer's speech, but suffered from following immediately after Nehru. I noticed that the Press next day cut out the bit at the beginning about himself. Baldev Singh spoke with evident sincerity. Claude Auchinleck in grey flannel shorts was pacing up and down most of the time. 'Pug' Ismay came in later. He has done a fine job behind the scenes. He hesitated to appear too confident about the immediate future, but I felt that much of his anxiety was relieved.

June 4th. DELHI TO KARACHI

I saw General 'Pete' Rees for a few minutes before we went down to the Palem Airport. His G.1, Lt.-Colonel W. Stewart of the 2nd Gurkhas, whom we met at Poona, is coming with us on the Tunis and Italy tour. We reached the airport at 11, but had to return to Delhi about 14.30 because a magneto in the York wouldn't behave itself. Finally, after a series of contradictory messages, we went back to the airport and were away soon after 19.30, reaching Karachi at 23.30. Douglas and Cecil Gracey were at the airport. They had arranged a dinner party, but that confounded magneto messed everything up. However, they came and sat with me while I ate a very late dinner at the hostel and moreover stayed until we went off to deal with the formalities of departure just after 1 a.m.

June 5th. KARACHI TO MALTA

We were airborne about 1,30. Peter and I bedded down in the after cabin. We reached Basra for breakfast about 6.30. I had about three hours sleep. An hour later we were airborne at 235 m.p.h. for Heliopolis where we came down at 12.30. We drove to the Palace Hotel, and had a fairly decent lunch after which I lay down till tea-time, when we drove back to the airport. The Egyptians were in their usual state of bloodiness with pompous customs and passport examinations. Bureaucracy is a worldwide malady due to human folly, but with them it resembles a venereal disease due to vice.

The flight to Malta was most agreeable. The sea by Sidi Barrani and Sollum was a more amazing blue than ever. Dusk was rapidly deepening when we passed Tobruk, but I could still make out the masts of the sunken ships. A huge golden moon, slightly gibbous, had risen. We came down at Malta just an hour before midnight. The shrines put up for the Corpus Christi processions were still illuminated. We were airborne again at midnight.

June 6th. MALTA TO DENCHWORTH

I achieved four hours' sleep before we landed at Heathrow at 6.30. The English heat wave had vanished and a cold tempestuous morn of early June was in full swing.

I was amused by a piece of genteel prudery at Heathrow. Next the 'Gentlemen' is not the 'Ladies' but the 'Ladies' Powder Room'. Why not closet?

Rain set in heavily to greet my return to Denchworth.

June 7th. DENCHWORTH TO LONDON

Peter and I went up to town and lunched with Major-General Denys Reid at the Naval and Military. Reid gave us a lot of advice about Italy. He commanded 10th Indian Division.

June 9th. LONDON

I had a long and extremely good talk with General Sir Geoffrey Scoones at the India Office. I lunched at the Oriental with Lt.-General Ouvray Roberts who commanded 23rd Indian Division. He was most helpful.

Peter Goodwin and I went to see the exhibition of Wyndam Robinson's sketches at India House. I liked the ones he did round Imphal and Kohima very much.

June 11th. LONDON

I went down to Little Hadham to see General A. E. Percival. The train was unable to pull in to Bishop's Stortford station. When

[tried to get out I was told to wait, and then the damned train vent right on to the next station which meant arduous telephoning ınd an hour's delay before I got back to Bishop's Stortford. The L.N.E.R. is not the Great Northern of old. Percival was inclined o be reserved at first, but later opened out more and was evidently pleased when I told him he should see what I wrote about Malaya before publication.

June 15th. LONDON

Up early and off to Gatwick at 8. The weather seemed more promising, and we took off about 11 in an Anson. We were twenty niles into France when Wing-Commander E. D. Crundall the Pilot aid that the weather forecast was bad and we returned to Croydon. Just as well. Another chartered Anson crashed in France that day. It was not very bumpy, but the real snag was the low cloud. I stayed at the Savile.

June 16th. LONDON TO NICE

We left for Croydon by car at 9. Passports and customs all over again, but everybody was amiably unobstructive. We came down at Le Bourget to re-fuel. Crundall had a difficult time. Evidently he Le Bourget people are trying to discourage privately chartered planes. We had a good lunch. A capital slice of ham and hardboiled eggs with a bottle of Graves—Chateau Olivier 1944. Peter Goodwin, ooking rather like Hamlet after he saw his father's ghost for the irst time, came rushing up from the men's place and begged me to go down and explain to the old lady presiding that she must go away. He said he had tried to hustle her out, but she would not budge. I explained the French custom, and he descended again, shaking his head.

The flight to Nice was steady and the view of the Alps sublime. Mont Blanc behaved exactly as a classic mountain should behave and so seldom does. On the starboard side a bank of cumulus ighted by the westering sun tried to compete, and put up a very ine show. We went up to 11,000 feet and came down on the Nice aerodrome about 18 o'clock. The Azure Coast was in coloured-poster attire, and it was good to be back. We put up for the night at the Queen's Hotel. Swedes, Belgians and Swiss provide the bulk of the visitors, but there were quite a few English tourists all looking as if they were at Southend.

June 17th. NICE TO TUNIS

There was an hour's delay at the aerodrome because the clerk who cashed Stewart's travellers' cheque at Le Bourget had forgotten to enter the amount in his passport. The taxi-driver shook his head "We are at the mercy of parasitic functionaries" he said to me "Fonctionnaires parasitiques." Finally we were airborne at 11. As I write that sentence it is noon and the mountains of Corsica still patched with snow on the top of Monte Cinto are rising out of white clouds to port. The sea is watered silk below, the sky above an unflecked blue.

It is now 13 o'clock and we are over N.W. Sardinia, Sassari to starboard and Lake Coghinas to port. Habitations are few and cultivations sparse, but there are plenty of roads. About half an hour later we came down at Elmas which is the airport for Cagliari I was moved to be standing on Italian soil after an absence of over twenty years and found myself talking the language fairly fluently *Correntamente*, yes, but not alas, always *correttamente*. The airport has been terribly knocked about, but we found a buffet where it was possible to drink some good vermouth at what seemed a delirious price, even with the lira at 2000 to the £1.

A young Italian Lieutenant pressed upon me the attractions of Sardinia.

"Although I am myself a Sardinian I have to admit that in the interior the people are extremely primitive and often very dirty. However, we have in Cagliari a *cercolo intellettuale* and you would find it worth your while to spend a few weeks here."

We reached Tunis about 16.30 and were met by Consul-General Gibbs, Vice-Consul Manning, and M. Caunsu who is second in command to M. du Boisberranger, the Chef du Cabinet, all of whom were extraordinarily helpful. Gibbs is leaving for Saigon in a few days to take Meiklereid's place. What a difference it makes when our Consuls and our Consul-Generals get on with the people with whom it is their duty to get on.

We had rooms at the Palace Hotel; but as they were unable to serve anything more than coffee and rolls we ate at the Majestic M. Caunsu informed us that the Chef de Cabinet was putting a car at our disposal all the time we were in Tunis, and as soon as our lodging was fixed we went round to call on M. du Boisberranger and thank him for this courtesy. He was sorry that the Resident was away and there would be no opportunity of giving me a formal dinner. Just before we left the Chef du Cabinet, M. Caunsu came in with a bit of red ribbon for me to put in my button-hole. I had happened to mention that in London I could only obtain the uniform ribbon of the Legion.

After leaving the Chef de Cabinet we went round to the Consu-

ate-General. The building is modern, but our Consulate-General
ere is the oldest of all and goes back well over 300 years. Many
egotiations must have been conducted in it to set free captives
aken by Sallee rovers.

June 18th. TUNIS

I had a good deal of rheumatism in the night, and the street noises n the early morning stopped any chance of dozing.

Sharp at 9 we were airborne on the way to the Mareth Line. We lew over Sousse, Sfax and El Djem, round which we circled twice or Peter to take some good photographs of the Roman amphi-heatre. From above, the Mareth Line is a jumble of hills over which aths like the tentacles of an octopus wave in every direction. I was pointed out the hill where the troglodytes live, but from 1,000 eet up there was no sign of them. A view of campaigning country rom the air is little more inspiring than a map, but time pressed and we could not explore all Tunis by road as I should have liked. From above the Wadi Zig Zaw looks such a simple proposition, and that's the deceptive part of a plane with a view.

We came down at Gabes and were met by Captain de la Rocque, who drove us to the house of General Dio, the Military Commander of Southern Tunis. The latter is a Breton with a chic Parisian wife. He was one of the first to throw in his lot with De Gaulle, and I noticed a large framed photograph of the French patriot, inscribed "Á mon compagnon". The house was not too arabesque and the rooms were cool and agreeable, shaded from the blazing sunlight outside. A wall of the dining-room was covered with Hitler relics —swastikas and eagles and Nazi daggers. One looked at them as one would have looked at the spears, clubs and totem poles collected by an explorer from savages.

The lunch was superlative. We went on eating and drinking for nearly two hours. The General expressed his intention of retiring to his native Brittany one day, but I noticed a glint in Madame Dio's eye which suggested that he was unlikely to get nearer to Brittany than the Parc Monceau. There are few things in life as agreeable as French hospitality at its best, and I should willingly have stayed talking for the rest of the afternoon; but there was still a good deal to see, and just before 15 o'clock we left the General's house and drove with Captain de la Rocque to Wadi Akarit, thirty kilometres away. Here is that range of arid and ferocious hills which was the scene of one of the greatest military exploits of the war. Near Wadi Akarit there is a fine austere monument to the men of the Fourth Indian Division. It is a monolith about eight feet high, on the four

sides of which are engraved the names of the fallen; and it stands a
the head of a steep flight of steps in as desolate a countryside as one
could imagine, looking across a waste of tumbled rocks and sand
and withered herbage to the grim mountain called Fatnassa and
Point 275, the eight-hundred-ft. hill nearest the road. The range
from there to Rumana is about four miles, and the Wadi Akari
itself runs in a great anti-tank ditch some ten miles to the sea. The
wind blew hard from the north-west: the sun blazed. All that now
remains of the battle are two of the Italian guns that were knocked
out by that brilliant military operation in the middle of the level
wasteland, and farther along a German tracked troop-carrier
rusting away.

We were airborne again at 16.30 and reached Tunis at 19 o'clock.
It was too late to explore the souk as we had intended. So we went
round with Gibbs to the summer house of the Consulate-General
which was presented to the British Government by the Bey of Tunis
about a century ago. It is an attractive arabesque house with a very
large garden, and with that bewitching and subtle effluence of the
South of which Browning knew the secret in words. Afterwards we
drove out to Sidi Bon Said where Gibbs was giving us dinner. Mrs
Gibbs unfortunately could not come with us. We passed by the
gates of the famous d'Erlanger villa to go to the restaurant which has
a large terrace overhanging the bay. The host declared that it was
too damp to dine outside, and I thought of how many times in
Mediterranean summers it had been too damp to dine outside and
of how many times, ignoring the precaution, I had dined outside
and paid for it with a fortnight's pain. It was a good dinner of which
the red mullet must be proclaimed the best I ever ate. We drank
with it a light *vin rosé*. It is strange that the Germans who love the
Mediterranean as much as any nation have never been civilized,
or even mentally cleaned by those lustral waters. It is so difficult
to avoid being civilized by the Mediterranean. Yet, when I remember some of those Riviera novels of the 'thirties, I wonder if it *is* so
difficult.

June 19th. TUNIS

We left the hotel at 8.30 to the minute for a long day's driving.
Our first objective was the glade a few miles from Ste. Marie du Zit
where von Arnim and his staff surrendered to General Tuker on
May 11th, 1943. It lies some fifty miles south-east of Tunis at the
base of the Cap Bon peninsula from which the Germans had hoped
to achieve another Dunkirk. All the way along the roadside there
was still plenty of flowers and the dry water courses were full of

oleanders in prodigal rosy bloom. I called the place of surrender a glade, but it is more accurately a fold in the low rolling hillside covered with lentisk, myrtle, cistus, juniper and rosemary. It was typical *maquis* or *macchia* with few trees, and every step one took was aromatic. The year's primal burst of bloom was past, but there were still flowers enough. I noticed many plants of a small starry St. John's Wort, a Tyrian purple bugloss, a brilliant violet linaria, yellow thistles, a graceful yellow umbelliferous plant, the most vivid blue eryngium I have seen, and best of all an echinops with very large heads of pure sapphire. I am not aware of having noticed this echinops in gardens, but it surely must be in cultivation at home.

Bill Stewart was with Colonel Showers of the 2nd Gurkhas when they arrived, before General Tuker of 4th Indian Division, to find about a thousand Germans on parade dressed up in their best to surrender. It was poetic justice that the Germans should surrender to three Second Gurkhas because the night attack through the defiles of the hills above Wadi Akarit when Subedar Lalbahadur Thapa of the 2nd Gurkhas won his V.C. was the decisive action of the Tunis campaign. 4th Indian Division began the fight for North Africa and it was 4th Indian Division which ended it. The whole place stank of burning rubber when Showers and Stewart got there because the enemy had been destroying all his transport, all, that is, except two caravans and two staff-cars. The caravan in which von Arnim lived is now at Poona. One of the staff-cars lies as a derelict souvenir among the myrtle and the rosemary. Stewart told me the Germans were still very cocky in May 1943 and seemed to think that their surrender in Tunis was a mere incident.

From this memorable spot we drove along to the village of Enfidaville, another forty miles south of Ste. Marie du Zit. Enfidaville is a pleasant spot wearing few marks of war, most of the gardens of the neat villas hedged with plumbago in full flower. The War Memorial of 1914-18 surmounted by the Gallic cock in full crow stands in the *Place*. I wonder if the exuberant vitality of that bronze bird ever seemed to the Germans a warning omen of the future.

We were unable to get up to the ridge, but from below it was easy to appreciate just what a formidable obstacle it was to our victorious advance. I looked with awe at the bald grey dome of Djebel Garci where the Rajputana Rifles, the 9th Gurkhas, and the Essex fought so gloriously. I saw the hill Takrouna on the eastern edge of the ridge, where a castellated village stands like a castle from a Doré picture. This was captured by the New Zealanders by an astonishing feat of arms. I saw, too, the wide stretch of open country at the foot of the ridge across which the 4/16th Punjabis—

the old Bo Peeps—advanced under very heavy shell fire as steadily as if across the dusty parade ground at home in Sialkot. The fathers of these men saved the line at Neuve Chapelle, and fought a great bayonet fight at Festubert.

Tunis is a country of olive groves. They are all planted on the same system, each tree, on account of the water problem, being allowed much more space than I have seen in the olive yards of Greece or Italy. The trees in Tunis may be any age from ten to a thousand years, but they are all as trim as the trees in a nursery Noah's Ark. The older groves are infernal to fight in, almost worse than the rubber plantations of Malaya. We saw where the Royal Sussex had a desperate battle among the olives.

We drove on from Enfidaville to reach Medjez-el-Bab across country, but before we set out we lunched in an avenue of young eucalyptus trees leading up to a farmhouse. The gums cast a scanty shade and the flies were legion. The cross-country road depressed our driver because owing to the dust he could not go at more than forty miles an hour. His average speed on good roads was a steady sixty, and he often got up to eighty. We turned aside past Medjez-el-Bab to drive up to a much shelled farm from which we had a good view of the country across which the 4th Indian Division drove a way between the 1st and 4th British Divisions to reach the open plain and allow the 7th British Armoured Division to race through for the final kill. Yes, it was indeed a fine poetic justice which ruled that the two Divisions which had arrived in Africa first should be the two to wind up so many months of African warfare.

Beyond Medjez-el-Bab at Massicault we found a tavern and drank several bottles of most welcome iced beer. Then we visited the cemetery at Massicault, which stands fairly near a German cemetery full of stone Maltese crosses, presumably meant to look like iron crosses. We got back to Tunis about 17 o'clock after an exhilarating day of sun, wind and very fast driving in an open car.

Gibbs took us round to see St. George's Church where there is a monument to 152 dead warriors of the 4th Indian Division. St. George's Church itself is modern, but the ground on which it stands belongs to the British Government and it has been the site of a church of some kind or another for over three centuries. At present it appears to be run for the purpose of converting Jews and for the spiritual health of those already converted, the missionary being appointed by the London Jews' Society. St. George's Church is built right in the middle of the native city and from the flat roof of the missionary's house one looks down on one side into Arab courtyards and on another into the Jewish quarter. On the flat roof across an lley a blindfold donkey was turning a water wheel. This provides ater for the public baths which are used by men and women on lternate days.

In the churchyard is a monument to John Howard Payne, the uthor of *Home Sweet Home*, who was born in 1791 and died in Tunis n 1852. In 1883 his remains were disinterred and taken across the tlantic to Washington where they now rest. On a gloomy November fternoon in the year 1912 I was walking along that endless main treet of Schenectady and feeling myself as gloomy as only that kind f street can make one feel in that kind of weather. I passed by a arge stuccoed house set back from the road behind a grove of lready leafless trees. A lot of small boys were playing some game vith a ball and wearing away with their feet what little grass was eft on the muddy expanse beneath the trees. I thought as I looked t this house in the November blight that it was the most depress-ng house I had ever seen, and that if I ever wanted to choose a etting for some melancholy or sombre tale of thwarted hope and rustrated lives I would choose as a perfect setting this gaunt tuccoed house with its dank leafless grove and muddy playground overed with green slime. Then on a pillar beside the gates, I saw n inscription which recorded that John Howard Payne, U.S.A. Consul in Tunis, had been born and brought up in this house. This ouse, in fact, *was* home, sweet home.

Gibbs and Manning dined with us at the Majestic, and toward he end of dinner word came that a press representative would like o interview me. I supposed this to be a journalist who had called ound at the Palace Hotel and for whom I had left a message with he porter to come on to the Majestic. The porter made a mistake nd the unfortunate interviewer waited for me an hour at the Palace Hotel before going away disgruntled. The press representative who alled at the Majestic had run me to earth in the interest of a rival paper, and turned out to be a most intelligent young French-voman, delicate-looking and *poitrinaire*, who spent well over an hour alking to me and wrote for *Tunis-Soir* about the best interview I iave ever had.

June 20th. TUNIS TO NAPLES

Gibbs and Manning were down at the aerodrome to see us off, but omething had gone wrong with the brake and they had to say good-bye before we were finally airborne at 10.30. They had taken a lot of trouble to make our visit fruitful, and I like to think that Meikle-eid in Saigon will be succeeded by a Consul-General as much in ympathy with the French as himself.

It was a silvery scirocco day, damp and hot with hardly any wind We made the Sicilian coast close to what is now called Agrigenti— Acragas to the Greeks, Agrigentum to the Romans, and Girgent to everybody else until Mussolini gave it the current name o Agrigenti. I was annoyed at not being able to sight the temples, bu consoled myself by recalling the expedition D. H. Lawrence, Franci and Jessie Brett Young made to Girgenti from Capri in 1920. I cannot remember whether it was Lawrence's hat or Francis's ha which blew away, but whichever it was, the other deplored to me the disturbance of the classic scene by chasing a runaway ha through the temples.

After a while mighty Etna appeared. The volcano looks almos more majestic from a plane than from the deck of a ship. It was when gazing at the last rosy flush of sunset upon the peak of Etna in 1916 that the best service cap I ever had blew off into the sea, the result of which was that I had to borrow a white naval helmet and wear it with khaki when I went to lunch next day with Admiral Mark Kerr in *H.M.S. Queen* at Taranto. It was a drenching day and I hoped to get on board the flagship almost unobserved. Alas, the awnings were up and the Italian Admiral and his Staff were all on the quarter-deck when I came on board because they were lunching with Mark Kerr as well as my humble self. To make one's way through that golden net of aiguillettes, saluting against the wrong headgear, was an ordeal of self-consciousness. That kind of thing upset us a lot in the old war. By the end of World War Two I don't believe that if a captain in the Royal Marines had boarded a battleship in a pyjama jacket, shorts, and a bowler hat, anybody would have raised an eyebrow.

The summit of Etna was shrouded in cotton wool this morning, and rain seemed imminent when we landed on the aerodrome at Catania. The officials here were much excited because apparently ours was the first strange plane which had landed since the Military Administration ceased. Half a dozen of them, all talking at once and contradicting one another about the procedure, dealt with the business of filling in the forms to be checked against our passports. Like all Mediterranean ink it was only just perceptibly coloured, and the pens were more like the quills of sea-urchins than pens. At last after interminable *chiaccieria*, the bureaucratic ritual was accomplished and we went off to eat *mortadella* and drink beer in the refreshment room.

The coast was much obscured over the Tyrrhenian Sea. Cape Palinuro loomed out of the dense rain. On such a day might the steersman of Aeneas have been drowned, and the profoundest pessimism of Cyril Connolly about his own creative vitality (and everybody else's) been justified.

We flew all round Capri where the air was clearer, and I was able to see how ruthlessly the trees of Ventrosa had been cut. I bought the whole front of Monte Solaro—the stomach of the mountain—in the spring of 1914. While negotiations were going on a wanderer from the Levant offered me for £400 seventeen carpets, three of them large silk Persians, the others Persians and Bokharas of the finest quality. Now, £400 was the exact sum I was proposing to pay for Ventrosa. I could not afford both and I chose the land. This was a bad mistake. The land to-day is worth five times what it was, but the carpets would be worth twenty-five times what I was asked for them in 1914. The Levantine must have stolen them, for they were ridiculously cheap even then.

Ventrosa was the only real bird sanctuary in Capri. Axel Munthe had a sanctuary below San Michele, but hardly any birds frequented its sparse Aleppo pines. In the ilex and arbutus groves and dense *macchia* of Ventrosa the birds flourished. The Capri flora numbers nearly 900 species, and there must have been at least six hundred of these growing on Ventrosa. I never saw butterfly orchises grow in such profusion as they grew there, and the *lithospermum rosmarinifolium*, which had been dug up by generations of tourists all over the rest of the island used to fall here in an azure cataract for 1,500 feet almost to the sea's edge.

The rain was pouring down over the Bay. The airport at Naples seemed derelict. Great puddles stood everywhere on the runways and the seating accomodation in the reception office had been improvised out of packing-cases. There was a bureaucratic flap here because neither Wing-Commander Crundall, the pilot nor Bronson, the wireless operator from County Kerry, had visas for Italy. Fortunately Crundall looks like a benign country parson, and even the most fanatical bureaucrat is softened by his amiable appearance, speech and manner. We pointed out to Naples that Catania had assured Crundall and Bronson that visas were unnecessary for the crew of a chartered plane. "That," said Naples scornfully, "is a *fesseria*." Jeaffreson, the representative of the Embassy's Public Relations Department who had come to meet us, was amiable. So was I. So of course was Peter Goodwin who is the very spirit of amiability. Jeaffreson and I agreed that without doubt it was a *fesseria;* but we amiably hoped that Naples would allow the crew to go on to Rome where they would be able to obtain a provisional *permesso di soggiorno* from the police. To this Naples, unable to resist our united amiability, finally agreed.

Jeaffreson had booked two rooms at the Continental and three rooms at the Vesuvio, the only two hotels which were functioning with reasonable comfort. Peter Goodwin and I went to the Continental, which has been really well done up. There is a new notice in all the rooms to say that a guest who breaks or damages any of the furniture or fittings will be charged for it on his bill, such has been the difficulty and expense of re-equipping the hotel.

I stood on the balcony of my bedroom exactly opposite the Castello del Uovo and gazed once more at the port of Santa Lucia after so many years. The air was haunted by the faces and figures of the past. The rain had stopped and the bay was in a golden glow. In the old days we used to stay at the Santa Lucia hotel and take the nine o'clock boat—the *Principessa Elena*—to Capri. Those topaz-bright November mornings after the chilly fogs of England and the long railway journey from Calais or Boulogne! The Santa Lucia Hotel had not yet opened again, but my balcony at the Continental looked out on the same heart-warming view. *O mihi praeteritos!* Those two exclamation marks are sighs not shrieks.

Neither the Continental nor the Vesuvio was able to feed its guests. The manager of our hotel recommended a visit to the Villa dei Principi at 74 Via Manzoni, Alto Posillipo, where he promised we should eat much better than at any of the Santa Lucia restaurants by the water's edge, which were always packed out. We did eat well, and I need hardly say I chose to begin with spaghetti of which I devoured a plateful almost as big as Vesuvius itself.

June 21st. NAPLES TO CAMPOBASSO

The waiter, one of those venerable ecclesiastical figures into which only Italian waiters who remain in Italy can develop, came in with my morning coffee to announce that the weather had recovered from its extraordinary behaviour of yesterday. It was almost as if he said, "the sun's apologies and he is shining again".

We were away soon after 10 in a large Lancia. We had meant to start at 9 but had forgotten to put our clocks forward. There was a lot of traffic on the road between Naples and Cassino, but we were in Cassino before noon. The town looks now like one of those boom towns which spring up in America after the discovery of gold or oil. We drove up as far as the top of Castle Hill, but the condition of the road made it impossible for so large a car to get to the top of the hill on which the monastery once stood, and I was disinclined to walk up and survey what I still consider was devastation caused by empirical tactics, the result of ill-considered and improvised strategy, and a link in the long chain of mistakes which marked the Italian campaign from the very beginning. The soft underbelly of the Axis became in fact a mere rhetorical figment after the failure to turn the turtle over on its back when Mussolini fell.

Not without bitterness I contrasted what had been done at Cassino with the wonderful restraint of the fighting for Mandalay Hill. I remember having an argument with a Canadian officer soon after the destruction of the Abbey. His point was that the noblest edifice in the world was less important than the life of one man. My point was that either that dead man had an immortal soul or he had not. If his soul was immortal he would recognize in eternity that his earthly body was well worth sacrificing to something greater than that earthly body. If on the other hand that man did not possess an immortal soul, I was not prepared to accord his life any more importance than that of a monkey. Do we really believe that the lives of a few Venetians were more important than the Acropolis?

After studying the melancholy topography of Monte Cassino we visited the British cemetery, which is in charge of an entertaining and competent New York Italian called Tony. Here beside the British graves are the graves of Hindus and Muslims. The shrubs and sapling trees were doing well, the borders glowed with the rich orange and black of gazanias above which fluttered many Clouded-Yellow butterflies and Scarce Swallowtails. We call them scarce in English, but in southern Italy the Scarce Swallowtail is commoner than our own Swallowtail. Of course the Scarce Swallowtail should not be included among our English lepidoptera. I doubt if it was ever even a casual visitor. Probably the two or three specimens caught were released from a breeding-cage.

After our visit to the cemetery we went down into the town and lunched at the Risorgimento Restaurant. Risorgimento is the key-note of Cassino to-day. On the top of the monastery hill the stones are already being gathered and stacked in preparation for rebuilding. The town is alive with the spirit of rebirth. Every face was alight with energy. Indeed, throughout this Italian tour, I have been impressed by the vitality and courage of the Italian people.

After lunch we drove on into the Abruzzi through Venafro, Isernia, and Cantalupo. The countryside was bright with flowers—poppies and broom, scabious and mullein. Every one of the Abruzzesi girls we passed had a beautiful face, a perfect figure and faultless carriage. I have not seen anywhere so many good-looking women in the course of a few hours. Celibacy here is unimaginable. Yet, the Abruzzi, I think I am right in saying, produces a higher percentage of priests than anywhere in Italy.

We reached Campobasso about 19 o'clock. It is an industrial city, but clean and orderly with streets shaded by closely clipped and trimmed holm oaks. The Grand Hotel at which we put up had been the headquarters of one of our military organizations when Campobasso was a rest camp. It was not a luxurious hostelry, but it was reasonably clean, and we enjoyed a simple dinner of spaghetti and eggs. I saw the young moon from my open bedroom window in a calm green sky. The standard of good looks among the girls of the countryside was maintained in Campobasso itself. I went to bed at 21 o'clock, for I had been in pain all day.

June 22nd. CAMPOBASSO TO CHIETI

My leg was still giving me jip when we started at 7.30 on what was to be a long and crowded day. The swifts were wheeling and screaming against the faded blue sky of the morning. The beauty of the countryside between Campobasso and Casacalenda was more powerful than the pain, and I drove for two hours in a rapture. It is limestone country, and the white road flung itself ahead of us for miles like a lasso. We travelled some of the way through the richly cultivated valleys of the foothills, some of the way round bald green hills. The cultivation displayed indomitable energy. The slopes on either side in the foreground were painted with the amber and gold of ripening corn in various shades; and in every sloping cornfield mighty trees such as you see in an English park provided contrasting shade, a luminous blue where it was aslant the sun. It was a landscape for Breughel, and he would have done justice to the human element—to the reapers in gaily coloured groups and to the horsemen who came riding along, each with a large long-haired goat on a lead, itself the colour of ripe corn. Goats do not like motor cars and when they saw ours approaching they would always leap aside off the road and drag the horsemen with them. In the grassy verges on either side there was as great a profusion of wild flowers as in any Alpine meadow—poppies, broom, a ladies' bedstraw twenty-four inches high and heavily scented, candytuft, love-in-a-mist, a brilliant crimson dianthus, larkspurs as blue as the finest ultramarine, corn-marigolds, a large crimson unscented pea, anchusa, a puce-coloured broomrape, and any amount of *clematis flammula* which I used to grow over the ruined house of the old privateer in Jethou.

The road on from Casacalenda to Larino was a succession of avenues—avenues of limes, of stone pines and Aleppo pines and acacia. There was one avenue of stone pines at the entrance of the Piano di Larino, the ground between their dark umbrellas on either side of the road covered with mauve-pink thistles in full bloom, a most unusual floral effect, for the thistles looked as if they had been deliberately planted, so thick were they. The harvest in the lowland of the Piano was full ripe, and Sunday was no interruption to its being reaped. Presently we crossed the River Biferno, the first of those rivers all the way up Italy which cost so many lives in the crossing of them. We skirted Termoli and drove north along the coast road beside the pale blue Adriatic that was quiet as velvet on this summer's day.

After crossing the Trigno we came to San Salvo, and went on past big fields of tobacco until, half an hour after midday, we reached Vasto. Here we looked at the Headquarters of the Eighth Army and remembered it was from this pompous municipal building that in November 1943 General Montgomery summoned spirits from the Vasto deep and proclaimed that the Eighth Army would be in Rome by Christmas. I wonder how much Livy he read at the school of which we are both alumni. We ought to have stopped in Vasto for lunch, but as there was still a great deal of ground to cover we decided to drive on and lunch in Casalbordino at 13 o'clock. However, when we reached Casalbordino we could not find a *trattoria* let alone an *albergo* or *ristorante*. So on we drove. Presently a signpost pointed to Torino, which much amused Vincenzo, our Neapolitan chauffeur. "Why leave out Rome?" he asked. The Torino in question was the small village of Torino di Sangro. By the time we reached it it was after 13.30 and we enquired hopefully whether there was a chance of getting a bottle of wine. The population of Torino di Sangro felt that something had to be done about it. A reconnaisance party was sent out and finally it was reported that a willing host had been found. We turned down into a small side street and came to a cross between a stable and a cellar. The host said we should have fish if we could wait half an hour, but we decided to be content with our hard-boiled eggs and the red wine of the country. There was a lot of health drinking and a great deal of excited conversation. "Brava gente," Vincenzo commented. Yes, fine people indeed. It will be long before I forget that sunny by-way and that cool cellar in which we drank the rough red wine of the country.

Our next objective was the cemetery at Torino di Sangro to which one of the party had volunteered to guide us, he having an uncle who worked there. He asked if we would afterwards give him a lift as far as Mozzagrogna, which we were only too glad to do.

The great cemetery at Torino di Sangro where over 3,500 dead warriors lie at peace occupies the most impressive site of the many cemeteries I have seen in all these months. It is reached by a private road running up at a steep angle from the main coastal road to Pescara and Bari. The expanse of white crosses takes up the whole of a semi-circular bluff some two or three hundred feet above the Sangro River, and the effect is of a vast half-amphitheatre of graves. Below, the Sangro winds down a broad valley from the Apennine to the sea. Northward the land rolls in great billows to a sky-line crenelated here and there by villages. Westward and north-westward the bastions of the Apennine, Maiella most prominent, towering indigo-dark against the sky. Eastward spreads the Adriatic, its waters on the morning we saw it that velvety Cambridge blue. Southward and level with the cemetery the countryside is intimate and fertile, a countryside of laden orchards and browsing cattle and lush grass. In due course the cemetery itself will become an extension of this little Arcadia it bounds; and I pray that, when they whose dear ones lie here visit this spot in the kinder years for which we hope, the beauty of the natural scene will shed upon their hearts a benison. I have felt nowhere a profounder sense of peace.

We drove on across the Sangro through Fossacesia to the village of Mozzagrogna in which at the end of November 1943 some of the most desperate fighting anywhere or at any time in the war took place. The perfect setting of a battle-scarred village is provided by the piazza of Mozzagrogna. The church in the centre has lost its roof by fire, and the flame-throwing tank which sprayed it with blazing oil still stands where it stood when Major Warner of the Royal Fusiliers blew off the turret from the window of a house looking down on it . . . Opposite the east end of the church on the other side of the piazza a life-sized *bersagliere* in bronze crowns the untouched memorial of the First World War. Round this the Gurkhas buried their dead.

At Mozzagrogna our friend from Torino di Sangro left us, carrying a small bundle of comestibles for the relatives whom he was going to visit.

We drove on to Lanciano and saw the house where Bill Stewart lived when he was second-in-command of the 1/2nd Gurkhas. We saw, too, the tobacco factory which had been used as a hospital and bombed by the Germans. We decided to take a chance and drive to Chieti by a third-class cross-country road instead of going round by Pescara. This would enable me to get a much better idea of the actual course of our fighting. Moreover, it was an opportunity to get a near view of an enchanting countryside. Vincenzo grew gloomier and gloomier. "Ma questa non è una strada," he kept muttering to me, and at intervals he would get out of the car to examine anxiously the springs and the tyres. We kept descending and ascending small deep valleys bosky with orchards and olives and bronzed with corn, and passing from time to time groups of

Memorial to the 4th Indian Division in the English Church, Tunis

The site of General von Arnim's surrender, near Sainte Marie du Zit

The Roman amphitheatre at El Djem

The ruined cemetery at Tollo

The battlefield of Cassino, from Route 6

The ruined church at Mozzagrogna

Sacro Speco, Subiaco

Castle Hill, above the town of Cassino

ending reapers in bright attire, the rhythmic pattern of whose abour rejoiced the eye like the backgrounds of mediaeval art. In he bottoms of these valleys streams ran through lush reeds and rasses and white cows grazed beside them. On the third ridge we aw ahead of us the shattered town of Orsogna, the road to which vas sometimes almost impassable on account of derelict German and Iew Zealand tanks. In a field behind one of these tanks men, vomen and children were reaping the corn and beside the now nerely obstructive monster was growing an unusually large clump f rest-harrow covered with spikes of rose and white flowers. That ough-rooted plant which baffles the iron teeth of the harrow had ere, as it seemed, arrested the progress of a tank. The whole scene vas a fine subject for a symbolical painting.

Orsogna itself is a wilderness of tumbled stone and brick and nortar and the people there still seem stunned by the shelling and ombing which they had to endure from both sides. For six months ur front line ran along the ridge eastward from Orsogna. Bill tewart got out of the car about a mile outside the town to go and ook at another house in which he had lived and found it exactly he same as he had left it more than three years ago. I walked through he arched gateway of the local cemetery and surveyed a macabre cene. Almost all the mausoleums had been destroyed and almost ll the lowlier graves had been torn open and their metal crosses ent and twisted by bombs and shells. As I walked round among he blasted cypresses and scraggy rose-bushes I was followed by a en with nine cheeping chicks which evidently thought I had rrived with food.

We drove on toward Chieti along what used to be our front line. he more one sees of this country, the more clearly one realizes that he whole of the Italian campaign was a vast improvization by which ven Generals of Alexander's or Montgomery's calibre were ewildered.

I recall from the drive from Orsogna to Chieti the village of Tollo s being more completely smashed up than any I saw. I recall in Iiglianico a group of red and rosy hollyhocks in front of a grey wall hich the dust had turned to a delicate study in pastel. I recall the erce slogans for the Republic painted in black on the walls of every illage through which we passed until suddenly we came to Ripa eatini and found the walls there covered with slogans for the Ionarchy in blue paint. I thought that if we stopped to enquire ere we should probably find that the parish priest possessed a trong personality. Among all these Vivas for the Republic or he King there was one Viva which expressed despair. On one wall somebody had painted "Vive Niente". Long live nothing

It was nearing sunset when we reached Chieti—a clean town o
40,000 inhabitants standing some 2,000 feet up and looking acros
the wide level valley of the Pescara to a superb panorama of th
Apennine, the jagged peak of Gran Sasso d'Italia clawing at th
majestic sunset. We sat for a few minutes in the small public garde
at the edge of the almost sheer hill on which Chieti stands to con
template the mighty view. After this I went into the Duomo, th
exterior of which was rebuilt just before the war with great skill an
taste in Romanesque style. Inside, this archiepiscopal cathedral i
entirely baroque, and I sat for awhile in meditation until the ros
cherubs faded into the dusky glooms above and the florid gilt candle
sticks upon the altar lacked lustre, and all was dim.

We found rooms at the Albergo Sole where we had a great dea
of courtesy but not much comfort, though we ate well at the adjoin
ing restaurant. My bed was nothing but a thin straw palliasse lai
on rigid metal laths, and the water in the basin ran only for a
hour. Moreover, at a critical moment of undressing the electri
light went out. Peter Goodwin and Bill Stewart were in a front roon
overlooking the main street, up and down which what seemed hal
the population of Chieti indulged in a congested promenade fron
dusk until the small hours of the morning. About two o'clock Pete
G. came into my room for the flit spray, declaring with what sounde
like a sob in the throat that he and Bill Stewart were being eaten b
myriads of fleas and that the people in the street would not sto
promenading up and down or stop talking. I told him the flit spra
might conquer the fleas but that I didn't see what use it would b
against the people in the street. Bill Stewart felt that he was bein
ill repaid for marching in with his Gurkhas to liberate Chieti whe
the Germans abandoned the Gustav line and went surging back t
the Gothic Line. As for me I slept well in spite of the bed and wok
next morning without pain.

June 23rd. CHIETI TO ROME

We were away by 9, Vincenzo in a cheerful mood at the prospec
of being able to drive really fast along one of the great main road
across the wide level valley of Pescara and into the Apennine by th
main pass from the south-east. At the end of this lies the ancier
and picturesque little town of Popoli, which was thronged fc
market day. We took the road to Rome by Avezzano not the one b
Sulmona. Both are equally beautiful; no people make mountai
roads as well as the Italians. The rain kept off while we were windin
up through gorges and circling ancient fortified villages and town

ach on the top of a different hill with a dominating castle; but hen we came down into the great plain rescued for agriculture by he draining of Lake Fucino a torrential thunderstorm broke over s and did not stop until we reached Avezzano on the other side of he plain.

The earthquake at Avezzano in January 1915 was the only time felt a shock on Capri, where it set all the cagebirds fluttering in larm. I was in the middle of writing *Guy and Pauline*. It was a bad arthquake, and the signs of it in Avezzano are everywhere evident hirty-two years later, to which has been added further destruction y bombs. We found a restaurant, and while we were at lunch the torm rained istelf out.

We drove on through those lovely towns of the Alban Hills, all f them drenched with history. Perhaps the most beautifully situated f all is Arsoli with that magnificent grove of ancient cypresses on a reen hill above the town. Arsoli, to judge by the slogans painted up, strongly royalist. Some miles farther on we left the main road to isit Subiaco. I wanted to reassure myself about the damage done y allied bombers. I found that a piece of the cloisters of the big nonastery of Santa Scolastica has been smashed and a good deal of ther damage done, but this building is most of it comparatively nodern. The smaller monastery of the Sacro Speco had by the mercy f God escaped damage.

The cave in which St. Benedict spent three years in communion vith the Divine Will is set in the hillside at the entrance of a deep avine at least a mile away from Subiaco itself. The monastery, vhich at present houses eight monks, was built piece by piece round his cave through the centuries. Long before there was any threat f bombers there must have been a fear lest rocks from the hillside bove should fall and crush the building which challenges by its osition the malice of nature. The evidence of this fear is to be found n a life-sized statue of St. Benedict in one of the small courtyards olding up his hand to avert the danger and inscribed: *Stay, O rock, o no harm to my sons*. His sons may have watched that arm held up to hield them when the bombs were falling all round the Sacro Speco. t seems fairly certain now that the attack was the mistake of a too nthusiastic American squadron which imagined it was bombing he retreating German Army instead of one of the most sacred nes in Christendom.

We were lucky enough to enquire the way up to the monastery om a young monk who at once jumped on the running board of he car and guided us through a courtyard to where one alighted or the ascent of some 200 steps through a grove of primeval holm

oaks, not one of which could have been less than a thousand yea
old. Dom Ignazio Giampaoletti was the perfect guide. When
expressed my eagerness to see the portrait of St. Francis of Assi
painted by one of the monks when he visited the monastery in 122
Dom Ignazio was not prepared to accept so positive a statemen
He would only allow that it might have been painted by a mon
Anyway, the portrait itself completely fulfilled all my expectation
The fact that it shows the saint without halo or stigamata is pro
that it was a contemporary portrait and the inscription 'Frat
Franciscus' suggests that it was painted by a monk. Even now, as
write about it away in India, those two eyes are looking at m
Nor was Dom Ignazio prepared to accept as more than a legen
the grafting of roses by St. Francis on St. Benedict's briars. Th
roses themselves were not in flower, and I am completely at a los
with only the vivid light green leaves before me, to say what kin
of roses they are, but I have seen nowhere any like them. Th
faithful have cured their ills by drying these leaves and taking the
as a powder.

The rain held off while we were walking down the steps to rejoi
the car, but we were no sooner inside than it came in a downpou
However, it stopped soon after we got back on the great Vi
Tiburtina Valeria, and Vincenzo was able to tear blissfully along
sixty miles an hour, once we had left Tivoli behind us.

The noise of Rome came as rather a shock to me. For so long th
eternal city had seemed to my mind's ear the quietest capital
them all. To find it to-day more of a pandemonium than Napl
was a blow. We put up at the Grand Hotel, which remains wh
the Grand Hotel always was. Esmé Howard, who is in charge
Public Relations at the Embassy, came round to find out how w
were getting on, and this was lucky because Crundall and Bronsc
had not been able to get their passports put right owing to the
lack of the necessary Italian to explain what they wanted. So it wa
arranged that they should go next morning to the Prefettura wit
the support of somebody from the Embassy to get them stampe
I went to bed early. Too many ghosts from my golden prin
haunted the corridors and saloons of the Grand Hotel.

June 24th. ROME TO FLORENCE

The *permesso di soggiorno* was obtained and we left the hotel at 1
for the Ciampini airport. I had spent an agreeable half hour with
parruchiere of the old school who gave me a perfect shave and trimme
my beard with a master's touch. He had been at the Grand Hot
for over thirty years and looked rather like Clive Bell, and like Cliv

ell he had solved the problem of significant form. We found the irport largely in the hands of Americans and I was not impressed y the competency of the management. Some bad fairy seems to urse the work of all airmen on the ground, leaving a good fairy to ook after them above. We were kept hanging about for nearly three ours before we were airborne and into the bargain had to endure ne of the worst lunches I ever ate. Vincenzo, our Neapolitan driver, eft as at the airport in high spirits; I fancy he had filled up his car vith six passengers at an exorbitant fee to drive them from Rome o Naples that afternoon.

The hold up by weather at the start of our tour had made it mpossible for us to devote the two days we had intended to levote to the campaign from Rome northward, and there is no ise pretending that flying over the country is the same thing. It was antalizing to peer down at the terra-cotta huddle of Assisi, at the ade-green Tiber and the olive-green Arno, at the bright new red oofs of the devasted city of Arezzo, and at lordly Perugia upon its ill. On the other hand, one got a better idea of Lake Trasimene rom above than if one had been driving beside its turbid water.

Everybody in Italy was extremely vague about which aerodromes vere and which were not functioning, and the aerodrome of Florence looked so completely empty in the golden light of the afternoon when we came down at 17.45 that we wondered if we were expected. However, all was well, and Mr. Greenleaves, the British Consul, had kindly sent his car to meet us. The peace of Florence after the din of Rome was quite exquisite. The very aerodrome itself managed to look beautiful in that serene and classic landscape. The sky was deep azure with snowy cumulus as artfully arranged as if the brush of a great painter had designed its pattern. The encircling hills were the perfection of chiaroscuro. Every cypress tree seemed to have been planted by a master.

We had an excellent tea at the Grand Hotel, which was in impeccable order. The furniture, the service, and the decoration were equally good. I enjoyed a brief illusion that the world had returned to sanity and civilization. The Grand Hotel in Rome had been as full of *nouveaux riches* as it always was, but the guests in the Grand Hotel, Florence, were as much a part of the scene as the minor figures of a quattrocento picture. No doubt we were lucky in dodging one of those parties of hideous Swedish or Swiss women who now infest France and Italy, as once upon a time Italy was infested by even more hideous German women. Perhaps if we had arrived on another day we should have found that dignified interior reverberating with gutturals. Young Swedish women are as a rule so

extremely attractive that the failure of their middle age is surprising
Moreover, the beauty of young Swedish women is not just a skin
deep business of lovely colour. They have good figures and fine bone
beneath the radiant flesh, and their blue eyes have a sensual allure
ment which the blue eyes of England achieve more rarely; but wher
I looked at these Swedish women bundling out of planes at airport
I sympathized with Strindberg.

We had the luck to reach Florence on the Feast of St. John th
Baptist, the chief patron of the city. To be sure, it meant that al
the galleries were shut, but it also meant that the heavy traffic o
business and industry was still. After tea I got hold of an ancient ca
driven by an ancient driver with some mysterious kind of petrol
substitute and took Peter Goodwin up to Fiesole. As we drove
through one piazza after another murmurous with ordered gaiety,
I committed the same mental apostasy as I did during a visit to
Cambridge on a day at July's end in 1943. I said to myself then that
Cambridge was now a more endearing city than Oxford, and that
if I had a son I should send him to King's College. This afternoon
I renounced my devotion for Rome and bowed down to the lilies
of Florence. This may seem a trivial matter to others, but for me it
was the equivalent of a radical change of faith.

It was in Florence that the emotional pleasure of revisiting Italy
after an absence of twenty-three years became so acute that a kind
of Pentocostal inspiration seized me and I found myself talking the
language with such fluency as to amaze myself and my listeners,
who could not believe that I had been so long away.
A clerihew from long ago chimed in my ears:

D. H. Lawrence
Has gone to live in Florence;
Compton Mackenzie
Would have called it Firenze.

It was a pleasure to be able to show Peter Goodwin one of the
world's classic views as we saw it from Fiesole on that June day,
and he responded to it with gratifying enthusiasm.

That evening I dined with Babka Vinci*, her husband Zeno and
the two Goffs who had driven her from England right across Europe
to Florence. Zeno Vinci kindly gave up his seat, so that I could
see the football match between combatants—they really were
combatants—in cinquecento costume. It was an unexpected treat
because it was the first time that the annual football match on St.
John's Day had been held since the war. The game is played—or
fought—in the Piazza della Signoria between the Whites from this

* Contessa Vinci.

side of Arno and the Greens from the other side of the river. The Piazza is turned into a true arena with sand. A round white ball is used, but the game partakes more of Rugby than Association. There are twenty players on each side. Our seats faced the flying Campanile which was as lovely in the floodlighting as one of the city's own lilies, and the Michelangelo statues appeared to be divine visitors who had descended from Olympus to gaze at mortal sport. There were thousands of spectators in tiers round the Piazza and every window in the houses round was full. The audience resembled an immense bouquet of flowers, and when at some crisis of the play they rose from their seats in excitement to shout "Bianchi!" "Bianchi!" or "Verdi! Verdi!" it was like a surge of petals. The game was extremely exciting, and I am glad to say it ended, as it should have ended, in a draw of one and a half goals each.

We had missed the opening procession round the arena, but we saw the same procession bring the spectacle to a close with a ceremonious salute to the Communist Sindaco of Florence sitting in the State Box. There was a bewildering variety of mediaeval costumes, and a cavalcade of the young bloods of the city clad in armour. I recall particularly twenty drummers in slashed doublets and full breeches of blue and yellow. Such a procession at home would have been marred by the self-consciousness of those taking part in it, but here the illusion was complete because every single performer in this pageant had gone back in spirit four centuries. Only our own Yeomen of the Guard might not have disgraced themselves at such a display.

After the match was over we went round to Baglione's and sat talking till 3.30 when Zeno Vinci added to my obligation by driving me back to the hotel. I cannot imagine a more perfect celebration of thus revisiting the glimpses of the moon than I enjoyed in Florence. Indeed, indeed, *hoc erat in votis*.

June 25th. FLORENCE TO RIMINI

We were away on the road to Rimini by 9, being driven in a Fiat by a *simpatico* chauffeur called Luigi. I intended to pay my respects to the *Primavera*, but we could not wait for the gallery to be opened. I was in a good deal of pain during the first part of our exquisite drive through the Umbrian Hills, but aspirin and the ravishing beauty of the Muraglione Pass combined to banish it. In these hills the chief floral beauties were the cornflowers, which had been entirely absent from the wealth of flowers in the Abruzzi. We pressed on through Forli to lunch in Cesena, and thence through the wide fertile plain to reach Rimini. I was enchanted to see painted on walls "Votate per Malatesta". It seems to me indescribably romantic to find Francesca's husband or lover standing as a candidate for a post-war Italian Parliament.

The cultivation in this part of the country was interesting—strips of cornland, of anything up to half a mile long but not more than a hundred yards wide, divided by fruit trees with vines trained over them. We reached Rimini about 15 o'clock and found rooms in what used to be the Savoia Hotel and is now called the Excelsior. Rimini has been terribly damaged; indeed nothing of historic or artistic interest remains. After booking our rooms we drove on toward San Marino, visiting first of all the large war cemetery with many Indian graves. The cultivation continued in the same style of long strips divided by vines and fruit, in some of which where the harvest had been reaped the corncocks were arranged in a symmetrical pattern, every individual corncock itself a work of art. The stacks, in the farmyards were all beautiful in design and perfect in workmanship.

Presently we entered the territory of the age-long independent republic of San Marino and went winding up that fantastic peak to its Gothic summit where the city of San Marino waits in a dream for tourists to return. I could fancy myself back in Capri before 1914. Outside the bars and the restaurants and the shops that sell postcards, earthenware, and postage stamps may be seen printed notices that English, French and German is spoken within. All the way up the steep *viale* to the prison which dates back to the tenth century we passed chairs set out invitingly on little terraces for the tourist to refresh himself with Moscato wine.

From the battlements of the prison one has a view of at least fifty miles of country over which the 43rd Gurkha Lorried Brigade performed prodigious feats of arms. San Marino itself was captured by the Camerons of the 11th Brigade of 4th Indian Division in a night attack. I had a long talk with Sammarini the keeper of the prison, and his jolly wife, who was a great cigarette smoker. He told me there had been English, German and Ukranian prisoners incarcerated up here during the war. At present there are four minor malefactors, one of whom was taking a stroll on the *terrazza* of the Sammarini house and gave me a cordial *buon giorno* as I passed. The other three gazed at us from the grated windows of their cells in the tower.

On our way down we looked in at the Duomo, which is a fairly modern building itself, but behind the high altar are the two beds hollowed out of the bare rock on which legend says that St. Marino and his friend St. Leo used to sleep. A notice by the cathedral door

The Sangro River, looking toward the Mozzagrogna ridge

The fortress of
San Marino

The view from
San Marino
over the
Marrechia River

Harvesting near Orsogna

In San Marino

The damaged Ponte Vecchio in Florence

Interior, Sant' Apollinaris di Classe

With Signora Giulia Goverti at Sant' Apollinaris di Classe (*at right*)

Keren dwarf (*at left*)

announced that a Requiem Mass would be held on some date next week for the eighty-odd victims of an air bombardment.

We passed over the Titan Hotel in favour of an extremely Gothic tavern on the Piazza, where we drank two bottles of sweet, grapy and fizzy Moscato wine which Peter Goodwin, looking as solemn as a President of the Wine and Food Society, declared was the best wine he had ever drunk. We also ate several slices of a hard almond-flavoured San Marino cake. The landlord was disappointed that we did not order a beef steak, which he told us was a speciality of his kitchen; but presently seven Swedish women escorted by a male Swede came in and ordered an enormous meal. Then they started writing picture-postcards and showing one another what they had been buying in a cataract of excited Nordic conversation. It was so like the Germans on Capri once upon a time. San Marino has a definite personality, I should like to revisit it some day and see the *Capitani Regenti* presiding like two consuls of old over some ceremony of this minute and ancient State.

We started back to Rimini at 17 o'clock and on the way visited the Gurkha cemetery where 660 Gurkhas from every regiment except the First lie far from Nepal. Peter Goodwin took one or two good photographs of this which we shall send to the Maharaja with the suggestion that some lily and amaryllis bulbs should be sent from Nepal with hemerocallis roots and seeds of some of the Nepalese shrubs to be planted in this cemetery where they would grow well. When I got back to London I mentioned this idea to the Nepalese Ambassador who, a gardener himself, warmly approved of it.

We dined well in Rimini. *Sepialini* and *tagliatelli* of Bologna were my choice. *Sepialini* are small squids. After dinner we sat listening to an excellent trio—violin, accordion and piano. Encouraged by our applause they played selections from *Madame Butterfly* and *La Tosca* with much passion. There was a roulette table in the next room, but not a single player visited it, and at midnight the croupiers and ourselves went off to bed.

June 26th. RIMINI TO NICE

We left at 9 to drive to Ravenna. Three or four miles before we reached the city we stopped to visit Sant' Apollinaris di Classe, which I think I am right in saying is the oldest complete church in Christendom. It was built about 550 A.D. 'Classe' is a reminder of the days when the sea came as far as this, and half the Roman fleet (*classis*) was based here. The round tenth-century tower has been knocked about by shelling, but the marvellous Byzantine mosaics in the apse are undamaged except for a piece out of the corner by one window. The mosaics exceeded all my expectations. The texture resembles tapestry, and is not smooth-seeming like later mosaics. Apparently this effect was got by using tesserae of different shapes and heights. The design is beautiful, the most striking part of it being the twelve apostles in the guise of lambs, a stem of madonna lilies between each one.

I had a long talk with Giulia Goberti the Custode, who is a little frail old woman of ninety not much more than four feet high. She told me about the bombardment when 200 of the villagers, old and young, had sheltered in a side chapel for six weeks. 176 shells had fallen all round the Church. "Cento settanta sei, signore mio," she quavered to me. "Cento settanta sei!" Her grandaughter informed me that the old lady still insisted on digging in the garden for a couple of hours every morning. I wish I could reproduce the expression compounded of pride and humility on her face as she protested she could not do otherwise. I heard that she was not able to get as much strengthening food as she required and I gave myself the gratification of handing her a 1,000-lire note. which seemed to her a fortune but is only the equivalent of ten shillings nowadays. She was flabbergasted by this sum and promised to remember me in her prayers every day. I parted from this loveable old woman with regret; luckily the photograph Peter G. took of us both was a good one.

We had no time to visit more than a fraction of Ravenna's wonders. We went to Dante's tomb and saw the grassy pyramid of earth which had been heaped above the sarcophagus containing the poet's bones to protect them from bombs. Now they are back in situ. The Dante Museum is not interesting. There is nothing in it hallowed by the poet himself. Framed addresses from societies learned in his work are mere displays of pedantic eloquence.

A competent and cultivated guide took us round the church of San Vitale, another sixth-century building, the mosaics of which are one of the superlative expressions of Byzantine art. We were also able to view the tomb of Julia Placida, the wife of the Emperor Honorius. Here the mosaics are Roman, and the highly conventional Byzantine design gives was to a more realistic style. These Roman mosaics are full of movement. St. Lawrence might actually be running to place himself on the flaming gridiron in an ecstasy of martyrdom. The light in this great sepulchre comes through alabaster windows, the colour of tralucent flesh. By Divine mercy only one Church in Ravenna was completely destroyed, and that not a building of the first importance; but the thought that San Vitale and Sant' Apollinaris di Classe might easily have perished sends a shiver through the mind.

On our way to Argenta we visited another cemetery where a few Indians lie buried, but we missed the cemetery at Argenta itself. We lunched in the little town where the German forces in Italy received their deathblow in the Battle of the Argenta Gap. Peter G. had envisaged the famous Argenta Gap as a kind of Thermopylae. He would wake up from a doze in the car, burbling about the Argenta Gap, which he expected to be photographically the crown and glory of our rush through Italy. Actually it was a gap of dry land amid the wide floods and salt marshes all round, and as there were no floods now there was nothing for Peter to photograph, except another battered little town.

After lunch we drove on to Lugo which was liberated by the Jaipurs, a crack battalion of the States Forces. In the Piazza there is a hideous Fascist Memorial which ought to have been blown up for aesthetic reasons. Some miles beyond Lugo we came to the Senio. Children were bathing down between the thirty-feet high flood banks of that river which was one of the bloodiest crossings of the ten rivers crossed by 8th Indian Division in that long Italian campaign. Flame-throwers were used here to set the banks alight and two V.C.s were won by the Division in that hell of fighting.

We had no time to visit Ferrara or Faenza, but drove on through level country to Bologna. I should like to have seen more of that city of arcades and towers and sausages, but time pressed ever more urgently and we reached the almost abandoned airport at 6 o'clock, much relieved to see the Anson waiting for us. We had an almost emotional parting with Luigi, our Florentine driver, who stood waving his hat to us when we became airborne at 16.45 and went on waving until he was lost to view.

Flying over Modena, Parma and Napoleon's battlefield of Lodi, we reached Milan at 18 o'clock. At Bologna they had warned us we should have trouble in Milan over the visas of Crundall and Bronson; but when we landed every official wanted nothing better than to help us, and no kind of obstruction was put in our way. Milan is entirely under Italian direction and seems to be functioning much more competently than Rome under American and a tiny bit of Italian and British direction. The head of the Sicurezza, Maresciallo di Carabinieri Alberto La Morgia, insisted on taking me off to have a vermouth with him while he gave me his views on the criminal folly of Mussolini's declaration of war.

"Of course we didn't fight with any heart, but if you had seen us fighting the Austrians, ah, then you would have seen men fighting like panthers."

We had intended to stay the night in Milan, but a messenger

came down from the hotel where we had booked rooms to say that they were absolutely full on account of the big fair. So, the weather being good, we decided to fly on to Nice and were airborne by 19 o'clock, all the officials speeding us on our way.

The flight along the Riviera di Levante in the roseate light of evening was miraculously beautiful. Genoa, Rapallo, Portofino, Mentone . . . what memories of the past were tumbling through my mind. We came down on the Nice aerodrome at 20.30. Here another wearisome argument with "parasitic functionaries" took place. There was a bank strike in Nice and nobody seemed to know how we should be able to cash our travellers' cheques. We must have been signing our names and filling up forms for nearly an hour before our taxi was allowed to take us on to an hotel. We decided not to stay at the Queen's again and asked the advice of the driver. He recommended the Hotel Chatham, which was extremely comfortable. The driver asked me if I knew Monsieur Mowgam, the distinguished British author. I took some credit to myself for guessing at once that he meant Somerset Maugham. Apparently he had had the privilege of driving Maugham on many occasions and had a great respect for him.

June 27th. NICE TO LONDON

We left the hotel before 9 o'clock, but were kept waiting two hours at the Nice aerodrome, which was again an antheap of officials. Just as we thought we were away at last Crundall had to go and get his weather report. He had to walk over half a mile from the aerodrome for another series of formalities to be concluded, and then walk back, which meant we were kept grilling in the sun for three-quarters of an hour. Finally we got away just after 11 o'clock French time. We had intended to fly to one of the Paris aerodromes, but we encountered strong headwinds and came down instead to re-fuel at Lyons which we reached at 13 o'clock. Here we had a baddish lunch, but the officials were helpful. I had not been in Lyons since the summer of 1900 and wished we could have had time to visit the city.

The weather report was not too good, and it looked as if we might have to spend the night in Paris, a tiresome prospect because Peter and I had to catch a train for York the following afternoon. However, our luck was in and we dodged the bad weather, to reach Croydon about 19.30 Greenwich time. There had been a cloudburst about lunch time, and the whole place, inside and out had been swamped, two feet of water had stood in the main waiting-room. All the officials were extraordinarily helpful and within half an hour we were on our way to London in a car. I said goodbye to Crundall and Bronson with real regret. Crundall was a perfect pilot. He was imperturbably cautious and with his thirty years' experience of the air and his country-parson kindliness he would reassure the most nervous passenger.

June 28th. LONDON TO YORK

Peter Goodwin and I left King's Cross at 15.30 in what was intended to be a fast train to York with a first stop at Peterborough. Nevertheless, for two hours the wretched train wandered about in Hertfordshire, stopping just outside station after station. In the end we arrived at York two hours late.

Our host and hostess, Lt.-General Sir Montagu Stopford, G.O.C.-in-C Northern Command, and Lady Stopford were marvellously serene under the stress of guests arriving an hour late for dinner, and I soon forgot all about the sins of the L.N.E.R. in their delightful company.

June 29th. YORK

I drove into the city in the morning. The Church of the English Martyrs is one of the most attractive small modern churches I have seen. York itself is almost spruce, and the walls look as if they had been built yesterday. My talks with General Stopford were as good as I have had with any general, and we enjoyed much laughter. I yearn to put down in print some of his stories, but I must gag myself. Mrs. Richardson was staying with the Stopfords. She was a prominent officer in Burma of the famous 'Wasbies'.

June 30th. YORK TO EDINBURGH

After a grand week-end Peter Goodwin and I left for Edinburgh in the morning and reached the house of Lt.-General Sir Philip Christison, G.O.C.-in-C Scottish Command, at tea time. I had a good talk with him about 15th Corps. Among other things he told me that one of the fundamental causes of the trouble in the Netherland East Indies was the repudiation in Holland of the Queen's broadcast in 1942, promising self-government to the Indonesians. When the situation was blowing up in 1945 Van der Plas repeated this broadcast from Batavia to calm people down, for which the only thanks he received from Holland was a threat of being proceeded against for high treason. The trouble with the Dutch seems to be that they are still living in the time of William of Orange. We left Edinburgh that night, but could not get sleepers to King's Cross.

July 6th. LONDON

Peter Goodwin and I called on Sir Kaiser Shumsher the Nepalese Ambassador in the afternoon. He had not been about much in London since he arrived because the raising of the Legation to an Embassy had kept him in a state of suspended animation.

I broadcast after the 9 o'clock news.

July 7th. LONDON

I had a long and absorbing talk at the Imperial Defence College with General Sir William Slim. He answered every question I put to him with complete frankness. John North told me an interesting story about him. Slim was at Gallipoli with a battalion of the Royal Warwicks, and at Sari Bair saw a charge by the 6th Gurkhas. He made up his mind that if he survived Gallipoli he would go into the Indian Army after the war and be a Sixth Gurkha. Montgomery, who was also in the Royal Warwicks, was in France at this time.

In the afternoon I had a long talk with Maj.-General Maltby who commanded our forces in Hong Kong. I went on afterwards to a Press tea-party at the India Office.

July 8th. LONDON

A talk with Maj.-General C. G. C. Nicholson about Kohima.

July 9th. LONDON

A talk with Maj.-General E. C. Mansergh who had to handle a tricky situation in Java as commander of 5th Indian Division.

July 10th. LONDON

I went down to Winchester to see General Sir George Giffard, and I had a most fruitful couple of hours with him, talking about the time when he was C-in-C 11th Army Group in S.E. Asia. General Giffard has not been in the public eye as much as some Generals, but I have met none to whom I have heard warmer tributes paid by other Generals. He was frank with me, and enlarged my knowledge considerably.

July 12th. LONDON

I went along to Hyde Park Gardens to say good-bye to Sir Ian Hamilton. He was noticeably frailer than a year ago, which at ninety-four is not surprising; but he was in good spirits. Peter Goodwin took photographs of us sitting on the terrace. I was smoking a cigar, and Sir Ian demanded a cigar for himself before being photographed.

July 16*th. LONDON*

Sir Ralph Glyn, our North Berkshire Member, who has a good grasp of the position in India and strongly reprobates any attempt to make Pakistan another Ulster, kindly secured me a seat at the Bar of the House of Lords to hear the debate on the Government of India Bill—the last debate that will be held on Indian affairs.

Lord Listowel read his speech, and I could not help regretting that there was no orator to introduce this momentous Bill. Lord Listowel was followed by Lord Templewood who spoke as neatly as the erstwhile Sammy Hoare always spoke. At the same time he managed to implant one or two spicules of doubt while protesting the Opposition's unequivocal support of the Bill. Lord Samuel came next with a brief, dignified and agreeably Ciceronian speech. It was Lord Halifax, however, who first made me feel that I was listening to the final words of a drama which had lasted nearly three centuries, and I should imagine that I was feeling what most of the Noble Lords themselves were feeling. It was a moving speech, and it was difficult to believe that the man who made it was in his sixty-seventh year, so little really much older did he seem than Edward Wood speaking in the Oxford Union forty-five years earlier. Lord Halifax was followed by Lord Pethick-Lawrence, whose ten years' seniority to his predecessor seemed fifty. I had to leave the House after this speech by the man who made such a profound impression on Indian opinion by his essential goodness.

July 17*th. LONDON*

Brigadier Chaudhuri came round to see me at the Savile. He commanded the Indian contingent in the Victory March and stayed a night with us at Denchworth in September '46. He should have a great career before him. A heavy responsibility rests on these Indian and Pakistan Brigadiers and Major-Generals, but I believe they will rise to the occasion.

I had a final long talk at the India Office with General Sir Geoffrey Scoones. He has been tremendously helpful over this rather hectic supplementary tour.

July 18*th. LONDON TO CASTELBENITO*

I lunched with Philip Dunne and the Editor of my favourite paper *The News of the World* in Bouverie Street.

Peter G. and I went down to the B.O.A.C. place in Buckingham Palace Road at 18 o'clock and we left for Heathrow in the bus half an hour later. I had a few words with Morgan who was purser in the flying boat *Castor* from Karachi to Habbaniya.

We were airborne in the York at 19.30 and came down at Bordeaux just as dusk was turning to night. We were refreshed with peaches and were airborne again less than half an hour later, coming down at Castelbenito in Tripoli some time after midnight.

July 19th. CASTELBENITO TO BASRA

I got about four hours sleep before we reached the foul city of Cairo. We drove to the Heliopolis Palace for lunch and were airborne again by about 15 o'clock. The York which crashed at Basra in a dust-storm was the one we were originally booked for, but somebody wanted an urgent priority and Jackman booked us for the next York. All the crew were killed, and the passengers are now in hospital at Basra.

We were lucky, with good weather all the way. We landed at Basra about 20 o'clock and had a tolerably good dinner before we went on again an hour later.

July 20th. KARACHI TO NEW DELHI

We reached Karachi about 6. Douglas Gracey rang up about 8.30 to say he had only just received the signal to say we were arriving, and I had a quarter of an hour with him before we were airborne again for Delhi. He and Cecil were in a state of domestic confusion because the Pakistan Government were taking on the military business of Karachi as the seat of the Dominion Government. He was wondering what his job was going to be in the new order. It ultimately turned out to be C.G.S. to Frank Messervy who is to be Commander-in-Chief of the Pakistan Army. Rob Lockhart is to command the Army of the Dominion of India, with Roy Bucher as his C.G.S.

We reached Delhi in time for lunch. The Chief, who is now to become Supreme Commander and preside over the unwelding of an army it had taken ninety years to weld into its present shape, was in good form.

July 21st. NEW DELHI TO SIMLA

We had a comfortable journey to Kalka, and reached Simla in time for lunch.

Since October 1st, 1946, I have travelled over 8,000 miles by sea, made over sixty flights totalling about 30,000 miles, driven over 9,000 miles by road and travelled over 3,000 miles by train. About 50,000 miles in all and 101 different beds. The Odyssey is over—at any rate for the present. I look back at these ten months and wonder if I have dreamed them.